The Philosophy and Practice of Coaching

The Philosophy and Practice of Coaching

Insights and issues for a new era

Edited by
David B. Drake
Diane Brennan
and
Kim Gørtz

JOSSEY-BASS
A Wiley Imprint
www.josseybass.com

Other Wiley Editorial Offices

John Wiley & Sons Inc., 111 River Street, Hoboken, NJ 07030, USA

Jossey-Bass, 989 Market Street, San Francisco, CA 94103–1741, USA

Wiley-VCH Verlag GmbH, Boschstr. 12, D-69469 Weinheim, Germany

John Wiley & Sons Australia Ltd, 42 McDougall Street, Milton, Queensland 4064, Australia

John Wiley & Sons (Asia) Pte Ltd, 2 Clementi Loop #02–01, Jin Xing Distripark, Singapore 129809

John Wiley & Sons Canada Ltd, 6045 Freemont Blvd, Mississauga, ONT, L5R 4J3, Canada

Wiley also publishes its books in a variety of electronic formats. Some content that appears in print
may not be available in electronic books.

Library of Congress Cataloging-in-Publication Data

The philosophy and practice of coaching : insights and issues for a new era / editors,
David B. Drake, Diane Brennan, Kim Gørtz.
   p. cm.
Includes bibliographical references and index.
ISBN 978-0-470-98721-6 (cloth : alk. paper)
1. Executive coaching. 2. Organizational learning. 3. Personal coaching. I. Drake, David B.
II. Brennan, Diane. III. Gørtz, Kim.

HD30.4.P46 2008
658.3′124–dc22

2007050379

British Library Cataloguing in Publication Data

A catalogue record for this book is available from the British Library

ISBN 978-0-470-98721-6

Typeset in 10/12pt Garamond by SNP Best-set Typesetter Ltd., Hong Kong
Printed and bound in Great Britain by TJ International Ltd, Padstow, Cornwall, UK

Diane: *To my husband Bill and daughter Ashley, for their endless love, inspiration and support, and to my parents Chet and Ann for giving me a great beginning.*

Kim: *I wish to thank my wife and my children for their beautiful presence and tremendous patience.*

David: *To Kim for the invitation, to Diane for her steady guidance, to my wife Gisela for her encouragement, and to my daughter Hannah for reminding me what really matters.*

Table of Contents

Table of Contents

List of Contributors

Merrill Anderson Merrill C. Anderson, Ph.D., is a business consulting executive, author and educator with over 20 years' experience improving the performance of people and organizations. Dr. Anderson is currently the chief executive officer of Cylient, a coaching-based leadership development firm that features MetrixGlobal™ evaluation services. He has over one hundred professional publications and speeches to his credit and he was recognized as the 2003 ASTD ROI Practitioner of the Year. He continues to be widely quoted in the international press on issues of strategic change and ROI (return on investment).

William Bergquist An international coach and consultant, author of 43 books, and president of a graduate school, William Bergquist, Ph.D., consults on and writes about personal, group, organizational and societal transformations. In recent years, Dr Bergquist has focused on the processes of organizational coaching, having co-founded the International Journal of Coaching in Organizations and the International Consortium for Coaching in Organizations. His graduate school (The Professional School of Psychology: PSP) offers Masters and Doctoral degrees in clinical and organizational psychology to mature, accomplished adults. PSP also participates in The Coaching Alliance multi-programme initiative that provides worldwide training, coaching, consulting, publishing and research services.

Diane Brennan Since the year 2000, Diane Brennan has been engaged internationally as an independent coach and consultant through her company, Brennan Associates, based in Tucson, Arizona. She interacts with organization leaders, physicians and business owners as an individual and team coach. Her expertise in this capacity has involved her in disciplines as varied as performance management, leadership development, conflict resolution and process improvement.

A Master Certified Coach with the International Coach Federation, Diane holds a Master's in Business Administration from Bloomsburg University in Pennsylvania and the distinction of Fellow in the American College of Medical Practice Executives. Prior to coaching, Diane spent over 20 years in senior management, executive and clinical practice positions within private and publicly traded healthcare organizations in the USA.

Vikki Brock An executive, leadership and mentor coach with over 20 years Fortune 100 leadership experience and 13 years as a successful entrepreneur, Vikki Brock, Ph.D., E.M.B.A. provides coaching services through Call Me Coach and is a coach-for-hire on large scale corporate coaching initiatives. Vikki graduated from University of Washington's Executive MBA Program in 1989 and completed her Ph.D. in Coaching and Human Development from the International University of Professional Studies in 2008. Her dissertation work on the evolution of coaching encompasses interviews of over 175 key influencers. She is on the faculty of the University of Texas-Dallas School of Management Coaching Program. An International Coach Federation Master Certified Coach (MCC) since 1998, she is also a Certified Executive Coach (CEC) with the Worldwide Association of Business Coaches.

Francine Campone Francine Campone, Ed.D., is a coach and consultant in private practice and has co-edited The Proceedings of the International Coach Federation Research Symposia for three years. She specializes in working with mature professionals making significant transitions in work and life, especially those in the non-profit and education sectors. Dr. Campone is a founding faculty member of the University of Texas at Dallas' graduate programme in executive coaching and teaches courses on coaching research and evidence-based coaching at that institution as well as for Fielding University.

David Clutterbuck David Clutterbuck is visiting professor at the coaching and mentoring faculties of Sheffield Hallam and Oxford Brookes Universities. He is co-founder of the European Mentoring and Coaching Council, where he chairs the UK research committee, and the author or co-author of 12 books on coaching and mentoring, the most recent being *Coaching the Team at Work*. He leads an international consultancy, Clutterbuck Associates, which specializes in helping organizations develop sustainable programmes of coaching and/or mentoring. He has recently completed the first longitudinal, quantitative study of mentoring to examine the relationship from both mentor and mentee perspectives.

Marcia Collins Marcia Collins, BA, co-founded Coach For Life, http://www.coachforlife.com, an accredited coach training company in 1996. Marcia was the lead author of all training materials for its two accredited coach training programmes that feature the Fulfillment Coaching Model™ that has Coaching the Human Spirit™ as its central theme. As a Master Certified Coach, Marcia continues to develop, articulate and facilitate those who are ready to experience as well as coach their clients with the power of Spirit and the elegance of human self-discovery. Marcia supported the founding of the Foundation for Inspired Learning, http://inspiredlearning.org, by donating her intellectual property on how to train facilitators to create thriving and sacred learning environments. Marcia graduated Magna Cum Laude in Computer Engineering.

Sabine Dembkowski Dr Sabine Dembkowski is founder and Director of The Coaching Centre in London & Cologne, www.thecoachingcentre.com. Together with her colleagues, she supports members of boards, executives and high-potentials in Fortune 500, DAX 30 as well as leading professional service firms across Europe. Before she established The Coaching Centre she was a strategic management consultant with A.T. Kearney and Monitor Company in London. Sabine is co-author (with Fiona Eldridge) of *The Seven Steps of Effective Executive Coaching* published by Thorogood in June 2006 (sabinedembkowski@thecoachingcentre.com).

David B. Drake David B. Drake, Ph.D., is the founder and Executive Director of the *Center for Narrative Coaching* in California (www.narrativecoaching.com). He teaches coaching skills for leaders, managers and teams and helps organizations develop integrated coaching and development strategies in organizations. David teaches narrative coaching skills to professionals around the world and is a subject matter expert for coaching-related research projects and programmes. David has a doctorate in Human and Organizational Systems from Fielding Graduate University in California. He has studied and taught Jungian narrative psychology, grief processes and rites of passage to deepen his ability to help individual and organizational clients make generative important transitions. David has written over twenty publications, papers and chapters on narratives, evidence and coaching. David writes on living your legacy now at www.coachingcommons.org.

Fiona Eldridge Fiona Eldridge co-founded The Coaching Centre and is MD in the UK. Much of her work centres on supporting leaders across the Public Sector. Previously she was Head of Leadership and Coaching at Veredus. In addition to her work for The Coaching Centre she is non executive chairman of Teaching Personnel and a non executive director of NHS Professionals – a Special Health Authority set up to manage the supply, cost and quality of the temporary workforce within the NHS. Fiona is co-author (with Sabine Dembkowski) of *The Seven Steps of Effective Executive Coaching* published by Thorogood in June 2006 (f.eldridge@thecoachingcentre.com).

Vicki Escudé Vicki H. Escudé, MA, Master Certified Coach, is CEO of Executive Leadership Coaching, LLC, and has over 20 years' experience in executive coaching, business ownership, writing, management and counselling. She is a senior associate and Coach Trainer for SECA, and is also on the Board of Directors and Coach Trainer for Success Unlimited Network, LLC. She was elected to the Board of Directors of the International Coach Federation for 2005–2008. She is on the faculty of the University of Texas-Dallas School of Management Coaching Program. Vicki graduated from Vanderbilt University, and received her Master's Degree from the University of West Florida in psychology and counselling. She received additional training with post-graduate work in testing and assessments, coaching training and facilitation.

Sandy Gordon Sandy Gordon, Ph.D., FAPS is with the School of Sport Science, Exercise and Health at The University of Western Australia, where he teaches Sport and Exercise Psychology and Coaching Psychology. He is a Registered Sport Psychologist, Fellow member of the Australian Psychological Society (APS), and member of both the APS Interest Group of Coaching Psychology (IGCP) and College of Sport Psychologists (CoSP). Accreditation also includes Advanced and Professional Development Executive coaching certificates from the Institute of Coaching and Consulting Psychology. He serves on three Editorial Boards and regularly reviews for several other periodicals that publish applied psychology research.

Kim Gørtz For the last five years, Kim's interest has increased in the field of organizational development, coaching, leadership, engagement and innovation from philosophical perspectives. He is currently working in Nordea Bank A/S & Learning Lab Denmark as an industrial Ph.D. where he is undertaking foundational research on coaching in business in relation to leadership development, increased engagement and innovation. Kim has run a 'Coach-Café' for two years now and his published works to date include *The Openness of Thought, Values in Leadership, Values with Meaning, Coaching in Perspective, The Philosophical Performance* and *Coaching from Philosophical Perspectives* (www.filosofisten.dk).

Kristina Gyllensten Kristina is a Chartered Counselling Psychologist and a coach. Kristina has recently completed her Doctorate at the Coaching Psychology Unit at City University, focusing on the experiences of coaching and stress in the workplace. She has co-authored a number of articles and a book chapter on this topic. She currently works as a therapist and researcher at a Centre for Cognitive Therapy in Gothenburg, Sweden and is also involved in the development of a new coaching organization, *adSapiens*, in Gothenburg where she is working as a coach and is involved in training courses.

Charles Hamrick With 18 years' experience in the management of multinational corporations and eight years' experience in coaching top executives of major global corporations, Charles Hamrick works with the challenges that people face in creating and meeting their goals in global settings. He has managed companies in most Asian countries, served in consulting and coaching roles with hundreds of executives, and has worked with members of the US Congress and Senate. He is a certified coach, with a professional education in engineering at undergraduate and graduate levels, psychology at graduate level, and holds an MBA. Charles speaks several languages including English, Japanese, Chinese and Korean.

Peter Jackson Peter Jackson is a coaching practitioner and lecturer, teaching on post-graduate programmes in coaching and mentoring practice at Oxford Brookes University. He holds an MSc in Organizational Behaviour from Birkbeck College, University of London and an MA in Coaching & Mentoring Practice from Oxford Brookes University. He is a member of the Council of the Association for Coaching, an AC accredited coach and former editor of the *AC Bulletin*. Previous publications have explored the nature of reflection in coaching, and how coaching practitioners conceptualize their practice. He previously worked in industry in IT and HR.

Travis Kemp Dr Travis Kemp is the Managing Director & Lead Coaching Psychologist of The Teleran Group Pty. Ltd. He is an educator, psychologist and human resources professional.

Travis is a founding national committee member of the Australian Psychological Society's Interest Group in Coaching Psychology and holds adjunct appointments as Lecturer in the University of Sydney's Coaching Psychology Unit, Research Fellow in the University of South Australia's International Graduate School of Business and Clinical Associate in the Discipline of Psychiatry in the School of Medicine at the University of Adelaide. Travis co-edited *Evidence-Based Coaching Volume One: Theory, research and practice from the behavioural sciences* and is co-editor of the *International Coaching Psychology Review*.

Peter J. Reding Peter J. Reding, BS, MBA, co-founded Coach For Life, http://www.coachforlife.com, an accredited coach training company in 1996. Peter helped to author the International Coach Federation's (ICF) core coaching competencies and has served as ICF's chairman of the Independent Ethics Review Board. Peter is one of the eight original founders of ACTO – the Association of Coach Training Organizations – and served as its executive director for two and a half years. As a Master Certified Coach, Peter coaches world-changing visionaries. Peter founded the non-profit Foundation for Inspired Learning, http://inspiredlearning. org in 2003. Peter speaks and writes about creating learning environments through his company Positively Brilliant International, http://www.positivelybrilliant.com. He earned his BS from Marquette University and his MBA from Pepperdine University.

Peter Webb Peter Webb is a Leadership Coach Psychologist specializing in wisdom-related performance in leadership effectiveness in the Asia-Pacific region. He holds an Honours Degree in Economics from the University of Queensland and a Masters Degree in Applied Science (Psychology of Coaching) from the University of Sydney. He is the immediate past Secretary of the Australian Psychological Society Interest Group in Coaching Psychology, and a lecturer in Coaching in Organizations for the Masters Degree programmes in coaching at the University of Sydney. Peter is also an Associate Program Director at the Melbourne Business School – Mt Eliza Executive Education Centre, and he has authored several publications on executive coaching and the development of wisdom through coaching.

Patrick Williams Dr. Patrick Williams is a clinical psychologist turned coach with almost 20 years of coaching experience. He has an MA in Humanistic Psychology and an Ed.D. in Transpersonal Psychology and was one of the first 25 Master Certified Coaches in the world to be credentialed by the International Coach Federation. Pat served on the ICF board from 2002–2005. He is also the founder of the Institute for Life Coach Training and author of numerous books and articles about coaching including the best selling professional's book *Becoming a Professional Life Coach: Lessons from the Institute for Life Coach Training*. Pat was awarded the first Global Visionary Fellowship by the Foundation of Coaching for his project *Coaching the Global Village*.

Foreword

Professor Stephen Palmer

Around the world, coaching has made in-roads into the personal and professional development arenas that were once the exclusive domain of therapists, consultants and trainers – each in their own setting. Coaching builds on psychotherapists' commitment to self-development and self-efficacy, consultants' commitments to thinking systemically and strategically, and trainers' commitment to learning and performance. However, in doing so, coaching brings a greater emphasis on proactive approaches, real-time change, and long-term gains. As such, qualified coaches and multidisciplinary coaching teams are increasingly being called on to enhance the levels of empowerment, development and performance in organizations and the broader society.

While many books have been published on coaching, they mostly seem focused on basic coaching skills and relatively simple models or methodologies for coaching conversation. They were often written in an enthusiastic style in which the authors based their claims of success on anecdotal evidence. However, in recent years there has been a gradual shift as more coaching books have introduced psychological theory and research to underpin their coaching model(s). An increasing percentage of them also include academic references and cite published research as a foundation for their approaches. We are also seeing more coaching–related journals being published, e.g., *International Journal of Coaching in Organizations, International Journal of Evidence Based Coaching and Mentoring, The Coaching Psychologist, The International Coaching Psychology Review*, and the newest one, *Coaching: An International Journal of Theory, Research and Practice*. Some of these publications are also being abstracted in well-known and prestigious databases such as psycINFO from the American Psychological Association.

Another sign of coaching's maturation and professionalization is the fact that the field is represented by one or more established professional bodies, e.g., the Association for Coaching, British Psychological Society

Special Group in Coaching Psychology, European Mentoring and Coaching Council, International Association of Coaching and the International Coach Federation. Crucially, they have developed codes of ethics and practice for their members. In addition, some have a coach training course recognition scheme and most have an accreditation and/or credentialing process so members can work towards recognition as qualified coaches by their peers and others. Similar to other professions, there is a healthy competition between the professional bodies to raise the bar on what they offer their members and society. In addition there are larger initiatives underway, such as The Coaching Commons, which are stimulating the next level of thinking about what coaching brings to organizations and the world.

As a result, the field of coaching now benefits from well-written and resourced books, evidence-based journals with peer-reviewed research, and a number of established professional bodies with codes of ethics and practice and credentialing processes for their members and providers. We can begin to make the case that coaching has arrived as it has gradually shifted from being an industry to a profession. Consequently, there will be higher expectations placed on coaches by their peers and service users. Already in the UK, organizations are asking potential coaches if they are accredited, receive on-going supervision and are knowledgeable about the field.

This book, *The Philosophy and Practice of Coaching: Insights and Issues for a New Era*, is timely as it covers many of the contemporary issues facing the profession, including a deeper understanding of the foundations for coaching, the applications of coaching, and the issues faced by organizations in their use of coaching. The insightful chapters are written by well-known experts in the field who have come together in this project. I really appreciated the wide-ranging and insightful reflections these practitioners have shared with us about their particular area of expertise. Their chapters provide the reader with excellent continuing professional education and development, a necessity for coaching in the 21st century.

The book lives up to Kim Gørtz's original concept as '*a way to bring a deeper inquiry and further philosophical reflection into the field of coaching so that both the field and the people involved will be nourished in creating the future in a more thoughtful, ethical and loving way.*' The book successfully links the past, the present and the future development of coaching as a profession.

Professor Stephen Palmer PhD
Director of the Coaching Psychology Unit,
City University, London, UK

Introduction

Diane Brennan, Kim Gørtz and David B. Drake

Dear Colleague,

We welcome you into the world of coaching and invite you to join us on a journey of discovery. As coaching continues to grow and mature, there is a need for a deeper conversation about its current state and its future directions. This book is designed to extend and enrich that conversation in provocative yet grounded ways. Our authors come from various backgrounds and locations around the world; we have internationally recognized coaches, educators, researchers and writers among us. The book offers you a unique opportunity to look inside their minds and practices as a way to reflect on your own. In doing so, we have taken a scholar-practitioner approach that is theoretically and evidentially sound yet approachable and useful for coaches.

The book showcases a variety of ways to integrate scholarship and research in one's practice by professionals who do so every day. In particular, we have asked the contributors to this anthology to help us open the 'black box' of coaching through a closer look at their thinking and their work. We asked ourselves, 'What makes coaching so powerful when it is done well? How does it work?' We see this book as a solid resource for everyone involved with creating the next generation of coaching and the next level of its contribution to a better world. We believe the time is right for this book as a doorway into a new era for coaching, one that is marked with greater sophistication, maturity and reach. We invite you into the conversation through this book as a way to support your journey.

The book's title, 'The Philosophy and Practice of Coaching: Insights and issues for a new era', grew out of the process of developing the book and reading the early drafts from the coaching experts we have assembled. The book was originally conceived of by Kim as 'a way to bring a deeper inquiry and further philosophical reflection into the field of coaching so that both the field and the people involved will be nourished in creating the future in a more thoughtful, ethical and loving way'. Kim's passion attracted most of the authors to our project. David came on board as the executive editor and Diane provided additional and invaluable leadership. Collectively, we were keen to address the philosophy of coaching, the 'why', in addition to the practice, the 'how'. We wanted to take coaches 'behind the scenes' to increase their abilities to reflect on their coaching work as part of helping us all to better understand, 'Why do we do what we do?' The second half of the title refers to the fact that we invited the authors to take a more personal stance on their topics such that readers would benefit even more from their insights on many of the key issues facing coaches today. We are clearly in a new period in the history of the world; our hope is that this book will be a stepping-stone into bigger and more daring conversations about how to help coaching rise to the occasion.

The book is divided into three sections: 'Foundations for Coaching', 'Applications of Coaching', and 'Organizations and Coaching'. Each chapter follows the same format: (1) the *context*: a brief theoretical and operational history of the topic relative to coaching as well as the compelling need(s) addressed by the author; (2) the *content*: current, significant and research-based material on this topic presented with a balance of breadth and depth; (3) the *connections*: how the key theories cited link to coaching practices in general and in the lived experience of the author(s) (so as to unpack the 'black box' of coaching in action; and (4) the *consequences*: the implications of the author's chapter for the further development of coaches and the future of coaching as a profession.

The first section, 'Foundations for Coaching', provides a solid introduction to three key issues facing coaching: (1) Where do we come from as a professional practice? (2) What are our obligations for self-development as coaching professionals? (3) How do we engage with coaching-related research to support our decisions and practice? These chapters address the need to link coaching to a past, present and future in ways that deepen our accountabilities, capabilities and possibilities.

Patrick Williams gets us started with a historical review of the extensive contributions from one hundred years of psychology and psychotherapy to what we know now as coaching. It is important for coaches to understand the source of many of the perspectives and techniques we use in our practices and to appreciate that the connections between the two disciplines may be greater than we think. *Travis Kemp* provides an excellent analysis of three key findings from social psychology and their role in helping us to understand the primacy of the coaching relationship and the importance of self-management to coaching mastery. He provides two practical models for coaches in support of these two aims. *David B. Drake* explores some key tenets from narrative psychology to demonstrate the process of moving from established theory to emergent practice and to offer ways to think narratively in working with client stories. He invites coaches to think about and engage the material that emerges in coaching conversations in new ways and, in doing so, to rethink their role as stewards of these stories. *Peter Jackson* asks the provocative question, 'Does it matter what the coach thinks?' as a platform to discuss the role of theory and evidence as a foundation for the practice of coaching. Of particular interest here is his call for coaching to move beyond the false dualisms inherent in a 'culture of pragmatism' in order to develop ourselves professionally and collectively. *Francine Campone* closes out this part with a wonderful review of three eras of coaching research as well as sharing her insights on where coaching is heading/needs to be heading in its relationship to research. Along the way, she provides some guidance on how to 'connect the dots' between theory, research and practice.

The second section, 'Applications of Coaching', provides a look at how coaching has been applied to address five important issues facing today's organizations and communities. In addition to gaining access to the authors' expertise, these chapters also provide a rare look at their lived experience in working with clients around their topic.

Sandy Gordon opens the section with a look at the application and advantages of a strengths-based approach to coaching. Drawing on research and experience in both sport and business, he demonstrates how appreciative inquiry coaching is well-suited to enhance clients' mental toughness and resilience as key developmental and performance drivers for success. *Charles Hamrick* continues with a fascinating set of stories and reflections on his own development as a leader and coach working across cultures. Drawing in particular on his in-depth experience in countries across Asia and his understanding of their cultures, he provides some important guidance for work as a global coach. *Kristina Gyllensten* looks at some of the research that has been done on the impact of stress in the workplace, including her own, and some of the early efforts to gauge the efficacy of coaching to address these issues with clients. Her work is important because it gives us a candid and inside view of what it is like researching a complex issue in organizations and the challenges of assessing the contributions of coaching. *Peter Webb* brings us a stellar review of the wisdom literature and how he is applying this work in his coaching practice. He shares his passionate belief in the urgent need for wiser leaders to address the challenging issues of our time and offers two models coaches can use to bring forth greater wisdom in their clients. *Peter J. Reding* and *Marcia Collins* take us on a journey through the development of their approaches to coaching, one that is aimed at bringing out the human spirit in clients. In doing so, they champion an experience-based epistemology and address some of the key issues in coaching about how to help people live from the place of their highest self. *Sabine Dembkowski* and *Fiona Eldridge* provide an overview of the process they went through in developing their coaching model. While there are hundreds of models used by coaches across the globe, it is not often that we get to learn about their formation. As an inspiration for us all to take a harder look at our espoused theories versus our theories-in-use (Chris Argyris),[1] they offer a client case to demonstrate their model in action.

The final section, 'Organizations and Coaching', provides a look inside the uses, expectations, impact and value of coaching the organization. Whereas the first section focused largely on the person-centred disciplines, psychology and philosophy as the bases for coaching, this part draws on[2] coaching's roots in organization-centred disciplines such as organizational development and leadership development. Accordingly, these authors address some of the key issues facing organizations that are seeking to create better and more sustainable results from coaching.

David Clutterbuck opens this section with a fascinating look at the origin and nature of teams in the workplace and what we can learn from this analysis in creating a more rigorous and unique approach to coaching teams. In addition to providing practical guidance on working specifically with teams, he challenges all of us to be more rigorous in developing a grounded knowledge base about our coaching clients and initiatives. *Diane Brennan* offers an extended case study of a coaching intervention with the leadership team of a healthcare organization. It traces the path of the project, the impact it had for the leaders and their staff, and the lessons learned; it serves as a very good example of reflective practice in action. *Vicki Escudé* follows with a look at some of the steps in creating a coaching culture within an organization. In doing so, she demonstrates how a set of individual coaching competencies can be used to assess an organization's level of readiness for a shift to a coaching culture and work with them in supporting that movement.

---

1 Argyris, C. (1991, May–June). Helping Smart People to Learn. *Harvard Business Review*, 99–109.
2 Drake, D.B. (2007) An Integrated Approach to Coaching: The emerging story in a large professional services firm. *International Journal of Coaching in Organizations*, 5(3), 22–35.

William Bergquist and *Vikki G. Brock* explore six different cultures of contemporary organizations and talk about how coaching needs to adapt within each one in order to be effective. The second half of the chapter is a fascinating look at the place of anxiety within each of these cultures, what that means for coaches, and how each cultural path can contribute to greater meaning in the workplace. *Kim Gørtz* takes us inside a large Scandinavian financial institution to look at how coaching was used to support their leadership development as they underwent a major change effort implementation. Drawing on the literature on Lean processes, flow and coaching, he demonstrates some of the challenges and opportunities of working with coaching in a systematic way across broader initiatives in organizations. *Merrill C. Anderson* closes the section with some critical insights based on his extensive work in applying return on investment (ROI) methods to evaluate coaching interventions. Many organizations are asking for more data on their coaching investments and outcomes, but we are only just beginning to understand how to generate meaningful data in this regard. He uses a case study to explore these issues and provide guidance on measuring the tangible and intangible results from coaching.

We invite you to dive into this book – both in places that are familiar to you and those that are less so. Be curious; explore with an open mind and heart. We hope it will challenge you to expand your thinking, reflect more deeply on your practice, and seek new ways to add value for your clients and the profession. We hope too that it will encourage you to unpack your own 'black box' in order to grow in your development and work as a coach. If coaching is to fully emerge as a true field of study, we need to adopt a greater discipline in engaging with and in sound scholarship and critical thinking. If coaching is to fully emerge as a profession – even if it is what Drake (2007, in press)[3] has called *postprofessional* in nature – we need a greater commitment to our own reflective practice and our willingness to do candidly for ourselves what we ask of our clients. This book was designed to help coaches and coaching programmes in these pursuits.

We have designed two resources to help you in this journey: (1) We have provided a set of questions at the end of each part of the book; there are 48 questions in all. Use them to reflect on what you have read and what you will take into your practice as a new awareness, new perspective or new action. *Imagine the impact on your development and*

---

3 Drake, D. B. (in press) Finding Our Way Home: Coaching's search for identity in a new era. *Coaching: An International Journal of Theory, Research and Practice.*

business if you intentionally addressed one question a week over the course of a year (assuming some time off for well-deserved holidays!). (2) We have built a website – www.practiceofcoaching.com – that features interviews with the authors, additional resources, and opportunities for interaction with other readers around the topics and the questions. Check it out.

Welcome to the journey!
David, Diane and Kim

Part I

FOUNDATIONS FOR COACHING

The Life Coach Operating System: Its Foundations in Psychology

1

Patrick Williams

This chapter charts the course of some of the psychological theorists of the twentieth century who laid the groundwork for the emergence and evolution of personal and professional coaching. Relevant evidence-based research and theories will be noted along with their application and significance in coaching today. It is important for professional coaches to know that quality coach training and education is based in a multidimensional model of human development and communication that has drawn from the best of humanistic psychology, positive psychology, integral psychology and others in this field. Coaching also draws from other fields such as organizational development, adult learning theory, and systems theory, but they are not the focus of this chapter.

It is important to cite the theories and research from the established field of psychology and note how specific techniques and/or skill sets can be applied in coaching conversations so that coaches can develop a greater variety of tools in communicating with clients. Many of the same techniques that originated in clinical psychology are useful in assisting clients to reframe their experience and to discover their strengths. These techniques include powerful questions, guided imagery (Psychosynthesis), empty chair technique (Gestalt therapy), time lines and future pacing (NLP), and even techniques and theory from Transactional Analysis (Eric Berne), client-centred counselling (Carl Rogers) and life-stage awareness (Carl Jung, Frederic Hudson,

The Philosophy and Practice of Coaching: Insights and Issues for a New Era.
Edited by David B. Drake, Diane Brennan and Kim Gørtz.
© 2008 John Wiley & Sons, Ltd.

Carol Gilligan, and Robert Kegan, among others). This chapter focuses particularly on the philosophy and practice of life coaching as it relates to high-quality human communication that empowers the client. Some nuances require adaptations for various cultures, but since coaching is a co-created conversation to empower the receiver of the coaching, an *expert/client paradigm* is intentionally absent. Many of the theories and techniques cited in this chapter are unique to Western cultures but can be adapted for use in most other cultures as well.

Life Coaching as an Operating System

Personal and professional coaching has emerged as a recognized career in the last decade and it has created new options for people who seek help with life transitions in finding a *guide* to partner with them in designing their desired future. While coaching has grown to incorporate a variety of specialized applications, the case can be made that life coaching as a whole-person, client-centred approach is the foundational operating system. As an operating system, the whole life approach is always in the background of the conversation, just like an Operating System (OS) in a computer system. Invariably, any specific focus of a coaching relationship will be interconnected to other areas of a person's life. If you have a client who wants to be a better manager, or make a career transition, you will find that conversations about their significant relationships, or their personal wellness, or their stress level could and should come up in the conversation. They are all intertwined in a whole person approach. For your coaching practice, this means that you need to be willing to open up conversations through asking questions about other areas of the client's life. What is working well? What is less than in satisfying? How do *energy drainers* in one area of the client's life *bleed over* into effecting their stated goals?

Before about 1990, there was little mention of coaching except in the corporate culture. Although there were a few people who were doing personal work and calling it coaching before that time. Vikki Brock (Brock, 2008) who has written some research on the origins of coaching notes that Results Unlimited in the UK was begun in 1980 and was providing life coaching. And Sir John Whitmore helped begin one of the first training schools in the UK in 1988 based on the 'inner game' theories of Tim Gallwey. Mentoring and executive coaching were resources that many top managers and CEOs utilized, either informally from a colleague or formally through hiring a consultant or psychologist who became their executive coach. This chapter documents the rise of life coaching within the broader movement of personal and professional coaching and its roots in psychology.

The rise in the profession can be seen in the following ways. The International Coach Federation was founded in 1995 but did not have a real presence until its first convention in 1996. The ICF has kept detailed archives of media coverage on coaching since the early 1990s. Two newspaper articles appeared in the US media in 1993 (there were reportedly earlier articles in the UK media in the 1980s), four in 1994 (including one from Australia), and seven in 1995. The majority of articles appeared in publications in the United States. Then, in 1996, a huge increase in publicity occurred, with more than 60 articles, television interviews, and radio shows on the topic of coaching. Every year since, media coverage has increased to hundreds of articles, radio programmes, and television venues such as *Good Morning America, Today,* CNBC, BBC, and others around the globe. The only books before 1990, that were written about coaching were geared to corporate and performance coaching. Since then, numerous solid books about life coaching, executive coaching, career coaching, wellness coaching and other specialties have been published, with more every year, and a few recent ones have even become national bestsellers. At last count, over 35 universities across the globe offer at least a certificate in coaching and an increasing number of universities offer graduate degrees in coaching. All of this is to show the rapid evolution of this profession globally with different roots in different parts of the world.

Life coaching was originally thought to have originated in the United States and has rapidly spread worldwide. But through more recent research and conversations with other coaches, it really started in the UK in the 1980s and then the work of Thomas Leonard and others in the US influenced its growth in the UK even more. I contend that coaching will soon reach a critical mass in society – people will have heard of coaching, know when they need a coach, know how to find a coach, and know the difference between partnering with a life coach versus seeking the services of a therapist or counsellor. Understanding coaching's historical roots provides current and prospective life coaches with a framework for understanding their profession and insights into future opportunities. This framework also helps life coaches place themselves squarely within the larger context of a profession that is still evolving. Life coaches will understand the present more accurately and become better prepared as life coaching expands in the twenty-first century if they looking across the diverse threads of the past upon which the work is based. An examination of the evolution of life coaching also helps counsellors and others from the helping professions to make the transition to life coaching by clarifying the similarities and differences between life coaching and their professions (Hart, Blattner, and Leipsic, 2001).

What Are the Roots of Life Coaching?

Coaching has a unique paradigm, but much of the foundation of coaching goes back many decades and even centuries. The draw to pursue life improvement, personal development, and the exploration of meaning began with early Greek society. This is reflected in Socrates' famous quote, 'The unexamined life is not worth living'. Since then, people have developed many ways of examining their lives, some useful and some not; some are grounded in theory and evidence-based, while others are made up and inconsistent in their helpfulness. What persists, however, is that people who no longer need focus on the pursuit of basic human needs – such as food and shelter – are beginning to pay attention to higher needs such as self-actualization, fulfilment, and spiritual connection. This is also why much of the world that lives in poverty and on the edge of survival does not concern themselves with dreams and big goals for their lives. Those have to be put on the back burner.

I have spent much time in Third World/developing countries and see that the coach approach can be helpful in empowering local villagers to be more resourceful, but they still need the resources to become available. The NGOs and nonprofit groups that supply food, water, housing etc., could benefit from a holistic coaching approach in order to create and empower sustainable changes that the *resource-poor* villagers can continue with assistance from *resource-rich* countries and foundations. Taking this global and integrative perspective for the power of coaching, we could do much for the view that coaching is mostly elitist and serves the rich and powerful primarily. Accordingly, more and more people have an intense desire to explore and find personal meaning, when the blocks to survival are eliminated and the ability to thrive supplants survival.

Coaching today is seen as a new phenomenon, but as a field it borrows from and builds on theories and research from related fields such as psychology and philosophy. So coaching is *a multidisciplinary, multi-theory* synthesis and application of applied behavioural change. As coaching evolved in the public arena it began to incorporate accepted theories of behavioural change as the evidence base for this new helping relationship (Williams, 2004). However, in recent years, more and more research has been done and evidence-based theories developed to begin creating a body of knowledge and evidence that coaching can call its own (Stober and Grant, 2006).

Contributions from Psychology

What has the field of psychology brought to coaching and what are the major influences? I would propose that there have been four major forces in psychological theory since the emergence of psychology in 1879 as a social science. These four forces are Freudian, behavioural, humanistic and transpersonal. Both the Freudian and behavioural models grew out of biology and were focused on pathology and how to 'cure' it. The humanistic approaches of Carl Rogers and Abraham Maslow were a response to the pathological model; they attempted to make space in psychology for those elements of being human that create health and happiness (Williams, 2007a). Finally, the transpersonal movement arose in the late 1960s in a further attempt to include more of what allows human beings to function at their best. Its focus was on mind, body and spirit and included studies and experiences of states of consciousness, transcendence, and what Eastern traditions and practices had to teach Western theorists and practitioners. A more recent approach, the integral model of Ken Wilber and others, is emerging and may become a fifth force, integrating all that has come before and offering a holistic and even multilevel view of the various modalities for understanding human development and our desire to evolve mentally, physically, spiritually and socially.

In recent years, several other approaches have arisen as adaptations of one or more of the original four and have been taking up by many coaches. Cognitive-behavioural psychology grew from a mix of the behavioural and humanistic schools. I say this because much of cognitive psychology embodied wisdom and leanings from behaviourism and even operant conditioning. But when the humanistic aspect was included, it became a way to use those techniques and theories of change to increase *choice* for the individual. In coaching, then, you can utilize what we know about shifting mindset and behaviours by using a process of inquiry and powerful questions that guide the client to understanding their ability to respond rather than react to their personal situations. Responding comes from viewing the multiple choices available in cognition and behaviour rather than just reacting habitually. Positive psychology builds on two key principles from humanistic psychology: a non-mechanistic perspective and a view of possibility as opposed to pathology as the essential approach to the client. Humanistic psychology arose as a counterpoint to the view of Freudian psychology and behaviourism that people could be viewed as controlled by unconscious and conditioned responses Humanistic psychology arose to promote the emphasis on personal growth and the importance of *beingness* and the phenomenology of the human experience. Along with each revolution in psychology, a changing image of human nature has evolved along with greater insights into how to effectively work with people. As noted above, Wilber's integral theory is adding to the holistic knowledge base upon which professional coaches can draw.

The Birth of Psychology

The field of psychology began as the investigation of consciousness and mental functions such as sensation and perception. *Webster's New World College Dictionary* (indexed 4th edition) defines psychology as 'a) the science dealing with the mind and with mental and emotional processes, and b) the science of human and animal behavior'. Much of the early influence on psychology came from the philosophical tradition and early psychologists adopted the practice of introspection used by philosophers. The practice of introspection into one's desires, as well as noticing and observing behaviours, thoughts and emotions are core practices for increasing client awareness and, as such, are cornerstones of a solid approach to coaching. Introspectionists were an early force in psychology in the late nineteenth century, with Wilhelm Wundt in Germany and Edward Tichener in the United States being two of the early pioneers of introspection as a method of understanding the workings of the human mind.

However, they eventually realized introspection was insufficient in the pursuit of validation for the young science of psychology because consciousness and mental functioning were difficult to study objectively. These challenges were part of the larger growing pains within psychology and echo many of the same challenges faced by coaching today. Psychology, like coaching today, went through many fits and starts and met with much debate in the milieu in which it developed. Even today, there is debate amongst various theories and approaches. So, the fact that this is occurring in the emerging field of coaching should not surprise us. It is healthy within coaching circles to have lively debates about what works and what is effective in order to increase our understanding of why various approaches work. Otherwise, it is just a fantasy and not backed up with evidence. The growing body of coaching-related research greatly assists the profession in meeting this need to have evidence that what coaches do with their clients actually works. Coaches today have a rich resource of studies and published research that can inform their practice and help articulate the efficacy of what they offer to clients. As a context for this research, let us take a quick tour of the growth of psychology and how its major thinkers set the stage for the coaching revolution.

William James was the father of American psychology. James preferred ideas to laboratory results and is best known for his writings on consciousness and his view that humans can experience higher states of consciousness. He wrote on such diverse topics as functions of the brain, perception of space, psychic and paranormal faculties, religious ecstasy, will, attention and habit. Because of his orientation, he gradually drifted away from psychology and in his later life emphasized philosophy, changing his title at Harvard to 'professor of philosophy'. Nevertheless, William James had a tremendous influence on the growth of the psychology profession, and he is still widely read today. One of his most historic books, *The Varieties of Religious Experience* (1994), is a treatise that offers much today on the topics of spirituality and transpersonal consciousness.

The First Wave: Freudian Psychology

Sigmund Freud influenced the first force in psychology. While psychology in the United States was struggling for an identity and striving for recognition by the scientific community, European psychology was being reshaped by the theories of Sigmund Freud. Freud created quite a stir in the medical community with his ideas and theories, but he finally gained acceptance in psychiatry with the 'talking cure' breakthrough – psychoanalysis. Freud brought us such terms as *unconscious*, *id*, *ego* and *superego*. His theories and practices soon began to gain acceptance in the United States as well. Some of Freud's followers went on to become well-known theorists as well – most notably **Carl Jung** (e.g., archetypes, psychological types, individuation and the shadow), **Alfred Adler** (e.g., the social self, compensation and inferiority/superiority), and **Karen Horney** (e.g., a neo-Freudian view of neuroses, isolation and helplessness as the root of anxiety). Over the years, as more people worked with Freudian ideas, the practice of psychoanalysis became more refined and more effective.

Many American psychologists began to combat Freudian theories as another non-verifiable, subjective pseudoscience of the mind. What was happening in almost parallel times were two major attempts to explain what 'a piece of work is man' and to understand what would explain pathological behaviour and what would prevent or create change in aberrant behaviours – the focus though was primarily still on the negative, the pathology and the problems of the human, not the positive drives that would come to be emphasized later in the twentieth century, especially with the rise of the humanistic theories and now in the twenty-first century the popularity of positive psychology (see Seligman, 2002).

The Second Wave: Behaviourists

As Freudian thought was taking shape in Europe and the United States, other theorists began to focus on measurable behaviour. Thus, the time was ripe for the emergence of behaviourism as the second major force in psychology, a movement led by **B. F. Skinner** and **John Watson.** Hundreds of years previously, Shakespeare had commented, 'What a piece of work is man?' The behaviourists took this literally and looked upon humans in the early twentieth century as *Homo mechanicus*, an object to be studied as any machine. *Homo mechanicus* was a machine whose mind was ignored and instead the focus was on behaviours that arose via automatic processes, leaving the humanity out of the equation. The behaviourists wanted an empirical psychology, one that could be tested and confirmed in a laboratory. Coming from more of a scientific background, these theorists felt that psychology would only survive if it were made more objective. They looked to create a model of human behaviour that could be shaped and moulded through conditioning and other techniques.

However, they were sharply criticized for neglecting the subjective realm of experience – personality, emotions and interior experience. It is worth noting, however, that the influence of the empirical model can still be seen in the emerging field of neuropsychology (most notably Daniel Dennett and William Calvin), an approach that reduces all of human experience to the functions of neurotransmitters and electrical signals. However, many of the cutting-edge researchers in neuropsychology are actually opening the door to considering such factors as *human energy field* and other findings that are allowing a blending of science and what previously made up parapsychology and spiritual practices that were the purview of the next two forces in the twentieth century.

The Third Wave: Humanistic Psychology

In the 1950s, **Abraham Maslow** and **Carl Rogers** initiated the third force in psychology, humanistic psychology, which focused on the personal, ontological and phenomenological aspects of human experience as opposed to the mechanistic and reductionist theories of Freudianism and behaviourism. Carl Rogers was more concerned with the 'fully functioning person' than he was with pathology. He believed that people needed love and acceptance from others in order to be fully functioning, and his work resulted in what came to be known as client-centred therapy. Likewise, Maslow was interested in how people find value and meaning in their lives, which resulted in his 'hierarchy of needs' model, and his use of the term self-actualization. Two important books are *On Becoming a Person* (1989) by Carl Rogers and *Toward a Psychology of Being* (1962) by Abraham Maslow.

The Fourth Wave: Transpersonal Psychology

Transpersonal psychology was originally a major theme in the writings of Roberto Assagioli, who spoke of transpersonal consciousness. There are many who believe that psychosynthesis actually represents a fifth force, but for the purposes of this chapter, it is included as an influence of the fourth force in psychology (Assagioli, 1991). Maslow eventually posited the fourth force, transpersonal psychology, which included mind, body *and* spirit. It delved into altered states of consciousness that were both naturally induced by esoteric spiritual practices such as meditation, chanting and dancing and chemically induced by LSD and other hallucinogens (as experienced and researched by Stanislov Grof, Timothy Leary and Richard Alpert *aka* Baba Ram Dass) as a way to explore the transpersonal realm. This research opened up our knowledge of the human mind and expanded our windows of perception and possibility.

Abraham Maslow suggested this new model when he designated the humanistic approach as a third force. As he emphasized that humanistic psychology was a major development distinct from psychoanalysis and behaviourism, he also anticipated fourth and fifth forces, which he labelled 'transpersonal' and 'transhuman' (Goble, 1970). In recent years, transpersonal psychology has joined forces with humanistic psychology in studying states of consciousness, spirituality and positive aspects of human life. In fact when positive psychology emerged in the 1990s, it seemed that many had forgotten the early influences of these two schools of thought and their positive approaches to human understanding and change.

Ken Wilber's *The Spectrum of Consciousness* (Wilber, 1977) revolutionized transpersonal psychology by combining Western psychology with Eastern spiritual practices – especially Tibetan Buddhism and Vedanta Hinduism – to create a comprehensive model of human development from the lowest stages (prepersonal) to the highest stages of nonduality (transpersonal). Wilber and others have refined this model even more over the last 30 years.

Major Figures

So who were the major figures from these four forces in psychology and what do they bring to modern day coaching? What follows is a historical review of the influence of psychology and the theories that relate to coaching. Through works such as *The Psychopathology of Everyday Life* (1901/1971), **Sigmund Freud** brought us the unconscious, transference, counter-transference, defence mechanisms and resistance. His theories, although strongly pathology-based, did allow the pursuit of our unconscious desires and unconscious mechanisms that influenced behaviour. Coaches, of course, today speak of the unconscious frequently, and probably often ask their clients to *look inside or at least to be more aware of thoughts, desires and motives just out of conscious awareness.*

Carl Jung made many important contributions to the development and terminology of psychology, including the spiritual realm, symbolism, the relevance of ancient wisdom, archetypes, life reviews, synchronicity, transpersonal consciousness, stages of life, individuation, the shadow and spiritual quests. Jung broke away from Freud in pursuing a more holistic, spiritual understanding of human motivation. He is quoted as saying 'who looks outside, dreams . . . who looks inside awakens'. That is a powerful quote for coaching today. Jung's views were often called teleological and future-driven. He became very much involved with what clients could learn from their life journey as they continued to create their desired future. They had more control over their lives than early Freudian theories would consider. Carl Jung is largely connected with the third and fourth forces of psychology because of his study of ancient and tribal cultures and the esoteric wisdom schools from around the globe. A major theory that tracks well with coaching is his concept of *individuation* – the process of becoming whole and realizing one's unique purpose and path. There is much literature on Jungian thought but for a good, short and easily accessible introduction to Jung's thought, see Chapter 1 of *Man and His Symbols* (1964), conceived and edited by Jung. Another good introductory text is *The Portable Jung* (Jung, 1976), edited by Joseph Campbell.

Alfred Adler worked on social connections, humans as social beings, the importance of relationships, family of origin themes, significance and belonging, and lifestyle assessment. His exploration of the big question ('What if . . . ?'), and the possibilities of 'acting as if' are techniques commonly used in coaching today. For coaches who work on issues related to social, corporate or family cultures with their clients, his theories of human nature are enlightening. He identified five key areas of influence on our everyday existence: social, love, self, work and spiritual; and three *life tasks* as he called them: (1) love and sexual relationship; (2) relationship to work and occupation; and (3) relationship to others and the culture. Both he and Jung believed humans had a teleological pull, a pull to create a desired future – a view at the heart of what professional coaches work toward with their clients! See *Understanding Human Nature* (Adler, 1998) for an introduction to his work.

Roberto Assagioli, the father of *psychosynthesis*, wrote about our ability to synthesize our various aspects in order to function at higher levels of consciousness. He introduced such terms as *subpersonalities, wisdom of the inner self, higher self,* and *the observing self.* He would be considered in the humanistic and transpersonal camps and major works to review from him are *Psychosynthesis: A Collection of Basic Writings* (Assagioli, 2000) and *Transpersonal Development: The Dimension Beyond Psychosynthesis* (Assagioli, 1991).

Karen Horney was an early, influential feminist psychiatrist. Her key theories involved irrational beliefs, the need for security, early influences on rational-emotive theory, and modelling the goal of 'self help'. She was a contemporary of Adler and an early influence on Carl Rogers. She was considered a theorist who supported humanistic theories and a work to read would be *The Collected Works of Karen Horney* (Horney, 1950).

Fritz Perls, founder of Gestalt therapy, worked with personality problems involving the inner conflict between values and behaviour (desires), introducing terms such as *top dog and underdog,* and practices such as *polarity* (black-and-white thinking), *the empty chair technique,* and *awareness in the moment.* Gestalt theory also valued the whole-person experience of the client, including mind, emotions, physicality and spirituality. Perls was influenced by Kurt Lewin's change theory and his work in figure–ground perspectives. He was a major influence in humanistic psychology and the holistic view of a person as a interaction of body, brain and being and that unconscious thoughts and feelings manifested themselves in many ways that could be understood with present focused inquiry. A major work for coaches to read would be *The Gestalt Approach and Eye Witness to Therapy* (Perls, 1973).

Carl Rogers developed a client-centred approach that suggested clients have the answers within them. He brought us the terms *unconditional positive regard* and *humanistic psychology.* He championed the practice of listening, reflecting and paraphrasing, and the value of silence and sacred space. The field of psychotherapy was strongly influenced by his works, *Client-Centered Therapy* (Rogers, 1951/2003) and *On Becoming a Person* (Rogers 1989/1996), and this influence carries over to coaching and its value for deep listening, co-creating the coaching space, client-driven processes, and viewing coaching as a partner to clients in their exploration of desired change.

Abraham Maslow introduced his hierarchy of needs and values. He reflected on *being needs* versus *deficiency needs,* the higher self, and our transpersonal potential. He is considered the father of humanistic psychology and did much research into the process of self-actualization. His theories apply well to positive psychology and coaching today leading toward an emphasis on *thriving* more than *surviving* or even just *striving.*

Virginia Satir can be seen as the mother of family therapy, as was experienced when I heard her say at Esalen Institute in 1970 that she could not explain the magic herself – she just did what she felt and intuited and let the family's issues surface in ways that she had fun with but also provoked deepening their awareness. She began to be called the Columbus of family therapy because she did not arrive where she started to go and did not really know where she was when she got there. She believed that a healthy family life involved an open and reciprocal sharing of affection, feelings and love. She was well known for describing family roles, e.g., *the rescuer, the victim* or *the placatory*, that function to constrain relationships and interactions in families. Her work, an early systemic look at relationships, has had a strong influence on coaching in the business context because many of the consultants at that time began to realize that her system theories and techniques for families were just as effective with dysfunctional work teams and managers. I personally used much of her techniques in my early executive coaching with executives at major corporations in the later 1980s and early 1990s. Her work, as seen for example in *Changing with Families: A Book about Further Education for Being Human* (Bandler, Grinder, and Satir 1976), was a key influence of the humanistic movement.

Viktor Frankl developed 'logotherapy' out of his personal experience during World War II. Influenced by existential philosophy and his own existential crisis, Frankl wrote *Man's Search for Meaning* (1959) while in a Nazi prison camp and later published it from the notes he had made on toilet paper. He is quoted as saying that the one freedom that could not be taken from him while in prison was his freedom to think, dream and create. Frankl introduced paradoxical intent into psychology – 'what you resist persists' or 'what you give energy to is what you manifest'. Coaches today use these same principles to assist their clients to focus on what they want and on creating desired outcomes. Frankl is cited today by many coaches as an exemplar of the importance of intention and the necessity of finding meaning in work and life.

Milton Erickson investigated hypnotherapy as well as *languaging* and the *double-binding* of the client. From his work, coaches have learned to focus on possibility and look for the uncommon approach to change, including the use of evocative and powerful questions as well as creative requests that were made of clients. Erickson is the father of American hypnotherapy and, along with Gregory Bateson, an early influencer of neuro-linguistic programming (NLP) created by Bandler and Grinder. They studied and recorded the techniques that made Erickson and Satir so creatively successful and masterful in a way that they did not even know what it was they did that created the magic, a framework that is used by many coaches.

Jeffrey Zeig and **Bill O'Hanlon**, students of Milton Erickson, intro-duced pattern interruption, the confusion technique, forced choice, assumption of the positive path, non-trance hypnosis, and unconscious competence. *Reframing* is another important coaching tool based in their work, used to help clients shift their view of a situation. O'Hanlon's works are particularly complementary to life coaching. A great new resource to read would be *Change 101: A Practical Guide to Creating Change in Life or Therapy* by Bill O'Hanlon (O'Hanlon, 2006).

In the 1970s, solution-focused approaches emerged; they put less focus on the problem and instead focused their energy into discovering and highlighting what works. Three well-known practitioners in this arena are **Insoo Kim Berg** and her husband, **Steve de Shazer**, and **Bill O'Hanlon**. Berg and Szabo (2005) wrote *Brief Coaching for Lasting Solutions*, which blends solution-focused theory and brief, short-term coaching sessions. The development of 'solution oriented therapy' has given rise to 'solution focused coaching' along similar lines.

Fernando Flores is a philosopher who took Austin and Searle's work (Solomon and Flores, 2001) on *speech act theory* and applied it to human interaction through conversations. One of the most useful coaching tools, making requests, is a legacy of his exploration of how language brings action into being. Flores was an early influence on Werner Erhard, and the EST training which later became Landmark Education, pro-grammes which influenced Thomas Leonard and his early curriculum at Coach University and Laura Whitworth and the curriculum of the Coaches Training Institute. Both Leonard and Whitworth worked closely with Werner Erhard in his organization in the 1980s. Julio Ollala and James Flaherty, both early creators in the ontological coaching theories and practices, are important figures here as well.

Martin Seligman promotes positive psychology as a strength-based approach to human fulfilment. In doing so, Seligman brought new emphasis to principles from humanistic psychology in looking at positive and generative aspects for human living. Its consistent focus is on building and utilizing strengths rather than weaknesses, and it can be applied to therapy as well as coaching and education. Seligman's work is highly useful to coaches and it is based in decades of research to back up the theories. Life coaching can certainly be viewed as applied positive psychology. Read *Authentic Happiness: Using the New Positive Psychology to Realize Your Potential for Lasting Fulfillment* by Martin Seligman (2002).

In addition to the contributions of the theorists discussed above, a vast array of research into lifespan developmental psychology has created an understanding of particular developmental trajectories that can be very helpful to coaches. **Daniel Levinson's** early work on the life development of Harvard graduates over their 50-year lifespan (*Seasons of a Man's Life* (Levinson, 1978)) yielded great insight into men's development within that age cohort. **Carol Gilligan's** work on girls and women generated insight into the ways in which women's moral, cognitive and personal development differed from men's development over the lifespan. **Robert Kegan** has developed theories and methods for assessing the development of levels of consciousness in human lifespan development.

Ken Wilber's integral approach to psychology built upon and went beyond the transpersonal approaches. Wilber synthesized the developmental models of several leading psychologists, including Freud, Piaget, Erickson, Kohlberg and Bandura for early development, and then added Jung, Graves, Gilligan, Aurobindo, Washburn, Kegan, Fowler, Underhill and dozens of others to produce a developmental model that generalizes 13 basic stages from birth up to total, nondual enlightenment. Wilber also proposes that all of human experience can be situated within a quadrant map, based on distinctions between the individual and the collective, and on the interior (subjective) versus the exterior (objective). A basic version of Wilber's quadrants in a coaching context might look like Figure 1.1.

Figure 1.1   The Client and The Context (Adapted from Wilber (2000); used with permission).

	Interior	Exterior
Individual	I Intentional (SUBJECTIVE) Emotional, Mental, Spiritual, Impulses, Perceptions Sensations, Level of Trust for Self, Other, World, Values, Beliefs, Moods, etc.	IT Behavioural (OBJECTIVE) Physical, Neurological, Body, Brain, Behaviour, Things Encountered, Neural Patterns, Physiology, etc.
Collective	WE Cultural (INTERSUBJECTIVE) Relationships, Community, Service, Morals and Ethics, Myths, Social Expectations and Rules, World View, Country of Origin	ITS Social (INTEROBJECTIVE) Systems and Institutions Rules, Patterns, Machinery

As coaches work with clients, Wilber's model can be very useful in understanding the origin and context of specific client issues. Although the quadrants are all interdependent, each one will present unique problems and provide the bases for unique solutions. For a basic understanding of Wilber's theories and their applicability to your coaching practice read, *The Essential Ken Wilber: An Introductory Reader* (Wilber, 1998).

Putting Theory into Practice

It is very important for those progressing as professional coaches today to understand how much of this theoretical foundation of coaching has become part of their ground of being rather than a technique they pull out of their pocket to use with a specific client, particularly those who transition into coaching from psychology or other helping professions (Williams, 2007). Some of this theoretical foundation has become infused in our culture as a whole, further deepening this ground of being. At the same time, the contributions of certain theorists (particularly more recent ones) offer a unique new lens through which to understand human behaviour and sometimes even help to shape an entirely new paradigm. The example below is an illustration of one such foundational influence as it applies to life coaching. I offer this here as a model that evolved from the field of addictions counselling to one that is prevalent in wellness programmes today. It is helpful for coaches to see how this model for assessing client readiness can be applied to coaching clients and what theory of technique for human behavioural change may be best applied depending on the client's stage of readiness for such change.

James Prochaska's theory of readiness for change can help coaches understand where they can most effectively enter the client's landscape of living. Prochaska's work emerged from the field of addiction counselling and research on which behaviour and style by the counsellor would best match the stage of the client's readiness for change. Prochaska (Prochaska, Norcross, and DiClemente, 1994) identified six well-defined, time-based stages that clients move through, although not necessarily in a linear way. This model can also be quite useful in coaching as a way to apply the appropriate strategies necessary to support the client's movement through the change and toward the desired state or behaviour.

What follows is a coaching example using the six stages. In it, the client's goals for coaching are that he wants to improve his health and begin an exercise routine.

(1) *Precontemplation*
At this stage, the client actually is not yet considering making a change. Clients sometimes are unaware of the need for a change or unaware of their current patterns or behaviours. If the coach sees that the client seems to be at this stage, the client is not ready to make big changes. When coaching a client at this stage, the initial exploration and assessment phases of coaching can be critical.

The client who wants to improve his health is already beyond this stage. It is not as if precontemplators cannot think of a solution – it is that they do not identify a problem. The client above has already identified a problem and has reframed it as a goal: to improve his health and begin an exercise routine. Coaches are unlikely to find clients at the precontemplation stage, unless perhaps they have been sent by their employer for a problem they have not identified on their own. Sometimes, however, a client comes to a coach for one reason and something else emerges over time. In this case, the client may be at the precontemplation stage around a particular issue.

It is important for coaches using Prochaska's model to recognize that the stage is related to the specific issue: a client may be at several different stages for several different goals, which requires flexibility on the part of the coach. The coach may be working with a client on work issues or on improving fulfilment in relationships when the client goes to the doctor and discovers his cholesterol and blood pressure are high, and the doctor recommends that he focus on his health. Here, the client has received *assessment data* from his doctor. Sometimes assessment data is utilized in coaching. These can be formal, as from a plethora of personality assessments available, or informal, as in the initial client interview, or use of the wheel of life model. In either case, a coaching strategy for moving a client from precontemplation to the second stage, contemplation, is to use assessment data. A coach would be looking to see if the client is accepting the information or denying that a problem exists that might need to be addressed.

(2) *Contemplation*
Clients at this stage are considering making a change and also may find themselves quite ambivalent about it, or they may not know what to do to make the change. They can endlessly weigh the pros and cons but not actually decide to get into action. The coach can assist the client at this stage to examine how the current situation and his habits, behaviours and patterns work for and against him. For this client who wants to improve health and initiate exercise, the coach might ask: 'What kind of exercise do you most

enjoy?' 'What will be the result if you keep things as they are and don't make any changes?' 'What are the pros and cons for you of initiating a regular exercise programme?' The client may be a busy executive who travels quite often and feels time-pressured. If so, the coach's role might be to help the client examine the consequences of allowing work to overtake his time and schedule to the detriment of his health. In addition, the coach helps the client explore the motivation to change versus the motivation to keep things as they are.

This is where a coach could use Perls' empty chair technique with the client. The coach would ask the client to map out the pros and cons of two poles of an issue – in this case, exercise programme or no exercise programme – and to identify the positive and negative aspects of each side. Then, the coach works with the client to have one part of himself take the pro side of the desire and then sit in an empty chair and give voice to the other side. This technique is a nonthreatening way to give voice to the inner dialogue that is just beneath the surface. The coach is an ally to help the client find a pathway for moving forward with more clarity and commitment. This technique of giving voice to different parts of the client is most often seen today as working with the *gremlin* or *inner critic* in coaching. The use of the empty chair technique could serve the client very well in not only making the internal dialogue external, but also to have some lively fun while they are at it. This does not have to be applied as it would in a psychotherapy situation but instead could be done in a lighthearted but profoundly insightful manner in coaching.

(3) *Preparation*

At this stage, the client is preparing to change – gathering information, assembling resources, checking out possibilities and preparing to act. This is where the focus on accountability in coaching can be paramount. The coach can help the client discover resources, identify what is needed, co-create possibilities and choices and with them the willingness and desire to move forward.

Helping the client move from contemplation to preparation can be a significant accomplishment in itself. The client begins to overcome the inertia that characterized the previous stage, where the only action was *thinking* about action. Coaches sometimes feel that they have failed if their client does not jump into action. Instead, it is important to recognize that the preparation stage is critical. The coach's work is to help initiate change; if the client is seeking health, for example, it is researching on the Internet local resources for health clubs, trainers, classes, or other health and fitness opportunities. This *is* movement – although sometimes the coach who is unfamiliar with Prochaska's work does not see it that way. With the model in mind, a coach can maintain the patience to allow the client to move through each stage, knowing that the client's ultimate success will be better ensured if each stage is addressed fully according to the client's unique needs.

(4)   *Action*

This is the classic stage where the client actually takes actions, practises new behaviours, and tries new things. The coach's role is to ensure that clients' actions are congruent with who they are and what they want. The work in the initial three stages to identify their own ways of taking action is empowering for clients. The ideas for action do not come from the coach's preconceptions or advice but, instead, have resulted from the co-creative process of coaching. This client's actions may include hiring a personal trainer, buying a piece of exercise equipment and using it, setting up a regular workout schedule, changing his diet, and so on.

(5)   *Maintenance*

At this stage, the client has maintained the chosen actions long enough to have created new habits and integrated them into the rest of his life. This usually indicates that new habits are being installed and are likely to last; coaching at this time continues to acknowledge and endorse the changes. The client's alliance with the coach increases the likelihood of enduring success, particularly with clients who may not have been successful at maintaining change in the past. If the client slips back into old habits or if circumstances change, the coach helps the client to reset his goals or recalibrate his actions.

Just as in car maintenance, occasional tune-ups and adjustments are needed to address the current situation. Clients sometimes believe that they can consistently maintain actions over time, no matter what. Yet life brings changes. This client may develop a health issue that requires that he change his preferred way of exercise and this may be more difficult than he expected. A new child in his family may require realignment of his use of time and energy.

(6)   *Termination*

Prochaska used this term because it reflected the fact that the client no longer needs a programmatic approach to the behaviour that needed changing. The new behaviour has become a natural part of the person's life, and it happens without much thought on the part of the person. For the client above, the exercise programme has simply become a part of what he does each week – a new habit, perhaps even a new joyful habit.

In coaching, stage (6) may not mean an end to the coaching per se. It may simply mean that the coaching will no longer focus on a particular goal – it has been *terminated,* so to speak. Some clients may feel that they have achieved their coaching goals. The coach helps the client recognize when ongoing maintenance coaching or coaching for new issues will benefit him.

It is important to keep in mind that *change is a process, not an event.* On any desired change, the client may cycle through these stages in a nonlinear fashion. These steps are not linear – they are spiral. For example, coaches commonly see a pattern in which the client commits to taking action by the next session, yet when he appears for the next session has moved back from the action stage to the contemplation stage. The coach's role is to support the client's movement through the cycle and to accept the client wherever he is in the moment.

Conclusion

The core of the coaching profession is grounded in sound academic and scholarly theories that preceded coaching, and it will be strengthened by the validation of theories and evidence-based research as the profession moves forward. All the amazing tools that have grown out of modern psychology support coaches in assisting clients to change as desired. As the recent emergence of positive psychology demonstrates, new developments become available all the time.

The hallmarks of coaching are its synthesis of tools from other fields and its proclivity for innovation. With all the research going on today, coaching is developing its own evidence-based theories. It has borrowed from what has gone before, much as psychologists borrowed from philosophers. As coaching grows as a profession, it will develop its own research base of effective strategies and tools within the unique relationship that is the coaching alliance. This chapter and those that follow are an attempt to glean the practical from the scientific. How do all the knowledge and theories inform your coaching business? How do you know what skills work best and also fit your style? Knowing that the skill sets and competencies are not invented out of thin air adds credibility to an emerging profession, and finding practical uses for the theories in coaching relationships makes a difference in people's lives.

Professional life and business coaches support clients in the search for, and in walking the new path toward, desired change. They do so by being able to bring *multiple perspectives* to the client work. They remain fully appreciative of the unique gifts and strengths of each individual client. At the same time, they can see how the client's work fits within the context of how human beings generally develop over the course of a lifespan.

Coaching has arisen as a profession, I believe, because of the shortage of real listening in our society today and for the lack of true connection that many people experience. All of these factors arise from the socio-economic conditions of rapid change, technology advances, and the instant availability of information. Carl Rogers said that counselling was like buying a friend; hiring a coach is similar. But, of course, it is much more than that. A coach is a partner who is hired to assist the client in going for greatness in any and all domains of his or her life. People may not always *need* a coach, but I believe they do *deserve* a coach. And like all true professions, there are different levels of mastery and competence. So in looking for a coach, interview several and do your research. You will be glad you did.

References and Bibliography

Adler, A. (1998). *Understanding human nature* (C. Brett, Trans.). Center City, MN: Hazelden.

Adler, A. (1956). *The individual psychology of Alfred Adler: A systematic presentation in selections from his writings* (H. L. Ansbacher and R. R. Ansbacher, Eds.). New York: Basic.

Albee, G. W. (1998). Fifty years of clinical psychology: Selling our soul to the devil. *Applied and Preventive Psychology, 7,* 189–194.

Albee, G. W. (2000, February). The Boulder model's fatal flaw. *American Psychologist, 55*(2), 247–248.

Allport, G. (1937). *Personality: A psychological interpretation.* New York: Holt.

Allport, G. (1955). *Becoming: Basic considerations for a psychology of personality.* New Haven, CT: Yale University Press.

Allport, G. (1961). *Pattern and growth in personality.* New York: Holt, Rinehart & Winston.

Assagioli, R. (1965). *Psychosynthesis: A manual of principles and techniques.* New York: Hobbs, Dorman.

Assagioli, R. (1991). *Transpersonal development.* London: Crucible Books.

Assagioli, R. (2000). *Psychosynthesis: A collection of basic writings.* Amherst, MA: Synthesis Center Publishing.

Bandler, R., and Grinder, J. (1975). *Patterns of the hypnotic techniques of Milton H. Erickson, M.D.* Cupertino, CA: Meta.

Bandler, R., Grinder, J., and Satir, V. (1976). *Changing with families: A book about further education for being human.* Palo Alto, CA: Science and Behavior Books.

Berg, I. K. (1994). *Family-based services: A solution-focused approach.* New York: Norton.

Berg, I. K., and Szabo, P. (2005). *Brief coaching for lasting solutions.* New York: Norton.

Berne, E. (1996). *Games people play: The basic handbook of transactional analysis.* New York: Ballantine Books.

Brock, V. G. (2008). *Grounded theory on the root, and emergence of coaching.* Unpublished dissertation.

Bugental, J. F. T. (1967). *Challenges of humanistic psychology.* New York: McGraw-Hill.

Calvin, W. H. (2005). *A brief history of the mind.* Oxford: Oxford University Press.

Dennett, D. (1991). *Consciousness explained.* Boston: Little, Brown.

de Shazer, S. (1985). *Keys to solution in brief therapy.* New York: Norton.

de Shazer, S. (1988). *Clues: Investigating solutions in brief therapy.* New York: Norton.

Erickson, M. H. (1990). *Uncommon casebook: The complete clinical work of Milton H. Erickson* (W. H. O'Hanlon and A. L. Hexum, Eds.). New York: Norton.

Fadiman, J., and Frager, R. (1976). *Personality and personal growth.* Upper Saddle River, NJ: Harper & Row.

Flaherty, K. (1998) *Coaching: Evoking excellence in others.* Burlington, MA: Butterworth-Heinemann.

Frankl, V. E. (1959). *Man's search for meaning.* New York: Pocket.

Freud, S. (1965). *New introductory lectures on psychoanalysis.* New York: Norton.

Freud, S. (1982). *Basic works of Sigmund Freud* (J. Strackey, Trans./Ed.). Franklin Center, PA: Franklin Library.

Freud, S. (1971). *The psychopathology of everyday life.* New York: Norton.

Gallwey, W. T. (2000). *The inner game of work: focus learning, pleasure and mobility in the workplace.* New York: Random House.

Gilligan, C. (1993). *In a different voice: Psychological theory and women's development.* Cambridge, MA: Harvard University Press.

Goble, F. (1970). *The third force: the psychology of Abraham Maslow.* New York: Harper & Row.

Haley, J. (1986). *Uncommon therapy: The psychiatric techniques of Milton H. Erickson.* New York: Norton.

Hart, V., Blattner, J., and Leipsic, S. (2001). Coaching versus therapy: A perspective. *Consulting Psychology Journal,* 53(4), 229–237.

Horney, K. (1950) *The collected works of Karen Horney* (2 vols). New York: Norton.

Horney, K. (1980). *The adolescent diaries of Karen Horney.* New York: Basic.

Hudson, F. (1999). *The handbook of coaching: A comprehensive resource guide for managers, executives, consultants, and HR.* San Francisco: Jossey-Bass.

Hudson, F. (1999). *The adult years.* San Francisco: Jossey-Bass.

James, W. (1994). *The varieties of religious experience: a study in human nature.* New York: Random House.

James, W. (1983). *The principles of psychology.* Cambridge, MA: Harvard University Press.

Jourard, S. M. (1974). *Healthy personality, an approach from the viewpoint of humanistic psychology.* New York: Macmillan.

Jung, C. G. (1964). *Man and his symbols.* Garden City, NY: Doubleday.

Jung, C. G. (1933). *Modern man in search of a soul.* London: Trubner.

Jung, C. G. (1953). *The collected works of C. G. Jung* (H. Read, M. Fordham, and G. Adler, Eds.). New York: Pantheon.

Jung, C. G. (1970). *Civilization in transition* (R. F. C. Hull, Trans.). Princeton, NJ: Princeton University Press.

Jung, C. G. (1976). *The portable Jung* (J. Campbell, Ed.; R. F. C. Hull, Trans.). New York: Penguin.

Kegan, R. (1982) *The evolving self: Problems and process in human development.* Cambridge, MA: Harvard University Press.

Levinson, D. (1978). *Seasons of a man's life.* New York: Ballantine.

Maslow, A. (1954). *Motivation and personality.* New York: Harper.

Maslow, A. (1962). *Toward a psychology of being.* Princeton, NJ: Van Nostrand.

Maslow, A. (1993). *Farther reaches of human nature.* New York: Arkana.

May, R. (1953). *Man's search for himself.* New York: Norton.

May, R. (1975). *The courage to create.* New York: Norton.

May, R. (1979). *Psychology and the human dilemma.* New York: Norton.

O'Hanlon, B. (1999a). *Guide to possibility land.* New York: Norton.

O'Hanlon, B. (1999b). *Do one thing different.* New York: Morrow.

O'Hanlon, B. (2006). *Change 101: A practical guide to creating change in life or therapy.* New York: Norton.

O'Hanlon, B., and Martin, M. (1992). *Solution-oriented hypnosis: An Ericksonian approach.* New York: Norton.

Perls, F. S. (1966). *Ego, hunger and aggression: A revision of Freud's theory and method.* San Francisco: Orbit Graphics Arts.

Perls, F. S. (1973). *The Gestalt approach and eye witness to therapy.* Ben Lomond, CA: Science & Behavior.

Perls, F. S. (1969). *Gestalt therapy verbatim.* Lafayette, CA: Real People Press.

Prochaska, J. O., Norcross, J. C., and DiClemente, C. C. (1994). *Changing for good: A revolutionary six-stage program for overcoming bad habits and moving your life forward.* New York: HarperCollins.

Rogers, C. (1951/2003). *Client-centered therapy.* Boston: Houghton Mifflin.

Rogers, C. (1989/1996). *On becoming a person: a therapist's view of psychotherapy.* New York: Houghton Mifflin.

Satir, V. (1964). *Conjoint family therapy: A guide to therapy and techniques.* Palo Alto, CA: Science & Behavior.

Satir, V. (1976). *Making contact.* Millbrae, CA: Celestial Arts.

Satir, V. (1991). *Satir model: Family therapy and beyond.* Palo Alto, CA: Science & Behavior.

Satir, V., and Baldwin, M. (1983). *Step by step: A guide to creating change in families.* Palo Alto, CA: Science & Behavior.

Seligman, M. E. (2002) *Authentic happiness: Using the new positive psychology to realize your potential for lasting fulfillment.* New York: Free Press.

Skinner, B. F. (1976). *About behaviorism.* New York: Vintage Books.

Solomon, R. C., and Flores, F. (2001). *Building trust: in business, politics, relationships, and life.* New York: HarperCollins.

Stober, D., and Grant, A. (Ed.). (2006). *Evidenced based coaching handbook.* New York: John Wiley & Sons, Inc.

Watson, J. (1913) Psychology as the behaviorist views it. *Psychological Review,* 20, 158–177.

Whitmore, J. (1995). *Coaching for performance.* Sonoma, CA: Nicholas Brealey.

Wilber, K. (1977). *The spectrum of consciousness.* Wheaton, IL: Quest Books.

Wilber, K. (1998). *The essential Ken Wilber: An introductory reader.* Boston: Shambhala Publications.

Wilber. K. (2000). *Integral psychology: Consciousness, spirit, psychology, therapy.* Boston: Shambhala Publications.

Williams, P. (1980). *Transpersonal psychology: An introductory guidebook.* Greeley, CO: Lutey.

Williams, P. (1997). Telephone coaching for cash draws new client market. *Practice Strategies,* 2, 11.

Williams, P. (1999). The therapist as personal coach: Reclaiming your soul! *The Independent Practitioner,* 19(4), 204–207.

Williams, P. (2000a, July). Practice building: The coaching phenomenon marches on. *Psychotherapy Finances,* 26(315), 1–2.

Williams, P. (2000b, June). Personal coaching's evolution from therapy, *Consulting Today* (special issue), 4.

Williams, P. (2004). Coaching evolution and revolution: The history, development, and distinctions that will define coaching on the most important organizational development in the future. *Absolute Advantage,* 3(4), 6–9.

Williams, P. (2007). Bordaline: Understanding the relationship between therapy and coaching, *Choice* magazine, 5(3), 22–26.

Williams, P. (2007a). The theoretical foundations of coaching: You mean this stuff wasn't just made up? *Choice* magazine, 4(2), 49–50.

Williams, P., and Davis, D. (2007). *Therapist as life coach: An introduction for counselors and other helping professionals, revised and expanded edition.* New York: Norton.

Williams, P., and Thomas, L. (2005). *Total life coaching: 50+ Life lessons, skills, and techniques to enhance your practice and your life.* New York: Norton.

Williams, P., and Menendez, D. (2007). *Becoming a professional life coach: Lessons from the Institute for Life Coach Training.* New York: Norton.

Zieg, J. K. (1994). *Ericksonian methods: The essence of the story.* New York: Brunner/Mazel.

2

Coach Self-Management: The Foundation of Coaching Effectiveness

Travis Kemp

Why this Topic?

There is an increasing effort within the field of coaching to exploring the application of evidence-based methodologies that have been successfully utilized within clinical psychology, counselling and psychotherapy (see Allcorn, 2006; Auerbach, 2006; Ducharme, 2004; Kilburg, 2004; Peterson, 2006; Sherin and Caiger, 2004). Less effort, however, has been made in exploring the unique relationship that is created between the helper and the client within the coaching context, despite many practitioners' and theorists' strong contention that it is this relationship itself that represents the central mediating factor underpinning the effectiveness of all such developmental interventions (Corey, 2004). As such, the coaching engagement can be conceptualized as a helper–client relationship within the overall context of the applied, positive and performance domains of psychology. In this chapter I will address the key elements and dynamics of the relationships that are formed in the coaching engagement and explore the opportunities for coaches to deepen their understanding and management of these inter- and intra-personal processes.

In the first part of this chapter I propose that, in contradiction to popular coaching belief, it is the coaching *relationship*, rather than any

The Philosophy and Practice of Coaching: Insights and Issues for a New Era.
Edited by David B. Drake, Diane Brennan and Kim Gørtz.
© 2008 John Wiley & Sons, Ltd.

specific coaching model or technique, that is the core determinant and catalyst for client change. It is important to clarify that this proposition does not, however, contend that *any* relationship constitutes a coaching relationship. Clearly there are both qualitative and functional differences between a relationship based on, for example, friendship, and those experienced in a coaching relationship. The latter are clearly articulated and entered into by both parties for the client's developmental purposes; they incorporate an explicit purpose, client-driven direction and outcomes, and mutually agreed parameters for challenge and accountability. As such, the quality of these relationships will more positively correlate with the quality of outcomes achieved by the client than will the coaching model used in the coaching engagement.

For some practitioners and theorists alike, this may come as a fundamental challenge to the prevailing rhetoric that espouses the comparative efficacy of 'unique' models and methodologies of coaching which are often presented by authors as proprietary intellectual capital. Instead, I utilize the evidence-based literature that supports the proposition that the client–helper relationship is the central mediating variable to the achievement of efficacious, client-driven change outcomes (Bordin, 1979; Connor-Greene, 1993; Greenson, 1967; Rogers, 1957; Horvath, 2000, 2001, 2006; Horvath and Greensberg, 1989; Kivlighan, 2007; Lilliengren and Werbart, 2005). Further, meta-analytical studies, such as those reported by Horvath and Symonds (1991), lend compelling support for this proposition. Building on this foundation, I introduce and illuminate the central role of the coaches' own self-understanding, self-management and continuous intrapersonal development in furthering the impact of the coaching engagement.

In particular, the chapter identifies the antecedent conditions, processes, and intrapersonal and interpersonal dynamics that are critical to developing professional, accountable and ethical foundations for coaching, and it highlights the similarities that are observable between helping relationships in allied professions and those seen in coaching engagements. To this end, the chapter builds upon previous comparisons of professional practice in these related fields (Corey, 2004; Egan, 2002). Emergent issues in coaching practice such as ethics (de Jong, 2006) and supervision (Hawkins, 2006) are also explored in the context of the coach's unique position and responsibility within the coaching relationship. Of specific applied value to the practitioner is the presentation of a practitioner model designed to operationalize a coach's unique development processes and highlight the positive client opportunities that emerge when she develops greater self-management mastery.

Why Self-Manage?

Self-management can be most succinctly defined as a developmental process in which coaches become increasingly aware of their unique cognitive, behavioural, perceptual and emotional systems and, through this process, develop an increasing capability to effectively manage their use in service to the client's development process within the coaching relationship. The importance of coaches actively participating in this process, a process that compels them to engage in the same introspective and reflective learning space that they expect of their clients, may appear self-evident; however, to date, it has been seldom addressed within the coaching literature. As the practice of coaching continues to seek recognition as a profession, and in particular, as a helping profession, coaches must continuously seek to engage in self-analysis and professional development to satisfy the core foundations of ethical practice that are expected of us by our clients and our peers from other helping professions.

To date, whether it is recognized or not, coaching has been heavily informed by the extensive body of knowledge accumulated across these related helping professions. As an example, Perrin and Newnes (2002) eloquently articulated the many challenges faced by therapists and psychologists in managing the multiple identities that the helper and client bring to the therapeutic relationship. Likewise, the coaching relationship brings with it a myriad of complex challenges in relation to the unique individual systems that we as humans bring to these relationships.

In beginning our exploration of these complexities, I turn to the extensive body of knowledge accumulated within the discipline of social psychology to explore the reasons why self-management may be so important to the effective practice of coaching. Social psychology can be described as 'the scientific study of how people think about, influence and relate to one another' (Myers, 1996, p. 6) and hence, understanding this body of knowledge is vital when considering how best to approach the coaching relationship. I have clustered four major principles from the social psychology literature which pertain particularly to the coaching relationship.

Principles from Social Psychology

Attribution Theory, Trait Inference and Stereotypes

Attribution theory (Heider, 1958) contends that people tend to explain others' behaviour by attributing it to either their internal dispositions, that is, their traits, motivations, values and attitudes, or to their external conditions such as the environment, situational circumstances and social influences. Further, Jones and Davis (1965) discovered that we often assume that people's intentions and dispositions correspond to their actions and behaviour. Thus the subsequent tendency is for people to generalize their attributions and assumptions to all similar people and situations. These two cognitive biases result in the emergence of stereotypes or an expectation that individuals within a specific group or subgroup will have a predetermined and consistent set of characteristics, beliefs or behaviours – a judgement made in the absence of specific data on that individual. The danger of these stereotypes when coaching specific client groups is clear. Without a strong awareness of the coach's potential for stereotyping, and the subsequent self-awareness and effective management of these tendencies should they exist, the positive coaching impact for clients who fall within that specific stereotype are significantly reduced and at worst, coaching becomes a negative and destructive experience.

Ross (1977) coined the term *fundamental attribution error* to describe the tendency one has as an observer of a situation to underestimate the situational factors contributing to that situation and overestimate the dispositional factors of individuals' behaviour within that system. This error is particularly pertinent to coaching within organizational or corporate settings, given the often problematic nature of working within groups and teams. Simply stated, if an undesirable situation or outcome arises for a group or team of which the observer is *not* a member, the observer will tend to attribute these undesirable elements to the dispositions, competencies and capabilities of the individuals within that group. Conversely, if a problem arises within a group of which the observer is also a member, that observer will tend to attribute those negative elements or outcomes being experienced within that group to situational factors that are then seen as being out of the direct control of the group members themselves. These behaviours often manifest in the form of blaming external impacts such as market and economy conditions for poor financial performance or other family members for disharmonious relationships at home.

Within the coaching relationship, many developmental opportunities emerge where the client is tempted to attribute blame to someone or something other than their own behaviour or performance. This is particularly the case if the client finds herself in a reactive and defensive cognitive framework rather than a proactive and accepting one (Kemp, 2005a). The coach in these cases is at risk of being drawn into the client's fundamental attribution error complex if she is not acutely cognizant of both her own investment in her client's improved performance and success and her client's investment in being seen to be making progress in the eyes of the coach. As a result, a coach's effectiveness as a catalyst and facilitator of a client's change process is arguably compromised if her predispositions are not actively surfaced and managed within her field of awareness and actions.

Behavioural Confirmation, Halo Effect and Belief Perseverance

A unique cognitive bias that humans have towards creating self-fulfilling beliefs or self-fulfilling prophecies creates a phenomenon known as *behavioural confirmation* (Snyder, 1984). Over time, people begin to behave as others expect them to behave, that is, the generalizations that are made by an observer of the behavioural patterns of another person they observe tend to directly influence the observer's interactions with that person in the future and hence, all subsequent interactions result in similar behavioural patterns being observed. This biasing effect gives rise to phenomena such as the *halo effect* (Thorndike, 1920). This effect causes one's judgement of a particular trait or set of traits observed within an individual as either good or bad and then subsequently, a further generalization of this judgement to the whole person is established. Once this judgement of an individual as 'good' or 'bad', or, as is often the case in organizations, a 'high' or 'low' performer, they persist, even in the face of evidence to the contrary. This cognitive bias is commonly known as *belief perseverance* (Myers, 1996).

Clearly, a lack of awareness of these cognitive biases places coaches in a compromising position when faced with either particularly attractive or repulsive behaviours or values demonstrated by their clients. A coach's inability to effectively manage these biases and maintain appropriate emotional, cognitive and behavioural boundaries within the coaching relationship is vital to the coach remaining effectual as a change agent for their client's development. Hence, the coach must develop the ability to identify what these unique friction points are for him and then establish a process and mechanism for adjusting and managing these perceptions and responses to the client within a coaching conversation. These two steps are critical in maintaining a positive experience for clients and the appropriate ethical standards for coaches.

The Coach's Achilles Heel

Perhaps one of the most potentially debilitating cognitive biases faced by a coach is his tendency to overestimate the accuracy of his beliefs and judgements and to be more attached to their confidence than to the pursuit of accuracy. This *overconfidence bias* (Gilovich, Griffin, and Kahneman, 2002), if left unchecked, compromises the coach's ability to create an accurate 'case conceptualization', and subsequently, to effectively facilitate the client's developmental process in the relationship. In coaching terms, this case conceptualization process involves the collection, ordering and interpretation of a complex set of data relating to the client which enables the coach to design a development process that best suits the client's style, needs and goals. Without this step, the coach's ability to provide an appropriate intervention model and development framework is compromised and the client's coaching outcomes may again be limited.

Once people lock in on these beliefs and judgements, and subsequently develop a strong level of confidence about them, they then begin to subconsciously filter data that enters their field of perception so that only data which supports their existing view of a person, situation or event enters their cognitive processes. This *confirmation bias* (Gilovich, Griffin, and Kahneman, 2002) establishes progressively stronger belief perseverance and severely limits the coach's ability to remain objective in the coaching relationship. By deepening their understanding of these human predispositions and their personal idiosyncrasies, coaches are more able to maintain their position as a neutral yet conscious facilitator on behalf of their clients' goals. By adopting this perspective when entering into the coaching relationship, coaches can proactively manage the potentially adverse influence of their fears, limitations, hopes and desires on their clients' process and, as a result, act in ways that keep their clients' needs and objectives at the forefront of the coaching relationship. This is particularly important in the formative stages of the relationship's development so as to provide a stable foundation for the coaching engagement.

Psychodynamic Influences

The subconscious aspects of Freud's psychodynamic realm add a further level of self-management complexity to the coaching relationship. Kilburg (2004) argues that this subconscious dynamic impacts significantly on the coaching relationship in a number of forms.

For example, transference can be described as the tendency for the client to respond to the coach in a similar pattern as he displays with others in his life who have similar characteristics and attributes and in which similar relationship dynamics exist. Further, the client's projections of unconscious or subjective perceptions, beliefs and attributes onto the coach add a further level of complexity to the coaching relationship dynamic. This complexity, when left unsurfaced and unexamined, potentially clouds the coaching relationship and the subsequent goal striving activity of the client.

Likewise, the subconscious reciprocity of this transference – or *counter transference* – on the part of the coach towards the client creates deeper challenges in the coach's pursuit of a client-centred and client-driven coaching relationship. At worst, failing to surface and manage this psychodynamic inherent in all coaching relationships can be potentially harmful to the client and professionally culpable and ethically questionable for the coach. However, at best, it can be seen as a natural consequence of all human relationships which, when used skilfully and intentionally, becomes a valuable tool for insight (McAuley, 2003) and provides a valuable context and framework for the relationship between coach and client. By actively engaging in the continuing process of inquisitive self-reflection, introspection and professional support, a coach is better able to identify his own psychodynamic patterns.

A simple illustration of the importance of these reflections is the impact of early familial relationships on adult behaviour patterns. A coach whose paternal relationship was emotionally disengaged, conflict-driven and aggressive as a child may respond to a client with similar behaviours in the same way in which he responded to his father during childhood. If these responses were positive and adaptive, this can support the client's deeper exploration of the impact that this behaviour has on others. However, if the coach failed to resolve an effective method of interaction with this parent, the same ineffectual or dysfunctional patterns of interaction may emerge again within the relationship with the client and, consequently, the coach's effectiveness in this relationship is compromised. The coach is therefore compelled, both professionally and ethically, to surface, explore and identify the potential impacts that their unique psychodynamic patterns may have on the client through the coaching relationship.

A coach is better able to maximize the positive impact of her skills and talents in a calculated, ethical and responsible way by raising her awareness and subsequently managing her cognitive predispositions to biases, patterns and psychodynamics. As a result, she can bring richness to the client's experience in the coaching relationship that may otherwise be at risk of becoming overly 'clinical' and 'formulaic' in its structure. By surfacing, managing and minimizing the negative impact of cognitive biases in the coaching relationship, and concurrently maximizing the opportunities for coaches' unique experiences and talents to surface within the relationship, clients' growth experiences can be positively enriched and are better able to achieve what Wesson and Boniwell

(2007) refer to as a 'flow-enhancing' coaching relationship (see Moore, Drake, Tschannen-Moran, Campone, and Kaufman (2005) on *relational flow*).

What can We Do? Introducing the Human Factors Lens

By developing and deepening our awareness of our unique internal system of thinking, behaving, perceiving and emoting we are better able to minimize the potentially negative impact of our 'blind spots' – those human factor elements that surface within the coaching relationship, which remain unknown to the coach himself and may/may not be unknown to the client. If they emerge, unmanaged, within the coaching relationship and are observed by the client, these inadequacies may cause the client to question the capability and professional skills of the coach. This situation, while clearly undesirable, is even more deleterious to achieving positive coaching outcomes when the coach's inadequacies remain unknown to the client as well. In the latter case, any negative impact of these blind spots remains undetected and, hence, unchallenged and uncontrolled – putting the client at direct risk of psychological injury.

Most importantly, it is the coach's ability to continuously reflect upon, illuminate and subsequently manage her unique personality constructs and cognitive schemas in a way that serves to support – but at minimum to 'do no harm' – to clients and their pursuit of their growth and development goals. I propose that by engaging in a structured and continuous cycle of self-reflection, illumination and self-management, the coach develops a deeper level of self-understanding and, subsequently, a refined level of personal capability in maintaining appropriate relationship boundaries between herself and client. By actively eliciting feedback from peers, supervisors and past clients, coaches develop the capability to effectively calibrate the way in which they are engaging with their clients in relationships and gain a deeper awareness of the specific cognitive and behavioural traits and tendencies that they have in response to a diverse range of clients and their situations. By integrating these insights and awareness into their conscious field of awareness, coaches are more able to notice, reframe and adjust these traits and tendencies. As a result, coaches are more able to integrate these insights in the moment and, therefore, more able to moderate and mediate their reactions and behaviours within the coaching relationship.

In Figure 2.1, the central developmental levers are clustered to form a conceptual framework to enable coaches to explore their internal environment as a starting point for this self-development process. The Human Factors Lens provides a means for coaches to reflect upon their current internal dynamics and explore the ways in which their organizing framework shapes their view of and response to the world around them. As coaches, we can use this lens to systematically reflect upon the four key questions (and their respective levels) that underlie the four human factor lenses (see Figure 2.1).

Firstly, by reflecting on our *cognition*, or thinking, we surface and explore the myriad of cognitive biases common to all humans. As a core developmental platform, the active process of reflecting on and capturing our own unique thinking patterns in addition to these inherent tendencies is a valuable starting point for our self-management challenge and provides a solid foundation for subsequent reflections. This process of 'thinking about our thinking', or metacognition, serves to surface and question the accuracy of our habitual cognitive patterns and our idiosyncratic variations on common cognitive biases.

Secondly, by reflecting on our *feelings* we begin to develop a deeper insight and awareness of the powerful impact that emotions have on

Figure 2.1 The Human Factors Lens.

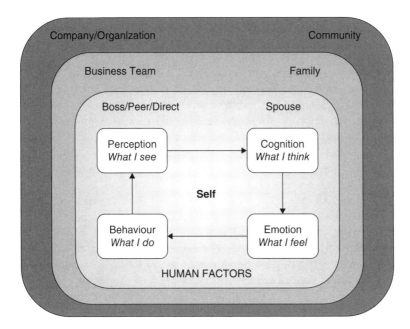

the other three human factors. If we can better understand how we respond and behave in the face of frustration, anger, elation and a myriad of other emotions that appear in coaching, we are more able to notice and manage the form and impact of these responses in the moment. This ability is particularly important in recognizing and shifting our response when experiencing client issues, language and behaviours that have, in the past, triggered strong emotions for us.

Thirdly, these very responses and *behaviours* in the context of emotional stimuli within coaching relationships, and their impact on both our immediate relationships and our environment, are a rich source of data for discerning and assessing our internal predispositions. As our behaviour is the most overt tool in the coaching relationship, and the most observable by the client, it is vitally important that coaches understand intimately their behavioural patterns and refine their repertoire in response to personally challenging situations and events in the coaching relationship. If a coach's tendency is to withdraw, for example, from strong interpersonal conflict, it is imperative that this issue be appropriately addressed outside of the coaching relationship to ensure that client outcomes are not adversely compromised by the coach's personal challenges. However, it is the awareness of this tendency through reflecting on patterns in both client types and client interactions that provides the opening for a coach to explore these issues.

Fourthly, we must examine our *perception* of the other people, situations and environments around us. By identifying and testing these perceptions through data gathering and feedback, any discrepancies in the coach's perceptual acuity can be identified and appropriate adjustments made. For example, if a coach perceives his client's withdrawn and non-conversant behaviour as aloofness and arrogance rather than contemplation and introspection, his response may be one of direct challenge and confrontation rather than one of support and empathy. Each of these two potential responses from the coach will have a markedly different impact on the client's coaching experience. If a coach has developed the tendency towards certain biases in viewing, interpreting and responding to types of situations, people, philosophies or events, his inherent tendency will be to reinforce these views. As previously discussed, these beliefs and perceptions tend to persist, regardless of conflicting data; it is therefore important for the coach to actively and frequently identify and challenge any generalizations, stereotypes or schemas that begin to manifest. The coach who stereotypes all accountants as 'emotional invalids' undermines his effectiveness when working with these types of clients even as they represent an opportunity for a closer look at himself along these lines.

These four key human elements can be drawn upon to understand how we as individuals interact across progressively broader relationships and environments – from those we have with our manager, peers and spouse to those we maintain with our profession, family, community and broader society. The continuous surfacing, reflecting on and managing of these intrapersonal/interpersonal complexities can be overwhelming for coaches if conducted in isolation from the appropriate developmental support. One of the hallmark methods used by the majority of long-established helping professions to maintain their standards is a relationship that is established between fellow professionals for the purpose of providing ongoing supervision. The establishment of a relationship with a credible and competent coaching supervisor is a critical step in ensuring ethical and responsible practice, and it provides a sound platform for the coach to continue her progressive self-development process outside of her professional coaching engagements.

This relationship is not a coach-the-coach relationship commonly established between coaching practitioners. Rather, this relationship is designed for the main purpose of continuing to surface and illuminate the 'unknown' self (Luft and Ingham, 1955) and to further deepen the coach's own understanding of how his unique human factors are manifesting in his coaching relationships. Often, coaches will bring specific coaching challenges or problems to their supervision sessions and, rather than be a forum for facilitated problem solving, the supervision conversation becomes one of analysis of the interpersonal relationship dynamics between the coach and his clients. Perhaps equally important is the external and impartial accountability that the relationship creates and the opportunity to open one's coaching practice to somewhat public scrutiny.

The intent behind this process is twofold. Firstly, by sharing about her normally private coaching practices – with the appropriate confidences in place and details respected – the coach's potential blind-spots and challenges can be identified, surfaced and discussed with a third party. This provides a high level of professional accountability and security to the service being provided to her clients. Secondly, this supervision relationship offers a place for the coach to identify those methods and practices that yielded positive client outcomes and to determine how best to generalize them to similar situations and clients in the future.

Once this relationship has been established, however, the first and most critical step for the coach is to continue the process of introspection and reflection on her self-concept, the construction of her unique 'self', and the subsequent impact of these insights on the way in which she attends to and relates to her client within the relationship. When a coach engages fully and openly in this human factors approach, the

Figure 2.2   The Self-Management Pyramid.

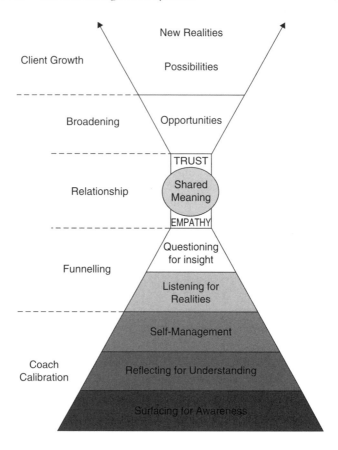

foundations for effective self-management are laid down and the subsequent benefits to the client and the coaching relationship are free to surface. The Self-Management Pyramid (SMP) was developed (see Figure 2.2) to more fully explain the introspective and reflective process by which the coach can come to achieve shared meaning and positive outcomes with his clients.

What's in it for the Client? An Introduction to the Self-Management Pyramid

Given the complexity of the human change process (Gilbert, 2002), coaches will be inadequate for the challenge of facilitating their clients' growth without first having an intimate and personal experience of the change process themselves. Perplexingly, this question remains largely under-addressed in the coaching literature and, surprisingly, is only found infrequently in the psychological and therapeutic literature. Hence, there are few guidelines or frameworks for coaches to utilize as a guide for their own continuing journey of growth and development.

It is for this reason that the Self-Management Pyramid (Kemp, 2007) was developed to provide a framework for coaches to contextualize the self-management process and clarify its role in supporting clients to actualize their goals in the coaching relationship. The framework explains the progressive antecedents of an effective and professionally impactful coaching engagement and positions the process of coach self-management as the foundation for a effective coaching relationship. This framework highlights the importance of the coach's own self-development in the coaching process as the basis for trust, shared insight and results; a proposition which to date has remained largely unexplored within the professional coaching literature.

Surfacing for Awareness

Beginning at the base of the model, the initial phase in a coach's self-development, and arguably the most critical to establishing a platform for effective self-management, is the progressive surfacing of the coach's existing beliefs, values, biases and prejudices. The core challenge of the coaching relationship lies in the inherent subjectivity and bias that exist within the coach himself and, given his role as facilitator and catalyst in the helping process, their impact on the client's developmental direction and process. In addition to the perceptual and cognitive processing flaws discussed previously, a coach's developmental, cultural, familial and spiritual experiences throughout his life journey add to the complexity of his perceptual and interpretive biases.

For example, a coach whose experience was one of a nuclear family with three siblings within a suburban, middle-class setting may be quite different from a client who experienced a single-parent family as an only child within an environment of financial hardship or relationship confusion. A coach's unique context influences his perceptions of his client's own unique context and, at times, may cloud his interactions with the client and his processing of the client's unique challenges. While the surfacing of these internal beliefs is critical within this phase of coach development, it is the validation and confirmation of the coach's self-concept that provides the foundation for understanding and effectively managing his behavioural patterns as shaped by this self-concept. To do this effectively, the coach must actively seek out formal and informal external feedback, in the form of psychological testing and profiling, multi-rater feedback, interviews and questionnaires and general feedback on professional impact and performance.

Reflecting for Understanding

Once surfaced, the coach's growing awareness of her human factors template becomes a foundation for reflection and, with supervisory assistance, the opportunity for deeper understanding and meaning is created. It is in this phase that the coach stands to gain the most significant breakthroughs in self-understanding and hence the most clarity in relation to the specific areas requiring targeted self-management. As the coach becomes aware of previously unknown elements of her thinking, behaviour, feeling or perception, these insights provide the content for deeper reflection and analysis in supervision and the source of meaning and insights for the coach. During this phase, the coach actively explores and challenges her bias complexes and the drivers of her current behaviour by exploring these personal values and beliefs, often through reflections on her familial and other significant relationships, e.g., the behaviours that were modelled, the 'stories' that were composed, and the reaction patterns that were formed. In doing so, the coach stands to gain an intimate understanding of her Human Factors Lens as the basis for this ongoing work.

It is during this phase that the skill and experience of the professional supervisor is mandatory and invaluable. Much more than simply a 'coach for the coach', this person is highly skilled in intrapersonal/interpersonal, psychological and developmental dynamics and is an experienced resource with extensive training in the helping professions. Without this support, the coach can at best become disillusioned with process but, at worst, be left confused and frustrated. At her best, the supervisor listens deeply for the coach's unique context and actively challenges his perceptions and behaviours where they seem inconsistent or inappropriate. The trust, lucidity and accountability that is built within effective supervisory relationships often provides a foundation for coaches' progressive personal transformation and their subsequent evolution as a helping professional. The supervisor–coach relationship is founded on a platform of fundamental positive regard and professional respect which allows for high levels of external scrutiny of the coach's own coaching behaviours and practice and ensures a level of ethical accountability that defines and differentiates the helping professions as unique.

Self-Management

Once the coach has developed a sufficient level of insight and self-understanding, she can then use these as the basis for what I'd refer to as a 'self-management plan' (SMP). Simply, the coach embarks upon a process of mapping her potential biases, blind-spots and conditioned beliefs within the coaching relationship and actively puts in place mechanisms for working through these elements to minimize their impact on the client relationship. Broadly, this may include setting up cues, creating disrupting thoughts, or scripting positive self-statements that will support the coach in her self-management within the relationship, particularly in situations that may be especially challenging for her. For example, a coach who has surfaced a persistent pattern of 'rescuing' her clients when they are faced with emotionally disturbing or difficult feedback may devise a SMP that disrupts this pattern when it surfaces in the conversation.

One way of doing this is to firstly identify the trigger that sets in motion this coach's habitual rescuing pattern. This may be a client's sudden silence, tears or agitation within a coaching conversation. As this trigger occurs, the coach may take three deep breaths, communicate an affirmation to the client that, with the support of the coach, he has the inner capability to work through this challenge successfully himself, and then complete a slow count to 30 to allow silence for the client to fully experience and engage with the emotion he is experiencing. The plan may continue with the coach asking a refocusing question that brings the client back to the uncomfortable place or issue that he is grappling with. This is important for the client's growth and development as it is often within this place of cognitive dissonance and tension that significant adaptation and learning can occur for the client as well as the coach.

Listening for Realities

As the coach continues to develop a deeper understanding of herself and a subsequent ability to internally manage and cognitively-behaviourally calibrate in adjusting for her internal biases, she develops the capability to listen to the intent behind the client's overt language and literal dialogue. This process of 'listening with the third ear' (Macran, Stiles, and Smith, 1999; Reik, 1948) allows the coach to begin to develop a more complete picture of the client's unique goals and challenges. As the coach's perceptual filters and processing biases are more mindfully managed within the coaching conversation, less data from the client's unique perspective and context is lost through the coach's filtering process and more richness from the client's own experience can be harnessed within the development process. In short, the coach is able to listen, hear and respond to the client and his unique goals and aspirations in a way that reduces the subjective influence of the coach's life experiences and personal values, opinions and judgements on these responses. Hence, the client's experience in the coaching relationship is one that is, as much as possible, of his own creation and in line with his own desires and goals.

Questioning for Insight

The importance of questioning in raising introspective self-awareness has been acknowledged previously (Clarkson, 2000), particularly in relation to the coach's ability to facilitate his own self-discoveries. Authors such as Overholser (1996) argue for the adoption of a position of 'ignorance' by the therapist within counselling relationships by utilizing a broadly Socratic method of interaction. This position of ignorance can be interpreted as the adoption of a mindset of an inquisitive and curious learner underpinned by genuine interest, concern and unconditional positive regard. By adopting this position, the coach creates the conversational and psychic space within the relationship to allow for the client's needs and reflections to surface. This method can be seen as being most effective when used with clients demonstrating high levels of motivation and resourcefulness.

With the coach actively engaged in the process of self-management, she is now able to craft progressively more refined yet evocative questions to facilitate her own insight and the insight of her clients. Much more than simply a set of open questions, insight-driven questions are those that stimulate a generative motivation for developing deeper personal awareness and reflection. Questions such as, 'If you were to change your view of the current situation, what would that allow for?' and 'What may be possible if you were to make the change you are describing?' invite the client to free himself of self-limiting beliefs and thought processes – what Albert Ellis (1967) founder of Rational Emotive Therapy described as the 'irrational shoulds and musts' that often limit coaching clients in setting goals.

Shared Meaning

The cumulative effect of moving through these foundational phases is the establishment of a relationship between coach and client that has, at its core, a sense of collective and shared meaning and contextual clarity. Once achieved, this is the pivotal point in the process of developing a generative coaching relationship (see Figure 2.2). The establishment of a clear and accurate purpose for coaching is difficult to achieve if the coach has not done her personal work or engaged in Socratic questioning of herself in the first instance. Further, I propose that the coach, by embracing and demonstrating the three 'pillars' of Carl Rogers' person-centred therapy – empathy, congruence and unconditional positive regard (Barrett-Lennard, 1998) – creates a relationship founded on a deep and shared trust, that, in and of itself, facilitates the emergence and utilization of the client's inner resources to support his pursuit of goals within the coaching relationship.

Client Outcomes

As a result of engaging fully in the initial five phases of the self-management cycle which are focused on generating awareness, insight and understanding, the coach can foster the kind of coaching relationship from which client-centred outcomes can flow naturally. In moving forward from a place of shared meaning, a higher level of trust and openness within the coaching relationship evolves, and their respective defensiveness dissipates. This broadening movement toward client growth allows for a rapid expansion of possibilities and opportunities to surface within and for the client, and with further clarification, the client can strengthen her commitment and resolve to the achievement of these goals.

As the client maintains her focus and action within coaching and moves into the maintenance phase of the change process (Prochaska, Norcross, and DiClemente, 1994), the probabilities of a new level of performance and self-mastery become more visible and achievable – further fuelling the client's motivation for continued efforts. For many clients, these emergent probabilities may have been previously unachievable and incongruous with their initial perceptions of their own potential and talent. Their autonomous negative thinking and self-limiting beliefs are effectively extinguished and the client is liberated from what is often an emotionally driven and habitual behaviour pattern in order to generate new positive self-thoughts and more desirable future opportunities and possibilities. By way of illustration, the following case story highlights the process, complexities and value of the self-management process for practising coaches.

Case Story

Jane grew up in what many would consider a privileged family. Her mother was a high school teacher who took time out when Jane and her younger brother were young to look after the them. When Jane and her brother started school, Jane's mother returned to an administrative role in the local high school. Her father was an executive with an international pharmaceutical company. A pharmaceutical scientist and PhD, Jane's father was described by most as being a driven perfectionist and archetypal provider. Uncompromising in his pursuit of excellence, his interactions with Jane and her brother were often more of a clinical and scientific critique of their performance as children rather than caring and nurturing reinforcement of their individuality. This environment rewarded technical and scholastic excellence and Jane found herself often at the top of her high school class – graduating at the top of her senior class and having the luxury of offers from the best universities in the country.

She went on to be trained as an electrical engineer; she completed an MBA in her early 30s as she rose within the global resources firm where she eventually spent 20 years of her career. However, on reaching a role as a senior vice-president, she had experienced a fundamental realization: she was not happy. Her marriage had fallen apart after 18 years when the second of her children had finished high school. Now, she was alone and immersed in an unrewarding and unfulfilling career. She made the decision to go it alone and to spend her life doing something that she was passionate about – helping others to find balance and meaning in their lives as she had during her sea-change experience. So executive coaching was an obvious choice for her as it was focused on human growth and it enabled her to help others to avoid the painful mistakes she had made in her career. Her demonstrable track record as a successful executive in a tough, male-dominated industry, together with her MBA, gave her the street credibility needed to effectively influence the senior executives with whom she worked.

However, at one point in her new role as a coach, Jane was faced with a big challenge in working with a particular client. She had always been prone to angry outbursts in her years as an executive, but she had managed to survive with her reputation and career intact. However, this time it was different. She was growing increasingly frustrated with this client, a senior vice-president of an international chemical company whose main products included pesticides and herbicides. A passionate and committed environmentalist, Jane struggled with her client's commercial activities, a fact that emerged in her coaching conversations in both direct and indirect ways, e.g., the occasional off-hand remark about organic produce or toxicity in the food chain. The further the coaching engagement progressed, the more ineffectual Jane felt that she was becoming. Her client was not making progress and they both knew it . . . she had to do something.

Being the committed professional she sought the counsel of a well-respected peer who suggested she consider seeking a supervisory relationship with a suitable professional. Jane was sceptical at first, but trusted her friend enough to made contact with the potential supervisor. Their initial meeting was relaxed and productive; Jane felt that this was someone who could help and they agreed to work together. Her supervisor encouraged her to gather her insights and reflections on how she currently felt about, thought about, saw, and behaved with her client and why she thought that those difficulties were occurring. Over the next four supervision meetings, Jane's supervisor helped her to explore the situation, the 'stories' she had created to describe the situation, and from where those stories may have emerged.

As Jane's level of trust in the supervision relationship increased, so too did the depth of her explorations. She began to see patterns in her behaviour with this problematic client that were similar to those patterns that she used as a child to cope with her father's emotional absence and demanding standards. As she attempted to engage with her clients, often unsuccessfully, she experienced feelings of emptiness, vulnerability and insecurity rising. Fear of not being 'good enough' for her clients; not being accepted by her clients; not being *loved* by her clients; all flooded her inner thoughts and emotions. As these emotions persisted, her efforts to connect with her clients became more co-dependent and frantic. She searched for ways that she could take her clients' problems away and make them happy. She watched herself compromising her own boundaries within the relationship in an effort to gain her clients' approval, taking on her clients' issues as her own, and 'crusading' on behalf of her clients to those who contributed to her clients' discontent. On one occasion, she had contacted the manager of a male client to express her concerns that she was being 'too hard' on him and should perhaps rethink her role as a leader.

As she reflected on these events more deeply, she began to see commonalities that appeared consistently across other similar clients with whom she was working. She also made several observations about the impact that she was – or was not – having in those relationships and the inappropriateness of several of her previous actions. When she came to these realizations, her initial response was one of embarrassment, shame and devastation but, with the support and counsel of her supervisor, she was able to process these insights effectively and positively and put in place an SMP to address her clients more effectively in the short term as she continued her own growth in the long term.

While they were personally challenging, the three months that she invested in this supervision relationship appeared to be paying dividends. For example, with the challenging client, Jane found herself listening with different ears, even in the face of her automatic resistance to some of his perspectives. She was becoming more tolerant and patient with him and less judgemental. She was beginning to understand him with a new level of nuanced understanding and, for the first time, could see that his underlying intentions and motivations were far more compelling and noble than she had originally thought. As a result of her shift in perception of her client, she had noticed a marked increase in his openness to her input and the level of trust that they enjoyed in their sessions.

By implementing her SMP and actively engaging in the three core levels of the self-management pyramid, she was better able to listen to and challenge her client through client-centred questioning. She was able to identify the triggers for her automatic behaviours more effectively and steer her interactions with her client towards a client-driven outcome rather than simply 'resist or rescue' him in difficult conversations. By effectively self-managing, Jane was able to effectively redefine the coaching relationship in transactional analysis terms (from that of parent to child to that of adult to adult) and hold her client accountable for his own behaviour and outcomes. In this process, her client began to identify and surface his own autocratic paternal patterns and this, in turn, facilitated new awareness and behavioural strategies within his leadership practice.

By the conclusion of the coaching relationship, Jane's client had made several important developmental leaps forward from both a business and personal perspective. He had put in place the necessary changes to support a better work–family balance and, as a result, was reporting significantly higher levels of satisfaction with his life and in his role as father to his two young girls. Jane's efforts to effectively manage her own unique biases and perspectives in the coaching relationship had enabled her client to more effectively engage with his – resulting in a coaching engagement which far exceeded both Jane's and her client's expectations.

Conclusion

The purpose of this chapter has been to provide a solid foundation for professional and ethical practice as a guide for coaches in delivering results-driven coaching interventions to their clients. Contrary to the predominant coaching dialogue to date, the coaching method or model utilized within the coaching relationship can be seen as a methodologically important, but by no means causal, variable in facilitating successful coaching outcomes for clients. The strong support from the evidence-based literature for the importance of the relationship created between the helper – in our case, the coach – and the client in achieving successful client development outcomes compels us as coaches to examine the phenomenon of the relations that coaches create with their clients. To this end, it is critical for all coaches to understand fully the unique dynamics between the four elements in their Human Factors Lens as a way to understand their predispositions in coaching and their opportunities for development.

This chapter has argued that to do this effectively requires a structured and progressive engagement of the coach in the process of personal development and has, therefore, offered the Self-Management Pyramid as a potential framework for guiding this process. By effectively surfacing, understanding and self-managing the inherent complexities of their inner world, coaches are able to create and sustain a client-centric and client-driven focus from which an effective coaching relationship can emerge. Within this relationship, the confounding impact of the coach's biases and habits are made explicit and managed appropriately. The initial step in this process for many coaches will be to identify and engage an appropriately qualified and experienced coaching supervisor. To elevate coaching practice to the status of a profession will require not only that coaches comply with the necessary training and standards requirements laid down by a truly representative, inclusive and non-partisan professional association, but also that they maintain a prescribed level of rigorous and accountable professional supervision. Frameworks and contexts such as those presented here will be important in helping us to do so.

It is through the process of linking existing social psychology literature to contemporary coaching practice; understanding the four human factors as a lens on our own perceptual, cognitive and behavioural processes; and disciplining ourselves to use tools such as these in professional supervision that we will advance our personal growth and professional practice as coaches.

References

Allcorn, S. (2006). Psychoanalytically informed executive coaching. In D. R. Stober and A. M. Grant (Eds.), *Evidence based coaching handbook: Putting best practices to work for your clients*. Hoboken, NJ: John Wiley & Sons, Inc.

Auerbach, J. E. (2006). Cognitive coaching. In D. R. Stober and A. M. Grant (Eds.), *Evidence based coaching handbook: Putting best practices to work for your clients*. Hoboken, NJ: John Wiley & Sons, Inc.

Barrett-Lennard, G. (1998). *Carl Rogers' helping system: Journey and substance*. London: Sage.

Bordin, E. C. (1979). The generalizability of the psychoanalytic concept of the working alliance. *Psychotherapy: Theory, Research and Practice*, 16, 252–260.

Clarkson, P. (2000). *Gestalt counselling in action* (2nd edn.). London: Sage.

Connor-Greene, P. A. (1993). The therapeutic context: Preconditions for change in psychotherapy. *Psychotherapy*, 30(3), 375–382.

Corey, G. (2004). *Theory and practice of counseling and psychotherapy* (7th edn). New York: Wadsworth.

de Jong, A. (2006). Coaching ethics: Integrity in the moment of choice. In J. Passmore (Ed.), *Excellence in Coaching: The Industry Guide*. London: Kogan Page.

Ducharme, M. J. (2004). The cognitive-behavioral approach to executive coaching. *Consulting Psychology Journal: Practice and Research*, 56(4), 214–224.

Egan, G. (2002). The skilled helper: A problem-management and opportunity-development approach to helping (7th edn). Pacific Grove, CA: Brooks Cole.

Ellis, A. (1967). Rational-emotive psychotherapy. In D. Arbuckle (Ed.), *Counseling and psychotherapy*. New York: McGraw-Hill.

Gilbert, R. L. (2002). *How we change: Psychotherapy and the process of human development*. Boston: Allyn & Bacon.

Gilovich, T., Griffin, D., and Kahneman, D. (Eds.). (2002). *Heuristics and biases: The psychology of intuitive judgment*. Cambridge, UK: Cambridge University Press.

Greenson, R. R. (1967). The working alliance and the transference neuroses. *Psychoanalysis Quarterly*, 34, 155–181.

Hawkins, P. (2006). Coaching supervision. In J. Passmore (Ed.), *Excellence in coaching: The industry guide*. London: Kogan Page.

Heider, F. (1958). *The psychology of interpersonal relations*. New York: John Wiley & Sons, Inc.

Horvath, A. O. (2000). The therapeutic relationship. From transference to alliance. *Journal of Clinical Psychology*, 56(2), 163–173.

Horvath, A. O. (2001). The alliance. *Psychotherapy*, 38(4), 365–372.

Horvath, A. O. (2006). The alliance in context: Accomplishments, challenges and future directions. *Psychotherapy: Theory, Research, Practice, Training*, 43(3), 258–263.

Horvath, A. O., and Greenberg, L. S. (1989). Development and validation of the working alliance inventory. *Journal of Counseling Psychology*, 36(2), 223–233.

Horvath, A. O., and Symonds, D. (1991). Relation between working alliance and outcome in psychotherapy: A meta-analysis. *Journal of Counseling Psychology*, 38(2), 139–149.

Jones, E. E., and Davis, K. E. (1965). From acts to dispositions: The attribution process in person perception. In L. Berkowitz (Ed.), *Advances in experimental social psychology* (Vol. 2). New York: Academic Press, p. 77.

Kemp, T. J. (2005a). The proactive behaviour framework: A reflective process for exploring thinking, behaviour and personal insight. In M. Cavanagh, A. M. Grant and T. J. Kemp (Eds.), *Evidence based coaching, Vol 1: Theory, research and practice from the behavioural sciences*. Sydney: Australian Academic Press.

Kemp, T. J. (2005b). Self management theory as grounding for executive coaching. *2nd Australian Evidence-Based Coaching Conference*, Sydney, July.

Kemp, T. J. (2007). Simplifying evidence-based practice: Applying the Human Factors Lens to the coaching process. *Opening Keynote Address, 3rd Australian Evidence-Based Coaching Conference*, Sydney, July.

Kilburg, R. R. (2004). When shadows fall: Using psychodynamic approaches in executive coaching. *Consulting Psychology Journal: Practice and Research*, 56(4), 246–268.

Kivlighan, D. M. (2007). Where is the relationship in research on the alliance? Two methods for analyzing dyadic data. *Journal of Counseling Psychology*, 54(4), 423–433.

Lilliengren, P., and Werbart, A. (2005). A model of therapeutic action grounded in the patients' view of curative and hindering factors in psychoanalytic psychotherapy. *Psychotherapy: Theory, Research, Practice, Training*, 42(3), 324–339.

Luft, J., and Ingham, H. (1955). The Johari window, a graphic model of interpersonal awareness, *Proceedings of the western training laboratory in group development*. Los Angeles: UCLA.

Macran, S., Stiles, W., and Smith, J. A. (1999). How does personal therapy affect therapists' practice? *Journal of Counselling Psychology*, 46, 419–431.

McAuley, M. J. (2003). Transference, countertransference and mentoring: The ghost in the process. *British Journal of Guidance & Counselling*, 33(1), 11–23.

Moore, M., Drake, D. B., Tschannen-Moran, B., Campone, F., and Kauffman, C. (2005). Relational flow: A theoretical model for the intuitive dance. Paper presented at the Coaching Research Symposium, San Jose, CA.

Myers, D. G. (1996). *Social psychology* (5th edn). New York: McGraw-Hill.

Overholser, J. C. (1996). Elements of the Socratic method: V. Self improvement. *Psychotherapy*, 33(4), 549–559.

Perrin, A., and Newnes, C. (2002). Professional identity and the complexity of therapeutic relationships. *Clinical Psychology*, 15, 18–22.

Peterson, D. B. (2006). People are complex and the world is messy: a behavior-based approach to executive coaching. In D. R. Stober and A. M. Grant (Eds.), *Evidence based coaching handbook: Putting best practices to work for your clients*. Hoboken, NJ: John Wiley & Sons, Inc.

Prochaska, J. O., Norcross, J. C., and DiClemente, C. C. (1994). *Changing for good: A revolutionary six-stage program for overcoming bad habits and moving your life positively forward*. New York: Avon Books.

Reik, T. (1948). Listening with the Third Ear: The inner experience of a psychoanalyst. New York: Grove Press.

Rogers, C. R. (1957). The necessary and sufficient conditions of therapeutic personality change. *Journal of Consulting Psychology*, 22, 95–103.

Ross, L. (1977). The intuitive psychologist and his shortcomings: Distortions in the attribution process. In L. Berkowitz (Ed.), *Advances in experimental social psychology* (Vol. 10, pp. 173–240), Orlando, FL: Academic Press.

Sherin, J., and Caiger, L. (2004). Rational emotive behavioral therapy: A behavioral change model for executive coaching? *Consulting Psychology Journal: Practice and Research*, 56(4), 225–233.

Snyder, M. (1984). When belief creates reality. In L. Berkowitz (Ed.), *Advances in experimental social psychology* (Vol. 18, pp. 116, 167). New York: Academic Press.

Thorndike, E. L. (1920). A constant error on psychological rating. *Journal of Applied Psychology*, 4, 25–29.

Wesson, K., and Boniwell, I. (2007). Flow theory: Its application to coaching psychology. *International Coaching Psychology Review*, 2(1), 33–43.

3 Thrice Upon a Time: Narrative Structure and Psychology as a Platform for Coaching

David B. Drake

Introduction

It all started with a simple question to Tom*,[1] 'How did you come to be a lawyer?'

In answering, he shared several stories about Bruce*, a lawyer who had been a mentor for him and the other kids in his neighbourhood. As a result of Bruce's influence, Tom carried into adulthood a strong value for justice and fairness and he eventually chose a career in law himself. As he and I moved from these stories to the present day, and stories of Tom's work in coaching other lawyers and developing new modes of mediation, there emerged a moment when it seemed important for the two sets of stories to meet. I said to Tom, 'I bet Bruce would be really proud of you right now'. In the profound pause that ensued, Tom was able to recognize for the first time a central narrative thread that ran through his life, share this recognition with someone else as a witness, and connect Bruce's gift with his path, his work and his vision for the future.

Although the 'narrative turn' in psychology and the other social sciences has largely occurred in the past 40 years, stories themselves have been integral to human communities since the dawn of time. We use them

---

1 The names with asterisks have all been changed to preserve anonymity.

The Philosophy and Practice of Coaching: Insights and Issues for a New Era.
Edited by David B. Drake, Diane Brennan and Kim Gørtz.
© 2008 John Wiley & Sons, Ltd.

to remember and organize our past, communicate about and negotiate our present, and envision and act into our future (Drake, 2005). Particularly in these largely postmodern times, stories enable us to (1) establish and sustain social identities; (2) discern influential cultural/contextual norms; (3) claim and navigate our formal and informal memberships; (4) negotiate our identity performances in key environments; (5) observe ourselves from other vantage points; (6) test and rehearse new selves; and (7) situate ourselves in a meaningful larger narrative. We can see some of these functions in Tom's story, e.g., the use of a story about Bruce to situate himself within a large narrative about his life path and purpose.

I find narrative work quite satisfying as it allows for the integration of the head and heart in ways that are often not otherwise possible. In his story workshops, Robert McKee (2004) talked about it this way, 'In real life we never get to experience the emotions of an event and its meaning in the same moment. The flow of time separates the two. Yet we have a great need to unify emotions and meaning, and good stories do this.' So stories serve as windows into the architecture of a client's psyches and the longing of their souls as well as the platform from which to build and express new ways of being in the world. In developing a story-based approach to coaching, I have engaged in a deep study of narrative psychology in order to build bridges between this established body of work and the emergent practice of coaching. In doing so, I created links between the *foundational knowledge* (Drake, 2007a, 2007b) I have gained through research and study and the *professional knowledge* I have gained through teaching and coaching.

This chapter outlines how a better understanding of narratives can contribute to the deepening of our coaching practices and increase our ability to create breakthrough moments with clients through the artful use of their stories. In particular, I draw on Burke's (1969) work on *dramatism*, the search for a person's motive (motivation) as the driver of their narratives, and his *Pentad*, the questions to unpack a story to discover these motives. The focus, therefore, is on the structure and elements of narratives as a key component in working with clients' stories.

The chapter is built around a three-level framework for narrative analysis in coaching conversations that I have developed from Burke's work and that of others (see Drake, 2003, 2004, 2005, 2007) as well as my own research. The intent is to help coaches understand more fully how to work fluidly and powerfully with the stories that emerge in sessions in order to help clients achieve their goals as seen through the seven aims above. For example, coaching around a promotion might focus on questions of membership (#3) or questions of identity (#4). In the final section, we will look more specifically at how to translate the three levels of this framework into coaching practice. The conclusion offers several recommendations for creating a narrative foundation for coaching. For now, let us set the stage with some of the backstory behind this approach to coaching.

The Backstory

My work with narratives in coaching was sparked, in part, by Clandinin and Connelly's (2000) use of Dewey in their research on the development of teachers to create a set of spatial-temporal terms that form a three-dimensional narrative inquiry space. It has also been guided by a lifelong interest in Jung's insights into the collective and unconscious influences on the self (Drake, 2003) and Freire's (1970) critiques of 'banking methods' of learning and development that overly privileged the dominant narratives. In my early research and work, I looked at clients' stories through a rites-of-passage lens (Drake, 2003, 2004, 2005) and, in doing so, I studied the people telling the stories, the stories they told, and their processes of narration. Using this initial three-part approach enabled me to triangulate the coaching conversations as a way to help people discover a meaningful path forward on their quest. Doing so helped the stories come alive in my coaching sessions and gave rise to a deeper curiosity about the conversational field. This chapter describes a three-level approach to client stories for the purpose of explicating the foundational links between narrative psychology and coaching, between theory and practice.

The title of this chapter is a play on the famous opening line from children's fables. It is used here to make a key point about stories in coaching. *Once upon a time* reflects the common focus on the narrator who tells the story and provides the setting – the cue that a story is coming and the context for the actions that will follow. This is the level of rapport and engagement with the audience, a relational process of mutual trust building. *Twice upon a time* refers to the focus on the story that is told and the problems and opportunities that are its core. This is the level of plot and purpose, a co-creative process of reciprocal understanding as the story unfolds. *Thrice upon a time* represents a focus on the field that is created in a coaching conversation between the coach, the client, and the narrative process; it is affected by the contextual stories that shape(d) each one. I contend that it is in/from this field that the possibilities inherent in the stories emerge through working with the elements (e.g., other characters, objects, places, images and metaphors) and the dynamics between them.

I have come to appreciate the importance of all three of these levels in thinking and working narratively with clients and teaching my work to others. The first level is about helping the client be fully present to himself and the setting for his story while creating a trusting space in which to do so. The second level is about advocating for the full story to emerge so that as much of the narrative material is available to be worked with through the conversation. It is at the third level where the breakthroughs most often occur, for it is here that the client reframes or rearranges the material in order to gain a new perspective, new sense of self, or new options for action. Working across all three levels with clients, stories can be seen as extensions of the client that are projected into the field, consciously and unconsciously, and thereby available for the work of the coaching conversation. As stewards for these narrative fields, coaches need to take as much interest in the process of narration as they do in the resulting narrative material in order to have access to more of the levers for change.

This layered, almost alchemical, approach to stories is based in an understanding that a given story emerges from the cognitive, discursive and social fabric that the coach and client bring to a session and create together once they are there. A story is inseparable from the context in which it is performed, lived and held (Boje, 1998; Rossiter, 1999). Any story told in a coaching session, even if it has served as a transformational vehicle for the client in that setting, must survive the retellings that will occur in other contexts if the client wishes to sustain the changes he or she has begun. Therefore, I focus on 'thinking narratively' (Drake, 2007b) as a comprehensive frame for coaching conversations rather than thinking of stories as just another tool. In doing so, I join with Boje (1998) and others who have taken the postmodern turn by shifting from the usual ways of thinking of *stories-as-objects* to a stance in which we see *stories-in-context*. It is about working with the story as it emerges in coaching as a mutual and dynamic process rather than as a unitary and static commodity.

This view is widely supported within the field of narrative psychology where there is a deep appreciation for the socially constructed, contextual and relational nature of narratives and identity as well as substantial support for nondominant standpoints and discourse. When coaching, I think of client stories as psychosocial constructions, *per*formed in the contexts of the client's life (and told in the context of a coaching session), rather than *pre*formed outside of any such communities, histories, or pedagogies. This view reflects the postmodern emphasis on *situated identities* (Ochs and Capps, 1996) and addresses Gergen and Gergen's (2006) request for 'an account of human change in which all that we have understood as distinctly psychological can be understood in terms of relational action' (p. 119). In closing, coaches can draw from the narrative psychology literature to develop and deploy ways to engage with their clients and their stories in profound new ways. The next section will introduce one of these tools for doing so.

What to Look for in a Story: A Three-Part Framework

It is helpful for coaches to understand the characteristics of narrative structure so they can work at all three levels with their clients' stories. Otherwise, it is hard to discern the nuances of their stories as they are co-narrated or know how to effectively work with them such that they yield meaningful insights for the client. Like any craft, we have to master the basics before we can improvise in a given situation. The following three-part model provides such a foundation for coaches to have their skills in working with clients' stories. It incorporates the five narrative terms central to understanding human action as defined in Burke's (1969) *Pentad*, Stein and Glenn's (1979) grammatical structure for stories, Ollerenshaw and Creswell's (2002) work on the problem-solution narrative structure approach, and story elements as described by McKee (2004) in his masterful work on narrative structure. I have added a sixth element to Burke's list, the *coda* (see Bruner, 2002), in order to address the action orientation in coaching and to support the *reincorporation* phase in clients' development as seen from a rites-of-passage perspective. The overall framework addresses Burke's five questions about action and narration: 'what was done (*act*), when and where it was done (*scene*), who did it (*agent*), how he did it (*agency*), and why (*purpose*)' (Burke, 1969, p. xv) as well as what it all means in the end for clients and their stories (*coda*).

Once Upon a Time: The Situation

The Situation incorporates the *setting* (Stein and Glenn, 1979; Ollerenshaw and Creswell, 2002), the *scene* (Burke, 1969), in which there is a *protagonist* (Stein and Glenn), and *agent* (Burke) about whom we care. Other elements and characters are also introduced, often foreshadowing events to come. Understanding the situation gives us the context for the story that is about to unfold and engages us in wanting to know what happens to the primary character(s). The context for the story is often one in which the character has experienced a disruption in the status quo that has upset the balance of forces in his life. He is driven to create a narrative to address the resulting gap that has emerged between his prior assumptions and expectations and his present reality and experience (McKee, 2004). In the process, the normative social and contextual narratives that shape(d) these expectations become more visible and thus more available for renegotiation. As both his expectations and his circumstances are called into question, the client sets forth to restore the lost equilibrium. Along the way, he will often be challenged to release old attachments for the sake of the search.

Twice Upon a Time: The Search

The Search involves an *act* (Burke), including the person's *internal reaction or response* (Stein and Glenn), and a sense of *agency* (Burke) on the part of the person as she attempts to *deal with the situation* created by the *initiating event* (Stein and Glenn). The quest is to identify what she believes will put life back into balance if it is achieved; the search for it forms the spine of the story (McKee). The choices the person makes here often reflect the person's attachment patterns and historic searches, character and attitude (an element Burke later added to his Pentad to tie the other five together), and mental models and subsequent capabilities for agency and communion (Bakan, 1966). Trials and tribulations, encounters with individual and collective shadows, the sense of being 'in-between', and the appearance of allies and guides are common here.

Thrice Upon a Time: The Shift

The Shift, what Burke referred to as the *purpose*, arises out of the *consequences of the actions* (Stein and Glenn; Ollerenshaw and Creswell) taken by the person on his or her quest. Unconscious desires often emerge over the course of the search – allowing the conscious desire to change – but ultimately the agent must make a choice as to which story line to pursue (McKee). The answer, the object of desire, is often found where the person must face the greatest challenge, answer the most essential question or make the hardest choice; however, the result may or may not be the one the person was originally seeking (McKee). This climax to the story brings with it a *resolution* to the quest but it must take into account all that has happened along the way. The Shift reflects what happens to the person (e.g., her sense of self, mental models, expectations, narrative strategies) as a result. It often ends with a *coda* (Bruner, 2002), a *moral of the tale* (Stein and Glenn), for the benefit of the person and others to whom he tells the story as well as a platform for new awareness and action.

Let me offer a case story to illustrate the three-part framework in action.

Situation: I worked with a regional organization that was experiencing great turbulence in the wake of the sudden termination of the CEO. Nancy* was a senior manager in her late 50s who was increasingly called on, formally and informally, to advocate for the management team and the staff in the midst of this unexpected leadership vacuum. She was resisting these pleas even as she was not clear about why she was doing so. The purpose for the initial coaching conversation was to understand what was happening for her in this situation so she could decide on a more definitive and authentic response in the organization. Her initial stories set the stage and surfaced the theme of 'I'm just one of the gang'.

Search: At one level, she seemed to be quite willing to let things drift along as they had always been. However, stories emerged in our conversation about pioneering older women in her family and the rites of passage they provided for daughters. A variety of other stories also came out about her place in important social systems, such as stepping into new roles with her children as they moved further into their 20s. There was a strong spatial theme to her stories as she talked about being 'caught in the middle', her moves and the migrations of her ancestors, and her reflections on parenting others. We worked with these images to see what they might mean in terms of the overall narratives of her life as a woman nearing 60 and as one seeking clarity about her place now in the organization.

Shift: Her 'object of desire' emerged through a deeper exploration of her stories about the women pioneers in her family, particularly in light of themes from the other stories. What stopped the story of 'just being one of the gang' was her realization that 'that's not true any more, is it?' She became aware in that moment that her lingering uncertainty reflected the fact that she was leaving behind a lifetime as a *youngest* to step into a new role as an *oldest*, a position that was quite new for her. In recognizing that 'it's my turn now to be an elder', she reframed her story about her place in her life, in her family, and as a leader in the organization.

The material in the coaching conversation with Nancy emerged from the stories themselves; as such, she was already signalling, albeit unconsciously at first, the developmental process that was under way through her choices of stories to tell and the ways in which they were told. It is important to note that clients rarely bring forward their stories in a coherent form or order; it is the coach's role to help bring them to the surface and work with the client to make new connections and new sense of them. Taken together, *Situation, Search* and *Shift* provides a useful structure with which to listen to, track and respond to the stories that clients tell us in the context of coaching conversations as a way to advance and deepen their impact. This approach is consistent with Chanfrault-Duchet's (1991) observation that the most crucial information is often seen in the ways in which the narrative itself is organized. I use this framework as a foundation and guide for my interactions with the narrative material that emerges when I coach, teach coaching, and work with organizations on their coaching strategies. It is based in a belief in the client as a human being or human system seeking to discover, express and manifest a story that is more fulfilling.

An important role for coaches in working with narratives is to be able to reflect back to clients their stories or elements of their stories in such a way that the larger patterns and strategies become clear for them. Working in this way with clients and across all three levels with their stories creates a much stronger foundation for change because it draws on the cognitive, discursive and social bases for awareness and behaviour in a systemic fashion. *Once upon a time* focuses on the narrator, his narrative strategies and the setting for his narration. *Twice upon a time* focuses on the story and the discursive factors at play in its construction in the coaching conversation. *Thrice upon a time* focuses on the field within the conversation, the story elements at play there and the larger social forces that shape its constellation – within the session and back in the client's life. Let us explore in more depth what it looks like to work at these three levels in building a narrative foundation for coaching.

Working at the Three Levels of Narrative

Introduction

A narrative approach to coaching is predicated on a trusting container in which clients are free to fully narrate their experience and work with the resulting material in service of their goals. As Stern (2004) noted, it is about expansion wherein 'the process [becomes one] of staying with or within each specific moment as it comes along, treating it more fully and endowing it with more import and deeper appreciation' (p. 208). This in-the-moment approach to coaching and the field in which clients' stories are shared (Drake, 2007a), makes sense given the contextual nature of narratives and identity. Not only can clients' narrative patterns be observed in action, but they can experience greater freedom in the process. For example, one of my clients repeatedly told stories in which he felt burdened. In our work we began to explore what it would be like for him – and the others around him – to not always be 'in charge' and thereby release his attachment to that frame and those behaviours. In the process, I also observed my occasional urge to take on the burdens of his distress. It was a reminder that as coaches we are not immune to the emotional and energetic dynamics that emerge; instead, it is all part of the field (Schwartz-Salant, 1998). The secret is to mindfully and artfully work with what emerges – within the coach, the client and the field – as the client's stories are narrated. With this client, he was able to take the awareness he gained through this search and experiment with a new story and a healthier approach to delegation.

A story-based approach is well suited for this attention to the field in coaching conversations because the two-way traffic between implicit and explicit dimensions, between signs and the signified, is inherent in the very nature of narratives. A pivotal contribution to coaching from narrative psychology is the recognition of the need to focus on the implicit dynamics of the coach–client relationship and the field they create together as a vehicle for change as well as the more familiar domain of the explicit content (Stern, 2004). In fact, it is through the interplay between context and content that stories gain much of their power for learning and transformation. Otherwise, client's stories devolve into mere chronicles and the process degrades from an embodied experience to an abstract analysis – neither of which is productive in coaching. To better understand these connections between narrative structure and psychology and coaching theories and practices, the following sections look at the three levels more closely to guide coaches in working with clients' stories once, twice, and thrice upon a time.

Situation (Agent/Scene)

> *Every man [sic] invents a story for himself – which he often, and with great cost to himself – takes to be his life.*
>
> (Max Frisch, 1972)

Once upon a time refers to the setting for the story and the person who tells it. It provides the background and the platform for the story as it is formed in response to a cognitive, emotional and/or tangible breach in the status quo. It is based in the fact that people use stories to narrativize (form narratives about) what happened, how they are experiencing what has happened, and what they imagine might happen now (Drake, 2003, 2005). These frames shape what is available to them at a given moment and thus influence the repertoire and range of their available responses. Working with clients' stories helps them to articulate and adjust, as needed, their narrative patterns in order to engage more fully in the developmental opportunities in front of them. As a coach, the focus in working at this level with stories is on developing a full sense of the situation, e.g., the context, the characters, and the fullest participation of the client as the narrator.

Coaching helps clients to increase their awareness of the stories they bring to their work and life, assess how well they are working (or not), and adopt narrativizing frames that yield more of their desired results. At the heart of this work for the client around 'who am I?' is the notion of a narrative identity situated in time and space. By mindfully staying within a narrative frame in the present moment, coaches can help the client work with the temporal and spatial dynamics of the stories themselves. For example, I had a client who continually spoke of what was not possible based on her experience in the past (time) within the configuration of her leadership team (space). When asked to imagine, in the moment, the possibility of restructuring her team (space), a new – and more satisfying – future opened up for her (time). In working this way, the person has the opportunity to transcend the problem as it has been constructed (White, 2007) in order to gain a new perspective from which to see alternatives.

An essential competency for coaches in this regard is the ability to stay in what I call 'storytime' and 'storyspace' – and support the client to do the same. One of the skills involved is to ask questions that keep the client grounded in the experience of her own narration in the session as opposed to detached through analysis or premature planning. For example, instead of asking, 'What could you do differently next time?', the coach can ask, 'What is happening for you right now as you are speaking about this action?' As Stern (2004) urged, 'one should let the flow accomplish its work and find its own immediate destiny' (p. 170).

Supporting clients to be grounded in their present experience, their internal and external narration, makes the past and future more readily available in ways that connect more powerfully to their ability to make changes. In part, this may be because the past, present and future are closely linked in stories and each one receives its meaning from the other two. As White and Epston (1990) observed, 'Since all stories have a beginning (or a history), a middle (or a present), and an ending (or a future), then the interpretation of current events is as much future-shaped as it is past-determined' (p. 10). In working this way, I mirror the client's proclivity to move in and out of the past, present and future in constructing stories with me by asking questions such as, 'Where are you right now?', 'When have you been here before?' and 'When might you be here again?'

Other situation-defining questions that I ask of myself in coaching include: (1) where does this client invest the most energy?; (2) where does she turn for guidance?; (3) where is there stuck or misplaced energy?; and (4) what work needs to be done in each temporal area in order for her to tell a new story about herself and with her life? A key part of this work is the need to 'break up the ossification of the links a client has constructed between the past, present and future so that new constructions are possible' (Boscolo and Bertrando, 1992, p. 121). Ultimately, it is about helping clients loosen their *narrative grip* on the past, present and/or future to make room for the formation of new stories to be told and lived.

We can see the value of working along temporal lines in the case of Susan*, a middle-aged manager who had been passed over for a promotion and was using coaching, in part, to be better prepared the next time. In working with her stories about what had happened, we discovered a disconnection between how she *recollected* herself ('I'm just a trainer'), how she *carried* herself now ('I'm well respected by the leadership team for my opinions on development') and how she *imagined* herself ('Women [like me] don't get promoted here'). Bringing the stories together in the same conversation allowed her to see the ways in which she downplayed her actual experience in deference to the stories she told about her past and future. We went on to explore how she could use the embodied self as the basis for her actions. We strengthened this stance by inviting her to recall experiences of this new story in the past (Hewson, 1991) in preparation for a meeting about her career with her boss.

Clients like Susan bring form and meaning to key experiences through creating and telling stories about them. Coaches can gain a sense of clients' *emplotment* strategies (Hermans and Kempen, 1993; Polkinghorne, 1988), their framing of the world and their place in it, by working with their stories. This process is useful to clients because evidence contrary to their strategies is nearly invisible to them (Polkinghorne, 2001). It is often the gaps, where reality does not conform to expectations, which serve as the catalyst for clients to take new action (Ibarra and Lineback, 2005) – for example, getting the promotion has not been as fulfilling as they had imagined; starting their own business has surfaced some of their limitations once hidden in a corporate system; retiring is bringing up their disappointments and fears about their life. These gaps in narration can be seen as a *breach* (Bruner, 1986; Riessman, 1993) for clients; they are what set in motion the Situation in which a story can be told. This narrative activity attempts to resolve the discrepancy between what was expected and what has transpired (Ochs and Capps, 1996). Coaches can listen for *demarcation signs* (Gergen, 1994) and *markers* (Strauss, 1997) in their clients' stories as a way to track these breaches. A key role in coaching is to invite and support clients to step into their stories in order to notice their habitual narrative strategies, e.g., 'I am a victim' or 'I have to do this all by myself', and create openings for a different strategy in response to the same situations. These strategies reflect the person's mental models about themselves and the world; they provide an opportunity for the coach to understand why the person does what she does – and how to help her change that behaviour if so desired (Siegel, 1999).

Clients perceive the world and act on the basis of the stories they tell and that are told about them. Accordingly, clients' experience is the natural consequence of how they construct, attend to, and respond to their world. However, their consequences are compounded by the fact that these experiences often enough corroborate their expectations such that their views of themselves and the world remain intact (Siegel, 1999). Swann and Read (1981) remarked: 'Through such processes, people may create – both in their minds and in the actual environment – a social reality that verifies, validates and sustains the very conceptions that initiate and guide these processes' (p. 371).

Keeping this in mind, coaches can help clients to more fully articulate their Situation through reflecting back to them some of the consequences of their narration. This is important because, as social psychologists have discovered, our explanations, our expectations and our behaviours all strongly affect one another (Sherman, Skov, Hervitz, and Stock, 1981). It is precisely at these junctures where their frames no longer work well, as a mismatch either with their environment or their goals, that new stories become possible. In those moments, coaches can help clients discern what is being asked of them in these stories (Drake, 2005), as we saw in Nancy's story with her call to a new leadership stance.

Coaching reunites people with their stories so they can be more conscious of their Situation, their place and role in their stories, and their options for new stories and new roles. Sometimes clients choose to leave behind an old story to make room for one that better serves them at this stage of their life. Sometimes two stories that seem unconnected are brought together to create a new connection or awareness about who they are and/or what they want to do in their current situation. Working at the level of *once upon a time* is about developing the relational and situational platform for the coaching process. The primary aim is to fully bring clients into their own stories as they emerge in the conversation and to increase their sense of authorship or, at minimum, take a more conscious place as the narrator. This level is critical in constellating the field with clients as the container for the next two levels.

Search (Act/Agency)

By refusing his web of constructions, she also cut him off from his supporting fiction.

(James Hillman, 1983)

Much of the work in the Search phase focuses on the clients' stories themselves and teasing them apart in order to make more visible, to themselves and others, their invisible identity processes and *theory of events* (Foucault, 1965). The process often surfaces important information relative to the clients' character, constructions and capabilities that can be used to further their goals. One way to surface this information is to listen for any implicit or explicit 'if–then' statements by the client, for example, *if* I work extra hard at pleasing my boss on this project, *then* I will get the promotion; *if* I have all the answers (or at least appear to), *then* people will respect me and need me (and never leave me). A core discipline for coaches in this regard is to not bite at the first 'hook' cast by the client but to be patient in discovering what they are called to do (*act*) and what they will need in order to be successful (*agency*).

However, one of the challenges in working with people and their stories is that the dominant narratives in their life tend to blind them to the possibilities that other narratives exist (Drake, 2007b). Therefore, coaches can help clients understand the tacit cultural forces that shape their views of the world and themselves, their language and behavioural choices, and more. If coaches want to support clients to change, they must be more conscious of the larger narratives in which their clients' identities are situated. This is important because people often do not recognize the contours and limitations of their available narratives until they try to cross these normative boundaries or seek to narrate their experiences or selves outside of them. Coaching can be quite effective in helping clients turn these narrative *breakdowns*, when the old story does not work any more, into openings for *breakthroughs* to new internal responses and/or external actions. It is here we see the value of stewardship in working with the narrative material of clients at these critical junctures where the building blocks of their identities are in play (Drake, 2007b).

The world, and particularly our significant others, have a role to play in signalling, by the way they listen, which of our stories are worthy of telling and how we can tell them. They shape our narrative range and our subsequent self-definition; we become the stories we like to tell (Schank, 1990), to varying degrees. This reflects Berger's (1963) socio-logical perspective that 'self and identity are not something "given" in some psychological sense, but they are bestowed in acts of social recognition. We become that as which we are addressed' (p. 99). However, the stories we tell others, we also tell ourselves. As Schank (1990) noted, this has the 'odd effect of causing us to see our own lives in terms of pre-established, well-known stories that can obscure the ways in which our actual situation differs from the standard story' (p. 147). Working with clients' stories in coaching has a lot to do with helping them distinguish between their life and the stories they and others tell about their life. The Search phase often includes working with stories of and openings for separation from and/or renegotiation with a client's key communities.

However, this is not always an easy process as clients often have ambivalence around change that may hinder their success in coaching. This echoes McKee's (2004) observation that confusion over a character's desire is at the root of most story problems. Therefore, it is important in working with the stories themselves that coaches discern what clients are trying to accomplish with this story – and for whom – as they negoti-ate the trials and tribulations of their search. A central role for the coach in this regard is to help the client identify the deepest purpose, the truest nature and significance of the quest. What does the client want that, if you gave it to her, would stop the story? (McKee, 2004) In part, shifts come about through exploring, 'What are the historic, though often unconscious, demands contained within his or her stories and to whom are they addressed' (Phillips, 1994). For such change to occur, there must be 'a breakdown of previously accepted understandings, a percep-tion that a once familiar event no longer makes sense, a penetration of the previously taken-for-granted' (Bruner, 1986, p. 53).

Coaches can help clients move through these in-between times where they have left behind the old story, set out on a vector toward resolution, but not yet fulfilled that quest. It is a time when clients' problems and longings become clearer. While the complications are often signalled from the beginning, they often intensify as clients engage in the deeper work of change. For example, a client who longed for healthier work habits came to face the fears he held at bay through avoiding home as much as possible. It was only then that the more profound purpose of our coaching work became apparent. The Search phase is about gathering the awareness and resources in preparation for this resolution and the shift in their stories, identities and actions. Working at the level of *twice upon a time* is about guiding clients to that threshold where they can discover and fulfil the deeper purpose for the journey that is their story.

Shift (Purpose/Coda)

The most serious threshold in every story calls forth our greatest fear or attachment to the world as we know it.

(Laura Simms, 2000)

Once the client becomes clearer about the stakes of the game as seen in his own stories, the focus is on working with the stories' elements to enable the client to discern a path of resolution. This aligns with Hermans' (2004) notion of 'dialogical space', wherein 'new relationships are established between existing story parts or new elements are introduced' (p. 175). Working narratively in a coaching session with what Freud called 'evenly suspended attention' (cited in Yalom, 2000) helps develop a *storyworld* (McLeod, 2004), a space for therapeutic emplotment (Mattingly, 1998) and transformative dialogue. Stern's (2004) research on the present moment and his conjectures about the 'intersubjective matrix' as the place of continuous co-creative dialogue point in this direction as well. He observed that 'the sharing creates a new intersubjective field between the participants that alters their relationships and permits them to take different directions together. . . . Changes occur by way of these nonlinear leaps in the ways-of-being-with-another' (p. 22). This field is particularly important at this third level in narrative coaching because of the focus there on the resolution, its meaning (coda) and what is gained as a result.

Taking a systemic perspective in this way is consonant with the complexities of adult development and change. Clients frequently come up against tough choices as well as attract wonderful opportunities in their efforts to tell a different story about and with their lives. Either way, the Shift phase is marked by turning points in the client's story (Ibarra and Lineback, 2005). This last step involves some form of resolution of the catalyst that sent them on the quest in the first place – though it may not be what they thought they were looking for when they began. Accordingly, it is important to support the client in stepping into his own story and where it is leading him. A common source of the fabled 'aha' moments for clients in these situations is when they are surprised by the ending to their own story as it has unfolded with the coach. For example, the client who, in telling stories about how she wants to improve in her current role, comes to realize that deep down what she wants to do is quit and do something else.

Again, these insights often come sooner and more powerfully if clients arrive at them from within the story that got them there and in which they will have to create a different ending. When they are invited to reflect on their stories in the moment, clients can expand their consciousness and be more aware of the choices they make and want to make about which stories will guide them and where these stories are headed. In the process, they may decide that (1) some of their old stories are no longer salient or defining (positively or negatively) – they just do not matter any more; (2) some stories may take on a new salience or defining nature; (3) some experiences need to be 'de-narrated' and allowed to drop back down into the sea of life; and (4) other stories are brought forth and 'thickened' (Geertz, 1978) as they better represent who and how they want to be in the world. The important point here is that the shifts have arisen from within the clients' own narrative material as it has surfaced in the coaching conversation.

In working at this level with the client's stories, in the field created between and beyond the coach and the client, the latter is often seeking to develop new relationships with her own stories to reframe the past, open up new possibilities in the present, or build a new platform for the future. As a result, the goal to help the client do the work to face the core challenges, answer the essential questions, and make the hard choices (McKee, 2004) to bring a new story about herself to life. This is the moment in both stories and coaching when clients ask, 'What am I to do now?' Working at the level of *thrice upon a time* is about helping clients shift their sense of themselves as the narrator, their stories as they are told (and heard), the relationships among the elements in their stories, and the ways in which they live these stories in and with their lives.

I believe that the role of coaches is to be a clear and loving mirror for clients such that they can openly bring their stories into coaching sessions and find there the resolution and reward they are seeking. In nurturing these fields within sessions, it is important to remember that, while their stories of the past and the future are influential in shaping their identity and their behaviours, ultimately, all problems are problems of the present and *now* is the only time frame for new action (Boscolo and Bertrando, 1992). Therefore, an important discipline for coaches is to stay within *storytime* and *storyspace* as much as possible when engaging with clients around the narrative material that is present in the coaching conversation.

Working in this way allows the clients to embed any shifts in awareness or capacity in their lived experience as an anchor for change (Drake, 2007b). A here-and-now focus is consonant with the present-orientation and in-the-moment nature of coaching and it has many advantages. It provides a safe laboratory in which to experiment with new behaviours and to experience new voices before trying them in the world (Anderson, 2004; Yalom, 2000). Coaches can serve as stewards for these narrative journeys.

Conclusion

For we make sense – or fail to make sense – of our lives by the kind of story we can or cannot – tell about it.

(Joseph Dunne, 1995)

Narrative psychology provides a valuable foundation for coaching in helping clients to achieve the changes they are seeking. This body of work contributes a vast resource for coaches wanting to understand the dynamics of narrative as it relates to clients' identity, cognition, communication and behaviour. It provides the basis for coaching with a clear mind and open heart. People come to coaching because at some level their old stories are not working any more and they are searching for a new story and/or a more fitting audience for the one they want to tell.

The stories that clients share in coaching conversations shed light on their efforts to reclaim, retain and/or reframe their larger narratives about who they are and who want to be in the world. These stories generally reflect the inherent tensions between their drive for continuity (and stability) and their yearning for discontinuity (and change). At the same time, these same stories contain clues for what will resolve this tension and, thereby, lead to a new story about themselves, their lives and/or others who matter to them. It is incumbent on coaches to have the pedagogical and practical tools to work with these stories in ways that are both honouring and transformative.

Working at the narrative level in this way enables coaches to glimpse the process by which clients construct and sustain their identity in/orientation to the world. My aim is to extend clients' positional repertoire so they are more able to move flexibly from one position to another as they move in and out of the stories they are a part of each day (Hermans, 2004). In *thinking narratively* in a coaching conversation, I place more emphasis on the experience and less on the rush to interpretation, meaning or action; I engage the elements of the stories even as I attune myself to the context in which it is co-narrated (Drake, 2007b). In my practice, I no longer worry much about which stories clients share first. Instead, I trust they will begin at the level at which they are ready. Narratives tend to be holographic in nature; the critical themes will be present in one form or another regardless of where clients begin. Therefore, I focus more on creating a rich narrative field, noticing what appears, and trusting that any one story or set of stories is a portal into the larger issues at play in terms of the clients' developmental or aspirational needs.

Accordingly, one of the disciplines in bringing a narrative approach to coaching is not to get caught up in the search for or appearance of dramatic stories. It can be seductive to impose, albeit unconsciously, our own normative values on others' stories. In my experience, it is more important to acknowledge the narrative themes as they emerge, to attend to the field that arises in the conversation about them, and to focus my work in powerful ways with these often simple stories. Understanding narrative structure provides coaches with a greater ability to discern the salient points as they emerge (or are absent). So, it is important to remember that

> clients' stories are not 'simply' stories. They are rich, dynamic manifestations of clients' struggles . . . Sometimes the coach can help the client move deeper into their story as a means to understand their narrative construction process and use the material in the story itself. At other times, it may be helpful to help the client move out of the story in order to deal more directly with the deeper issues . . . there is usually more going on than is being told. (Rennie, 1994, p. 242)

As part of our due diligence as professionals, it is also incumbent upon coaches to be aware of the repertoire of life-stories we consider plausible and can therefore allow or even hear. What are the acceptable shapes of a life we find ourselves promoting based on our training, professional/business pressures and aesthetic preferences (Phillips, 1994)?

At the core of this work is a deep commitment to creating nonjudgemental yet generative spaces in which clients can work with their own narrative material as a pathway to their development and satisfaction. In tracing some of the contributions of narrative psychology to strengthen coaches' capabilities to do so, I have identified three parts to this narrative approach. *Once upon a time* is focused on helping clients to step more fully into their role as the narrator of their life's story and clarifying the Situation in the stories they've shared. Working at this level sets the stage for clients to understand who they are and how they got where they are; to trust the coach as a narration partner so they are increasingly able to tell the whole story; and to candidly recognize the journey they are on together. *Twice upon a time* is focused on creating space for the whole story to be told and deepening the Search. Working at this level is about helping clients identify the central breakdowns in their stories and lives as openings for breakthroughs; identify and acknowledge their resources; and discover the deeper purpose for their journey. *Thrice upon a time* is focused on the field in the conversation, the narrative elements in play, and supporting a Shift. Working at this level is about helping clients bring together elements within their stories such that the resolution of the problem and the completion of their quest become possible.

Coaches can engage their clients at all three levels – the narrator, the story and the story elements – in partnering with them for the desired results. I have advocated here for a relational approach that focuses on the dynamics of the narrative field rather than a transactional approach that focuses on the stories as mere objects. In the end, we walk with our clients on a journey they are narrating with us every time we meet. Often, it is not until the end, when they are reflecting on the lessons learned, the moral of their story, that they truly grasp how far they have come. I will close as I began, with a story. This one comes from a fascinating book by Tarlow and Tarlow (2002) that brings together an anthropological respect for indigenous wisdom with a postmodern awareness of the digital life.

> Aborigine trackers are the best in the world, able to follow a man even years after he has walked through a dry desert terrain. An anthropologist asked one of these expert trackers how he did it. The tracker responded, 'Oh, it's easy. We walk with him.' He does not look for clues; he enters the time and space where the journey occurred. He knows how to walk in the same world as the event he seeks. (p. 205)

References

Anderson, T. (2004). 'To tell my story': Configuring interpersonal relations within narrative process. In L. E. Angus and J. McLeod (Eds.), *Handbook of narrative and psychotherapy: Practice, theory, and research* (pp. 315–329). Thousand Oaks, CA: Sage.

Bakan, D. (1966). *The duality of human existence: Isolation and communion in Western man.* Boston: Beacon.

Berger, P. L. (1963). *Invitation to sociology.* Garden City, NY: Doubleday.

Boje, D. M. (1998). The postmodern turn from stories-as-objects to stories-in-context methods. *Research Methods Forum.* Retrieved January 7, 2006, from http://www.aom.pace.edu/rmd/1998_forum_postmodern_stories.html

Boscolo, L., and Bertrando, P. (1992). The reflexive loop of past, present, and future in systemic therapy and consultation. *Family Process*, 31, 119–130.

Bruner, J. (1986). Ethnography as narrative. In V. Turner and E. M. Bruner (Eds.), *The anthropology of experience* (pp. 139–155). Chicago: University of Illinois Press.

Bruner, J. (2002). *Making stories: Law, literature, life.* Cambridge, MA: Harvard University Press.

Burke, K. (1969). *A grammar of motives.* Berkeley, CA: University of California Press.

Chanfrault-Duchet, M.-F. (1991). Narrative structures, social models, and symbolic representation in the life story. In S. B. Gluck and D. Patai (Eds.), *Women's words: The feminist practice of oral history* (pp. 77–91). New York: Routledge.

Clandinin, D. J., and Connelly, F. M. (2000). *Narrative inquiry: Experience and story in qualitative research.* San Francisco: Jossey-Bass.

Drake, D. B. (2003). *How stories change: A narrative analysis of liminal experiences and transitions in identity.* Unpublished doctoral dissertation, Fielding Graduate Institute, Santa Barbara, CA.

Drake, D. B. (2004). *Creating third space: The use of narrative liminality in coaching.* In I. Stein, F. Campone, & L. Page (Eds.), Proceedings of the Second ICF Coaching Research Symposium (pp. 50–59). Quebec City, Canada: International Coach Federation.

Drake, D. B. (2005). *Narrative coaching: A psychosocial method for working with clients' stories to support transformative results.* Paper presented at the Second Australia Conference on Evidence-Based Coaching, Sydney, Australia.

Drake, D. B. (2007a). An integrated approach to coaching: The emerging story in a large professional services firm. *International Journal of Coaching in Organizations,* 5(3), 22–35.

Drake, D. B. (2007b). The art of thinking narratively: Implications for coaching psychology and practice. *Australian Psychologist* (Special Issue on Coaching Psychology), 42(4), 283–294.

Drake, D. B. (2008). Evidence in action: A relational view of knowledge and mastery in coaching. In K. Görtz and A. Prehn (Eds.), *Coaching in perspective.* Copenhagen: Hans Reitzel Publishers.

Dunne, J. (1995). Beyond sovereignty and deconstruction: The storied self. *Philosophy and Social Criticism,* 21(5/6), 137–157.

Eakin, P. J. (1999). *How our lives become stories.* Ithaca, NY: Cornell University Press.

Foucault, M. (1965). *Madness and civilization: A history of insanity in the age of reason.* New York: Random House.

Freire, P. (1970). *Pedagogy of the oppressed.* New York: Seabury Press.

Frisch, M. (1972). *Tagebuch.* Frankfurt, Germany: Suhrkamp.

Geertz, C. (1978). *The interpretation of cultures.* New York: Basic Books.

Gergen, K. J. (1994). Mind, text, and society: Self-memory in social context. In U. Neisser and R. Fivush (Eds.), *The remembering self: Construction and accuracy in the self-narrative* (pp. 78–104). Cambridge, UK: Cambridge University Press.

Gergen, M. M., and Gergen, K. J. (2006). Narratives in action. *Narrative Inquiry,* 16(1), 112–121.

Hermans, H. J. M. (2004). The innovation of self-narratives: A dialogical approach. In L. E. Angus and J. McLeod (Eds.), *Handbook of narrative and psychotherapy: Practice, theory, and research* (pp. 175–191). Thousand Oaks, CA: Sage.

Hermans, H. J. M., and Kempen, H. J. G. (1993). *The dialogical self: Meaning as movement.* San Diego, CA: Academic Press.

Hewson, D. (1991). From laboratory to therapy room: Prediction questions for reconstructing the 'new–old' story. *Dulwich Centre Newsletter,* 3, 5–12.

Hillman, J. (1983). *Healing fiction*. Woodstock, NY: Spring.

Ibarra, H., and Lineback, K. (2005). What's your story? *Harvard Business Review*, 83(1), 65–71.

Mattingly, C. (1998). *Healing dramas and clinical plots: The narrative structure of experience*. New York: Cambridge University Press.

McKee, R. (2004). Story seminar (notes), 10–12 September. Los Angeles, CA.

McLeod, J. (2004). The significance of narrative and storytelling in post-psychological counseling and psychotherapy. In A. Lieblich, D. P. McAdams, and R. Josselson (Eds.), *Healing plots: The narrative basis for psychotherapy* (pp. 11–27). Washington, DC: American Psychological Association.

Ochs, E., and Capps, L. (1996). Narrating the self. *Annual Review of Anthropology*, 25, 19–43.

Ollerenshaw, J. A., and Creswell, J. W. (2002). Narrative research: A comparison of two restorying data analysis approaches. *Qualitative Inquiry*, 8(3), 329–347.

Phillips, A. (1994). *On flirtation*. Cambridge, MA: Harvard University Press.

Polkinghorne, D. E. (1988). *Narrative knowing and the human sciences*. Albany, NY: State University of New York Press.

Polkinghorne, D. E. (2001). The self and humanistic psychology. In K. J. Schneider, J. F. T. Bugental, and J. F. Pierson (Eds.), *The handbook of humanistic psychology* (pp. 81–99). Thousand Oaks, CA: Sage.

Rennie, D. L. (1994). Storytelling in psychotherapy: The client's subjective experience. *Psychotherapy*, 31(2), 234–243.

Riessman, C. K. (1993). *Narrative analysis* (Vol 30). Newbury Park: Sage.

Rossiter, M. (1999). Understanding adult development as narrative. *New directions for adult and continuing education*, 84, 77–85.

Schank, R. A. (1990). *Tell me a story: A new look at real and artificial memory*. New York: Charles Scribner's Sons.

Schwartz-Salant, N. (1998). *The mystery of human relationship: Alchemy and the transformation of the self*. New York: Routledge.

Sherman, S. J., Skov, R. B., Hervitz, E. F., and Stock, C. B. (1981). The effects of explaining hypothetical future events: From possibility to probability to actuality and beyond. *Journal of Experimental Social Psychology*, 17, 142.

Siegel, D. J. (1999). *The developing mind*. New York: Guilford Press.

Simms, L. (2000). Crossing into the invisible. *Parabola: Myth, tradition and the search for meaning*, 25(1), 62–68.

Stein, N. L., and Glenn, C. G. (1979). An analysis of story comprehension in elementary school children. In R. O. Freedle (Ed.), *New directions in discourse processing* (Vol. 2, pp. 53–120). Greenwich, CT: Ablex.

Stern, D. M. (2004). *The present moment in psychotherapy and everyday life*. New York: Norton.

Strauss, A. L. (1997). *Mirrors and masks: The search for identity* (2nd edn). New Brunswick, NJ: Transaction.

Swann, W. B., Jr, and Read, S. J. (1981). Self-verification processes: How we sustain our self-conceptions. *Journal of Experimental Social Psychology*, 17, 351–372.

Tarlow, M., and Tarlow, P. (2002). *Digital aboriginal: The direction of business now: Instinctive, nomadic, and ever-changing*. New York: Warner Books.

White, M. (1995). *Workshop Notes*. Retrieved September 21, 2005, from www.dulwichcentre.com.au

White, M. (2007). *Maps of narrative practice*. New York: Norton.

White, M., and Epston, D. (1990). *Narrative means to therapeutic ends*. New York: Norton.

Does It Matter What the Coach Thinks? – A New Foundation for Professional Development

4

Peter Jackson

Introduction

This chapter is about knowing where you stand and why that is important. My aim in writing it was to build a picture of how we understand what we do as professional coaches. My hope is that, by sharing this picture, readers will be in a better position to discover more about why they do what they do and be motivated to take further their explorations of that question. That undertaking is, I believe, an essential part of acting in a professional manner and will benefit coaches, their clients and the market in general.

The meteoric expansion of the coaching industry has been well documented (see Jarvis, 2004; Grant and Cavanagh, 2004). Even so, it is important to acknowledge that growth itself is not necessarily smooth but tends to proceed in sequences of periods of gradual, organic, change punctuated by discrete jumps or reappraisals. Jumps can be traumatic. Periods of gradual change can go on too long. Those of us who work in a business context recognize that when these are not managed effectively, a business can find itself battling against the shadow of its former self: former nationalized industries struggle with commercialization; great entrepreneurial projects struggle to move on from the influence of their founders. The growth of the coaching industry to date has been like

The Philosophy and Practice of Coaching: Insights and Issues for a New Era.
Edited by David B. Drake, Diane Brennan and Kim Gørtz.
© 2008 John Wiley & Sons, Ltd.

one of those periods of gradual change, and, like a fast-growing business, risks leaving structural weaknesses in its wake. These cracks are small as yet, but as the edifice grows, so does the strain. People have predicted the dangers of poor practice or the imminent demise of another 'flash in the pan' industry. I do not want to be sensationalist and I am not clairvoyant, but it seems never too early to attend to foundations. And we can do this both as individual practitioners and as an industry.

But how do these wider issues relate to how the coach thinks? The connection for me is that there is a process of constructive investigation we need to undertake in order to deal with these issues. By investigating how we structure our practice we will be more able to build more robust foundations – both individually and collectively. Moreover, I would also argue that there are barriers, albeit largely artificial, that appear to stand between practitioners and this constructive investigation. These barriers are embedded in a professional culture in coaching that has arisen as a result of semantic and philosophical positions that are characteristic of this particular stage of the industry's development. In terms of the industry's growth, it may be time for a jump, a moment to reassess where some ideas have come from and where they are going. Let us first, then, stand back briefly and take a perspective on some of the drivers of current thinking in the field.

A Perspective

It is widely acknowledged that coaching is a young discipline of professional practice, though with roots in several more-established fields of knowledge. Its growth has been primarily market-led to date. However, a number of other activities related to greater professionalization have accompanied this growth, including increases in the number of:

- professional associations from just one or two in the mid-1990s to dozens of regional and international bodies in 2007;
- postgraduate level educational programmes (the first Masters course in the UK, for example, opened to students in 2001, and has been followed by a number of others, now extending into professional doctorates);
- PhD submissions on coaching-specific topics (see Grant and Cavanagh, 2004); and
- peer-reviewed journals focused on the discipline of coaching.

In fact, these latter activities have followed behind practice. Witness, for example, the fact that many practitioners claim coaching activity stretching back much longer than these 10 years, and that some of the key practitioner texts (e.g., Clutterbuck, 1985; Parsloe, 1992; Whitmore, 1992; Gallwey, 1974) date from the 1990s, 1980s and earlier. The significance of this order of events is that it reflects the change sequence I described previously, insofar as structured reappraisal has naturally followed on from gradual organic change. It is only within the context and momentum of a generally unstructured development of the industry that more and more voices have gathered around the mechanisms of step-change. To restate my purpose: it is to examine the nature of this context and momentum in order to transform our practice more effectively and to give focus to the move towards professionalization.

I would contend that this history of market-led activity has created a 'can-do' culture of pragmatism. It is attractive to talk about coaching as a practical discipline. It is a solution, not an idea; it is about outcomes not processes. Framing coaching in this way implies an action-orientation and speaks to a marketplace that wants results. However, we must not confuse the map with the terrain. This culture of pragmatism – through the values it espouses, and the structure of science on which it is based – is a frame that speaks to the market. At the same time it obscures issues of practice, professional development and the maturation of the profession.

This frame need not be permanent; it can be challenged. In teaching at a postgraduate level, I have had the privilege of witnessing highly competent and successful practitioners benefit from approaching their practice in new ways. They talk about gaining confidence, becoming more able to understand the strengths of taking different perspectives, and becoming more able to make more conscious choices in their practice. In essence, they become more flexible and more able to respond to unpredictable situations – even if using knowledge they already had. These are not the outcomes of simply gathering information or new techniques or of modelling other people's practice. It is the result of examining the foundations and assumptions of their own practice, questioning what they hold to be true, and engaging with the uncertainties of how we really know what we know. These are three requests coaches regularly make of their clients yet often fail to make of themselves as an unintended dominance of the culture of pragmatism.

As a result, the focus of this chapter is not coaching techniques themselves, but the nature of the thinking that gives rise to them. Some readers may find this uncomfortable. I hope so; I do. I seek to challenge the existing model after all and, in doing so, open up greater opportunities for professional development and professional practice.

The discussion starts with an explanation of what I mean by the 'culture of pragmatism'. I have said that this is a culture that creates a barrier to professional progress as it has arisen in the coaching profession; I will argue that it does so because it obscures the nature of evidence and theory. However, pragmatism as a philosophical formulation could play a significant and legitimate role in coaching practice – a view explained briefly in relation to pragmatic philosophers Peirce, James and Dewey. Understanding the origin and nature of pragmatism's practical orientation helps us to understand the shortcomings of its modern expression in coaching. In order to differentiate theory from different types of evidence, I look at the dominant model of empirical investigation proposed by Karl Popper whose thought in many ways reflects that of the pragmatists. By investigating a further dimension of tacit knowledge from learning theorists, I introduce a model that can be used to guide coaches in the development of their practice. This model provides a framework and logic that will both make sense of many of the professional development activities that are already in place and, I hope, inspire readers to take up further activities.

Pragmatism in Practice

What is the 'Culture of Pragmatism'?

I have argued that a culture of pragmatism has arisen from the dominant influence of practical and commercial concerns in the development of coaching as a discipline. Practitioner-oriented literature has led the way in spreading the popularity of coaching and in sharing skills across the practitioner population. It has carried with it a tendency to emphasize practical over theoretical considerations. I have tried to suggest that this is a legitimate and valuable concern. It is also an entirely legitimate part of the process of the development of the discipline. However, close examination suggests that it tends to present the relationship between theory and practice in a way that does not help the development of the profession. In this section, I will look at how this culture is expressed and propose some thoughts about what that means for coaching's future.

Here I would like to take a simple example from a well-regarded practitioner text by Chapman, Best, and van Casteren (2003) which claims that, 'This book is not about speculative theory, about what might happen. It's about what has happened and how it was achieved' (p. 16). Later, they write 'Unlike some of our more academic counterparts, we present only those models that have worked in the past for real clients' (pp. 16–17).

What are the authors saying here? We will see later that the view that theory derives from experience is a legitimate proposition, but in these small extracts there is a conflation of theory with speculation and academia with the *un*real. In fact, the authors are not guilty at all of eschewing theory even if they think they are – the whole book is theory, based as they quite fairly say, on their own practice. In the course of this practice they have picked up existing theory and applied it, finding some things work and others do not. Their frustration is understandable: 'We have observed too many coaches attempting to "shoehorn" an existing model into a coaching transaction when it is clearly inappropriate' (p. 22), but this does not justify a position that could logically be represented as '*theory* ≠ *what works*'. This is, and must be seen as, a false dichotomy. The authors' fundamental claim is that their theory – that is, their expectation of what will work to what end, in what situation – is more powerful than another, or perhaps, '*my theory* > *your theory*'. They may be right, but why do they pretend to be atheoretical? I cannot answer this for them, but one of the authors is very direct in saying that, 'As a coach, colleagues and clients describe my strength as commercial focus and directness. I can only concur' (p. 3). This stance seems to me to be very much part of the culture of pragmatism.

This is, of course, just one example. However, I have heard similar preferences routinely expressed by students (e.g., 'I haven't used any theories because I'm not a theorist'). It is also natural that providers of coaching services might be keener to talk about their proprietary 'system' (which has outputs) than their attitude or thinking (which does not appear to do so). In 2003 I carried out a small pilot study (unpublished) into the use of theory by UK-based individual practitioners. Of my respondents, (1) some were aware of the theoretical source of some techniques they used, especially when they were derived from therapy; (2) others were overtly and consciously pragmatic ('science doesn't matter to NLP' one told me); (3) another said that theory was 'important', but quoted practitioner literature as illustration rather than a theoretical source; and (4) none actually described scientific theory or evidence among their criteria for either the initial adoption of techniques into their toolkit or the subsequent application of those techniques in specific situations. Rather, coaches appeared to adopt techniques when either they had direct experience of a technique working well for them as a subject or they can imagine it doing so.

In my introduction, I argued that the culture of pragmatism was holding back the process of building better professional foundations for the discipline of coaching. It does so because it creates a faulty frame of reference for the ongoing development of disciplinary knowledge. In both the literature-based and interview-based examples I have given above, coaches have claimed not to use theory. This is a false claim based on a false understanding of what theory is. In essence, any decision based on a cognitive decision-making process, any form of action or intention based on a reasonable expectation of a particular outcome in a particular circumstance, can be thought of as a theory. We act on theory all the time: some are conscious theories, some are unconscious, some are personal and some are public. The claim not to use theory, in effect, obscures from scrutiny the basis of this decision-making, and this is why I argue that it is a faulty frame of reference.

My first step in constructing an alternative frame is to clarify an issue of semantics. A brief description of the background of pragmatic philosophy is included here in order to discriminate between that philosophy and the cultural claims made in its name. In fact, the central ideas of pragmatic philosophy are very pertinent to coaching practice – constituting a strong theme in practical approaches and techniques – and provide a powerful link between theory and practice.

The Pragmatic Tradition

It is interesting that 'pragmatic' has come to mean in everyday terms, 'practical', 'down-to-earth' or, in some senses, in opposition to 'theoretical' or 'idealistic'. Pragmatic philosophy developed in America in the late nineteenth and early twentieth centuries and was a response to the increasing distance between analytical philosophy and everyday practical questions of how one should live one's life. It is usually traced back to three main figures, all American: Charles Sanders Peirce, William James and John Dewey. It is marked in particular by its stance on what constitutes knowledge (the area of philosophy known as epistemology) and it is in relation to this stance that the term pragmatism came to be applied. It is important to stress that pragmatic epistemology does not constitute a rejection of theoretical concerns, but is an approach to ensuring that those concerns are oriented towards effects in the real world.

Pragmatism proposes an epistemology of utility. The three writers mentioned formulated this in different ways. Peirce, concluding that the search for a definitive epistemology was futile, focused in particular on what emerges from the process of collaborative enquiry; Dewey on what is warranted in practice through competent enquiry; and James on what seems to work best in practice. In this we hear echoes of attitudes to knowledge that we find among present-day practitioners.

Neuro-linguistic programming (NLP), for example, explicitly embodies James' epistemology as a way of enabling behavioural change. O'Connor and McDermott (2001) tell us that beliefs are distinct from facts, that what we believe affects our actions, and that some beliefs may be more helpful than others. In order to change a negative belief we might ask, 'What belief would I rather have?' (p. 152), or 'How will my life be better with the new belief' (p. 153). This is pragmatic epistemology in action. In effect it is saying, 'we should choose the construction of reality that suits our purpose'.

It is not just at the level of technique that we can see the impact of pragmatic epistemology, but also in the 'principles' or 'foundations' that practitioners and writers claim for their coaching approach. As one example among many, Rogers (2004) describes as a 'principle' of coaching that 'the client is resourceful' (p. 7). She refers to it also as a 'belief'. Rogers also illustrates how such principles have a direct effect on coaching practice, 'It follows from the first belief that the role of the coach is not advice giving' (p. 7). I am by no means alone in claiming that the coach's thoughts affect their actions!

So, pragmatism is concerned with basing our knowledge on collaborative enquiry (Peirce), competent enquiry (Dewey), or simply on what works (James). These ideas are expressed in some techniques and principles of coaching. In the same way that our own assumptions frame our thinking and therefore our behaviour, epistemology underpins how we understand evidence. In the next section, I explore this fundamental connection as the next step toward reframing coaching's relationship to theory.

Knowledge, Theory and Practice

If our assumptions affect how we operate, then it follows that our assumptions about the nature of knowledge affect what we choose to accept as evidence. I will take another example from teaching here. On a programme about coaching in organizations we use a sample case study. The case has a lot of historical, financial and organizational information. When I ask students what stands out for them, I typically get a range of different answers. Some people notice the relationships; some people go straight to the financial indicators; some people analyse the role of the HR policies in place. In noticing certain aspects of the organization as more significant than others, students typically reflect their professional experience: the OD consultant, the accountant, the HR manager, are all demonstrating that different perspectives create different constructions of reality.

So, as coaches, how do we form expectations of how the world works? How do we form theory? What is the science of coaching? Perhaps we should ask what are the most useful answers to those questions. I would like to base my discussion of the role of theory and evidence in coaching on Karl Popper's (1959, 1972) model of the development of scientific knowledge. Popper's philosophy of science can be criticized for internal conflicts (see Hindess, 1977), and the idea that scientific method can be applied to understand the social world in which coaches undeniably operate can be questioned. Nonetheless, its concept of theory survives these issues and provides a model that helps us to understand how we choose what we do.

Popper's starting point was to clarify the 'demarcation' between metaphysics – what we might think of as abstract philosophy in everyday terms – and empirical science. He saw this as a way of ensuring that speculative issues of philosophy could be held as distinct from demonstrable facts of science. The essential demarcation he made was between inductive and deductive methods. Inductive methods can be seen as the logical advancement from axiomatic statements that could be held to be true in their own right towards the consequences of those statements, namely second-order truths, and so on. Deductive methods, on the other hand, take possible truths – hypotheses – and subject them to testing, by observing whether the logical consequences of these hypotheses are in fact borne out in practice.

Popper (1959) differentiates very clearly between hypotheses and personal convictions: 'Can any statement be justified by the fact that K. R. P[opper] is utterly convinced of its truth? The answer is "No"' (p. 46). Yet, this is not a rejection of convictions or of logical induction that may themselves generate the hypothesis in the first place; demarcation simply says that they are not relevant to the empirical investigation of hypotheses. In summary:

> We must distinguish between, on the one hand, *our subjective experiences or our feelings of conviction*, which can never justify any statement [. . .] and, on the other hand, the *objective logical relations* subsisting among the various systems of scientific statements, and within each of them. (Popper, 1959, p. 44) (Popper's italics)

I suggested earlier that the culture of pragmatism essentially claims that *'theory ≠ what works'*. Instead, Popper's model implies that a more useful demarcation is between theories that are empirically testable and theories that are not. Theory, in Popper's sense, is about nothing other than observable facts in the real world. All propositions of cause and effect are essentially theoretical, but not all are empirically testable. In placing theory and practice in opposition, the culture of pragmatism creates a false reality: that we must choose between pointless theory and proven practice; and that one is wrong and the other is right. In so doing, it ignores the differentiation between (1) specific experiences of the world and models that can be reliably generalized to wider application; and (2) personal convictions and hypotheses that are empirically supported.

It is not, therefore, a debate over theory. This is a false debate. The debate is rather over what constitutes evidence. This is why I said that the false dichotomy '*theory ≠ what works*' could be reformulated as '*my theory > your theory*'. Now we can take this a stage further and say that the claim is actually '*my evidence > your evidence*'. The culture of pragmatism's false reality hides this claim. When such claims remaining hidden, the practical consequence is that we are at risk of the following:

- believing there to be evidence for specific interventions where there is none – or, more frequently, believing the evidence to be stronger or more applicable to a particular circumstance than is actually the case;
- dealing with clients as if they are the same as us, thereby confusing our own perceptual filters and biases with reality; and
- failing to identify accurately our own professional limitations.

What kind of programme is this for professional development and the maturation of the profession? I concur with Drake (2008) that, 'every choice we make in coaching is already based on some type of evidence – even if it is just the latest book we read'. We owe it to our clients and ourselves to work to become more transparent and diligent about the evidence on which we are basing our practice.

What Evidence Do We Use?

This discussion brings us to a lot of questions around how to practise. Is professional practice merely the application of empirical evidence? Is coaching not a science *and* an art? Is there a place for intuition?

Certainly empiricism should have a strong influence. Grant and Cavanagh (2004) have identified the elaboration of theoretically grounded approaches to coaching and the development of an empirical research-base as two of three key challenges for the coaching industry as it seeks to professionalize. In my Introduction I mentioned some of the phenomena of professionalization that have followed the market-led development of practice, namely the growth of professional associations, the development of postgraduate university coach education, and the expansion in the number of coaching-specific doctoral theses. Each of these developments in different ways demonstrates a concern with evidence and goes some way to making that evidence available to the serious practitioner: professional associations through forums, accreditation and 'best practice' guidance; universities through developing the capabilities of practitioners as critical researchers in their own right; and doctoral studies through the generation of genuinely new knowledge.

However, in critiquing the culture of pragmatism, I am not simply taking a contrary stance in favour of empirical investigation. Indeed, it has its own shortcomings. The criticism can be made that empirical evidence tends to be narrow in its application. Drake (2008) writes, 'Most quantitative research strives for internal validity to allow for rigorous testing and is thus susceptible to a limited ability to generalize beyond the sample studied'. While Schön (1991) argues that this atomization of knowledge, what he calls the model of 'technical rationality', makes it difficult for the practitioner to solve problems holistically. This perhaps is the point of Chapman et al.'s (2003) complaint, quoted previously. To illustrate this very real point, I once asked an academic organizational psychologist, whom I considered immensely knowledgeable and creative, whether he had considered doing more consultancy in business; in reply he said, 'Organizations don't want to pay to be told that there's no evidence that what they're doing will work'. Empirical evidence is just one source of evidence, and I am arguing not for one source over another here, but for clarity.

There is a parallel to this in academic research. Academics choose different approaches to discovering knowledge (methodology) and use different tools to do it (methods). Their choice of methodology is determined by the nature of the enquiry and to some extent the researcher's stance on what constitutes knowledge (epistemology). It is an important principle in academic research that the basis of claims of evidence should be transparent to the reader. Academics are at pains to clarify the assumptions they carry into a piece of research (including epistemological ones), the approach and methods they use, and, as precisely as possible, the conditions prevailing at the time. The point is that by providing a clear and transparent account, the researcher enables readers to form their own assessment of the research. This allows informed critique and debate, which in turn furthers our state of knowledge. In professional practice we may be able to apply the same principle: providing the same degree of transparency when we make claims for an approach or technique, whether those claims are made publicly or are implicit in our decision-making, would allow us to examine more closely the validity of those claims. What is required in order to do this is a clear model of the different types of evidence that we use. So what are they?

The starting point is epistemology. Popper described his approach in passing as 'deductivist' (Popper, 1972, p. 30) and contrasted it to 'our subjective experiences or our feelings of conviction' (p. 44). He described standards of empirical evidence very effectively. Yet Popper's model, *on its own*, would seem to devalue the artistry that is so inherent in professional practice and the value that is often placed on a more subjective sense of what is the right way to proceed in the moment. In order to understand the breadth of types of evidence that we use, we need to look where Popper did not.

The experience of students with whom I work illustrates the interplay of objective and subjective responses. During the course of an eight-month practicum many students, especially those less confident in their existing coaching experience, describe a typical arc. From a state of uncertainty and anxiety at the outset, they absorb as many coaching techniques and tricks as they can – to the point sometimes where they confuse themselves. Over time, they settle into preferences. By the end of the practicum they report being less concerned with technique and more concerned with paying attention to the relationship. Many students account for this as the process of moving from 'conscious incompetence' to 'conscious competence' to 'unconscious competence' (source unknown),[1] and often quote Whitworth, Kimsey-House, and Sandahl's (1998) concept of 'dancing in the moment'.

There are a number of explanations for this process. Dreyfus and Dreyfus (1986) introduced a five-level model of expertise, rising from 'novice' to 'expert', where the expert's skill 'has become so much a part of him that he need be no more aware of it than he is of his own body' (p. 30). Eraut (2000) describes the process of knowledge becoming 'routinised', such that access to it becomes almost automatic (literally, like riding a bike). In a similar way, Prietula and Simon (1989) describe how experts progressively 'chunk' patterns of information into single units as a way of retaining more information and more complex information than would otherwise be possible. As the expert recognizes and applies these 'chunks', the knowledge is reinforced and extended, and becomes less conscious. What is common to these explanations is that tacit knowledge or intuition is not some mysterious miasma, but the accumulation of experience. Hence our 'feelings of conviction' as Popper described them, may well be based on real-world experience, albeit experience that might evade explanation. Where Popper is certainly correct, is that they may not be subject to the deductive rigour he describes, and that the strength of our feelings of conviction cannot be taken as a measure of their reliability.

---

1 The original source of the (un)conscious/(in)competence model has been much debated, but without conclusion.

These interpretations emphasize individual experience in the process of creating knowledge. The practicum students mentioned above, however, are not learning alone. In the course of seminars and supervision we are able to create opportunities for them to test their interpretations with fellow students and experienced practitioners, to hear the ideas of others and to try them out for themselves. During this programme I have noticed two further types of knowledge creation that involve interaction with others. Firstly, the group as a whole tends to develop a consensus on certain topics. For example, we spend a certain amount of time looking at definitions of coaching and mentoring. There are plenty of definitions available and they are not entirely consistent. However, each successive cohort tends to come to a similar working consensus: that coaching is generally facilitative and process-oriented, while mentoring has a greater element of the transfer of knowledge. This does not necessarily make it 'right', but there is a process going on here of establishing a shared understanding with which the group decides (more or less) to go forward. Secondly, there is a process of imitation. Practitioners at all stages of development will model aspects of their practice on other respected individuals (see Bandura, 1977). With the practicum students this shows up as students trying out approaches and ideas that are put forward by peers, or in the practitioner literature, adopting (then adapting) approaches used by their practice supervisors, or picking up ideas from practical demonstrations and professional networking events that we run.

In practice, individuals will treat all these experiences as evidence, but there are essential differences between these types of evidence. If we are to make our own practice transparent to scrutiny and develop the body of knowledge, we need to understand the strengths and weaknesses of each of these ways of knowing: *empirical evidence* (objectivity); *experiential evidence* (subjectivity); *common agreement* (consensus or culture); and the *evidence of respected role models* (good practice). Let us examine each in turn.

Four Types of Evidence

Knowing Based on Empirical Evidence along the Lines of Popper's Hypothetico-deductive Method, Expressed as Objective Knowledge

This is the 'science'. The hypothetico-deductive method produces results that can be very clearly calibrated for qualities of validity and generalizability. In this respect the information can be shared relatively unambiguously and, by the same token, critically evaluated, extended, or contradicted by further research. It is considered to be unbiased and strongly predictive within bounds. It is criticized as an approach, especially in social contexts, for its mechanistic assumptions of human behaviour and the inherent restrictions on the applicability of findings. In other words, it simply does not reflect how professionals deal with complex situations. Schön's (1991) critique of the model of technical rationality argues that a focus on objective knowledge in professionals' formation results in a depth of specialization that becomes a trap and, in which, 'it is tempting, if the only tool you have is a hammer, to treat everything as if it were a nail' (Maslow, 1966, pp. 15–16). It is also a common phenomenon that the complex conditions under which statistical data are examined get lost in the translation from scientific to everyday language, leading to misleading interpretations presented in, for example, the popular press and lifestyle magazines. We must take on board both the strengths and the weaknesses of empirical evidence.

Coaches should therefore seek to understand fully the conditions and complexities of empirical knowledge, understand the strengths and weaknesses of different methodologies, and be wary of secondary sources. Neither is it enough simply to say that empirical evidence is lacking – as a community of professionals it is up to us to encourage, support and participate in the generation of knowledge.

Knowing Based on Previous Personal Experience, Expressed as Intuition

This is the professional 'gut feel', the 'hunch'. The strengths of this type of knowing are that it is immediately accessible to the practitioner, almost without thinking and that it is highly flexible to situations that may be very complex or in many respects dissimilar to previous situations encountered. It is practised art, Dreyfus and Dreyfus's (1986) 'mature and practiced understanding' (p. 30). The very strengths of this type of knowing also highlight certain risks. Dreyfus and Dreyfus express this in terms of automatism: 'The expert driver becomes one with his car, and he experiences himself simply as driving, rather than as driving a car' (p. 30). Yet, in this state, who has not had the experience of forgetting parts of a familiar journey or, as has happened to me, accidentally driven to work instead of to the supermarket? It is in the nature of this 'knowing' that we do not question it. We may have set off down the wrong track. Similarly, it may not be clear how much experience our 'hunch' is based on. What is the dividing line between the wisdom of experience and an unwarranted belief based on an unfortunate incident? When we feel a hunch, do we know how many experiences it is based on? In summary, it may be difficult to differentiate, without the conscious effort of self-examination.

Coaches should therefore make explicit self-examination a priority. This might take the form of coaching, supervision, or reflective practice.

Knowing Based on Consensus, Expressed as Culture

This is the kind of thing that might be prefaced by 'we all know that . . .', or 'obviously . . .' (or sometimes by references to supposed dictums of Confucius or Einstein). Culture carries an enormous amount of information very efficiently. It allows the individual to focus attention on the particular and the problematic rather than the routine. It creates 'safe' options for which the individual is unlikely to be criticized. However, cultural knowledge is tacit; it can be misread; and it can make claims that are unsupportable at a conscious level (for example, discrimination). Critical theorists use the term 'ideology': 'Ideologies are hard to detect since they are embedded in language, social habits, and cultural forms that combine to shape the way we think about the world' (Brookfield, 2005, p. 41). Brookfield further notes that, 'whenever we catch ourselves saying "obviously" to ourselves we know ideology is lurking close by' (p. 66). For the purposes of this discussion the concept of ideology is useful because it demonstrates how beliefs can be embedded not only in what we think, but in how we think about what we think.

Like Brookfield, we should beware the obvious.

Knowing Based on the Performance of Role Models, Expressed as Good Practice

This is the imitation of respected others. Vicarious experience has the benefit that it is highly transferable, subject to a degree of scrutiny (through being observed), and can be readily transformed into personal experience. On the other hand, adoption of vicarious experience can be subject to very personal qualities such as the charisma of the role model and mood. As a source of evidence it can be accepted (or rejected) uncritically and transform into a specific subculture. As such it is liable to risks similar to those inherent in consensus/culture, though here it may be easier to identify as coming from an external source. We should, therefore, be alert to approaches that may be doctrinaire or dogmatic. Any practice must be open to question.

Guidelines for Evidence in the Practice of Coaching

I have included in the descriptions above some of the risks or fallibilities of the various types of evidence as well as some assertions of what might mitigate those risks. There is further benefit, however, in looking at the landscape of evidence as a whole and formulating a programme that accounts for the interrelationships between them. Seen in this light, professional development can be seen as a programme consisting of three main strands: making the sources of evidence explicit; benefiting from as wide a landscape of evidence as possible; and mitigating the risks inherent in the weaknesses of each type. The final section of this chapter suggests ways we can do this, whether or not these strands are already part of a coach's practice. In either case, I hope that the argument I have presented gives added meaning to them.

The challenges of developing the profession and the nature of evidence-based practice, in particular, have been discussed to great effect by Grant and Cavanagh (2004) and Drake (2008) respectively. I do not seek to replace those discussions, but to lend them more support. By presenting this model of types of evidence, I believe the methods used in professional development for coaches can progress to become more apparent and logical. In this section I will look at the three strands of development identified above and suggest the practical actions practitioners might take.

Make the Sources of Evidence Explicit

I would not suggest here that we should become paralysed by self-analysis. This is not about putting things in the way of the flow of our practice, but about thinking about it constructively. This can be achieved by establishing the habit of enquiry. This might be done through coaching, supervision, journalling, or reflection on critical incidents. The important thing is that the question is asked, 'where did I get that idea from?', on what authority do I have it?' The consequence of answering this question is twofold: firstly, we may notice an over-reliance on certain types of evidence – and therefore opportunities to grow in other areas; secondly, we may identify personal theories that when exposed to the 'light of day' we choose to investigate further, or simply drop completely.

Seek Benefit from as Wide a Landscape of Evidence as Possible

In one sense, this activity fits most easily with the provision of professional development by employers, industry bodies and academic institutions: professional forums, practical demonstrations, short courses, conferences, journals and literature. There is, however, an opportunity to go further than this. Rather than having a haphazard programme, the individual practitioner can link their continuous professional development (CPD) to the previous strand. It therefore becomes an opportunity to focus on broader influences (rather than just more).

Mitigate the Risks Inherent in the Weaknesses of Each Type of Evidence

I have identified inherent weaknesses in each type of evidence: the narrow applicability of objective, empirical evidence; the susceptibility to personal bias in the 'hunch' or 'gut feel'; the risk of discrimination inherent in unexamined cultural norms; the possibility of uncritical 'followership' behind charismatic role models. It is not hard to imagine how each of these could compromise the coach's quality of service to their client. Again, I would argue that simply by engaging with the process of identifying our sources of evidence, asking on what authority we hold something to be true, we will go some way to managing these risks. However, there is more we can do and this consists in transforming one type of evidence into another, thereby enriching our own practice and the body of knowledge available to others. Here are some examples.

- Professional good practice is transformed into personal experiential knowledge simply by putting it into practice. Intuitive individual knowledge is transformed into professional good practice by being made explicit to the professional community at large (through physical demonstration, or written media).
- Cultural knowledge is transformed into empirical knowledge by making it explicit and undertaking research. Empirical knowledge is transformed into cultural knowledge by repeated dissemination and explanation.

If I were to summarize further the implications of this analysis I would recommend the following: examine the bases of practice through supervision and reflective practice; seek out forms of knowledge that are less familiar to you; contribute to the discipline by sharing the knowledge you have.

Conclusion

I started this discussion by looking at the 'culture of pragmatism', arguing that its inherent opposition of theory and practice was not helpful to developing the profession and professional practice. A discussion of the nature of theory and practice showed that this opposition was false.

Coaching is a discipline of application, but this can be misunderstood to mean that theory and evidence are not important. We all operate according to theory and the evidence we use is the measure of the theory. In this respect coaching is similar to any area of application of social science. Fay (1996) argues comprehensively that the advance of social science is not helped by false dualisms (for example, between the individual and society as an appropriate level of analysis; between seeing individuals as wholly responsible or as a product of their society; between meaning and cause; and most tellingly between subjectivity and objectivity). The culture of pragmatism argues a false dualism. It is an artefact of the history of the development of coaching. Now we must move on, reframe the epistemology of coaching, and adopt one that allows and encourages development of the discipline and its practitioners.

Theory and practice are not alternatives, but a range of shades and indeed of tones. As a discipline, and as practitioners, we must be committed to an active engagement with the full spectrum of evidence – empirical, intuitive, best practice, cultural – and be prepared to examine the basis of our own preferences through supervision, reflective practice and exposure to peer review. This is what professional development now means.

References

Bandura, A. (1977). *Social learning theory*. Englewood Cliffs, NJ: Prentice Hall.
Brookfield, S. (2005). *The power of critical theory for adult learning and teaching*. Maidenhead, UK: Open University Press.
Chapman, T., Best, B., and van Casteren, P. (2003). *The executive coach: Exploding the myth*. Basingstoke: Palgrave.
Clutterbuck, D. (1985). *Everyone needs a mentor: fostering talent at work*. London: IPD.
Drake, D. B. (2008). Evidence in action: A relational view of knowledge and mastery in coaching. In K. Görtz and A. Prehn (Eds.), *Coaching in perspective*. Copenhagen: Hans Reitzel Publishers.

Dreyfus, H. L., and Dreyfus, S. E. (1986). *Mind over machine: The power of human intuition and expertise in the era of the computer.* New York: Free Press.

Eraut, M. (2000). Non-formal learning and tacit knowledge in professional work. *British Journal of Educational Psychology*, 70, 113–136.

Fay, B. (1996). *Contemporary philosophy of social science.* Oxford: Blackwell.

Gallwey, T. (1974). *The inner game of tennis.* New York: Random House.

Grant, T., and Cavanagh, M. (2004). Toward a profession of coaching: Sixty-five years of progress and challenges for the future. *International Journal of Evidence Based Coaching and Mentoring*, 2, 1.

Hindess, B. (1977). *Philosophy and methodology in the social sciences.* Hassocks, UK: Harvester Press.

Jarvis, J. (2004). *Coaching and buying coaching services.* London: CIPD.

Maslow, A. H. (1966). *The psychology of science.* New York: Harper & Row.

O'Connor, J., and McDermott, I. (2001). *Way of NLP.* London: Thorson.

Parsloe, E. (1992). *Coaching, mentoring and assessing: A practical guide to developing competence.* London: Kogan Page.

Popper, K. (1959). *The logic of scientific discovery.* London: Hutchison.

Popper, K. (1972). *The logic of scientific discovery (3rd edn).* London: Hutchison.

Prietula, M. J., and Simon, H. A. (1989). The experts in your midst. *Harvard Business Review*, 67(1), 120–124.

Rogers, J. (2004). *Coaching skills: A handbook.* Maidenhead, UK: Open University Press.

Schön, D. A. (1991). *The reflective practitioner: How professionals think in action.* Aldershot, UK: Avebury.

Whitmore, J. (1992). *Coaching for performance.* London: Nicholas Brealey.

Whitworth, L., Kimsey-House, H., and Sandahl, P. (1998). *Co-active coaching.* Palo Alto, CA: Davies-Black.

Connecting the Dots: Coaching Research – Past, Present and Future

5

Francine Campone

Introduction

Describe the colour blue. . . . Writing about coaching research is a little like writing about the colour blue; everyone agrees it exists but each person experiences it somewhat differently. Nonetheless, without it, our shared experience of the world would be significantly impoverished. Readers may remember from their schooldays that the colours of the spectrum are visual manifestations of energy wavelengths. Violet, the first colour on the spectrum, shows where wavelengths are first visible. Blue, next to violet, reflects a slightly longer wavelength, more energy moving toward heat (red). Before the appearance of the first coaching research articles in the 1950s, coaching – as a distinct practice – was almost invisible. The earliest coaching research presented first glimpses of this new field of practice. More recent coaching research extends and amplifies the earlier works, making the blues of coaching more visible.

This chapter offers an overview of coaching-related research literature and suggests how this can support the emergence of coaching as a professional practice. I also offer specific strategies to help coaching practitioners use research in their ongoing professional development and in their journey to coaching mastery. Understanding the evolution of coaching research can help practitioners better appreciate the origins

The Philosophy and Practice of Coaching: Insights and Issues for a New Era.
Edited by David B. Drake, Diane Brennan and Kim Gørtz.
© 2008 John Wiley & Sons, Ltd.

and development of coaching (the past) and apply cutting-edge practice and evidence in coaching (the present and future).

One challenge in writing this chapter was deciding what to include. Like coaching practice, coaching research draws on the methods and protocols of diverse disciplines and is still evolving into its own distinctive form. I am broadly inclusive of print materials that explore, in a rigorous and systematic way, some aspect of coaching theory, models, processes or practice. My intention is not to provide a comprehensive and scholarly review of the coaching literature but to stimulate practising coaches and scholars of coaching to further explore the literature discussed. In the concluding section of this chapter, I will suggest specific ways that coaches can draw on research to deepen their practice.

I use a chronological scheme which reflects the 'colours' of coaching research as it is emerging. The past, encompassing 1955 to 2003, is the 'violet' era. The literature of this period shows coaches staking out the new territory of coaching by defining purposes and practices, and articulating early models borrowed from other fields. The present 'blue era' begins in 2003 (as with the spectrum, the segments slightly overlap) and continues to the time of this writing. The literature of this period brings a more scientific edge to the investigations, introduces new energy in the form of contributions from additional disciplines, and brings both academic and practitioner concerns to the conversation. The future starts now. Accordingly, I see blue starting to give way to green, a more organic research approach and agenda that adds energy and extends the learning from the past. In the sections below on the past and present, I offer an overview of research themes and venues and discuss the implications for coaching practitioners and the coaching field. The future is, of course, purely predictive and speculative. Even so, I offer thoughts about future directions for coaching research based on my experience in the field and potential implications for the practice and field of coaching.

Without the colour blue, the sky, the sea, cornflowers and blueberries would be mere ghostly images. Blue gives these aspects of our world their distinctive appearance, visible to all who view them. Without a solid body of research, the practice of coaching lacks substance and definition; it is a 'ghost' of consulting psychology, organizational development and other root disciplines. Coaching research provides coaches with a distinctive set of models and language for the work we do and the evidence that allows us to make sound professional decisions in the application of the models. It makes visible the energy and thinking that underpins the work of coaching. Research also provides coaches with models for assessing their own practices and outcomes. For the field of coaching as a whole, a body of coaching research provides tangible evidence of how and why the practice works.

As Grant (2004) noted, coaching research is critical if coaching is to develop as a professional field. Irene Stein (2004) writes 'we see the need for further definition of the theoretical foundations for the concept of coaching itself' (p. viii). Echoing and extending these observations, Stober (2005) encourages reflective practice to develop both the field and practitioners. The need for coaching research continues as a theme in the present and looking to the future (Campone, 2006; Page and Stein, 2006).

Numerous authors have noted that coaching has its roots in a variety of disciplines. As we move coaching toward the status of profession and ourselves as professionals, coaching research serves three important purposes. First, as Irene Stein (2004) foretold, a field of coaching studies is emerging which presents the conceptual framework for coaching as a discipline and the theoretical bases for sound coaching practice and for the professional preparation of coaches. This theoretical foundation must rest on empirical, scientifically sound and valid studies. Second, practitioners in coaching – like their colleagues in any other field – have a professional responsibility to maintain currency and a self-reflective edge as practitioners in order to best serve their clients. Here, too, the growing body of accessible coaching research literature serves to meet this need. Third, as internal and external coaches and business-owners, we rely on sound and reliable data to demonstrate value to clients and potential clients and to assess the state of the marketplace.

It is my hope that this chapter will encourage readers to pursue the primary sources in more detail and to incorporate a 'researcher mind' and documented best practices in their work with clients. It is my further hope that readers will undertake research as individual practitioners in the field and collaboration with practitioners and scholars contributing to the field of coaching studies.

The Three Eras of Coaching Research

Looking Back (1955–2003)

On our time spectrum, this is the 'violet' period when coaching moved from invisibility as a management technique or training strategy into its own light as a specific approach to human and organizational development. In the research literature of this period, pioneering coaches staked out the territory by exploring boundaries between coaching and therapy, discussing the purposes of coaching, and presenting strategies for coaching which are drawn from the authors' backgrounds and experiences. These early articles investigate what coaches do and with whom they work. Many offer 'how-to' guides outlining the early coaching methods and techniques that have now become an integral part of coach training curricula and practice. Toward the end of this period, the next wave of articles appeared with definitions of coaching that are still in use today. They investigated the application of borrowed models and theories such as the human change process in specific coaching contexts.

For practitioners, insight into the literature of this era offers glimpses of coaching's roots in a corporate context. The beginnings of what Drake (2008) refers to as professional knowledge and foundational knowledge are hinted at here. Most of the studies are drawn from the authors' own experiences and most – especially prior to the 1990s – are case studies or descriptive articles with little empirical evidence. In considering the research and writing of this period, we are reminded of the somewhat thin ground on which coaching stood in its early days and the great knowledge void which is typical of a very young field.

For my review of this era, I relied on two key sources: an article by Kampa-Kokesch and Anderson (2001) and an excellent annotated bibliography provided by Dr Anthony Grant.[1] In reviewing the mostly practice-based articles in a special issue of *Consulting Psychology: Research and Practice*[2] and coaching-related articles in journals from the fields of psychology, training and development, and management, Kampa-Kokesch and Anderson found six themes: (1) definitions and standards; (2) purpose; (3) techniques and methodologies; (4) comparisons with counselling and therapy; (5) credentials; (6) recipients (p. 208). The authors note that 'the psychological literature makes a unique contribution to the technologies and methodologies theme' (p. 209), calling attention to a phenomenon which continues to this day. They also note that psychology's early contributions drew on case studies to illustrate key points and they cite several examples of theory-based models, noting especially Laske's interdevelopmental model.[3]

---

1 The full bibliography which resulted from Dr Grant's search is included as an appendix to his article in the Proceedings of the First ICF Research Symposium. Copies of the updated bibliography may be obtained by contacting Dr Grant directly at anthonyg@psych. usyd.edu.au

2 *Consulting Psychology: Research and Practice*, (1996), 48 (2). See original article for Kampa-Kokesch's full citations.

3 Laske's most recent and comprehensive publication on the model is *Measuring Hidden Dimensions: The Art and Science of Fully Engaging Adults* (2006), Interdevelopmental Institute Press.

Some books in this era were early efforts to overlay a coaching language and framework on models borrowed from other fields: Robert Hargrove's (1995) text on transformative learning principles in an executive coaching context; O'Neill's (2000) book on using a systems approach to coaching executives; and Kilburg's (1996, 1997, 2000) texts on coaching from a psychodynamic perspective. In addition to the process-oriented literature, Kampa-Kokesch and Anderson found seven existing empirical studies of executive coaching in this period.

Six of the seven identified empirical studies were scattered throughout journals in business, management literature and psychology literature, and the seventh was a doctoral dissertation listed only in *Dissertation Abstracts*. This paucity reflects the absence of a cross-disciplinary venue for coaching research and a field-specific orientation to the practice during this early period of coaching. It also points to the challenges facing early coaches seeking coaching research articles.

Dr Anthony Grant (2004) was among the first to bridge research in the established disciplines of psychology and organizational development and the nascent field of coaching. As keynoter to the First Annual International Coach Federation Research Symposium, Grant (2004) presented the results of a study in which he examined articles about coaching that appeared in academic peer-reviewed journals in the behavioural sciences. An updated version (Grant, 2005) was used as a source for this chapter. By conducting a search on the term 'coaching', Grant identified 417 published papers appearing in the business literature between 1955 and 2005. Papers on mental health issues, education/peer tutoring or athletic coaching were excluded. Grant identified 105 (25%) of the papers as empirical studies, mostly 'uncontrolled or group case studies' (p. 1).

In a nutshell, Grant (2004) found three themes in these studies: '(a) reports on internal coaching conducted by managers; (b) the beginnings of more rigorous academic research on internal coaching and its impact on work performance; and (c) research which reflects on and examines external coaching by a professional coach' (p. 6). He characterized the prevalent methods of data gathering and reporting as 'descriptive articles; empirical evaluations based on case studies; and empirical evaluations based on group studies' (Grant, 2004, p. 6).

The first published peer-reviewed article on coaching appeared in 1955 in *The Harvard Business Review*, suggesting coaching as a development intervention with engineers moving into management positions. Early studies addressed coaching by managers or senior employees for specific improvements such as work safety, sales productivity, or interpersonal communication skills. The first doctoral research on coaching appeared in 1967 and marked the beginning of academic study of coaching-specific topics. As levels of coaching-related doctoral research increased in the 1990s, coaching research, especially empirical research, gained momentum. As coaching became a means of exploring and supporting the mechanisms and processes of human change, more studies focused on examining coach–client relationships. The first peer-reviewed empirical study of the impact of life coaching appeared in 2003.[4]

The coaching-related research of the 1990s also turned toward a new audience – professional coaches with an interest in theoretical issues. Discussion articles about the nature, practice and evaluation of coaching continued to appear and soon became the majority of published literature in the field. The first comprehensive literature review of executive coaching was published (Grant, 2004) and the distinctions between coaching and therapy and definitions of coaching were further explored. The scope of the sources in Grant's bibliography reflects the changing and increasingly global nature of coaching research. From 1955 until 1969, articles on coaching appeared primarily in *The Harvard Business Review*, *Training and Development Journal* and *California Management Review*. Studies published in the last decade (1996–2006) have been conducted or published in the United Kingdom, Australia, Canada, New Zealand, Holland, Japan, China, South Africa, Belgium, El Salvador, Czechoslovakia, Russia and the United States.

Present (2003–2007)

In the present era, coaching research starts to show up as 'blue'. Corporate coaching is no longer linked with athletic coaching and articles on leadership coaching start to edge out those on remedial coaching. Research shows a stronger infusion of theories and models from the fields of psychology (e.g., emotional intelligence, positive psychology and adult development) and from organizational development (e.g., Appreciative Inquiry). There is evidence of other influences on coaching as well (e.g., meditation and mindfulness, quantum physics, neuroscience, communications theory, Jungian and narrative psychologies, and systems theory. The literature began to include references to coaching beyond the corporate context, including explorations of wellness coaching, life coaching and pastoral coaching, for example. A new dialogue appeared on how, why or whether to measure return on investment (ROI) from coaching.

---

4 A. M. Grant. The impact of life coaching on goal attainment, metacognition and mental health. *Social Behavior and Personality*, 31(3), 253–264.

For practitioners, the literature of this period offered a larger and more complex vision of coaching purposes and principles, transcending the business development framework of the earlier period. The venues for creation and dissemination of coaching research expanded during this era as well, offering coaches greater access and the opportunity to become more informed practitioners. The pace of coaching research accelerated, meaning that practitioners who wish to stay on the cutting edge must include ongoing expansion of their knowledge base to stay current. Of the 417 papers cited in Grant's bibliography, 82% were published after 1996; 76% of the empirical studies have been published since 2001.

Grant's database was limited to print journals in business and psychology, the predominant sources for articles on coaching until 2003. That year, the first International Coach Federation (ICF) Research Symposium was held in Denver, Colorado, as a one-day pre-conference workshop and it offered a new venue for sharing coaching research. Papers recommended for presentation through a peer-review process were published in *The Proceedings of the First ICF Research Symposium* (2004), offering the first cross-disciplinary literature on the theory and practice of coaching. Proceedings co-editor Irene Stein (2004) introduced the first volume as 'Beginning a Promising Conversation' (p. viii), noting that the process of planning for the symposium brought together a community of coaching researchers and scholar practitioners that had not previously existed.

The presentations and papers at that and subsequent ICF Research Symposia demonstrate the growing diversity within the field of coaching and coaching research. Papers examined coaching models from psychology (a cognitive approach in 2003, adult development in 2003 and 2004, and the use of narrative liminality and behavioural psychology in 2004) and organizational development (Appreciative Inquiry and adaptive coaching in 2005). Theoretical models are also represented: archetypes of the coach role, coaching as dialogue and the use of metaphor in 2003, and evidence-based coaching and relational flow in 2005. The growing global dimensions of coaching showed up in studies of coaching in South America and the Philippines (2004), South Africa (2005) and China (2006) and with indigenous college students in Canada (2004).

The International Journal of Coaching in Organizations (IJCO) first appeared in 2003, offering a mix of articles and empirical studies in each themed issue. A special issue with a focus on coaching research was published in 2005 (vol. 3, no. 1). That issue offered a review of recent studies with a focus on methodologies, case studies of specific interventions, two articles on coaching particular populations, and two articles on ROI methods. The IJCO has devoted issues to other issues, for example, organizational coaching around the world (2003); coaching in closely held enterprises (2005); coaching and neuroscience (2006); and coaching collaborative ventures (2006).

A growing interest in measures of coaching outcomes and in the application of specific models in coaching is seen in the articles appearing in *Consulting Psychology Journal: Research and Practice* during this period. The fall 2004 (issue 56, no. 4) edition included studies of several conceptual approaches in executive coaching: cognitive-behavioural, rational-emotive, action frame theory and psychodynamic approaches. Subsequent issues have included one or more articles on coaching-specific research.

The voice of psychology in the field of coaching has taken on new energy in two accessible locations on the World Wide Web: *The International Journal of Evidence-Based Coaching and Mentoring* (IJEBCM) and *The International Coaching Psychology Review*. *The International Coaching Psychology Review* is also published in hard copy, available to members of the British Psychological Society. In August 2003, the IJEBCM (http://www.brookes.ac.uk/schools/education/ijebcm/vol1-no1. htm) published its first issue. Based at Oxford Brookes University in the United Kingdom, the publication maintains a consistent editorial position that emphasizes the importance of research and theory to the development of coaching as a profession. The studies published in the journal investigate coaching outcomes, the application of specific coaching models and coaching competencies and behaviours in organizational and other contexts. *The Coaching Psychologist* is published three times each year by the British Psychological Society Coaching Psychology Special Interest Group in print and is accessible online (http://www. bps.org.uk/coachingpsy/publications/thecoachingpsychologist.cfm). *The International Coaching Psychology Review* appeared in April 2006 with print and online-accessible versions (http://www.bps.org.uk/ coachingpsy/publication). The editorial in that first publication held that 'it is a matter of urgency to promote the development of coaching psychology at an academic and practitioner level' (p. 10). Thus, the material is scholarly and presumes a fairly high level of familiarity with core theories and models in the field of psychology. *The International Coaching Psychology Review* is published under the joint auspices of the British and Australian Psychological Societies. Those organizations, in collaboration with universities in Australia and the United Kingdom, have hosted several research forums in conjunction with coaching conferences.

Perhaps the richest source of coaching research in the present is found in doctoral dissertations. A search of *Dissertation Abstracts* using the keyword 'coaching', excluding 'athletics' and 'schools', and published in English in the past five years yielded 166 results. Eliminating those that were not coaching-specific still left 134 approved dissertations. As might be expected, a significant number of these examined some aspect of organizational, leadership or executive coaching. An equal number explored coaching in other sectors, including educational settings (schools and universities) and church leadership development. Six dissertations explored physical or mental health-related coaching. Dissertations on life and personal coaching examined the construct of happiness, skills and strategies used in coaching for creativity and problem solving, and coaching for motivation. Special populations studied included men at mid-life, abrasive executives, and African-American women. Dissertation studies linked coaching with adult development theory, cognitive development and models of transformational change.

Future: Trends, Opportunities, Possibilities (2007 forward)

In the absence of a crystal ball, I can only speculate about the future of coaching research. However, I propose four trends I believe warrant further discussion and consideration within the coaching community. These echo, in part, recommendations made in by Grant (2004) and Kampa-Kokesch and Anderson (2001) as well as current authors. They also reflect my own biases and beliefs about the best directions for engaging research as an engine in moving coaching from a practice to a profession.

First, I propose that research on empirically documented coaching models and theories will gain strength and broader acceptance within the field of coaching. The models put forward in the web-based journals are persuasive and link theory with practice, offering practitioners a sound basis for choice in action. Fillery-Travis and Lane's (2006) provocative question, 'Does coaching work or are we asking the wrong question?', opens new directions for a more nuanced investigation of what it is we are doing as coaches and what, exactly, we are seeking to measure. The development of valid models offers a sound basis from which such investigations can be launched. Such literature can inform the development of coaching preparation and education and provide purchasers of coaching services with a basis for informed selection and consumption. Research in this arena need not be limited, however, to the models and theories from the field of psychology. As the diversity of coaching-related dissertation topics suggest, empirically grounded models of coaching may arise in the fields of medicine and health, education, pastoral preparation and community development. Such models may also arise as the result of interdisciplinary and cross-disciplinary research collaborations.

Second, I foresee a larger and deeper pool of questions that can be investigated by coaching researchers and practitioners. Linley (2006) notes, 'the nature of the research question that we choose to ask is possibly the most important decision we will ever make' (p. 3). He suggests that to bridge the academic–practitioner divide, researchers would do well to consider: who the research is for and with; what is most critical to investigate; where the study is taking place (context); when – the time frame of the investigation; why or to what end we would undertake the investigation. In proposing coaching as a *postprofessional* practice, Drake and Stober (2005) conclude that 'coaches must regularly engage in reflective practice and systematic inquiry to gather and integrate both experience and research-based evidence in their work'. They further propose 'a hybrid approach that integrates rigorous analytical research and vigorous reflective practice' (p. 21).

Third, in my ideal future research world we collectively build a more complex, interdisciplinary research agenda. While Linley encourages readers to look to the field of psychology for models, other disciplines may offer equally useful models and perspectives. For example, education researchers apply models for programme needs and outcomes assessments and may employ collaborative action research methods among others. They are aware of the challenges of demonstrating causality in the classroom, lessons which may be useful in the study of coaching impacts and outcomes. Measures of ROI may combine methods from the fields of psychotherapy and business.

An interdisciplinary research agenda requires that we have a means of sharing information, skills and findings globally and across disciplines. One challenge inherent in this cross-disciplinary approach to coaching research lies in creating consensus in the coaching community about valid and appropriate methodologies. In virtually every review and commentary cited in this chapter, the authors have concluded with strong recommendations for research which is more rigorous, scientific, theoretically grounded and beyond case studies and anecdotes. It does not yet appear to me that the coaching community has a shared understanding of those research paradigms or that there is general agreement on the value of such studies. An additional challenge is that, at present, we lack an interdisciplinary venue for peer review and publication of such studies.

The International Coach Federation has reformulated the formerly preconference Research Symposium into a research track within the general conference. While this represents a possible gain in greater interaction between coaching researchers and practitioners, the interdisciplinary forum provided by the Research Symposium Proceedings has been lost. However, a new journal, *Coaching: An International Journal of Theory, Research and*

Practice, is slated to appear in spring 2008 (Routledge). The promotional website advises that the journal 'aims to develop novel insights and approaches for future research. Broad and interdisciplinary in focus, articles published will include original research articles, review articles, "interviews", technique reports and case reports. It offers an international forum for debates on policy and practice' (http://www.informaworld.com/smpp/title~db=all~content=t762290973~tab=summary). The journal is being produced in collaboration with The Association for Coaching and the editor-in-chief is Dr Carol Kauffman, a distinguished researcher and member of the Harvard University faculty.

This leads to my fourth projection: an increasing use of the Internet as a venue for developing, implementing and disseminating coaching research. For this research agenda to be useful, coach practitioners must have the ability to locate and evaluate coaching research, and to skilfully and appropriately apply the insights and information to their own coaching practices. Drake and Stober (2005) suggest that, 'The evolution of the open-source movement in software development may provide useful clues in shaping alternative approaches to professional consensus and development' (p. 13). Free-access resources such as The Foundation of Coaching Research Repository (http://www.thefoundationofcoaching.org) provide scholars with a venue for sharing papers and ideas, and practitioners and scholars with an easily accessible way of searching for and accessing coaching research papers. As more and more university-affiliated coaching preparation programmes come online, I would anticipate greater familiarity with and use of these resources to collect and share data and to engage in open-ended discussions using blogs and other forums. The final element in this picture of the future is the incremental inclusion of research literacy in all recognized coach preparation and education programmes.

Connecting the Dots

The past eras of coaching research staked out new territory for coaching, making visible what had previously been invisible. Early authors created practices, models and theories for coaching that drew heavily on their own individual training and experiences. The present era is characterized by the emergence of new voices and the enlargement of the territory beyond corporate coaching. A group of research-oriented coaches have initiated conversation about coaching research and created a coaching research community. The future involves building bridges between coaching researchers and practitioners and further diversifying the fields and contexts in which coaching is practised and studied. When we connect the dots of coaching research past, present and future, what is the picture that emerges?

I see three areas where these connections can move coaching, individually and collectively, from derivative practice to an integrated, full-fledged profession. The first area involves revisiting and critically examining the coaching theories, strategies and models put forth in the earliest period of coaching research. Such examination and reassessment can be done by practitioners in their own coaching interactions as well as by coaching researchers. For practitioners, I put forward a simple tool I use in some of the evidence-based coaching classes I teach. In those classes, I encourage the learners to conduct their own informal field research using a reflective journal. The *events* section of the reflective journal requires coaches to note and document critical incidents in the course of a coaching interaction: the client's verbal and body language, the content of the exchange, the 'cues' that the coach picked up suggesting that the brief moment is important. The coaches are also asked to document their own thinking, their 'left-hand column': the unarticulated assumptions, expectations, interpretations and theories they are holding as the exchange takes place. In the *actions* section, the coach notes what she actually said or did with the client. The outcomes section invites the coach to reflect on the exchange and to formulate some learning which will help the coach to be equally or more effective in a similar situation. In their reflections, the learners are invited to pay attention to the theories and models they are applying in coaching and to examine the fit between their mental models of coaching and actual experience. Because many coaches have been trained in models and techniques that originated in the early years of coaching research, the use of such reflective journals adds empirical evidence to the efficacy and impact of applying those models in practice.

The use of such a reflective journal brings together the four knowledge types as outlined by Drake (2008): professional and foundational knowledge with personal and contextual knowledge. This is just one small way to practise reflectively while continuing to grow our coaching repertoire and give it depth. Coaching mastery entails not only repetitive application of existing coaching skills but thoughtful self-observation, self-correction and extension of our knowledge. In my classes, learners share their journal observations and reflections and we collectively consider what the data suggest about elements of the specific coaching model we are studying. Engaged practitioners could form similar action-learning groups to contribute to the refinement and evolution of early coaching models and materials.

There is a second opportunity to link past and future by building cross-niche relationships using interactive resources for shared learning.

At the beginning, coaching was rooted firmly in a corporate context. As the diversity of research topics and sources in the present shows, coaching now takes place across a broad spectrum of contexts and venues. These niches have emerged in part to meet client need and marketing considerations. Nonetheless, I believe that cross-fertilization of theories, methods and ideas can only serve to enhance the coaching provided in each arena. For example, what might corporate coaches learn from pastoral coaches? How can a working knowledge of ROI concepts in the business coaching sector help wellness coaches demonstrate value?

The third opportunity is a function of the fact that more and more coaching research is available on the Web. As such, it is easier for practitioners to access research articles which offer alternative points of view about the coaching process in which an individual was trained. Articles may offer evidence for why one approach may be more effective than another with a particular client, enabling a more informed choice in working with the unique nature of each individual. Reading the literature of coaching research also offers practitioners different models for systematic and rigorous investigation of their own practice-related questions. Take, for example, the question of demonstrating return on investment. By reading a variety of research articles on this particular issue in the literature of business coaching, an educator coach can formulate a more clear idea about initial agreements and coaching goals, what constitutes measures of success, and valid means of gathering data to document both the process and the outcomes.

I am by no means the first, nor is it likely I will be the last, to trumpet the need for a body of research if coaching is to become a profession. I believe we can move this agenda forward individually and collectively. The concept of *collective intelligence*[5] offers a useful touchstone for how we can accomplish this. Engaging in and sharing coaching research provides material for critical analysis, discussion, debate and dialogue within the coaching community. This, in turn, helps us all distinguish what is sound and what is unsound in the field. Reflectively and thoughtfully integrating the knowledge generated by research into individual practice moves coaching practice toward a higher order of complexity. By including research as a foundation of coaching practice, we can extend the knowledge from the past and present and move coaching beyond the colour blue to a full spectrum of professional practice.

---

5 Which may be defined as 'the capacity of human communities to evolve towards higher order complexity and harmony through such innovation mechanisms as differentiation and integration, competition and collaboration'. (http://www.community-intelligence.com/blogs/public).

References

Bennett, J. L., and Campone, F. (Eds.). (2006). *Proceedings of the Fourth International Coach Federation Coaching Research Symposium.* Lexington, KY: International Coach Federation.

Blog of Collective Intelligence. http://www.community-intelligence.com/blogs/public.

Campone, F., and Bennett, J. (Eds.). (2005). *Proceedings of the Third International Coach Federation Coaching Research Symposium.* Lexington, KY; International Coach Federation.

Campone, F. (2006). Riding the waves: A quantum framework for coaching research. In F. Campone and J. L. Bennett (Eds.), *Proceedings of the Third International Coach Federation* (pp. 152–160). Washington, DC: International Coach Federation.

Drake, D. B. (2008). Evidence in action: A relational view of knowledge and mastery in coaching. In K. Gørtz and A. Prehn (Eds.), *Coaching in perspective.* Copenhagen: Hans Reitzel Publishers.

Drake, D. B., and Stober, D. R. (2005). *The rise of the postprofessional: Lessons learned in thinking about coaching as an evidence-based practice.* Paper presented at the Australia Conference on Evidence-Based Coaching.

Fillery-Travis, A., and Lane, D. (2006). Does coaching work or are we asking the wrong question? *International Coaching Psychology Review,* 1(1). Retrieved http://www.bps.org.uk/document-download-area/document-download$.cfm?file_uuid=FA4844B9-1143-DFD0-7EFD-9CAF8FFC87C2&ext=pdf on June 16, 2007.

Grant, A. M. (2004). Keeping up with the cheese! Research as a foundation for professional coaching of the future. In I. F. Stein and L. A. Belsten (Eds.), *Proceedings of the First ICF Coaching Research Symposium* (pp. 1–19). Washington: International Coach Federation.

Grant, A. M. (2005). *Workplace and executive coaching: An annotated bibliography from the peer-reviewed business literature* (September 2005). Unpublished paper. Coaching Psychology Unit, University of Sydney, Australia.

Hargrove, R. (1995). *Masterful coaching: Extraordinary results by impacting people and they way they think and work together.* San Francisco: Pfeiffer/Jossey-Bass.

Kampa-Kokesch, S., and Anderson, M. Z. (2001). Executive coaching: A comprehensive review of the literature. *Consulting Psychology Journal: Practice and Research,* 53(4), 205–228.

Kilburg, R. R. (1996). Toward a conceptual understanding and definition of executive coaching. *Consulting Psychology Journal: Practice and Research,* 48, 134–144.

Kilburg, R. R. (1997). Coaching and executive character: Core problems and basic approaches. *Consulting Psychology Journal: Practice and Research,* 49, 281–299.

Kilburg, R. R. (2000). *Executive coaching: Developing managerial wisdom in a world of chaos.* Washington, DC: American Psychological Association.

Linley, A. (2006). Coaching research: Who? What? Where? When? Why? *International Journal of Evidence-Based Coaching and Mentoring,* 4(2). Retrieved from http://www.brookes.ac.uk/schools/education/ijebcm/vol4-no2-reflections.html.

O'Neill, M. B. (2000). *Executive coaching with backbone and heart: A systems approach to engaging leaders with their challenges.* San Francisco: Jossey-Bass.

Page, L. J., and Stein, I. F. (2006). Framing the dialogue: Unlocking issues surrounding coaching research. In F. Campone and J. L. Bennett (Eds.), *Proceedings of the Third International Coach Federation* (pp. 141–150). Washington, DC: International Coach Federation.

Stein, I. F. (2004). Introduction: Beginning a promising conversation. In I. F. Stein and L. A. Belsten (Eds.), *Proceedings of the First ICF Coaching Research Symposium* (pp. 1–19). Mooresville, NC: Paw Print Press.

Stein, I. F., and Belsten, L. A. (Eds.). (2004). Proceedings of the First ICF Coaching Research Symposium. Mooresville, NC: Paw Print Press.

Stein, I. F., Campone, F., and Page, L. J. (Eds.). 2005. *Proceedings of the Second ICF Coaching Research Symposium.* Washington, DC: International Coach Federation.

Stober, D. (2005). Coaching eye for the research guy and research eye for the coaching guy: 20/20 vision for coaching through the scientist-practitioner model. In I. F. Stein, F. Campone, and L. J. Page (Eds.), *Proceedings of the Second ICF Coaching Research Symposium* (pp. 13–21). Washington, DC: International Coach Federation.

The International Coaching Psychology Review. S. Palmer and M. Cavanaugh (Eds.). http://www.bps.org.uk/coachingpsy/publication.

The International Journal of Coaching in Organizations. Forest Park, IL: Professional Coaching Publications.

The International Journal of Evidence-Based Coaching and Mentoring. E. Cox (Ed.). http://www.brookes.ac.uk/schools/education/ijebcm.

Reflections on Foundations for Coaching

David B. Drake

This section provided a solid introduction to three key issues facing coaching: (1) Where do we come from as a professional practice? (2) What are our obligations for self-development as coaching professionals? (3) How do we engage with coaching-related research to support our decisions and practice? These chapters addressed the need to link coaching to a past, present and future in ways that deepen our accountabilities, capabilities and possibilities. Whether you are new to coaching or consider yourself a seasoned professional, we invite you to reflect on the following questions as a catalyst for new ways of seeing yourself, your clients and your practice.

1. Patrick Williams – The Life Coach Operating System: Its Foundations in Psychology

(1)   What sources from within psychology do you draw on most significantly in your thinking about and doing coaching? Consider creating a mind map and/or a timeline of your major influences in terms of your development as a coach.

(2)   How has your developmental path shaped your practice (e.g., what you look for, what you may miss)? At this stage in your career, where do you want to deepen your knowledge and where do you need to stretch your knowledge?

(3)   What is the key insight/inspiration you are taking from this chapter in terms of your development as a coach?

The Philosophy and Practice of Coaching: Insights and Issues for a New Era.
Edited by David B. Drake, Diane Brennan and Kim Gørtz.
© 2008 John Wiley & Sons, Ltd.

2. Travis Kemp – Coach Self-Management: The Foundation of Coaching Effectiveness

(1) What insights did you gain about your 'Achilles heel' in coaching relationships through reading about the social psychology principles? If we think about ourselves as *wounded healers*, how can you use this developmental edge to spark your growth?

(2) Which of the four human factors do you find it easiest to access and remain aware of when you are coaching? Which lens would you like to improve on in your practice and what is one step you can take in this direction?

(3) What is the key insight/inspiration you are taking from this chapter in terms of your self-management as a coach?

3. David B. Drake – Thrice Upon a Time: Narrative Structure and Psychology as a Platform for Coaching

(1) What is your 'story' about what it means to be a coach and how do you, therefore, tend to participate in the storytelling process with your clients? What client stories do you attract and engage in versus those you avoid and disengage from? What is that about?

(2) How comfortable are you with working within *storytime*, the domain of 'thrice upon a time', and with the elements of the field?

(3) What is the key insight/inspiration you are taking from this chapter in terms of your role as a coach relative to your clients' stories?

4. Peter Jackson – Does it Matter What the Coach Thinks? – A New Foundation for Professional Development

(1) To what degree is coaching caught in a 'culture of pragmatism' and what does that mean to you? Which of the four types of evidence do you tend to favour in making choices and communicating about your work? What is the next step for coaching and for you?

(2) If theory is neither synonymous with 'what works' nor oppositional to practice, what needs to shift in terms of your practice and its promotion (e.g., examining your assumptions, questioning what you hold to be true, and engaging with the uncertainties of how you really know what you think you know)?

(3)   What is the key insight/inspiration you are taking from this chapter in terms of your epistemology as a coach?

5. Francine Campone – Connecting the Dots: Coaching Research – Past, Present and Future

(1)   How has your view of and relationship with research and evidence changed over the time you have been coaching? What do you see when you 'connect these dots' between theory, research and practice?

(2)   What do you make of the four trends Francine Campone has identified? Which one are you motivated to help advance in order to increase the collective intelligence with coaching? How will you do so?

(3)   What is the key insight/inspiration you are taking from this chapter in terms of your scholarship as a coach?

Part II

APPLICATIONS OF COACHING

An Appreciative Inquiry Coaching Approach to Developing Mental Toughness

6

Sandy Gordon

Introduction

Recent research on mental toughness in sport has increased our understanding of what is required to sustain wellbeing and high levels of performance in pressured environments. In this chapter, a brief review of the mental toughness (MT) literature is presented as well as two models of how this research in sport has been mapped onto business settings to understand how these coveted psychological attributes can be developed and supported. In addition, the principles of Appreciative Inquiry (AI) and Appreciative Inquiry Coaching (AIC) are described to illustrate the theory and vision behind a recent paradigm shift in promoting change in business settings. Finally, examples are provided of how a strengths-based coaching approach, such as AIC, can facilitate the development of MT.

What is Mental Toughness?

Within scientific and coaching communities in sport, mental toughness is acknowledged as being one of the most important attributes in achieving performance excellence (Bull, Shambrook, James, and Brooks,

The Philosophy and Practice of Coaching: Insights and Issues for a New Era.
Edited by David B. Drake, Diane Brennan and Kim Gørtz.
© 2008 John Wiley & Sons, Ltd.

2005; Jones, Hanton, and Connaughton, 2002; Orlick, 1998). Since Fourie and Potgieter's (2001) pioneering qualitative study of mental toughness in South Africa, a burgeoning line of inquiry has emerged from various parts of the world that include the USA (see Gould, Dieffenbach, and Moffett, 2002), the UK (see Bull *et al.*, 2005; Fawcett, 2005; Jones *et al.*, 2002; Thelwell, Weston, and Greenlees, 2005), India (see Gordon and Sridhar, 2005), and Australia (see Gucciardi, Gordon, and Dimmock, in press; Middleton, Marsh, Martin, Richards, and Perry, 2004). This research has focused on understanding the phenomenon of mental toughness from the perspective of athletes and coaches and has identified a myriad of characteristics ascribed to mental toughness.

As is illustrated in Table 6.1, numerous common characteristics have been identified across these studies such as self-belief, concentration, motivation, thriving on competition, resilience, handling pressure, positive attitude, quality preparation, goal setting, determination, perseverance, and commitment. In addition, some unique characteristics have also been identified, e.g., team unity, religious convictions, ethics, sport intelligence, safety and survival, coping with success and failure, risk taking and exploiting learning opportunities. Gordon and his colleagues (Gordon, Gucciardi, and Chambers, 2007; Gucciardi, Gordon, and Dimmock, in press), utilizing a Personal Construct Theory (PCP) framework (Kelly, 1955/1991) in their research in Australian football, also identified specific situations in which mental toughness is required as well as the behaviours/actions and characteristics ascribed to mentally tough performers. Coaches can draw on these findings to encourage their clients to identify specific situations that are particularly problematic so they can focus on solutions to those circumstances. As a result, mental toughness goals for behaviour change are subsequently more aligned to actual demands as perceived by the client.

Despite the parallel demands in and significant links between sport and business that have been identified recently (Gordon, 2007; Jones, 2002), no research on mental toughness in business settings has been undertaken. However, targeting executives and teams in the business world, Bull (2006) developed a mental toughness model (see Figure 6.1), derived from research in elite cricket (Bull *et al.*, 2005), in which he identifies four components of mental toughness that can be developed through coaching: (1) *turnaround toughness*, the ability to bounce back from adversity and setbacks; (2) *critical moment toughness*, the ability to execute a performance at a specific time under pressure; (3) *endurance toughness*, the ability to stay physically strong and mentally focused during times of relentless workload commitments; and (4) *risk management toughness*, the ability to make tough decisions and take the risky option to maximize performance. According to Bull, each of

Table 6.1 Overview of the identified characteristics of mental toughness.

Loehr (1986)	Fourie and Potgieter (2001)	Jones et al. (2002)	Middleton et al. (2004)	Gordon and Sridhar (2005)[a]	Bull et al. (2005)[a]	Fawcett (2005)[a]	Thelwell et al. (2005)[a]
Self-confidence	Confidence maintenance	Unshakeable self-belief to achieve competition goals	Self-efficacy	Motivation and commitment	'Never-say-die' and 'go-the-extra-mile' attitude	Commitment and determination	Total self-belief in achieving
Negative energy	Coping skills	Unshakeable self-belief that you possess unique qualities and abilities that make you better than the rest	Mental self-concept	Resilience	Thrives on competition	Effective mental application	Wanting to be involved at all times
Attention control	Cognitive skill	Insatiable desire and internalized motives to succeed	Potential	Self-belief and optimism	Willing to take risks	Handing pressure	Positive reactions
Visual and imagery control	Discipline and goal-directedness	Ability to bounce back from setbacks as a result of increased determination to succeed	Personal best (motivation)	Positive perfectionism	Belief in quality preparation	Self-control and discipline	Handling pressure
Motivation level	Motivation level	Thriving on the pressure of competition	Value (or importance)	Handling pressure	Determination to make the most of ability	Self-confidence and self-belief	Know what it takes to get out of trouble
Positive energy	Competitiveness	Accepting that competitive anxiety is inevitable and knowing that you can cope with it	Task familiarity	Focus	Self-setting challenging goals	Physical coping ability[b]	Ignore distractions and remain focused
Attitude control	Physical and mental requirements (prerequisite)	Not being adversely affected by others' good/bad performances	Goal commitment	Sport intelligence	Resilient confidence and belief in making the difference	Training and situation toughness	Emotion management

Table 6.1 *Continued*

Loehr (1986)	Fourie and Potgieter (2001)	Jones et al. (2002)	Middleton et al. (2004)	Gordon and Sridhar (2005)[a]	Bull et al. (2005)[a]	Fawcett (2005)[a]	Thelwell et al. (2005)[a]
	Team unity	Remaining fully focused in the face of personal life distractions	Perseverance		Independent and self-reflective	Coping with success and failure[b]	Having a presence that affects opponents
	Preparation skills	Switching sport focus on/off as required	Task-specific attention		Clear thinker (decisive, honest self-appraisal)	Safety and survival[b]	Control of outside issues
	Psychological hardiness	Remaining fully focused on the task at hand in the face of competition-specific distractions	Stress minimization		Robust self-confidence (overcome self-doubts, self-focus)	Coping with stress and anxiety[b]	Enjoy the pressure associated with performance
	Religious convictions	Pushing back the boundaries of physical and emotional pain, while still maintaining technique and effort under distress in training and competition	Positivity		Competitiveness with self and others	Knowing oneself[b]	
	Ethics	Regaining psychological control following unexpected, uncontrollable events (competition-specific)	Positive comparisons		Exploiting learning opportunities	Undivided attention[b]	

[a] Sport-specific research.
[b] Adventurer/explorer sample.

Figure 6.1 Bull (2006) model of mental toughness.

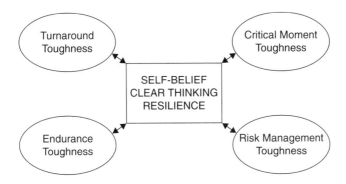

these components contributes to the enhancement of three factors that are directly related to peak performance in business: self-belief, clear thinking and resilience. Mentally tough performers in business settings deliver optimal performances under pressure by maintaining unshakeable confidence in their ability to perform tasks and stay focused, persevere through adversity when circumstances get tough, and bounce back quickly from setbacks and failure.

Similarly, Jones and Moorhouse (2007) drew on research among high achievers in both business and sport settings (Jones and Spooner, 2006) and among world champion athletes, professional coaches and sport psychologists (Jones *et al.*, 2002, 2007), in proposing that mental toughness can be developed in business settings. As illustrated in Figure 6.2, Jones and Moorhouse believe that mental toughness is comprised of four 'pillars' that form the foundation of sustained high performance: (1) keeping your head under stress; (2) making your motivation work for you; (3) staying strong in your self-belief; and (4) keeping focused on the things that matter. Both of these approaches (Figures 6.1 and 6.2) are important resources in addressing situations in the workplace that many business leaders find challenging and in engaging them in mental skills exercises designed to enhance reactions to these circumstances. Informed by their respective research, the authors provide valuable insights on the nature and development of mental toughness. Both of these models on mental toughness in business settings can be used to enhance high-performance leadership and professional development programmes in the workplace (Gordon, 2007). However, rather than relying on mental skills training, I believe we need to develop a richer understanding of how best to facilitate the acquisition of mental toughness.

Few studies of mental toughness thus far have examined psychological factors using a developmental framework. Research with gifted and

Figure 6.2   Jones and Moorhouse (2007) model of mental toughness. (Jones, G. and Moorhause, A. (2007) Developing mental Toughness: *Gold Medal Strategies For Transforming Your Business Performance.* Reproduced by permission of Spring Hill publishers.)

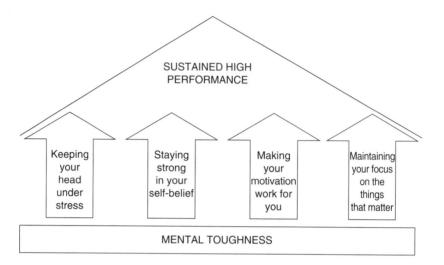

talented schoolchildren (Csikszentmihalyi, Rathunde, and Whalen, 1993; Gagne, 1996, 2003) and athletes (Bloom, 1985; Côté, 1999; Côté, Baker, and Abernethy, 2003) has highlighted the important role that both coaches and parents play in facilitating desirable psychological attributes associated with mental toughness. Gould, Dieffenbach, and Moffett (2002) investigated both the psychological characteristics and development of Olympic champions. Both questionnaire and interview data from 10 Olympic champions (winners of 32 Olympic medals), their coaches (*n* = 10), parents, guardians and/or significant others revealed that these athletes could be characterized by: the ability to cope with and control anxiety; confidence; sport intelligence; the ability to focus and block out distractions; competitiveness; a hard-work ethic; the ability to set and achieve goals; coach-ability; high levels of dispositional hope; optimism; adaptive perfectionism; and mental toughness/resilience. The results also revealed that a number of individuals and institutions influenced the athletes' psychological development, specifically their community and immediate family, nonsport as well as sport environment personnel, and the sport process itself. Coach and family influences were particularly important and ways in which these sources influenced the athletes were both direct, such as teaching or emphasizing certain psychological lessons, and indirect, such as involving modelling or unintentionally creating certain psychological environments.

More recently, Connaughton, Wadey, Hanton, and Jones (2007) re-interviewed participants from a previous study on identifying mental toughness (Jones *et al.*, 2002) and focused their examination specifically on the development of mental toughness. Findings from their semi-structured interviews with seven international level athletes indicated that:

> the development of mental toughness is a long-term process that encompasses a multitude of underlying mechanisms that operate in a combined, rather than independent, fashion. In general, these perceived underlying mechanisms related to many features associated with a motivational climate (e.g. enjoyment, mastery), various individuals (i.e. coaches, peers, parents, grandparents, siblings, senior athletes, sport psychologists, teammates), experiences in and outside sport, psychological skills and strategies, and an insatiable desire and internalized motives to succeed. (Connaughton *et al.*, 2007, p. 1)

Taken together, research on the development of talented children and of top athletes appears to suggest that mental toughness could be an innate disposition – something they 'just have' – and/or something they 'develop' over time. For example, the general consensus from research of both elite level cricketers (Gordon and Sridhar, 2005) and Australian footballers (Gucciardi *et al.*, in press) was that, in addition to an inherent level of mental toughness, observers (teachers, parents and coaches) agreed that mental toughness could also be *caught* (informally socialized through key networks) and *taught* (formally trained and coached). For example, the environmental effects that are influential in the acquisition of a variety of desirable psychological characteristics through socialization and the important roles both coaches and parents play in positive youth development have been identified by Bloom (1985) and Côté (1999) respectively. Similarly, the significance of formal teaching and coaching of mental skills has been highlighted in studies of elite athlete development by Gould *et al.* (2002) and Jones *et al.* (2002). Research by Bull *et al.* (2005) – arguably representing the most systematic examination of the topic – provides some important practical recommendations for coaches on how to influence the development of mental toughness.

Bull *et al.* (2005) sought to gain a better understanding of how mental toughness is conceptualized in elite cricket, and to determine how players developed the qualities of mental toughness. Twelve English cricketers, identified by 101 coaches as being among the mentally toughest during the previous 20 years, were interviewed. Four themes were identified from an analysis of their interview transcripts and the findings were subsequently disseminated among England's cricket coaching and playing population. The study points to the fact that the role of coaches in assisting players who are already highly developed technically and mentally involves collaborative discussion on choice of reaction and attitude towards tough environments and experiences rather than simply training or teaching mental skills.

The first theme, *environmental influence*, provides the foundation for the development of mental toughness. In the formative years, parental influence and childhood background were identified as the primary contributors together with secondary factors such as needing to 'earn' success, having opportunities to survive early setbacks, and being exposed to foreign cricket. Having a *tough character* was the first of three themes focusing on the individual player, and it included common personality characteristics such as resilient confidence, independence, self-reflection and competitiveness with oneself as well as others. The third theme of *tough attitudes* was considered an important component for the successful exploitation of tough character. These attitudes include a never-say-die mindset, a go-the-extra-mile mindset, thirst for competition, a belief in making a difference, exploiting learning opportunities, a willingness to take risks, a belief in quality preparation, the determination to make the most of ability, and the tendency to self-set challenging targets. The final theme of *tough thinking* relates to cognitive strengths most desirable in and around competitive events, such as clear thinking (e.g., good decision-making, keeping perspective, honest self-appraisal) and robust self-confidence (e.g., overcoming self-doubts, feeding off physical conditioning, maintaining self-focus).

The evidence on the development of mental toughness so far seems to suggest that while some mental toughness is simply inherited, an inestimable amount can undoubtedly be *caught* (socialized) and *taught* (coached). Further research in sport and other performance environments is needed to pinpoint exactly 'what' needs to be taught 'by whom' and 'how,' and also what experiences young people should be exposed to and when. In addition, do these experiences need to be activity-specific or even activity-related and/or is there a role for mentoring, storytelling and account-making in promoting mental toughness?

The next section introduces Appreciative Inquiry as a philosophy and approach well suited to developing mental toughness through coaching. Like other strengths-based strategies, it builds on the 'natural' mental toughness characteristics already present within the client. Based on my initial experiences using it in both business and sport settings, it has much to offer.

Appreciative Inquiry

Ap-pre′ci-ate, *v.*, *1. Valuing; the act of recognising the best in people or the world around us; affirming past and present strengths, successes and poten-*

tials; to perceive those things that give life (health, vitality, excellence) to living systems. 2. To increase in value – for example, the economy has appreciated in value. Synonyms: value, prize, esteem, and honor.

In-quire', *v., 1. The act of exploration and discovery. 2. To ask questions; to be open to seeing new potentials and possibilities. Synonyms: discover, search, systematically explore, and study.*

(Cooperrider and Whitney, 2005, p. 7)

As detailed by Watkins and Mohr (2001), Appreciative Inquiry (AI) was first conceptualized at the Weatherhead School of Management at Case Western Reserve University in 1980 by doctoral student David Cooperrider and his thesis supervisor Sruresh Srivastva, who had both been engaged in an organization change project. They discovered first of all that the traditional organization development (OD) approach of problem diagnosis and feedback simply sucked the energy for change right out of the system. As more problems were discovered the more discouraged people became, and the more discouraged people became the more they blamed each other for the problems. The authors also discovered that their intervention work became more powerful when they actually let go of the very idea of intervening. Instead of *intervention* they chose to frame their task as *inquiry*. They became students of organizational life – to learn, discover and appreciate everything that gave life to the organization when it was most vibrant and successful. Cooperrider and Srivastva's subsequent data analysis was effectively a radical reversal of the traditional problem-solving approach. Instead of detailing root causes of failure they focused instead on the root causes of success. They called their approach 'appreciative inquiry'; their classic article, 'Appreciative inquiry in organizational life', appeared a few years later (Cooperrider and Srivastva, 1987) and articulated the theory and vision behind an exciting paradigm shift for the field of OD and change.

While AI began as a theory-building process, it has also been called a philosophy, a revolutionary force, a transformational change process, a life-giving theory and practice, and even a new world-view. For the purposes of this chapter, AI is regarded as a positive, strengths-based operational approach to change, learning and development that seems most suitable to coaching mental toughness.

According to Watkins and Mohr (2001), the two essential components of AI are its five core principles and five core processes. As illustrated in Figure 6.3, these principles and processes are understood to have emerged from theoretical and research foundations grounded in social constructionism, the 'new' sciences (positive psychology, strengths-based coaching, chaos theory, self-organizing systems, biology, quantum mechanics), and research on the power of imagery. The five core principles and five emergent principles that serve as the basis for AI are

Figure 6.3   Structure of Appreciative Inquiry (adapted from Watkins and Mohr, 2001).

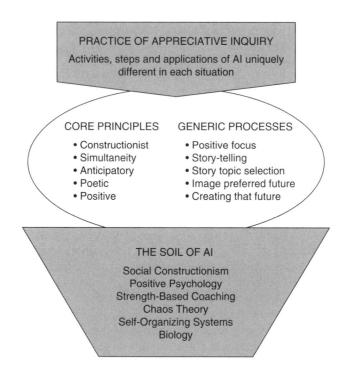

summarized in Table 6.2; for application purposes, I see the overall guiding principles as follows:

● *Appreciate* – yourself and other people in the change process
● *Apply* – your experience and knowledge of what works and what is possible
● *Provoke* – your imagination and creatively envision a desired future
● *Collaborate* – share, affirm and coordinate with others in the process

The other half of AI, the five generic processes, are listed in sequence for ease of comprehension as follows (Watkins and Mohr, 2001, p. 39):

(1)   Choose the positive as the focus of inquiry.
(2)   Inquire into stories of life-giving forces.
(3)   Locate themes that appear in the stories and select topics for further inquiry.

Table 6.2 Summary of Appreciative Inquiry's core and emergent principles (adapted from Kelm, 2005; Whitney and Trosten-Bloom, 2003).

Five core principles	Definition
The constructionist principle	Words create worlds • *Reality is constructed through language* • *It is a subjective vs. objective state*
The poetic principle	Whatever we focus on, grows • *Focus on success we create more success* • *Focus on problems we create more problems*
The simultaneity principle	Change begins the moment we ask questions • *Inquiry is intervention* • *All questions are leading questions*
The anticipatory principle	Image inspires action • *Human systems move towards images of their future* • *Positive images create positive futures*
The positive principle	The positive core • *Consists of strengths, achievements, unexplored potentials, assets* • *Building strengths is more effective than correcting weaknesses*

Five emergent principles	Definition
The wholeness principle	Wholeness brings out the best • *We are part of a bigger 'whole' or interconnected web of relationships* • *Bringing stakeholders together stimulates creativity and builds collective capacity*
The enactment principle	Just try it • *We must 'be the change we want to see'* • *Just try a new behaviour that aligns with what you want, and build from there*
The free choice principle	Free choice liberates power • *When free to choose people are more committed to perform* • *Free choice stimulates excellence and positive change*
The awareness principle	Social and self-awareness • *Understanding and integrating the AI principles* • *Reflection on 'automatic thinking' is important*
The narrative principle	We construct stories about our lives • *Stories are transformative* • *We can change our stories to help bring us more of what we want*

(4)   Create shared images for a preferred future.
(5)   Find innovative ways to create that future.

Underlying all generic processes is *social constructionism*, which Cooperrider first wrote about with consulting partner Diana Whitney,

> Simply stated – human knowledge and organizational destiny are interwoven. . . . We must be adept in the art of understanding, reading, and analysing organizations as living, human constructions. Knowing stands at the center of any and virtually every attempt at change. Thus, the way we know is fateful. (Cooperrider and Whitney, 2005, pp. 14–15)

Each of the above processes, as part of a larger whole, overlaps with the others. However, before the first question is asked, AI begins by obliging clients to choose 'the positive' as the focus of enquiry as the launching point for all that follows. Various models and approaches for applying AI using the five generic processes have emerged; one of these models, the 4-D model described below, is widely used and contains all five of the core generic processes.

The '*Appreciative Inquiry 4-D cycle*' (Figure 6.4) can be used to engage participants in a narrative-based process of positive change. The AI cycle can be as rapid and informal as a conversation with a colleague or as formal as an organization-wide process involving every stakeholder group, such as a 4-day AI Summit (Ludema, Whitney, Mohr, and Griffin, 2003). As described by Cooperrider and Whitney (2003, pp. 16–17), the four key processes in the AI 4-D cycle are:

Figure 6.4   Appreciative Inquiry 4-D cycle (Cooperrider and Whitney, 2005).

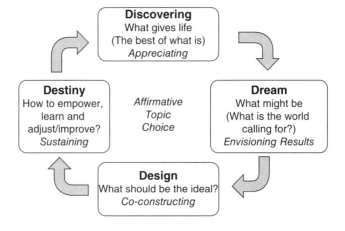

(1) *Discovery*: Mobilizing the whole system (individual, group/team) by engaging all stakeholders in the articulation of strengths and best practices. Identifying the 'best of what has been or what is'.

(2) *Dream*: Creating a clear results-oriented vision in relation to discovered potential and in relation to questions of higher purpose, such as, 'what is the world calling us to become?'

(3) *Design*: Creating possibility propositions of the ideal organization, articulating an organization design that people feel is capable of drawing upon and magnifying the positive core to realize the newly expressed dream.

(4) *Destiny*: Strengthening the affirmative capability of the whole system, enabling it to build hope and sustain momentum for ongoing positive change and high performance.

At the centre of the cycle is the *affirmative topic choice* which is the starting point and most strategic aspect of any AI process. Selection of topics itself provides opportunities for the system (individual, team/group, organization) to set a new course for the future.

A brief example of the 4-D cycle in action through the questions asked of a recent sport client (female golfer) is as follows:

Affirmative topic: What the client wants to change: 'My ability to handle stress'.

(1) *Discovery*: 'When you do handle stress what is happening? What is already working that you need to do more of?'

(2) *Dream*: 'Imagine you woke up tomorrow and the above was always the case, what changed in your habits?'

(3) *Design*: 'How will you act differently to make the above work more often?'

(4) *Destiny*: 'Now execute the above plan, live your "possibility statement", be the change identified as necessary for improvement.'

Appreciative Inquiry Coaching

Appreciative Inquiry continues to be examined by researchers who investigate both its theoretical and conceptual underpinnings. Its applied utility has elicited similar interest; one of the most recent developments and adaptations is an appreciative approach to coaching. According to Sloan and Canine (2007), Appreciative Inquiry Coaching (AIC) is the practical application of the core AI principles to the process in which a trained coach is engaged by a person (or by an organization on behalf of the person) to function as a counsellor and adviser. In addition, Sloan and Canine believe AI Coaching is highly effective for various coaching purposes, e.g., leadership, development and working relationships, and the AI principles and AI 4-D cycle provide an excellent guiding framework for the coaching process. While they recognize other comparable methods and training institutions that prepare people to act as coaches, Sloan and Canine believe

> the AI philosophy and practice is in and of itself the ideal process for both enabling people in organizations to become more aware of their own strengths and abilities in ways that increase their effectiveness in all parts of their life and to create robust support for change in the client's social system. (Sloan and Canine, 2007, p. 1)

Like AI, the essence of Appreciative Inquiry Coaching (AIC) holds that human systems are *heliotropic*, meaning they will move toward the 'generative and creative images that reside in their most positive core – their values, visions, achievements, and best practices' (Watkins and Mohr, 2001, p. xxxi). The following assumptions inherent to both AI and AIC about life, people and the change process itself, form the basis of Orem, Binkert, and Clancy's (2007, p. 26) model of Appreciative Coaching:

- In every society, organization, group or individual something works.
- What people focus on becomes their reality.
- Reality is created in the moment, and there are multiple realities.
- The act of asking questions of an organization, group, or individual influences the group or individual in some way.
- People are more confident and comfortable in their journey to the future (the unknown) when they carry forward parts of the past (the known).
- If people carry parts of the past forward, those parts should be what is best about the past.
- It is important to value differences.
- The language people use creates their reality.

Developing Mental Toughness Using Appreciative Inquiry Coaching

Both Bull (2006) and Jones and Moorhouse (2007) believe mental toughness can be developed and that doing so is as critical for workplace performance as it is for sport performance. 'More than ability, more than experience, more than education, in today's fast moving, highly competitive world, it's a person's level of mental toughness that will determine who succeeds and who fails. That's the case in the Olympics and it's true in the workplace' (Jones and Moorhouse, 2007, p. 28). As we saw in Figures 6.1 and 6.2, key components of mental toughness, the core competencies or skills that need to be learned, and means of acquiring these competencies through mental skills training have been identified. However, the following Appreciative Inquiry Coaching (AIC) approach to developing mental toughness is a significant departure from traditional approaches to mental skills training that might be used by performance psychologists. In the following section, several elements of AIC are featured to illustrate how its approaches can be used to create new thinking and imagined futures.

The first step in this approach to coaching, however, involves identifying mental toughness and an exploration of what the term means to each coachee. This is a necessary first step because coaches need to help coachees understand what mental toughness is and is not, when it is required and when it is not required, and how, in general, coachees personally construe their realities. Coaches can use the questions that follow – adapted from previous research using a Personal Construct Psychology (PCP) framework (Gordon *et al.*, 2007) and embedded in the AI 4-D cycle – to guide them in their explorations of mental toughness with clients. Coaches can ask each set of questions from the 4-D model in turn – allowing plenty time for reflection – and summarize the mutual understanding in each part of the cycle prior to proceeding to the next one.

Discovery

- Describe what you consider 'mental toughness' (MT) to be. Can you offer a definition, phrase or quote to describe it?
- When have you displayed MT?
- What was the situation which required you to be mentally tough and describe those situations which do not require MT?
- Having identified a situation which required MT, what do you think are the characteristics that distinguish mentally tough individuals from mentally weak individuals? What attitudes or beliefs do you consider to be the opposite of each of these characteristics?
- What do you consider to be the observable behaviours associated with each of these MT characteristics?
- What do you think your co-workers/peers would contend to be characteristics of a mentally tough individual and the role of these characteristics?

Coach's Focus in This Stage

- Establishing a positive connection between coach and client
- Leading the client to a more empowering perspective
- Affirming a sense of the possible
- Cultivating and supporting the client's belief in a positive future (Orem et al., 2007, p. 206)

Dream

- Imagine one night while you were asleep a miracle occurred and when you woke up you were mentally tough as you have just described, in all situations that required MT. How would you know you were MT?
- What would be different?
- What changed in your habits?
- Who would be the first to notice these changes?
- What will they say or do, and how will you respond?

Coach's Focus in This Stage

- Encouraging the client to create images of possibilities
- Inviting the client to give voice to his/her preferred future
- Affirming the client's dream (Orem et al., 2007, p. 206)

Design

- How will you act differently to make the above work?
- How best can you develop mental toughness?
- Are there 'significant others' who you feel play a crucial role in the development of mental toughness?
- What do you think these individuals do to help? What do they not do?
- Are there any techniques or methods that you have experienced which you feel influences the development of MT?
- Think of someone you know who you would characterize as being mentally tough. How do you think he/she developed this mental toughness?

Coach's Focus in This Stage

- Assisting the client in bringing the dream into focus
- Affirming the reality of the dream
- Supporting mindful choices and actions (Orem *et al.*, 2007, p. 207)

Destiny

- Reflecting on what you really want and where you are right now regarding MT, what do you see as the most significant changes you could make that would help you get what you want?
- What one small change could you make right now, no matter how small, that would improve your MT? The change does not have to be a physical action – it could be a shift in thinking or attitude.
- Just try it. Do this small change today that will move you in the direction of what you want and when it feels comfortable or becomes a habit, consider making another small change using the same small steps.

Coach's Focus in This Stage

- Helping the client recognize his/her dreams in the present
- Enabling the client to expand his/her capacity to create the dream
- Supporting the client in holding faith when the going gets tough
- Saying *namaste*[1] when coaching comes to a close (Orem *et al.*, 2007, p. 207)

The above process can be applied in exploring each MT attribute a coachee has identified as important in pursuit of his or her goals. Coaching each of the four key MT attributes identified by Jones and Moorhouse (2007) would involve a similar approach:

(1) *Keeping your head under stress* – controlling the amount and nature of the stress you experience so that you can remain composed in weighing the situation and making important decisions.
(2) *Staying strong in your self-belief* – maintaining a source of robust belief and confidence in your qualities and abilities required to achieve best performance goals.

---

1 *Namaste* is a polite Indian (Hindu) gesture (a bow) of farewell or greeting made with the hands held chest high and both palms pressed together.

(3)   *Making your motivation work for you* – ensuring your desire and determination to succeed is founded on positive and constructive motives that keep you optimally motivated and enable you to recover from performance setbacks.

(4)   *Maintaining your focus on the things that matter* – regulating your focus so that the many demands you encounter do not distract you from key priorities.

Orem *et al.* (2007) have identified a number of ways in which AIC can be used by coaches through: (1) embracing it as the primary coaching model and approach; (2) employing it as an additional tool within established coaching practice; and (3) applying selective elements as appreciative language, questions and tools to enhance other coaching methods. They also suggested that the underlying theory, principles and stages of AIC could be used in training managers and supervisors in an educational or training context. They used four key steps to introduce AIC into their own practice:

(1)   *Addressing worldview*
      Worldview is understood by researchers (see Koltko-Rivera, 2004) to be an essential component of human nature and encompasses a person's beliefs and values. In the Discovery stage, Orem *et al.* (2007) use questions to help reveal how clients see themselves in the world such as: 'What are your three most important values?'; 'Describe your beliefs about what motivates people?'; 'What do you not believe?'

(2)   *Using appreciative language*
      Because language matters, especially in coaching, Orem *et al.* (2007) began reducing the usage of certain 'problem-solving' phrases from the business world, e.g., goals, action plans, skill gaps and status quo and introducing other words, e.g., affirmation, images, dreams and potential – which led to a more generative orientation among their clients.

(3)   *Understanding what clients bring*
      In addition, Orem *et al.* (2007) realized that because each client presents with different levels of experience and facility in the areas of self-analysis and self-discovery, understanding what the client brings to coaching was very important.

(4)   *Becoming familiar with the stages and principles*
      Finally, Orem *et al.* (2007) found that the visual image of the four stages in the 4-D cycle (Figure 6.4) was easier for clients to understand than the list of the five core principles (Figure 6.3). However, they still took clients through the whole process because it was

the best way of helping them become familiar with the stages and processes of appreciative coaching; they also found reflection and observation the most effective ways of helping clients link the theory of AIC to the practice.

Having used AIC in helping professional athletes develop their mental toughness, the author has witnessed the immediate impact of using appreciative language in particular. Adapting questions from Orem *et al.*'s (2007) Client information form I created a form which coachees complete prior to the first meeting (see Table 6.3). I have received very positive feedback from athletes about this preliminary step to coaching, such as: 'I felt great just from thinking about past successes. I really should do that much more.' 'Reflecting on what I did back then, made me realize what I want to do more of right now.' 'The images were affirming and made me feel more proud of myself and of what I've achieved. I've realized that I've taken too many peak experiences for granted.'

I have also borrowed ideas from Orem *et al.* (2007, pp. 199–200) on self-reflective questions I use following each of my coaching sessions. For example:

- What did my client say was most important to accomplish in this session?
- What stage (Discover, Dream, Design, Destiny) were we in? What evidence demonstrated this?

Table 6.3 Client information form (adapted from Orem *et al.*, 2007).

Prior to our first discussion on mental toughness, please respond to the following questions

1. Describe your three greatest achievements to date that you would attribute to your mental toughness?
2. What made these accomplishments stand out for you?
3. What have you incorporated into your current game plans from your past accomplishments?
4. How could you use more of what you've learned from these accomplishments to assist you in making future changes?
5. List five adjectives that describe you when you are in 'the zone':
   - Physically
   - Emotionally
   - Mentally
6. What are you learning and accepting about yourself at present?

- What evidence did I see of an Appreciative Inquiry Coaching principle (e.g., Constructionist, Simultaneity, Poetic, Anticipatory, Positive)? Which one(s) did I see and how was it demonstrated?
- In what ways did I use the client's existing successes and strengths in co-designing a desired future?
- To what degree was the client's language positive? To what degree were my questions and responses couched in positive language?

Summary

Appreciative Inquiry (AI) focuses on supporting people and getting them to tell their own stories of positive development. It acknowledges that while coachees may have 'failed' or felt pressure to perform better, they are also resourceful and they have been successful in the past. Like other strengths-based coaching orientations, AI has been accused of being naive and idealistic in the way that it focuses on positive experiences and ignores or suppresses accounts of negative experiences (Reed, 2007). However, its social constructivist framework helps coachees in thinking about their world as they would like it to be, and in exploring how 'the positive' can contribute to their development in a different way from other coaching approaches.

In terms of enhancing daily living using AI, both Kelm (2005) and Stavros and Torres (2005) appear to have made transferable applications of AI convincingly possible. Increasingly, there are stories of how AI has effectively cultivated peak performance leadership in the workplace and how appreciative organizational practices have been used to create strategic competitive advantage (Anderson et al., 2001; Ludema et al., 2003). Readers are encouraged to look at www.aiconsulting.org/success for specific 'success stories'. Both Bull (2006) and Jones and Moorhouse (2007) have noted, however, that in contrast to sport personnel, business personnel are seldom shown how to develop and maintain their mental strengths. This gap is a natural opportunity for coaches equipped to help their business clients develop greater mental toughness as an aid to enhanced development and performance. Appreciative Inquiry Coaching (AIC) seems particularly well suited to this task. Perhaps it can become the point of difference business is looking for in developing and enhancing wellbeing among personnel, attracting and retaining talent, and building and sustaining high-performance leaders and cultures?

Based on my own research and coaching experience in both business and sport settings, I believe mental toughness can be coached, and that strengths-based strategies such as AIC are better suited for this purpose than any other coaching approaches. Coaches and those charged with the responsibility of coordinating coaching and leadership development programmes are encouraged to browse the resources on the AI Commons website www.appreciativeinquiry.case.edu/ and the books referenced in this chapter – particularly Cooperrider, Whitney, and Stavros (2005) and Ludema *et al.* (2003). Finally, I would like to conclude with a final word from Orem *et al.* (2007, p. 201):

> All coaches want their clients to succeed, and they help them achieve success using whatever approach seems most effective. We also think that, beyond success, flourishing is important to our clients, to the country, and to the world. If we as coaches find ways to help people flourish, we will have done our jobs well. If we can help clients accept themselves as fully capable and autonomous agents in making choices, if we can help them master their environments, have positive relations with those around them, and pursue a purpose about which they feel passionate, we have contributed to a more empowered and effective human family.

References

Anderson, H., Cooperrider, D., Gergen, K. J., Gergen, M. M., McNamee, S., and Whitney, D. (2001). *The appreciative organization.* Chagrin Falls, OH: Taos Institute.

Bloom, B. S. (1985). *Developing talent in young people.* New York: Ballantine.

Bull, S. J. (2006). *The game plan: Your guide to mental toughness at work.* Chichester, UK: Capstone.

Bull, S. J., Shambrook, C. J., James, W., and Brooks, J. E. (2005). Towards an understanding of mental toughness in elite English cricketers. *Journal of Applied Sport Psychology,* 17, 209–227.

Connaughton, D., Wadey, R., Hanton, S., and Jones, G. (2007). The development and maintenance of mental toughness: Perceptions of elite performers. *Journal of Sport Sciences,* 26(1), 83–95.

Cooperrider, D. L., and Srivastva, S. (1987). Appreciative inquiry in organizational life. In W. A. Pasmore and R. W. Woodman (Eds.), *Research in organizational change and development* (Vol. I). Greenwich, CT: JAI Press.

Cooperrider, D. L. and Whitney, D. (2005). *Appreciative inquiry: A positive revolution in change.* San Francisco: Berrett-Koehler.

Cooperrider, D. L., Whitney, D., and Stavros, J. M. (2005). *Appreciative inquiry handbook: The first in a series of AI workbooks for leaders of change.* San Francisco: Berrett-Koehler.

Côté, J. (1999). The influence of the family in the development of talent in sports. *The Sports Psychologist,* 13, 395–417.

Côté, J., Baker, J., and Abernethy, B. (2003). From play to practice: A developmental framework for the acquisition of expertise in team sports. In J. Starkes and K. A. Ericsson (Eds.), *Expert performance in sports: Advances in research on sport expertise* (pp. 89–110). Champaign, IL: Human Kinetics.

Csikszentmihalyi, M., Rathunde, K., and Whalen, S. (1993). *Talented Teenagers: The roots of success and failure.* Cambridge, UK: Cambridge University Press.

Fawcett, T. (2005). Perceptions of mental toughness from adventurer/explorer/ 'medal winning' elite athlete and elite coach perspectives: A grounded theory analysis. In T. Morris, P. Terry, S. Gordon, S. Hanrahan, L. Ievleva, G. Kolt, and P. Tremayne (Eds.), *Psychology promoting health and performance for life: Proceedings of the ISSP 11th World Congress of Sport* [CDROM]. Sydney: International Society of Sport Psychology.

Fourie, S., and Potgieter, J. R. (2001). The nature of mental toughness in sport. *South African Journal for Research in Sport, Physical Education and Recreation, 23,* 63–72.

Gagne, F. (1996). *A thoughtful look at talent development.* Montreal: University of Quebec Press.

Gagne, F. (2003). Transforming gifts into talents: The DMGT as a developmental theory. In N. Colangelo and G. A. Davis (Eds.), *Handbook of Gifted Education* (pp. 130–140). Boston: Pearson Education.

Gordon, S. (2007). Sport and business coaching: Perspective of a sport psychologist. *Australian Psychologist, 42,* 271–282.

Gordon, S., and Sridhar, C. (2005). Identification and development of mental toughness in elite cricket. In T. Morris, P. Terry, S. Gordon, S. Hanrahan, L. Ievleva, G. Kolt, and P. Tremayne (Eds.), *Psychology promoting health and performance for life: Proceedings of the ISSP 11th World Congress of Sport* [CDROM]. Sydney: International Society of Sport Psychology.

Gordon, S., Gucciardi, D., and Chambers, T. (2007). A personal construct psychology perspective on sport and exercise psychology research: The example of mental toughness. In T. Morris, P. Terry, and S. Gordon (Eds.), *Sport psychology and exercise psychology: International perspectives (pp. 43–55).* Morgantown, WV: Fitness Information Technology.

Gould, D., Dieffenbach, K., and Moffett, A. (2002). Psychological characteristics and their development in Olympic champions. *Journal of Applied Sport Psychology, 14,* 172–204.

Gucciardi, D., Gordon, S. and Dimmock, J. (in press). Towards an understanding of mental toughness in Australian Rules football. *Journal of Applied Sport Psychology.*

Jones, G. (2002). Performance excellence: A personal perspective on the link between sport and business. *Journal of Applied Sport Psychology, 14,* 268–281.

Jones, G. and Moorhouse, A. (2007). *Developing mental toughness: Gold medal strategies for transforming your business performance.* Oxford, UK: Spring Hill.

Jones, G., and Spooner, K. (2006). Coaching high achievers. *Consulting Psychology Journal: Practice and Research, 58*(1), 40–50.

Jones, G., Hanton, S., and Connaughton, D. (2002). What is this thing called mental toughness? An investigation of elite sport performers. *Journal of Applied Sport Psychology, 14,* 205–218.

Jones, G., Hanton, S., and Connaughton, D. (2007). A framework of mental toughness in the world's best performers. *The Sport Psychologist, 21,* 243–264.

Kelly, G. A. (1991). *The psychology of personal constructs: A theory of personality* (Vol. 1). London: Routledge (original work published 1955).

Kelm, J. B. (2005). *Appreciative living: The principles of Appreciative Inquiry in personal life.* Wake Forest, NC: Venet.

Koltko-Rivera, M. E. (2004). The psychology of worldviews. *Review of General Psychology,* 8(1), 3–58.

Loehr, J. E. (1986). *Mental toughness training for sports: Achieving athletic excellence.* Lexington, MA: Stephen Greene Press.

Ludema, J. D., Whitney, D., Mohr, B. J., and Griffin, T. J. (2003). *The appreciative inquiry summit: A practitioner's guide for leading large-group change.* San Francisco: Berrett-Koehler.

Middleton, S. C., Marsh, H. W., Martin, A. J., Richards, G. E., and Perry, C. (2004, July). *Discovering mental toughness: A qualitative study of mental toughness in elite athletes.* Paper presented at the 3rd International Biennial SELF Research Conference, Berlin, Germany.

Orem, S. L., Binkert, J., and Clancy, A. L. (2007). *Appreciative coaching: A positive process for change.* San Francisco: Jossey-Bass.

Orlick, T. (1998). *Embracing your potential.* Lower Mitchum, SA: Human Kinetics.

Reed, J. (2007). *Appreciative inquiry: Research for change.* London: Sage.

Sloan, B., and Canine, T. (2007, May). Appreciative inquiry in coaching: Exploration and learnings. *AI Practitioner: The International Journal of AI Best Practice,* May, 1–5.

Stavros, J. M., and Torres, C. B. (2005). *Dynamic relationships: Unleashing the power of appreciative inquiry in daily living.* Chagrin Falls, OH: Taos Institute.

Thelwell, R., Weston, N., and Greenlees, I. (2005). Defining and understanding mental toughness within soccer. *Journal of Applied Sport Psychology,* 17, 326–332.

Watkins, J. M., and Mohr, B. J. (2001). *Appreciative inquiry: Change at the speed of imagination.* San Francisco: Jossey-Bass/Pfeiffer.

Whitney, D., and Trosten-Bloom, A. (2003). *The power of appreciative inquiry: A practical guide to positive change.* San Francisco: Berrett-Koehler.

7

Focus on Cultural Elements in Coaching: Experiences from China and Other Countries

Charles Hamrick

Introduction

At the nexus of culture and coaching lies the opportunity to expand our consciousness, and thereby expand our ability to serve others. By consciousness, I mean both the myriad of our perceptions of our environments, and also our relationship with our environments. Typically, we stretch our perceptions, our tangible views of our world and the broader world of judgement and understanding of that world, into actions and behaviours in an expression of how we view our universe. These actions and behaviours are not always supportive of our goals and objectives. By relationship, I am suggesting those aspects of dialogue and sharing, of wonder and curiosity, of exploration and opening that allow us to reshape our behaviours into purposeful and meaningful expressions that support our values, principles, goals, objectives, vision and intention. This characterization is useful to the exploration of how, as coaches, we do what we do across cultures, and do that most effectively.

Calling upon the cultures of India and China, this chapter looks at coaching from an Eastern perspective. The Upanishads are a collection of Indian teachings of spirituality and philosophy dating back nearly

The Philosophy and Practice of Coaching: Insights and Issues for a New Era.
Edited by David B. Drake, Diane Brennan and Kim Gørtz.
© 2008 John Wiley & Sons, Ltd.

three millennia. The word 'Upanishad' means *sitting down beside*. From this place, sitting beside our clients, coaches have an opportunity of equality, of understanding our perceptions and those of our client, and of transforming those perceptions into behaviours and expressions in tune with our client's vision. The character 'Shen' in Chinese is derived from a pictograph of an earthen altar and a lightning bolt, together meaning to enlighten. With the addition of two strokes representing a person, the character transforms into the meaning to stretch, and with a few more strokes, the character transforms into the meaning of spirit or God. Thus, gurus of ancient China were often called *spirit stretchers*. These two concepts form the substance of my personal view of coaching in an intercultural context; that is, to sit beside the client with a view to stretch ourselves into consequential positive expressions of our true intention and purpose.

Often we see the outcomes of culture without understanding the cultural process. Learning is the 'software of the mind' (Hofstede, 1999) by which we learn from our environments to behave in certain ways, with people often judging the world by what is familiar. The effects become that all of us experience discrimination and stereotypes; however, money and power often buffer us from the effects of discrimination. The outcomes of culture are that we seek the company of those most familiar to ourselves. People resist change and the unfamiliar, rarely sharing or giving up power voluntarily.

Over the next few pages, culture is explored with the purpose of strengthening our coaching skills and competencies, and then venturing deeper into our consciousness itself. M. J. Bennett (Bennett, 1993), speaks to six stages of development as people experience intercultural situations: Denial, Defence, Minimization, Acceptance, Adaptation, and Integration. This is useful reading for any coach working across cultures; however, as coaches, we venture beyond the stages of development in the model, to a deeper understanding of ourselves and transformation of our consciousness. Seeing ourselves as we truly are helps us to connect with others. The maxim 'Know yourself, know the other' spans Earth from the Greeks at Delphi to Sun Zi in China. Yunus Emre, the Turkish poet and Sufi mystic asked, 'If you know not who you are, what's the use of learning?' (Yunus, 2007).

There is another, more defining, element to this. Sun Zi went on to say that to distinguish between the sun and moon is no great test of vision. Miyamoto Musashi, the Japanese samurai, in the *Book of Five Rings*, reiterated, 'What is big is easy to perceive; what is small is difficult to perceive'. To give an example of the meaning behind these quotes, I have often been approached, when reading a book in Chinese, with the question, 'Do you read Chinese?', followed by, 'Read this', as the person points to a line. These queries are not ones of veracity, rather to understand my communication ability, whereupon the person can then most effectively relate. Over dinner with a Japanese Sensei (honoured teacher), I ventured, 'I understand that there are multiple levels of the story of the 47 Ronin' (a classic story in Japanese history), to which he responded, 'Tell me what you know'. I mentioned the three levels that I understood, and he sat back, reflected, and then softly spoke, 'Let me tell you about the seven levels of the 47 Ronin'.

Does this mean that, as coaches, we must learn the deepest levels of a culture in order to communicate and coach? Not necessarily; however, it does mean that we must be willing to learn, greatly willing to listen and enquire into those aspects of culture relevant to the process at hand, less willing to espouse our own theory of the universe. These then are our first lessons as global coaches, to understand ourselves and others, beyond just the metaphorical difference between the sun and the moon.

Walking the streets of the Ginza in Tokyo in the summer of 1970, I learned the second of many lessons in moving across cultural borders. Recently graduated from university, my curiosity about the world led to acceptance of a job in Korea, and my father gave me a small pocket-knife just before departure. Grasping the small knife in my pocket, I wandered the streets amazed at the numbers of people, the way I towered above them, the unintelligible signs and speech, and the seeming absence of order. After about an hour of venturing down narrow lanes, I asked myself, 'What am I doing?' – and went over to a trash can and threw the knife in, assuring myself that I would never again have need to fear those different than myself.

This fear manifests itself subtly and amoeba-like, shifting to fit both personal environments and global conditions. Whether Cold War mentalities or alarm over bearded men from the Middle East, fear strikes at the core of our ability to have truly open dialogue with peoples unlike ourselves. Edward W. Said remarked in *Culture and Resistance*, 'Culture is a way of fighting against extinction and obliteration'. The entire process of coaching through intercultural lenses will be explored later; however, at this point, a key understanding is that from a place of awareness, arrived at through exploration of ourselves and others, we can springboard through fear to a place of practical, palatable and effective action.

Closely related to this fear is judgement, how we view others who may seem different from ourselves. As we seek to let go of judgement, all becomes our teachers. Walking the streets of Ropponggi in Tokyo, I saw a man coming at me down a back street. Tilted to one side, he was stumbling, though with a great intensity. My first reaction was to wonder if he wanted money, or something. Then I asked myself to be quiet and observe. From a coffee shop on the main street, I watched him over the next few weeks, as he would leave his home, stumble along, every few minutes leaning against a wall to catch his breath. He would go down to the corner, turn around and walk home. As Hafiz said,

> There is no one in this world
> Who is not looking for God.
>
> Everyone is trudging along
> With as much dignity, courage
> And style
>
> As they possibly
> Can.

The third macro-lesson that I learned about cultures came two years later as I was jogging down a path in the Malaysian forest at dusk. With a stream gurgling through fern-covered stones, the sun setting through the trees and fog, and cicadas beginning their nightly vigil, jutting from a bundle of bamboo, a reed drifted in the soft breeze. At the very tip perched a butterfly, with white and black bespeckled wings fluttering in synchrony with the leaves of the canopy of trees. The sight stopped me in my tracks, and I stood there for several minutes rapt in the beauty, startled by a thundershower back into the reality of needing to return to my waiting and dry car. That evening I went into a bookstore to look up that particular butterfly, and seeing its photo, purchased the book and went home, only to read, 'Not a particularly interesting species of genus . . . and species . . . ,' whereupon I threw the book into the garbage can, perhaps to unite with the penknife of my first venture to Japan.

It is worthwhile to review these three lessons, as they are essential for a coach working across borders. We reflect upon ourselves, learn who we are, our intentions, how we use our intentions to manifest our personal reality, and adjust accordingly. We overcome fear, looking at people through fresh and innocent eyes, with a curiosity that allows us to explore. We go beyond analysis to a view from the balcony, watching all around us from a place that allows us to see a larger perspective. As Lao Zi said, 'Soften your glare'.

Cultural Norms and Fallacies

In each other's eyes, we not only see different substance, we also perceive in fundamentally different ways. A few years ago I went to a cultural seminar in Shonan, Japan, and a professor at one of the universities talked about how Americans view Chinese and Japanese similarly, Chinese view Japanese and Americans in comparable ways and Japanese view Chinese and Americans likewise. Americans, in his research, tended to look at physical characteristics and how Asians appeared inscrutable. Chinese tended to view Americans and Japanese as misusing their economic and political power. If one reads the history of the shift in power in Asia in the late 1800s and early 1900s, this point would be very clear. By looking at the map and seeing Japan sandwiched between two large, powerful nations in China and America, one can guess as to their thoughts. The point is clear, it is not only the essence that is seen differently, it is the process of seeing that is itself dissimilar.

There are many borders, with many effects. Borders encircle language, religion, values, law, politics, technology, education and social order. These kaleidoscopic lenses impact our decision making, views of risk and innovation, reward systems, event horizons, processes, concepts of loyalty and relationships.

This global diversity leads borders to take many forms. In broad terms, these forms encompass individual, cultural and environmental diversities. At the individual level, gender, physical qualities, age, personality type, sexual orientation, education, marital status, experience and wealth all offer defining parameters. The cultural plane is defined by race and ethnicity, national origin and language, music and arts, religious beliefs and spirituality, value systems and acceptable behaviours. Environmental factors include country and ethnic business styles, industrial and corporate policies and cultures, economic and technological bases, negotiating styles and geographical location.

My experience is that whereas North Americans tend to look through individual lenses, with a blend of culture, Asians tend to look through environmental lenses, also with a touch of culture. These views lead to tendencies to ask different questions, observe dissimilar attributes, and come to diverse conclusions. The American may astutely observe the physical differences and opinions of the Chinese sitting across the table, but it is likely that the Chinese is seeking to understand the principles under which the American is operating.

The views of a global coach are multidimensional: we look inward to a new culture, outward from our own culture to the universal community, and within our own culture to reflect back into ourselves. As we gaze into another culture from the outside, it is often useful to have a model with which to view behaviours and values, and these will be discussed next. As we observe other cultures, we can begin to see relationships between cultures and then relate them to ourselves. This reflection intensifies within our own culture, as we learn that each person can be a teacher to us.

For example, we may perceive Chinese, Japanese and Korean cultures to be similar, whereas in reality, there are great differences, in virtually all of the dimensions just discussed. Even the use of the Chinese characters takes on subtleties in meaning with profound behavioural shifts between the cultures. For example, in China, if one has a good understanding and balance of the concepts of *guanxi, mianzi* and *renqing* (relationship, face and human feeling), relating can be like hitting a tennis ball in the sweet spot of a racquet. However, in Korea and Japan, relating is more like playing tennis with a loosely strung racquet, because the relationship concepts of Confucianism, Buddhism and Daoism underwent dramatic changes as they were absorbed over the centuries. It is not that it becomes an unfair advantage, as all play with nearly the same tools and processes; it is just that the game is different, and it behoves us to learn the specialties of each culture.

Cultures are complex, so generalizations are often useful to render multidimensional concepts relevant. Cultures have often been referred to as icebergs, with values and beliefs lying under the surface, behaviours above, and the visible a small fraction of the whole. Cultures are also like kaleidoscopes. We speak of such cultural dimensions as power distance, independence, relationship, pragmatism, uncertainty avoidance and community, yet in practice, they tend to overlap in an ever-changing myriad of colours, intensities and clarity.

Whereas discovery and labelling and discriminating may lead to advancement of certain forms of science, taking that science into the world of comparative beauty and worthiness often leads to inappropriate application of measurement and labels. Carlos Romulo, a Philippine diplomat, once remarked that Americans were like diamonds and Filipinos like pearls. The metaphor is powerful. The cut diamond is sharp, clear, often stands alone, and commands attention. The pearl is subtle, opaque, stands in strands, and begs attention ever so softly. Yet, who can truly judge the relative value?

The derivation of cultural theories and frameworks can lead to erroneous conclusions, and the results themselves are often not fine-grained enough to offer possible solutions to intercultural dilemmas. Two social scientists, Geert Hofstede and Fons Trompenaars use dimensions to explain cultural differences, and their works are highly recommended for those wishing to expand their understanding of cultures. In the same breath, search beyond the sun and moon towards what is really going on.

As an example, one of the more relevant dimensions to intercultural interactions is that of Specificity and Diffusion in Trompenaars' work. In Specific cultures, aspects of life are differentiated, relating is rather more direct, and one's moral stand is independent of the person being addressed. In Diffuse cultures, separate aspects of life are interconnected, relating is more circuitous and vague, and one's expressed morality is more dependent upon the context. Another way to look at this across cultures is that in the West, behaviours tend to drive relationships: as we behave, so goes our relationship. In Eastern cultures, relationships drive behaviour: as is our relationship with another, we behave accordingly.

The rub is this: in the questions in the research instruments often lie imbedded cultural assumptions. For example, one of the questions relating to Specificity and Diffusion has to do with whether one would assist in the painting of the employer's house at the weekend. Imbedded in the cultural assumption is that this measure of whether or not one paints the house is related to a dimension that measures a culture somewhere between the two ends of the spectrum.

This assumption does not withstand scrutiny. In India, when asking the question to many Indian friends and clients, they have asked, 'Why would any boss ask that? Labour is cheap.' Or the implication would be relative to the former colonialism under which India existed. In far reaches of China, in State Owned Enterprises (SOEs) in which people are bound together in strict social orders, one may assist with the painting; however, in Shanghai, many business executives kind of roll their eyes, muttering something about a *laowai* (friendly term for a foreigner) not understanding Chinese culture. So, two errors arise, one in inappropriately skewing the statistical results, and then falsely assuming that as people move out of SOEs in western China, that culture is changing because Chinese are moving towards the Western end of the dimension.

This is not to say that cultures do not change, and in fact, politics often overrides culture. As Calvin in the comic strip *Calvin and Hobbes*, quipped: 'History is the fiction we invent to persuade ourselves that events are knowable and that life has order and direction. That's why events are reinterpreted when values change. We need new versions of history to allow for our current prejudices.'

Still, Trompenaars and Hofstede are highly supportive in their work of the need to understand how cultures differ. As coaches, we must go beyond the generalizations to apply the learning appropriately. These generalizations are also useful in stepping back and looking at cultures in a larger perspective. For example, we speak of American culture as valuing independence, self-reliance, pragmatism, action, change and equality. Though the USA is composed of many sets of cultures, whether of Latino, Asian, African or European origins, from a cultural satellite, America looks much different from any of the component cultural aetiologies.

This rubs over into such countries as China. People from China's Northeast behave very differently from people from the South or West;

food and values both take on diverse expressions. When asking Chinese about the breadth of their culture compared to America, most with whom I have spoken say broader, some even saying that Chinese culture is really flat, like sand. Yet, through this cultural diversity lies a consistency of philosophy, language and behavioural culture that has existed in basically the same form for over three thousand years.

Confucius and Coaching

This consistency has enormous implications for coaching theory and application. Three great teachers exemplify Chinese thought, philosophy and relationship: Confucius, Lao Zi and Buddha. From the turmoil of the Warring States (771–221 BCE), rose the Hundred Schools of Thought, with a multitude of great philosophers and thinkers illuminating, challenging and expanding the ideas of the three teachers.

Before exploring these implications for coaching, we must back up to what German philosopher Karl Jaspers called the Axial Age, the period from 800 BCE to 200 BCE, during which similar revolutionary thinking appeared in China, India and the Occident. Karen Armstrong in *The Great Transformation* (2006) speaks about this period during which all the great world religions came into being, recoiling from the violence that marked their existence. The four ancient river cultures – Nile, Tigris and Euphrates, Indus and Ganges, and Yellow – merged into two general patterns of belief systems, that of the Mediterranean and that of the Orient. Eventually, Greek rationalism formed a sort of synthesis with monotheism in Europe, and Buddhism made its way across the mountains into China, and onward to Korea and Japan, giving rise to two radically different thought systems, those of Occident and Orient.

In broad terms, these cultures are expressed by the Western penchant for scientific thought and content of belief and the Eastern affinity for flexible credos and practice. In more concrete terms relative to coaching, Confucianism, Daoism and Buddhism merged in China to become an authentically Chinese answer to Western political and religious culture.

As a coach working with Chinese, the three teachings form a highly practical coaching metaphor with enormous implications for coaching across cultures. Confucius spoke to relationship and virtue, regarding life not as a tradition, rather as a question, inquiring into answers of civilization. He started with the family, expanding our relationship abilities outward into community, country and humankind. He spoke to attributes of people as they applied to these relationships, concepts of humanity, courtesy, uprightness, knowledge and integrity.

The Chinese characters themselves speak to the embodiment of the virtues: the character for humanity has the symbol of a person and that of duality, people in dialogue. That for courtesy contains the symbols for spirit and for ceremonial bowls, uniting spirit with formality. Uprightness joins the symbol for a goat with that of a person, signifying how we are responsible and accountable for that which is ours. Knowledge becomes an arrow coming from the mouth, and integrity becomes notes from a horn that heralds one who speaks the truth. Confucius taught the Four Freedoms, with the master free from obstinacy, egoism, foregone conclusions and arbitrary predeterminations. His devotion to learning was 'for the sake of the self'. He advocated the Middle Way, basically what has the ability to make you happy also has the ability to make you sad; therefore choose a way appropriate to the moment.

In my personal work with Lao Zi's *Dao De Qing*, three great themes emerge in resonance with coaching practice. The first is dealing with paradox, ambiguity and flow:

- 'The Way that can be told is not the Way.'
- 'If you want to become whole, let yourself be partial. . . . If you want to be reborn, let yourself die.'
- 'The highest good is like water. Water gives life and does not strive. It flows in places men reject and so is like the Tao.'

The second theme is very personal, holding three treasures:

- 'The first is compassion, by which one finds courage.
- The second is simplicity, by which one finds strength.
- And the third is not putting self first, by which one finds influence.'

The third theme, highly relevant to coaching, speaks to three forms of leaders:

- 'One who leads through fear.
- One who leads through organization.
- When the master leaves, the people say, "We did it ourselves"'.

Buddha spoke deeply to a major aspect of the coaching process. We live in a world of distress and dis-ease, yet there is a place of peace, and there is a way from the distress to peace, that of following a path of integrity in action, thought, intention, mindfulness and contemplation.

There you have it, coaching in a nutshell: relationship, natural flow and personal discovery. Together, they lead to effective action and practice that internalizes into an expression that takes us back to a place in which we can further explore who we are, where we wish to go, and what are we going to do to get there.

Coaching Globally; Being a Global Coach

What does it take to live globally, to coach globally? The first criterion, in my experience, is one's ability to learn from experience. This entails curiosity and the enjoyment of challenges, being open to understanding self, and seeking feedback about behaviours. The second is the ability to manage complexity and function in ambiguous circumstances. Together, these allow one to seek to understand cultures, ever adaptable and flexible, responsive to cultural cues, able to reevaluate priorities in tune with an ever-expanding personal consciousness.

Other strengths and attributes include acceptance, which evolves respect; knowledge, which demonstrates interest; our interaction, which energizes our relationships, and flexibility, which synthesizes the others. Recall the aforementioned self-understanding, absence of fear, and ability to move beyond paradigms. Together, we are getting close to a set of competencies and attributes that define a coach able to move across borders. Now, we turn to the process of doing so.

The Chinese have a saying that, 'intention drives spirit; spirit drives power'. Spirit in this case refers to a deep-seated universal energy which connects all humanity. Power is the mental, spiritual and emotional ability to act, a faculty which mobilizes the outcomes. A wise and dear friend and teacher often challenges me by saying, 'Intention is the building block of the outcome'.

Thus, as coaches, we coach to multiple levels. We coach towards intention and awareness, enquiring into a person's awareness of their own awareness, so to speak. We coach to people's strengths, their abilities to harness their energy into places of success. We coach to success itself, that manifestation of our intention and passion. In all levels, we coach towards the person's awareness of intention, strengths and success. We also coach towards understanding evolving desires and how to apply them into new ways of being and expression.

In engineering school, I learned to apply frameworks, models and paradigms to problems that required solution. In living in Asia over the years, I have learned that it is not the model that works, rather the ability to leave a model behind and explore new territory. When we get attached to a model and then apply it, especially working across cultures, we often try to fit round pegs into square holes.

The way that I look at it is twofold. First, models are there to serve, to promote learning, to remind us until we internalize the learning. They are there to also serve as tribute to the authorities. This is true whether it is a P&L statement, a form, or a structure to record the progress and development needs of a patient in a hospital. Both speak to health, one of an organization, the other of a person. The authorities in either case require them. So, to paraphrase a Master – we give to the authorities what is theirs and to the universe what is of service.

What models enlighten in one case may obscure in another. Measurements, models, paradigms and notions of good, bad, right and wrong, are all training wheels until you get to a place where you totally flow with the person beside you, and also flow from within your being. This is that flow which calls to a loss of sense of time, total immersion in service, using all aspects of our abilities, total connection with all there is. However subtle, a model disconnects us, serving as a veil which hides who we are and also who the person is whom we are serving. It is no different from subtle models of culture.

The Process of Coaching

At the risk of violating my own premise, a highly adaptive model for the process of coaching is one grounded in the thoughts of Lao Zi and Aristotle, and which much later resurfaced in Husserl. Aristotle and Husserl spoke to a concept of epoché, a sort of intense nonjudgement, allowing ourselves to resonate with those around us. Lao Zi spoke of it in terms of emptying and exploring what is not; i.e., 'We look at it, and we do not see it. We listen to it, and we do not hear it. We try to grasp it, and do not get hold of it'.

As coaches, we seek to understand another's experience, what they notice and what they desire. We sit beside, looking at the universe together, asking the question, 'Is your universe friendly?' We then explore, positively, compassionately and nonjudgementally, not poking, rather inviting towards discovery of internal sources. As we explore and come to a place of awareness, we discover that on the flip side of the awareness coin lies inspiration, the inspiration to act in new ways, seek goals more in line with who we are.

From here, we dive into action, overcoming fears, fears of failure, of what others may say, of our own limits. We learn new actions, prototype new ways of behaving, and then practice until the new ways become internalized. This internalization leads to transformation, that transformation mentioned at the beginning of the treatise, that which leads to understanding our connection with all that exists. This leads back to experience, except a new level, a different expression. From there we start the emptying process again, except at a higher energy level.

This process of experience, exploration, awareness and action, is grounded in the classics, spanning millennia, transversing places and cultures. Lao Zi would probably smile.

My experience is that, in actual coaching sessions, this process leads to two outcomes. One is a place of silence, a place where all has been said. Often, we in the West are uncomfortable with silence. However, it is the place from which the second outcome gathers strength – the palatable action plan that allows us to manifest our intention and live in a state of joy.

I would challenge all of us as coaches to expand our own consciousness, experiment with it, learn to let go of paradigms and trust that which is within. It is time for us in coaching to come to a place in which we drop all vestiges of separation and move in totality with those we serve. This universe has become too fast-moving, too diverse, too much towards a tipping point, to allow anything but Grace to guide us. I do not mean Grace in a religious context. I mean it from a place of innocence, guided from within, without judgement, pre-forgiving all.

References

Armstrong, K. (2006). *The great transformation*. London: Atlantic Books.
Bennett, M. J. (1993). Towards ethnorelativism: A developmental model of intercultural sensitivity. In R. M. Paige (Ed.), *Education for the intercultural experience* (2nd edn), (pp. 21–71). Yarmouth, ME: Intercultural Press.
Hofstede, G. (1999). *Cultures and organizations: Software of the mind*. New York: McGraw-Hill.
Yunus, E. (2007). Knowledge should mean a full grasp of knowledge, retrieved on 20/8/07 from http://www.poetry-chaikhana.com/E/EmreYunus/Knowledgesho.htm.

8 Coaching and Workplace Stress

Kristina Gyllensten

Introduction

Stress in the workplace is a serious problem. Different types of interventions are used in order to address workplace stress and different types of professionals are involved in this work. Although coaching is an intervention that is not commonly associated with stress reduction, it has been suggested that coaching can be useful in tackling stress (Hearn, 2001).

Unfortunately, there appears to be a lack of literature on coaching and stress and a lack of research investigating the impact of coaching on stress (Gyllensten and Palmer, 2005a). Consequently, the focus of this chapter will be on deepening our understanding of coaching and workplace stress. It is intended to be of use to individuals who are involved in developing stress reducing/preventing interventions in the workplace, and individuals who are interested in research on the evaluation of coaching services as they are applied to workplace stress. I begin by outlining the key topics related to coaching and workplace stress, and then outline the relevant research in this area. The findings from a research study focusing on coaching and stress, conducted by the author and Dr Stephen Palmer, will be outlined. I close with recommendations for future research and a conclusion that summarizes the key lessons learned.

The Philosophy and Practice of Coaching: Insights and Issues for a New Era.
Edited by David B. Drake, Diane Brennan and Kim Gørtz.
© 2008 John Wiley & Sons, Ltd.

Coaching

A number of different coaching definitions have been proposed. For the purpose of this discussion I will use Grant's (2001a, p. 8) definition of coaching in the workplace as 'a solution-focused, result-oriented systematic process in which the coach facilitates the enhancement of work performance and the self-directed learning and personal growth of the coachee.'

Various theories and approaches are used in the practice of coaching. Indeed, it has been suggested that the practice of coaching is based on a mix of concepts and methods from domains such as traditional organization development, adult education, management training, industrial/organizational psychology, and generic consultation skills (Kilburg, 1996). Grant (2001a) proposes that the discipline of psychology, in particular, has the potential to greatly contribute to the field of coaching through provision of a theoretical grounding and carrying out of scientific research. Indeed, the field of coaching psychology is being developed in places such as Australia and the UK (Palmer and Whybrow, 2005). Coaching psychology is embedded in the discipline of psychology as well as incorporating other skills, models and approaches from other disciplines that have a positive impact on individuals' wellbeing (Palmer and Whybrow, 2005).

Workplace Stress

Workplace stress is a serious problem that is related to a number of negative psychological, physiological and economical outcomes (Health and Safety Executive, 2001). A survey by the Health and Safety Executive (HSE) found that half a million people in the UK believed that they were suffering from stress, anxiety or depression that was related to their work. It was further estimated that 12.8 million days were lost due to work-related stress, anxiety or depression (Jones, Huxtable, and Hodgson, 2004). Moreover, a survey of 47 million European workers found that 28% of the workers reported that they were suffering from stress (Employment and Social Affairs, 1999). Of the employees taking part in an American survey 40% reported that their job was 'very or extremely stressful' (National Institute for Occupational Safety and Health, 1999). These surveys highlight that workplace stress is a problem in both Europe and the USA.

Stress can be defined in a number of different ways. Palmer, Cooper, and Thomas (2003, p. 2) propose the following definition of stress: 'stress occurs when the perceived pressure exceeds your perceived ability to cope'. This cognitive definition of stress highlights the individual's perception of pressure. A definition of workplace stress that is focusing more on the external pressure is proposed by the HSE (2001, p. 1); 'work-related stress is the adverse reaction people have to excessive pressures or other types of demand placed on them'. A definition of stress that originates from the Occupational Safety and Health Service in New Zealand is 'Workplace stress is the result of the interaction between a person and their work environment. For the person it is the awareness of not being able to cope with the demands of their work environment, with an associated negative emotional response' (Occupational Safety and Health Service, 2003, p. 4). When considering stress as measured in the research study that will be presented in this chapter the terms 'stressors' and 'strain' are important to define. Environmental factors that may be sources of stress are called stressors and the individual's reaction to the stressors is called strain (Cooper, Dewe, and O'Driscoll, 2001). The 'model of work stress' shown in Figure 8.1 (adapted from Palmer, Cooper, and Thomas, 2004) highlights the relationship between the potential hazards, symptoms and negative outcomes of stress.

Figure 8.1   A model of work stress.

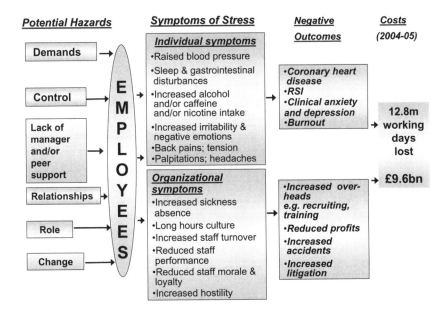

Coaching and Stress

It has been suggested that coaching can be useful in reducing stress (Busch and Steinmetz, 2002; Jones, 1996; Mangell and Neld, 2003; Meyer, 2003; Willis, ND; Zeus and Skiffington, 2003). Indeed, the British Chartered Institute of Personnel and Development (2004) suggests that reduction of stress is one of the common benefits of coaching. Coaching is used, therefore, by individuals and organizations, in order to improve performance, achieve goals and manage stress (Palmer, Tubbs, and Whybrow, 2003). This chapter is focused on individuals and stress, but coaching can also help to identify and change organizational stressors. For example, patterns may emerge in coaching individuals that may require strategies for addressing organizational issues, e.g. structures, conditions, processes and expectations that are contributors to stress.

The experience of stress is unique to each of us and what is stressful for one person is a positive challenge for another. By being flexible, based on the client's particular needs, coaching can be useful in addressing a number of different problems that may be triggering stress reactions. Indeed, coaching can be effective in tackling and preventing workplace stress both in direct and indirect ways. Hearn (2001) suggests that stress can be tackled directly in coaching by helping the person to identify the sources of stress, find strategies for change, and develop lasting solutions. In addition, coaching could also have an indirect effect on stress by helping an individual to improve in a specific area as a way to reduce the sources of stress related to their perceived shortcomings in the area targeted by the coaching intervention (Gyllensten and Palmer, 2005a). For example an individual may feel very stressed prior to, and while, making presentations. Coaching could help the individual to challenge and reframe unhelpful beliefs contributing to their distress as well as to improve their presentation skills. As result of coaching the person would experience less stress and while presenting, be more able to manage any stress that did arise, and be more relaxed preparing for future presentations. Another example of where coaching can be helpful is with the stress associated with procrastination (Neenan and Dryden, 2002). With people for whom putting things off creates stress, coaching can help these individuals to challenge unhelpful beliefs relating to the procrastination, e.g. 'I can do this tomorrow' or 'This is too boring', and develop more helpful behaviours. As a result these individuals are better equipped to reduce their procrastination and decrease any stress that does emerge by putting things off.

So far this discussion has only focused on individuals and stress but it is also possible that coaching could help to identify and change organizational stressors. For example, if key personnel are coached they may want to focus on strategies for changing organizational issues.

Research Studies on Coaching and Stress

As stated previously there is a lack of research investigating coaching and stress (Gyllensten and Palmer, 2005a). Nevertheless, a number of case studies highlight the reduction of stress as one of the benefits of coaching. Moreover, a small number of qualitative and quantitative studies have investigated stress as one of the factors upon which coaching may have an impact.

Case studies that have found that coaching reduced the clients' stress levels have been reported by Ascentia (2005), Hearn (2001), Marotta (1999), and Palmer, Cooper, and Thomas (2003). A case study using a multimodal approach which describes executive coaching with a female senior executive is presented by Richard (1999). The coaching took place over ten months during which the executive was responsible for major changes within the organization. Problems were assessed and discussed within the modalities of behaviour, affect, sensation, imagery, cognition, interpersonal and drug/biology domains. Within this model, outlined by Richard (1999), the coach assesses these seven dimensions and consequently plans cognitive-behavioural interventions within each modality. According to the client, the coaching helped her to cope with the stress and demands at work, and she reported improved relationships outside work. A number of different interventions and modalities were used, including: modifying cognitive responses, seeking support from a manager, learning strategies for dealing with problem employees, and developing time charts. These case studies highlight that coaching can be useful in reducing stress although this was not necessarily the only, or main, focus of the coaching.

Wales (2003) conducted a qualitative study exploring managers' experiences of coaching. The coaching was used as a development tool and was tailored to each individual's needs and goals. The data were analysed using a phenomenological approach and 'stress management' and 'work/life balance' were two of the themes that emerged. Many of the participants reported that they were experiencing high levels of stress at the start of the coaching. However, after the coaching the managers reported feeling calmer, more tolerant, less angry and more able to deal with pressures from work and personal life. According to Wales (2003) the coaching provided a safe environment where the managers could discuss their anxieties, identify coping skills, and try different behaviours. Moreover, some coaches encouraged discussions regarding causes of stress, and stress-reducing techniques. The managers also experienced an improved ability to be proactive in the management of the different roles in life. They reported taking more ownership of the decisions affecting themselves and their families.

Another study combined quantitative and qualitative methods to investigate the effects of coaching in a group of Executive Directors (CompassPoint Nonprofit Services, 2003). The most common personal goal for the participants was improving their effectiveness in dealing with work/life balance; the fourth most common goal was reducing stress. Three survey items related to perceived levels of work stress and burnout were included and scored, but there were no significant changes between the baseline test and the final post-coaching test on these items. Despite the lack of statistical differences in the survey results it was reported, in the qualitative part of the study, that coaching in fact helped several of the participants to reduce stress and burnout. They indicated that coaching had helped them to reduce their stress by encouraging them to take time regularly for themselves and by highlighting the importance of self-care. Moreover, it was found that, following the coaching, the participants felt better equipped to cope with any future feelings of burnout. Overall, the participants reported being very satisfied with their coaching experience with a mean of 4.6 on a five-point Likert-scale (CompassPoint Nonprofit Services, 2003). Interestingly, the qualitative research appears to suggest that coaching is useful in the reduction of stress whereas the quantitative part of the CompassPoint Nonprofit Services' (2003) study does not support this suggestion. The authors pointed out that work-related stress and burnout are complex processes affected by many different factors.

The effects of cognitive, behavioural and cognitive-behavioural coaching approaches were investigated in a quantitative study conducted by Grant (2001b). The sample consisted of students and it was reported that all three coaching approaches significantly reduced test anxiety. Changes in levels of depression, anxiety and stress were also investigated and only the cognitive coaching was found to significantly reduce depression and anxiety. Levels of depression, anxiety and stress were not significantly reduced in the behavioural and cognitive-behavioural coaching. In addition, Grant (2003) conducted a further study that evaluated the effects of life coaching upon goal attainment, meta-cognition, depression, anxiety and stress in a sample of post-graduate students. The coaching was based on cognitive behavioural theory and solution-focused principles. Interestingly, although mental health was not targeted in the programme Grant (2003) found that levels of depression, anxiety and stress were significantly reduced post coaching. Improved quality of life and goal attainment were further benefits of coaching. In view of these results Grant (2003) suggests that future research should investigate the usefulness of life coaching in the enhancement of wellbeing.

These studies show mixed findings regarding coaching and stress. The case studies report that coaching helped to reduce stress, although this was not necessarily the focus of the coaching. The qualitative studies found that coaching helped to reduce stress (Wales, 2003; CompassPoint Nonprofit Services, 2003) whereas the questionnaire data showed that stress was not reduced in CompassPoint Nonprofit Service's (2003) study. However, Grant (2003) found that stress was reduced despite the fact that it was not targeted in the coaching. Thus, it could be suggested that Grant's qualitative studies support the notion that coaching can be useful in the reduction of stress in an indirect manner.

One Case: A Study Investigating Coaching and Stress

The following section will outline the findings from a study investigating coaching and stress. This section will outline a summary of all three parts of the study, a more detailed account of each of the parts have been published elsewhere (Gyllensten and Palmer, 2005b, 2005c, 2006). The aim of the study was to investigate whether coaching could help to reduce perceived stress in the workplace. The research study consisted of three parts.

Part I

Part I of the study measured stress before and after coaching comparing a coaching group ($N = 16$) and a control group ($N = 15$) in a sample of employees from a UK financial organization. The coaching group received an average number of four coaching sessions. The coaching intervention did not follow a specific protocol; rather, it was focused on the specific issues the coachees wanted to focus on. An important part of the coaching was reflective listening. The GROW model (Whitmore, 1992) was used. Various techniques were used including affirmation cards, imagery exercises, cognitive restructuring and assertiveness training. The control group did not receive any intervention. Stress was measured by the means of a valid and reliable stress questionnaire, the Depression Anxiety and Stress Scales (DASS)–21 (Lovibond and Lovibond, 1995). Pre-coaching the coaching group and the control group reported similar levels of depression, anxiety and stress. Post-coaching levels of anxiety and stress had decreased more in the coaching group

Table 8.1 Summary of participants' DASS scores after coaching.

	Depression Max. = 42		Anxiety Max. = 42		Stress Max. = 42	
	Mean	S.D.	Mean	S.D.	Mean	S.D.
Coaching group N = 16	7.50	8.18	2.63	3.63	9.25	8.70
Control group N = 15	6.80	5.39	4.80	5.44	12.13	9.99
Total N = 31	7.16	6.87	3.68	4.64	10.65	8.98

compared to the control group, and were lower in the coaching group compared to the control group (see Table 8.1). Nevertheless, these differences were not significant when mixed ANOVAs (used to test significant differences between groups, pre- and post-coaching) were performed. Moreover, levels of depression had decreased more in the control group compared to the coaching group. In summary, the results indicated that the coaching did not significantly reduce stress. However, individuals in the coaching group reported high levels of coaching effectiveness with a mean score of 6.43 on a seven-point Likert-scale. Thus, the study did not find statistical differences in the levels of stress between the coaching and control group but the participants reported that they found the coaching highly effective. It would have been useful to learn more about in what way the coaching had been effective.

Part II

Part II of the study investigated the relationship between coaching and stress. Employees from the UK finance organization and from a Scandinavian telecommunications organization participated (N = 103). The participants in the coaching group received an average number of four coaching sessions. Stress levels were measured in a coaching group and control group (again using the DASS–21) after the first group had received coaching. Both groups reported similar levels of depression, anxiety and stress. Multiple regression analyses showed that participation in coaching did not have a relationship with lower stress levels. However, participants once again reported high levels of coaching effectiveness with a mean score of 5.64.

Part III

A qualitative methodology was used for Part III of the study. Employees from the two participating organizations were interviewed about their experiences of coaching ($N = 9$). The interviews were analysed by using the Interpretative Phenomenological Analysis method (Smith and Osborn, 2004) and four main themes emerged. 'Management of stress' was identified as a main theme and coaching was found to help participants reduce stress indirectly by improving their confidence, saying 'no' to extra work, and by improving problem-solving skills. Participants reported that their ability to cope with stress was improved by coaching and many would consider using coaching to deal with future stress problems. Nevertheless, the study also found that coaching also had the potential to cause stress by being perceived as 'a waste of time' and as being unproductive by failing to lead to any action. 'The coaching relationship' was a further main theme. The relationship was valued by participants and viewed as very important for effective coaching. Important aspects of the relationship were trust and transparency. Another main theme was 'confidence'. Coaching helped to improve confidence and related benefits included improved job performance, more assertive behaviour, and benefits outside of the workplace. Finally, 'coaching = investment in staff' was identified as a main theme. The fact that the organization provided coaching was viewed as a sign that the employer cared for and valued their employees.

Summary of the Research Study

The three parts of the study produced mixed different findings. Part I found that coaching did not significantly reduce stress and Part II found that participation in coaching was not associated with lower levels of stress. However, one of the findings from Part III was that coaching did reduce stress indirectly. A possible explanation for this discrepancy is that the participants who were interviewed in Part III may have represented a minority of individuals who found that coaching was useful in reducing stress. Other coaching clients may not have reported such positive experiences regarding coaching and stress. Another explanation may be that larger numbers of participants were needed in order to find significant differences between the groups in Part I of the study. Indeed, the tests in Part I did not have a sufficient number of participants in order to have a power of 0.80 (this being the minimum level of power recommended according to Clark-Carter and Marks (2004). Thus, the lack of power is an important limitation of the study. Nevertheless, high levels of coaching effectiveness were reported by participants in both Parts I and II of the study. Thus, the coaching could have been effective at tackling the specific issues targeted in coaching while failing to significantly reduce levels of stress.

Future Research

As workplace stress is a serious problem and the practice of coaching is spreading, it is possible that there will be a growing interest in using coaching to tackle stress. If this is the case it is important that further research is conducted in order to investigate the effectiveness of coaching. Both naturalistic studies, investigating the effectiveness of coaching as it is practised in the workplace, and randomized controlled trials with larger sample sizes, are needed. Grant (2003) found that cognitive-behavioural and solution-focused life coaching improved mental health and it would be useful to investigate the effectiveness of specific coaching approaches in reducing workplace stress.

It is also important that further qualitative studies are conducted as they often have the potential to capture the richness of the coaching experience. This research could investigate which aspects of the coaching were useful, and at what points, in terms of alleviating stress and developing better stress prevention and response strategies in people. In addition, future research could also investigate the discrepancy between qualitative and quantitative approaches, found both in the current study and in previous research.

Conclusion

This chapter has addressed the topic of coaching and stress, and the idea that coaching could be useful in tackling stress. There is little research focusing on this topic; nevertheless, a few research studies and case studies have reported that coaching was useful in reducing stress. Moreover, this chapter has presented research where the coaching did not necessarily focus on reducing stress. It is likely that coaching specifically targeted at reducing the perception of stress is the most effective intervention if stress is the main issue. Finally, it is important to remember that stress is a complex and dynamic phenomenon and many factors, other than coaching, can influence individuals' levels of perceived stress. Indeed, different interventions, focusing both on the individual and on the organization, are needed in order to tackle this serious problem.

References

Ascentia. (2005). Case studies. *International Journal of Evidence Based Coaching and Mentoring*, 3(1).

Busch, C., and Steinmetz, B. (2002). Stress management and management. *Gruppdynamic und Organizationsberatung*, 33, 385–401.

Chartered Institute of Personnel and Development (CIPD) (2004). Training and development 2004. Retrieved 1 September, 2005, from http://www.cipd.co.uk.

Clark-Carter, D., and Marks, D. F. (2004). Intervention studies: design and analysis. In D. F. Marks and L. Yardley (Eds.), *Research methods for clinical and health psychology* (pp. 145–165). London: Sage.

CompassPoint Nonprofit Services. (2003). Executive coaching project: Evaluation of findings. Retrieved 28 January, 2005, from *www.compasspoint.org*

Cooper, C. L., Dewe, P. J., and O'Driscoll, M. P. (2001). Organizational stress: A review and critique of theory, research and applications. London: Sage.

Employment and Social Affairs. (1999). *Health and safety at work: Guidance on work related stress – Spice of life – or kiss of death?* Luxembourg: European Commission.

Grant, A. M. (2001a). Towards a psychology of coaching. Retrieved 12 May, 2003, from *www.psych.usyd.edu.au*.

Grant, A. M. (2001b). *Coaching for enhanced performance: Comparing cognitive and behavioural approaches to coaching.* Paper presented at the 3rd International Spearman Seminar: Extending Intelligence: Enhancement and new constructs, Sydney.

Grant, A. M. (2003). The impact of life coaching on goal attainment, metacognition and mental health. *Social Behaviour and Personality*, 31, 253–264.

Gyllensten, K., and Palmer, S. (2005a). Can coaching reduce workplace stress? *The Coaching Psychologist*, 1, 15–17.

Gyllensten, K., and Palmer, S. (2005b). Can coaching reduce workplace stress? A quasi-experimental study. *International Journal of Evidence Based Coaching and Mentoring*, 3(2), 75–87.

Gyllensten, K., and Palmer, S. (2005c). The relationship between coaching and workplace stress: A correlational study. *International Journal of Health Promotion and Education*, 43, 97–103.

Gyllensten, K., and Palmer, S. (2006). Experiences of coaching and stress in the workplace: An interpretative phenomenological analysis. *International Coaching Psychology Review*, 1, 86–97.

Health and Safety Executive (HSE). (2001). *Tackling work-related stress: A manager's guide to improving and maintaining employee health and well-being.* Sudbury: HSE Books.

Hearn, W. (2001). The role of coaching in stress management. *Stress News*, 13(2), 15–17.

Jones, J. D. (1996). Executive coaches. *Mississippi Business Journal*, 18, 5–7.

Jones, J. R., Huxtable, C. S., and Hodgson, J. T. (2004). *Self-reported work-related illness in 2003/2004: Results from the labour force survey.* Sudbury: HSE Books.

Kilburg, R. R. (1996). Executive coaching as and emerging competency in the practice of consultation. *Consulting Psychology Journal: Practice and Research*, 48, 59–60.

Lovibond, P. F., and Lovibond, S. H. (1995). *Manual for the depression anxiety stress scales*. Sydney: Psychology Foundation.

Mangell, L., and Neld, M. (2003). Coaching and mentoring in Sweden. *The International Journal of Mentoring and Coaching*, 1(1).

Marotta, P. (1999). Power-coaching for executive women. *Independent Practitioner*, summer.

Meyer, J. L. (2003). Coaching and counselling psychology in organizational psychology. In M. J. Schabraq, J. A. M. Winnburst, and C. L. Cooper (Eds.), *The handbook of work and health psychology* (pp. 569–583). Chichester, UK: John Wiley & Sons, Ltd.

National Institute for Occupational Safety and Health. (1999). Stress. Retrieved 11 April, 2003, from http://www.cdc.gov/niosh.

Neenan, M., and Dryden, W. (2002). *Life coaching: A cognitive behavioural approach*. Hove, UK: Brunner-Routledge.

Occupational Safety and Health Service. (2003). Healthy work: Managing stress in the workplace. Retrieved 1 September, 2005, from www.osh.dol.govt.nz/order/catalogue/3.shtml.

Palmer, S., Cooper, C., and Thomas, K. (2003). *Creating a balance: Managing stress*. London: The British Library.

Palmer, S., and Whybrow, A. (2005). The proposal to establish a special group in coaching psychology. *The Coaching Psychologist*, 1, 5–11.

Palmer, S., Cooper, C., and Thomas, K. (2004). A model of work stress to underpin the Health and Safety Executive advice for tackling work-related stress and stress risk assessments. *Counselling at Work*, winter, 2–5.

Palmer, S., Tubbs, I., and Whybrow, A. (2003). Health coaching to facilitate the promotion of healthy behaviour and achievement of health-related goals. *International Journal of Health Promotion and Education*, 41, 91–93.

Richard, J. T. (1999). Multimodal therapy a useful model for the executive coach. *Consulting Psychology Journal: Practice and Research*, 51, 24–30.

Smith, J. A., and Osborn, M. (2004). Interpretative phenomenological analysis. In G. M. Breakwell (Ed.). *Doing social psychology research* (pp. 229–254). Oxford: Blackwell.

Wales, S. (2003). Why coaching? *Journal of Change Management*, 3, 275–282.

Whitmore, J. (1992). *Coaching for performance*. London: Nicholas Brealey.

Willis, P. (ND). Coaching worked for Radio 4's 'Ruth', but is personal coaching for stress the right approach for everyone. Retrieved 1 September, 2005, from http://www.lauriate.com/Documents/Personalcoachingforstress.pdf.

Zeus, P., and Skiffington, S. (2003). *The complete guide to coaching at work*. New York: McGraw-Hill.

9 Coaching for Wisdom: Enabling Wise Decisions

Peter Webb

The Purpose of Coaching

What the world needs now . . . is wise leadership! Now, more than ever, our collective fate rests in the hands of leaders who decide and act either wisely or foolishly. Masterful coaching has the potential to both enable and ennoble leaders for our sustainable common good.

Wisdom, according to the late American historian Barbara Tuchman (1984), is 'the exercise of judgment acting on experience, common sense and available information' (p. 4). Anything less is 'folly'. And folly in leadership is as pervasive now as it ever was. 'Know my son, with how little wisdom the world is governed,' advised Count Axel Oxenstierna, Chancellor of Sweden, 1632–1644, during the Thirty Years' War (Tuchman, 1984, p. 8).

There is no doubt we want our leaders to have more rather than less wisdom when it comes to making difficult decisions affecting our lives. But how do we know who is wise and what a wise decision is? In the rapidly changing environment of both commercial and government enterprises what seems a wise thing to do today can easily be deemed folly over time, and often within a very short time.

Business leaders, particularly, must make operational and moral decisions in the face of unprecedented complexity. Expertise, intelligence and experience are necessary but no longer sufficient to enable leaders to make far-reaching (and potentially catastrophic) decisions in a world of permanent incompleteness. The ultimate consequences of the continued 'march of folly' are now too great to ignore. What is needed is

The Philosophy and Practice of Coaching: Insights and Issues for a New Era.
Edited by David B. Drake, Diane Brennan and Kim Gørtz.
© 2008 John Wiley & Sons, Ltd.

a way to bring reason, compassion and creativity together to facilitate decisions for the common good, not just for private gain or unbalanced small group interests. The way to do this is through the intentional activation of wisdom in leaders.

Empirical studies show the domain of wisdom overlaps with intelligence, personality and adult development. Yet, like EQ (emotional intelligence), certain components of wisdom appear open to improvement through interventions such as coaching.

Kilburg (2000, p. 228) first made the claim that 'executive coaching, when done well, deliberately facilitates the emergence of wisdom in clients'. This was the starting point for my own discoveries about coaching and wisdom. 'Executive coaching may best be considered as a pre-eminent learning framework for inspiring leaders to apply wisdom decision-making processes and tolerance of complexity through chaordic systems to achieve a common good' (Webb, 2005, p. 92). Kilburg (2006) continues to make the same assertion (albeit with somewhat less confidence) that 'perhaps we can improve the odds that individual executives and dedicated executive groups will be better able to think, feel, and act wisely more routinely' (pp. 329–330). If it is possible to coach for wisdom, then surely coaching can have no higher purpose than to elicit wisdom-related performance in leaders worldwide.

The Nature of Wisdom

Wisdom is an ancient topic. Yet the study of wisdom in psychology is quite recent. 'The subject is complex and elusive,' noted Birren and Fisher (1990) in the first compilation of psychological thought on wisdom, 'but one that clearly seems worthwhile to pursue' (p. 330).

The emerging domain of wisdom has four major constructs of relevance to coaching:

(1) Wisdom as a system of expert knowledge (the 'Berlin wisdom paradigm', e.g., Kunzmann and Baltes, 2005).
(2) Wisdom as a property of a person (e.g., Ardelt, 2005).
(3) Wisdom as interaction between person, task and situation (e.g., Sternberg, 2005a).
(4) Wisdom as a 'mapping' process (Kilburg, 2006).

Arising from research into ageing at the Max Planck Institute for Human Development and Education in Berlin, Baltes and Smith (1990) defined wisdom as 'expert-level knowledge in the fundamental pragmatics of life' (p. 95). Smith, Staudinger, and Baltes (1994) described five dimensions of wisdom-related knowledge:

(1) *Rich factual knowledge*: general and specific knowledge about the conditions of life and its variations.
(2) *Rich procedural knowledge*: general and specific knowledge about strategies of judgement and advice concerning matters of life.
(3) *Lifespan contextualism*: knowledge about the contents of life and their temporal (developmental) relations.
(4) *Value relativism*: knowledge about differences in values, goals and priorities.
(5) *Uncertainty*: knowledge about the relative indeterminacy and unpredictability of life and ways to manage it.

These five dimensions are considered as criteria for measuring 'wisdom-related performance' in individuals using 'think aloud' protocols in response to difficult dilemmas in life. Using this approach, Baltes and his colleagues have been able to determine that wisdom-related performance is not necessarily age-dependent (one can see foolish 'baby boomers' and wise 'Gen Y's'!). Performance increases sharply during adolescence and young adulthood, but on average remains relatively stable throughout life with peak performance more likely in the 50 to 60 age group (Staudinger, 1999).

Wisdom seems to overlap IQ and EQ, but it is a unique dimension according to Staudinger, Lopez, and Baltes (1997). They found 40% of the variance in wisdom-related performance could be predicted by measures of intelligence, personality and their interface. But intelligence alone contributed only 2% of the variance, as did measures of personality alone. While there seemed to be a coordinative aspect of wisdom-related performance between intelligence and personality, 15% of the variance came uniquely from the 'intelligence–personality' interface (specifically cognitive style and creativity). An additional 22% of the variance came from parallel measures of wisdom-related performance using the five wisdom criteria.

In the Berlin wisdom paradigm, wisdom is described as a 'metaheuristic' – a high-level system of knowledge and frameworks – that helps individuals make difficult decisions about the conduct and meaning of life. It includes knowledge about the limits of knowledge and the uncertainties of the world – a knowledge with extraordinary scope, depth, measure and balance – and is used for the good or wellbeing of oneself and others; and while it is difficult to achieve and specify, it is a perfect synergy of mind and character, knowledge and virtue and it is easily recognized in others (Baltes and Staudinger, 2000).

However, recognizing wisdom in others presumes that there are characteristics that reside within the person. Wisdom has traditionally been conceptualized as an idealized state or an endpoint of adult development. Jung (1964) described a dream of being a wise old woman or a wise old man and Erikson (1950) defined wisdom as the eighth stage of psychosocial development. Wisdom may be the ultimate expression of behavioural complexity within an individual, the 'fifth order of mind' according to Kegan (1994), and reached by very few adults. Yet, Staudinger (1999), in suggesting that wisdom-related performance is relatively stable throughout the lifespan, opens up the possibility that everyone may posses more or less 'wisdom resources'. In much the same way, Goleman (2001) utilizes the idea of 'emotional intelligence competencies' to explain the situational activation of EQ in individuals.

People with a recognized high level of wisdom might reasonably be expected to have developed positive personality characteristics, such as maturity, integrity, and generativity, and to have overcome negative personality characteristics such as neuroticism or self-centredness. Ardelt (2003) measures wisdom by assessing the attributes and personality characteristics of wise individuals. She identifies the simultaneous presence of three dimensions of personality as both necessary and sufficient for a person to be considered wise:

(1) The *cognitive* dimension: a desire to know the truth and attain a deeper understanding of life, including knowledge and acceptance of the positive and negative aspects of human nature, of the inherent limits of knowledge, and of life's unpredictability and uncertainties.

(2) The *reflective* component: self-examination, self-awareness, self-insight and the ability to look at phenomena and events from different perspectives.

(3) The *affective* component: sympathetic and compassionate love for others.

Surveys have been developed to measure similar person-centred characteristics of wisdom such as the SAWS (Self-Assessed Wisdom Scale) (Webster, 2003), the Servant Leadership Questionnaire (Barbuto and Wheeler, 2006), and the Wisdom Development Scale (Brown and Greene, 2006), but Ardelt's 3D-WS (Three Dimensional Wisdom Scale) is so far the most promising, reliable and valid instrument for measuring latent variable wisdom (Ardelt, 2003).

In contrast, Sternberg (2005a) suggests that wisdom may emerge as a combination of both person characteristics and decision-making style within the particular situational context. Wise decision making is in the balance – in knowing what to do on what task in what situation and against what timeframe. From the PACE (Psychology of Abilities, Competencies, and Expertise) Center at Yale University, Sternberg (2005) has defined wisdom as 'in large part a decision to use one's intelligence, creativity, and experience for a common good' (p. 37).

Sternberg's 'balance theory of wisdom' (1998) is based on tacit knowledge which refers to 'knowing how' rather than 'knowing what'. Tacit knowledge is an aspect of practical intelligence that helps individuals solve everyday problems by utilizing knowledge gained from experience. As expected, tacit knowledge increases with experience (more so with how the experience is used rather than the amount), correlates only modestly, if at all, with IQ and personality, and it provides significant prediction of job performance beyond conventional IQ (Sternberg, 2003). The 'balance theory' defines wisdom as 'the application of tacit knowledge as mediated by values toward the goal of achieving a common good (a) through a balance among multiple intrapersonal, interpersonal, and extrapersonal interests and (b) in order to achieve a balance among responses to environmental contexts: adaptation to existing environmental contexts, shaping of existing environmental contexts, and selection of new environmental contexts' (Sternberg, 1998, p. 353).

Wise leadership however, is a special case and goes beyond the mere balance of competing interests and responses, according to Sternberg's (2005a) WICS (Wisdom, Intelligence, Creativity Synthesized) model of leadership. It must involve synthesizing intelligence (academic and practical/tacit), creativity (skills and attitudes), and wisdom (balancing interests and responses, moderated by values, in pursuit of a common good) to achieve wise outcomes for all possible stakeholders.

Similarly, Kilburg (2006) makes the claim that wisdom in leadership, particularly in executives of large commercial and government enterprises, is a special case. Taking a lead from the Berlin wisdom paradigm he defines executive wisdom as 'an expert system in the fundamental pragmatics of organized human life' (p. 47). He suggests a methodology called 'wisdom mapping' for encouraging the emergence of wisdom in executive decision making. Any situation faced by the leader is mapped onto a pathway that starts with the initial story and conditions, and then follows six areas of awareness:

(1) *Self-awareness*: the individual executive.
(2) *Family awareness*: the person's nuclear and families of origin.

(3) *Group awareness*: the group with whom he or she works most closely.
(4) *Organization awareness*: the organization(s) that the executive leads.
(5) *Situational awareness*: the complex situation that the leader faces at any point in time.
(6) *Moral and ethical awareness*: the moral and value lenses that often unconsciously influence the behaviour of the leader.

'When all six of these types of awareness illuminate the daily performance of a leader, he or she has the highest probability of exercising Executive Wisdom' (Kilburg, 2006, p. 141). Executive wisdom emerges as a result of *discernment* (a combination of rational and intuitive perception), *decision making* (time frame, perspective and planning), and *action* (implementation) linked dynamically and interactively with each other through *experience, feedback* and *evaluation* (Kilburg, 2006).

Enhancing Wisdom

There are three ways in which wisdom-performance may be enhanced:

(1) Life experience (e.g., Brugman, 2006);
(2) Teaching skills and ways of thinking (e.g., Sternberg, 2001a); and
(3) Short-term interventions (e.g., Glück and Baltes, 2006).

Wisdom is not merely the product of age but it does seem to emerge in the course of learning from life (Brugman, 2006). Certain experiences can lead to the cumulative development of wisdom such as being a parent or a mentor, living through individual and historical life events, reaching a level of equanimity in the face of the end of life, as well as professional training. For example, clinical psychologists were found to perform at least as well as 'wise persons' in wisdom-performance experiments (Smith, Staudinger, and Baltes, 1994; Baltes, Staudinger, Maercker, and Smith, 1995).

Can wisdom be taught? Sternberg (2001a, 2001b) has developed a curriculum for teaching wisdom to sixth-grade children. His course on wisdom 'encourages students to develop their own values while understanding multiple points of view', and 'can be made part of any subject matter, because wisdom is a way of looking at the world' (Sternberg, 2002, p. B.20). He teaches students the usefulness of *interdependence*: how to recognize and *balance* their own interests, those of other people, and of institutions; that the *means* by which the end is obtained matters, not just the end; the roles of *adaptation, shaping* and *selection,* and how to *balance* them; how to form, critique and integrate their own *values* in their thinking; and the importance of *inoculation* against the pressures of unbalanced self-interest and small group interest (Sternberg, 2001a, p. 238).

Social collaboration appears to enhance wisdom. Pascual-Leone (2000) acknowledges the role of mentors in facilitating the 'external path' to wisdom (for mentors, read 'coaches'). Staudinger and Baltes (1996) found that participants who discussed life problems with a significant other person and then reflected on the conversation before responding outperformed a standard-instruction control group in wisdom-performance. However, an equal effect was found in participants who only imagined discussing the problem with a significant other person. In the 'philosopher's dream' intervention, participants who were instructed to imagine travelling to various regions of the world on a cloud and to reflect on the differences in cultures and peoples before responding to wisdom tasks showed higher levels of wisdom-performance than a control group (Böhmig-Krumhaar, Staudinger, and Baltes (2002), reported in Glück and Baltes (2006, p. 680)).

This suggests that wisdom-related knowledge may be latent in people until activated by a wisdom-task or when faced with difficult life problems. Asking the question, 'try to give a wise response' to a difficult life dilemma seemed to enhance wisdom-performance, particularly in those who had high wisdom resources to begin with (crystallized intelligence, life experience, and the personality-interface factor 'Self-regulation and openness toward growth'). However, for those who were low on all three wisdom resources, asking the question caused a decrease in their wisdom-performance (Glück and Baltes, 2006).

Similarly, Kilburg (2006, p. 62) asks executives (who might reasonably be expected to have at least a moderate level of wisdom resources) a series of questions to support the emergence of wisdom such as, 'What is the wisest thing you have ever done as a person or as a professional? If you are a leader in an organization, what is the wisest decision or action you have ever taken? What made the decision or action wise? When and how did you know it was wise? What criteria did you use to judge its merits?'

Using questions *intentionally* to activate the individual's conceptions of personal wisdom depends on their developmental preparedness, their level of engagement with the coach, and the particular outcomes expected of the coaching assignment. If however, coaching is a deliberate intervention to move the client along 'the path of progressive development' (Kilburg, 2001, pp. 256–257) toward some higher level of functioning as a person, and particularly as a leader, for the achievement of agreed goals (e.g., O'Neill, 2000; Peltier, 2001; Greene and Grant, 2003), then eliciting wisdom resources is consistent with the practice of coaching.

Coaching for Wisdom

I define coaching as an intentional dialogue between a leader in an organization and a coach who uses a wide variety of behavioural techniques and methods to shape a *journey* from one place of identity and meaning to another place – from which the leader can more *wisely* manage his or her own life and the life of the organization.

Following from Lenhardt (2004), I conceptualize the journey as a cyclical model of coaching narrative which transitions from what is *apparent* (and evident) to what is *potential* (and discoverable), and back again (Figure 9.1). There are two levels of meaning in what is apparent:

(1) The *environment*, consisting of the structures and systems through which the individual operates.
(2) *Behaviour*, which involves communication methods, relationship management and managerial style.

The next three levels of meaning represent potential for discovery:

(3) *Attitudes,* which calls into question the individual's beliefs and values, those that govern his or her life, work, relationships, whether to trust or not to trust, and how he or she sees the world.

Figure 9.1 The coaching journey.

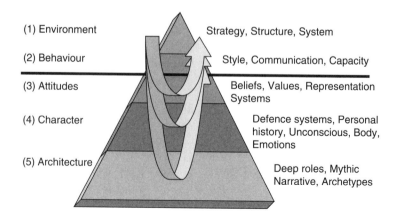

(4)   *Character*, as an aspect of personality, where the person's defences and unconscious beliefs, developed over their life history, reside.
(5)   *Architecture*, which constitutes the most intimate development of the person, beyond the defensive and blocking systems, to the essential nature of human consciousness or 'spirit', and the recognition of mythic narratives and archetypes that give deep insight to 'life, the universe and everything' (Webb, 2006).

In order to elicit wisdom-thinking, wisdom-decision-making and wisdom-performance I use an intentional coaching process – following Drake's (2007) narrative coaching model – which I call the FORMAT model of coaching for wisdom (Figure 9.2). This is a way of conceptualizing the coaching journey from what is apparent for the client to what is potential and back again. FORMAT stands for: Framework – Observations – Reflections – Meaning – Actions – Test.
    Each coaching session takes the following course:

(1)   *Framework*: This is the most visibly apparent domain of the client's experience – the context, the current conditions he or she faces at the moment. The key question here is, 'What's the story?' The next stage is:
(2)   *Observations*: What is the client seeing in the present situation? What takes their attention? What behaviours are they aware of in themselves and others? The key question is, 'What do you notice?' Next is:
(3)   *Reflections*: This is the transition space between what is external and apparent and what is internal and potential. Now the client explores their own awareness and interpretation of things at the attitudes level of meaning. The key question is, 'What do you value, and why?' Next is:
(4)   *Meaning*: The most profound realizations and understandings take place at the levels of character and architecture. The client is encouraged to review his or her story from different perspectives. The use of myths and archetypes can help connect the client with their deepest sense of identity. Here is the Socratic question, 'What is truth (in this situation)?' This is where the client's latent wisdom resources are most likely to be aroused. The next stage is:
(5)   *Actions*: To retrieve value from these understandings the client must contemplate potential actions – what might it be possible to do about the situation. This is transitioning back to the 'real world' and the key question is, 'What are your options?' The final stage is:

(6)   *Test*: Now it is time to 'prototype' the suggested action steps – to consider the practical implications of each action and what obstacles might need to be overcome. The key question is, 'Which of these actions will work?'

At the top of the cycle the client goes back into the *Framework* of their story with new insights and actions. And this, in turn, draws the dialogue back into observations and reflections for deeper understanding of meaning. Depending on the nature of the relationship between the coach and the client, both may be prepared to spend longer periods of time at the deeper levels before returning to the 'apparent world' with fresh insights and realizations (see Figure 9.2).

When conducted well with clients who are ready, I have seen a kind of personal 'wisdom compass' emerge from this process, partly from the individual's 'implicit theories of wisdom' (Bluck and Glück, 2005), but also as a co-constructed (between coach and client) practical template for how to make difficult decisions in the face of uncertainty.

For example, Allen, a regional general manager for a major Australian bank was facing an unusual dilemma. He had been asked to accept either the position of Head of Retail Banking, or the position of Head of Investment Banking. Both positions were equally attractive, and he was free to choose either one! Should he seek to develop his leadership skills by taking the retail banking role? Or should he stay in the invest-

Figure 9.2   The FORMAT model of coaching for wisdom.

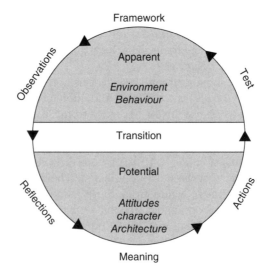

ment banking line of service from where he derived his expertise? Allen had undertaken a lot of leadership training and personal development up to this point in his professional life so he had a highly intelligent and functional grasp of career-critical decision making. But he simply could not make up his mind on this one.

Following the FORMAT model, our coaching narrative spent a lot of time in the *Meaning* area. From here Allen developed a kind of 'checklist' of *Actions* derived from recalling how he had made successful decisions 'with no right answers' in the past. The list included things like 'I try to see the whole rather than the parts', 'core values (what is important to me)', 'I am prepared to back myself, and at the same time ask, am I being honest with myself?' He agreed to *Test* these actions with reference to other strategic decisions he was making at the time. At one of our follow-up sessions Allen *Observed* that these criteria seemed to suit his decision-making style quite well but he *Reflected* that he was no closer to making a decision on which position to take. However, in the *Meaning* stage Allen embedded these components into a deeply resonant story which we co-constructed about being a winemaker. This was the key. Allen subsequently made the decision to take up the Head of Investment Banking and not long afterwards he found that this position gave him greater scope than he had foreseen to exercise the leadership skills he sought. For Allen this was a wise decision.

Bob was a long-serving business development manager for an international manufacturing firm. The company was being acquired by a competitor and he was faced with three options. Should he stay with the company and almost certainly have to relocate his family from Australia to South Africa? Should he breach his contract and negotiate a similar position with the takeover company? Or should he look for another job altogether? Each decision carried long-term consequences for his career and for his family. Acting too soon might deny some of the emerging possibilities. Waiting too long could risk losing any certainty. Bob's decision was further complicated by his ambition to pursue a general manager role. As part of the coaching journey, Bob produced a drawing which summarized the components of 'how to make a wise decision' for him. He drew three concentric circles. In the middle he placed his core value, 'God'. Around the next circle he placed important *interests*: 'family focus', 'shared success', 'spiritual wellspring', 'healthy body and mind'. And in the outer circle he placed the *responses* available to him such as, 'tolerance', 'servant heart', 'accounting skills', 'industry knowledge', 'risk–reward', 'church community'. It occurred to me that Bob had re-created Sternberg's (1998) balance model but with a circumplex layout! He went on to make a successful decision about what to do with his career during a tumultuous takeover and I recognized his drawing as a new way to conceptualize the use and application of wisdom resources (see Figure 9.3).

Drawing from Sternberg (2005b), Kunzmann and Baltes (2005), Kilburg (2006) and Ardelt (2004), I define *wisdom in leadership* as:

(a) the application of the five wisdom criteria of the Berlin wisdom paradigm, drawing from tacit knowledge and personality characteristics (cognitive, reflective and affective),
(b) through the acknowledgement of core values,
(c) balancing the interests of self, stakeholders and the organizational community,
(d) by adapting, shaping or selecting appropriate responses,
(e) in order to achieve a sustainable common good.

Furthermore, coaching to elicit wisdom resources directs the attention of the client to the processes of discernment, decision making and action, while facilitating reflection and insight through experience, feedback and evaluation (see Figure 9.3).

The next steps in my research are to assess wisdom-performance before and after coaching and against matched controls using a person-centred instrument such as Ardelt's (2003) 3D-WS together with more open-ended approaches as suggested by Kunzmann and Stange (2007). Contrary to Kilburg (2006) I believe wisdom resources reside in all of us to a greater or lesser degree. We resort to our own 'wisdom compass' to address the difficult and ambiguous life decisions for which there are no

Figure 9.3   A wisdom compass.

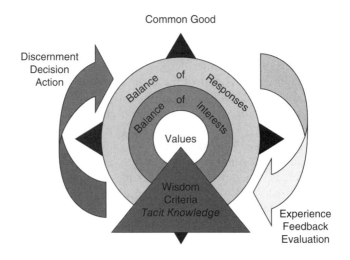

right answers. In this way, wisdom might be perceived as another kind of strategic decision-making tool, yet with far greater depth, range and meaning for positive human relationships within sustainable organizations. Asking the right questions at the right time can trigger the client's latent wisdom resources. This demands of coaches to both deliberately foster wise responses in their clients and to be wise themselves!

Ultimately, I believe the highest purpose for coaching in troubled times must be to make the leaders' implicit wisdom resources more explicit and to help them shape those resources into a personal 'compass' to make wise decisions in the service of a common good. The emerging field of wisdom in psychology suggests ways in which coaches can rise to that challenge. Our planetary survival may very well depend on it.

References

Ardelt, M. (2003). Empirical assessment of a three-dimensional wisdom scale. *Research on Aging*, 25(3), 275–324.

Ardelt, M. (2004). Wisdom as expert knowledge system: A critical review of a contemporary operationalization of an ancient concept. *Human Development*, 47(5), 257–285.

Ardelt, M. (2005). How wise people cope with crises and obstacles in life. *ReVision*, 28(1), 7–19.

Baltes, P. B., and Smith, J. (1990). The psychology of wisdom and its ontogenesis. In R. J. Sternberg (Ed.), *Wisdom: Its nature, origins, and development* (pp. 87–120). New York: Cambridge University Press.

Baltes, P. B., and Staudinger, U. M. (2000). A metaheuristic (pragmatic) to orchestrate mind and virtue toward excellence. *American Psychologist*, 55(1), 122–136.

Baltes, P. B., Staudinger, U. M., Maercker, A., and Smith, J. (1995). People nominated as wise: A comparative study of wisdom-related knowledge. *Psychology and Aging*, 10(2), 155–166.

Barbuto, Jr, J. E., and Wheeler, D. W. (2006). Scale development and construct clarification of servant leadership. *Group and Organization Management*, 31(3), 300–326.

Birren, J. E., and Fisher, L. M. (1990). The elements of wisdom: Overview and integration. In R. J. Sternberg (Ed.), *Wisdom: Its nature, origins, and development* (pp. 317–332). New York: Cambridge University Press.

Bluck, S., and Glück, J. (2005). From the inside out: People's implicit theories of wisdom. In R. J. Sternberg and J. Jordan (Eds.), *A handbook of wisdom: Psychological perspectives* (pp. 85–109). New York: Cambridge University Press.

Brown, S. C., and Greene, J. A. (2006). The wisdom development scale: Translating the conceptual to the concrete. *Journal of College Student Development*, 47(1), 1–19.

Brugman, G. (2006). Wisdom and aging. In J. E. Birren, K. W. Schaie, and R. P. Abeles (Eds.), *Handbook of the psychology of aging* (6th edn), (pp. 445–476). San Diego, CA: Academic Press.

Drake, D. B. (2007). The art of thinking narratively: Implications for coaching psychology and practice. *Australian Psychologist*, 42(4), 283–294.

Erikson, E. (1950). *Childhood and society*. New York: Norton.

Glück, J., and Baltes, P. B. (2006). Using the concept of wisdom to enhance the expression of wisdom knowledge: Not the philosopher's dream but differential effects of developmental preparedness. *Psychology and Aging*, 21(4), 679–690.

Goleman, D. (2001). An EI-based theory of performance. In C. Cherniss and D. Goleman (Eds.). *The emotionally intelligent workplace*. San Francisco: Jossey-Bass.

Greene, J., and Grant, A. M. (2003). *Solution-focused coaching: Managing people in a complex world*. Edinburgh Gate, UK: Pearson Education.

Jung, C. (1964). *Man and his symbols*. London: Aldus Books.

Kegan, R. (1994). *In over our heads: The mental demands of modern life*. Cambridge, MA: Harvard University Press.

Kilburg, R. R. (2000). *Executive coaching: Developing managerial wisdom in a world of chaos*. Washington, DC: American Psychological Association.

Kilburg, R. R. (2001). Facilitating intervention adherence in executive coaching: A model and methods. *Consulting Psychology Journal: Practice and Research*, 53(4), 251–267.

Kilburg, R. R. (2006). *Executive wisdom: Coaching and the emergence of virtuous leaders*. Washington, DC: American Psychological Association.

Kunzmann, U., and Baltes, P. B. (2005). The psychology of wisdom: Theoretical and empirical challenges. In R. J. Sternberg and J. Jordan (Eds.), *A handbook of wisdom: Psychological perspectives* (pp. 110–135). New York: Cambridge University Press.

Kunzmann, U., and Stange, A. (2007). Wisdom as a classical human strength: Psychological conceptualizations and empirical inquiry. In A. D. Ong and M. H. M. van Dulman (Eds.), *Oxford handbook of methods in positive psychology* (pp. 306–322). New York: Oxford University Press.

Lenhardt, V. (2004). *Coaching for meaning: The culture and practice of coaching and team building*. Basingstoke, UK: Palgrave Macmillan.

O'Neill, M. B. (2000). *Executive coaching with backbone and heart: A systems approach to engaging leaders with their challenges*. San Francisco: Jossey-Bass.

Pascual-Leone, J. (2000). Mental attention, consciousness, and the progressive emergence of wisdom. *Journal of Adult Development*, 7(4), 241–254.

Peltier, B. (2001). *The psychology of executive coaching: Theory and application*. New York: Brunner-Routledge.

Schwartz, B., and Sharpe, K. E. (2006). Practical wisdom: Aristotle meets positive psychology. *Journal of Happiness Studies*, 7, 377–395.

Smith, J., Staudinger, U. M., and Baltes, P. B. (1994). Occupational settings facilitating wisdom-related knowledge: The sample case of clinical psychologists. *Journal of Consulting and Clinical Psychology*, 62(5), 989–999.

Staudinger, U. M. (1999). Older and wiser? Integrating results on the relationship between age and wisdom-related performance. *International Journal of Behavioral Development*, 23(3), 641–664.

Staudinger, U. M., and Baltes, P. B. (1996). Interactive minds: A facilitative setting for wisdom-related performance? *Journal of Personality and Social Psychology*, 71(4), 746–762.

Staudinger, U. M., Lopez, D. F., and Baltes, P. B. (1997). The psychometric location of wisdom-related performance: Intelligence, personality, and more? *Personality and Social Psychology Bulletin*, 23(11), 1200–1214.

Sternberg, R. J. (1998). A balance theory of wisdom. *Review of General Psychology*, 2(4), 347–365.

Sternberg, R. J. (2001a). Why schools should teach for wisdom: The balance theory of wisdom in educational settings. *Educational Psychologist*, 36(4), 227–245.

Sternberg, R. J. (2001b). How wise is it to teach for wisdom? A reply to five critiques. *Educational Psychologist*, 36(4), 269–272.

Sternberg, R. J. (2002). It's not what you know, but how you use it: Teaching for wisdom. *The Chronicle of Higher Education*, 48(42), B.20.

Sternberg, R. J. (2003). A broad view of intelligence: The theory of successful intelligence. *Consulting Psychology Journal: Practice and Research*, 55(3), 139–154.

Sternberg, R. J. (2004a). WICS: A model of educational leadership. *The Educational Forum*, 68(2), 108–114.

Sternberg, R. J. (2004b). Words to the wise about wisdom? A commentary on Ardelt's critique of Baltes. *Human Development*, 47(5), 286–289.

Sternberg, R. J. (2005a). WICS: A model of leadership. *The Psychologist-Manager Journal*, 8(1), 20–43.

Sternberg, R. J. (2005b). WICS: A model of giftedness in leadership. *Roeper Review*, 28(1), 37–44.

Tuchman, B. (1984). *The march of folly: From Troy to Vietnam*. New York: Ballantine.

Webb, P. J. (2005). Inspirational chaos: Executive coaching and tolerance of complexity. In M. Cavanagh, A. M. Grant, and T. Kemp (Eds.), *Evidence-based coaching, Vol. 1: Theory, research and practice from the behavioural sciences* (pp. 83–95). Bowen Hills, Queensland: Australian Academic Press.

Webb, P. J. (2006). Back on track: The coaching journey in executive career derailment. *International Coaching Psychology Review*, 1(2), 68–74.

Webster, J. D. (2003). An exploratory analysis of a self-assessed wisdom scale. *Journal of Adult Development*, 10(1), 13–22.

10 Coaching the Human Spirit

Peter J. Reding and Marcia Collins

This chapter explores what it takes to create a coaching relationship that connects the client with his unique Human Spirit, his most personal and powerful resourcefulness. The 'Human Spirit', as used in this chapter, can be seen as the melding of two key elements:

(1) An eternal benevolent Spirit (e.g., God, Higher Power, Divine Presence, Creator, or however it is named by the client) characterized as:
    (a) a force that connects all
    (b) a divine and organizing intelligence
    (c) accessible to all
(2) The individual human expression of this Spirit through our:
    (a) core values
    (b) life purpose
    (c) unique combination of natural talents

In each of the four sections below, we outline some key concepts and steps a coach needs to master in order to facilitate the client's reconnection to his Human Spirit as his most potent source of self-identity and expression of who he truly is in his everyday life. We contend that this resourcefulness is not in the client's mind, body or emotions, but in the client's Human Spirit. The sections in this chapter are based on four questions we see as the foundation for this exploration in serving our clients:

The Philosophy and Practice of Coaching: Insights and Issues for a New Era.
Edited by David B. Drake, Diane Brennan and Kim Gørtz.
© 2008 John Wiley & Sons, Ltd.

(1) What need is met by coaching the Human Spirit?
(2) What informed coaching the Human Spirit?
(3) How can I coach the Human Spirit?
(4) What are the implications of coaching the Human Spirit?

What Need is Met by Coaching the Human Spirit?

Coaching's Promise

Coaching's promise to clients is to support them to move forward in the direction of what they want. Every trained coach we know, whether new to the coaching profession or the most masterful of coaches, can do this with varying degrees of skill . . . and we know there is so much more. The client thrives when a coach is prepared to facilitate the client to explore deeper into his heart and soul to discern what he really needs to be fulfilled. In doing so, the client begins a metamorphosis through a powerful and deeply personal alignment process.

In this process, we can ask ourselves as coaches, 'Do we accept our responsibility to support the client to be clear that what she says she wants is really what she wants?' and 'Do we own the obligation to support our client to anchor his stated wants, needs, goals, and dreams to something that is innately and uniquely important to him?' If coaching is to fulfil its promise to the world and to human development, the answer to these two questions has to be 'YES'. The great news is that some coaches are already doing this with their clients and, as a result, their clients are thriving like never before. As the profession of coaching matures, coaches are being called on to go deeper with their clients. Coaching clients who are ready to go beyond the productivity of life are looking for coaching relationships that facilitate deeper explorations for the meaning of their life, deeper connections with their innermost guidance which is sourced from their unique Human Spirit, and a deeper understanding of their questions of 'Who am I?' and 'Why am I here?'

Transcending the Superficial Doingness or Productivity of Life

When clients say they want to change jobs, become a better manager, or write a book – and attempt to do so without aligning their goal, dream or aspiration to their innermost Human Spirit – the results are seldom satisfying. The time and energy devoted to its achievement, and often even the achievement itself, is frequently unfulfilling beyond the temporary high that is experienced, and is destined to become, at best, a frustrating cycle and, at worst, a destructive habit. As examples, we have heard ourselves and our clients say: 'I thought. . . . would be much more satisfying than it turned out to be' or 'There's got to be more to life than. . . .' or 'I have been ignoring the most important things in my life by pursuing. . . .' or 'I need more balance in my life'.

Two of the steps we recommend here are as follows:

(1)   Facilitate each client to get to know her unique Human Spirit.
(2)   Facilitate each client's awareness to choose (or not choose) alignment with her unique Human Spirit in her daily actions.

We will explore these steps in further depth in the third section, 'How can I coach the Human Spirit?'.

Knowing Your Self is an Inside Job

Clients from around the world are yearning to know themselves, be themselves and act in alignment with themselves. In our view, this is by definition an inside job. It can, in fact, only come from deep inside the client; it cannot come from the coach. This is also true in families; it cannot come from the parent. Every child has his own unique purpose, set of core values and combination of unique talents quite apart from his family of origin. While parents, culture, community and even gender may inform the experiences of each individual, the individual is one-of-a-kind in all of history. A coach is there to assist in the discovery of: Who are you? What is your ultimate purpose? For what or whom are you to be an advocate? What contribution are you to share with your world? What are you here to express?

These questions are important for coaches to remember in working with clients as they have been bombarded from birth with messages from external voices, e.g., parents, culture, religion, mass media and peers, about 'this is who you are . . .', 'this is who you are supposed to be . . .', 'this is what I want you to become'. These messages may or may not be beneficial or in alignment with what is ultimately true for the individual. Coaching can work with people to recognize and consciously examine the external messages they have internalized, albeit unconsciously, in forming their personal operating system and belief system, that have never been brought into alignment with their unique Human Spirit.

For example, a parent who has consistently told his son that his safety and security resides in getting a job at the local factory may stifle his son's exploration of his innate curiosities and the utilization of his natural talents. Later in life, as the son is holding on to his current job 'for dear life', despite his obvious disdain for this job, he may seek out a coach for support. In supporting him to get to know himself more fully, the coach can take him on a journey to reconnect with his Human Spirit – via his core values, life purpose and unique talents – and discern what parts of his current job (versus a desired job) align or do not align with the nature and needs of his Human Spirit.

As masterful coaches we have the privilege and the responsibility to invite our clients to reconnect to, articulate, bring awareness to, and consciously choose to (or not choose to) align with their unique Human Spirit. By accessing the client's Human Spirit – versus his ego – as a source of wisdom and benevolence, the client is naturally guided to both his and society's highest benefit. It has been our experience, in working with and teaching this model of coaching since 1996, that clients are humbled when they are reconnected to their unique Human Spirit. They often find it much easier to forgive, have compassion, be of service to their world, and live more purposeful lives.

What is Really Mine versus What is Yours (That I have Assumed is Mine)?

Modern-day personal coaches (life coaches, executive coaches, success coaches, etc.) have the potential to guide the client on the innate and ancient quest to 'know your self' as a means to discover the innermost core values, life purpose and unique talents that are the elements of his unique Human Spirit. The modern-day coach can support the client to discern, perhaps for the first time in her life, where she has internalized someone else's truth and where she can reclaim her own innermost identity.

The philosophy, principles and practices of *Coaching the Human Spirit*™ that are outlined in this chapter are universally applicable for every coach who practises with the belief that the client is the absolute source for his own best answers. The use and integration of these principles can deepen the coaching experience and provide an accelerated effectiveness for the client to achieve her goals and aspirations and experience the deep personal satisfaction of fulfilment.

What Informed Coaching the Human Spirit?

When we began our company in 1996, we were captivated by the primary founding principle of modern-day coaching: *each client is the source of his own best answers.* We sought to understand how best to support clients and new coaches to increase their capacity to discover and draw on these answers in order to lead more fulfilling lives and help others do the same.

Our initial inquires were:

(1)   Where exactly is the coaching client going to 'source his own best answers'?
(2)   How can the professionally trained coach best support their client to 'source her own best answers'?

We have come to see that coaching the Human Spirit is about facilitating the client to discover her deepest and most resourceful place in order to source her own best answers and experience the highest level of fulfilment she is willing to receive in the moment. Accordingly, we based our Fulfillment Coaching Model™ and work on three philosophies:

(1)   The most resourceful place where a client can access his own best answers is through his connection with his sense of a benevolent and loving Spirit, God, Divine Presence, or Higher Power. For our purposes, we refer to this as *Spirit.*
(2)   When Spirit is uniquely and humanly expressed through the combination of the following three elements we refer to these as the *Human Spirit:*
      (a)   core values
      (b)   life purpose
      (c)   natural strengths and talents
(3)   Each person experiences a deep sense of fulfilment when she:
      (a)   knows her Human Spirit
      (b)   aligns her daily planning, decisions and actions with her Human Spirit
      (c)   acknowledges herself when she is true to her Human Spirit

The Origins of the Model

In part, this model emerged from our study of many of the spiritual traditions of the world and the wisdom they offer. Some of the key principles we have drawn from them include:

- A divine presence is in and available to everyone.
- What you focus on expands.
- At some level every person is whole, perfect and complete.
- We create our lives consciously or unconsciously.
- We each have a unique purpose.
- We each have our own path of learning.

An essential component of the foundation for working with these principles was the need to develop a clear sense of who you are.

Know Your Self

Know your self . . . this famous line and ancient quest is as compelling today as it was for those who came before us. We can build on Shakespeare's now famous challenge and say, 'To be or not to be [your self] – that is the question'. This is still the question for every human being today. While time has changed many aspects of our outer world – such as the way we travel, make our living and communicate – the primal call from our inner world rings true even today. We must still answer the question: *to be or not to be* our self.

In earlier times, Socrates challenged his audiences by pronouncing that an unexamined life was not worth living and, in doing so, invited them to undertake a personal and inner journey. However, it takes courage to examine one's life. Closer to our own era, the American writer and philosopher Henry David Thoreau, observed that, 'most men [sic] lead lives of quiet desperation and go to the grave with the song still in them'. Thoreau lived a simple and reflective life. In doing so, he advocated self-expression and following your own conscience. He also knew that in order to do this you had to take the time and energy to know your self, be your self and live your life fully as your song. In our time, coaching is positioned well to support those who are ready and have the courage to examine their life.

In today's world, this theme of self-discovery and drive to know one's self is central to every coaching interaction. It is relevant to the teenager seeking to know her own identity and path, to the man seeking to know how to best provide for his family, and to the retiring woman seeking to create her unique legacy. The more the coach knows about the client's Human Spirit and supports the client's reconnection to his own Human Spirit, the more able they are to collectively anchor every client decision, plan, goal, aspiration, vision and action to what brings the client the greatest fulfilment.

Accessing the Human Spirit

It is important to acknowledge here that the Human Spirit is always available. Just as a seed has its own DNA that stores its identity, purpose and steps to manifest its purpose, so too each human being has a unique Human Spirit that stores and strives towards the individual's best and brightest self – regardless of life circumstances, age, difficulties or current misalignment of life choices. So coaches can help their clients discover more about their seeds, the storehouse of 'Who am I?' in the following ways:

- *How am I to be . . . in the various roles or positions or actions that I am engaged?* In coaching we call this our *core values*; they reflect and guide the client's *beingness* as the client engages in the *doing-ness* in life. The client can *be* happy or *be* resentful as he goes to work each day.
- *What am I here for?* In coaching we call this our life purpose. This offers the coach the foundation to ask the client, which of the many alternatives best serves her life purpose? A client makes better, more courageous, and life-affirming decisions by knowing and aligning with her life purpose. By bringing life purpose into the coaching relationship the client's greatest contribution can be made and her personal fulfilment is maximized.
- *How am I to contribute or make a difference?* What gifts and talents do I have that will assist me in contributing to my world? In coaching these are identified as the client's natural strengths or innate talents. Much of coaching is based on helping clients recognize, appreciate and apply them in service to their core values and life purpose.

Another important role the Human Spirit plays is as a magnet that tugs us towards living in alignment more often and fully with what brings our greatest fulfilment. Each of us has a choice to be conscious or unconscious about hearing and following our Human Spirit's guidance. The question is not, 'Do I have this inner guidance?' We believe every person does. The question is, 'Am I willing to be open to, trust and follow my Human Spirit's guidance?' The Human Spirit is an inner guide that combines the navigational properties of a gyroscope, to keep us upright and centred by living in alignment with our core values and utilizing our natural talents, with the directional properties of a compass, to keep us moving in the direction of our individual and unique life purpose. In our experience as teachers and coaches, the extent to which a person's life choices, actions, decisions, direction and focus are aligned with his Human Spirit is indicative of his state of peace, fulfilment, happiness and feeling of vibrancy. As such, there is a direct correlation between alignment with his Human Spirit and his level of fulfilment.

We built our coaching models and processes on two principles:

(1) See, hear and treat the client as her 'Human Spirit' before, during and after every coaching interaction. This mindset is held by the coach regardless of how the client sees herself, hears her critical voice, or holds on to any limiting beliefs she may have in the moment.
(2) Accept where the client is at, no matter what. Believe the client is learning, or in some other way benefiting, from being where she is right now.

How Can I Coach The Human Spirit?

The New Coach's Transformation

The challenge for most new coaches we train is to make the personal transition from giving advice to letting go of their own agenda in favour of the client's agenda. Most new coaches are quite comfortable giving advice to friends, family and associates about how they 'should be' doing something to improve their life and/or achieve their goals. In fact, most of them have been sought out over their life for their ability to give such advice. They have become good at it, are proud of supporting their loved ones, and are now seeking to learn a formal structure so they can get paid to do this. The good news is that they care deeply for people's wellbeing. However, they also come to recognize the down-sides of their old ways of 'supporting' people, including:

(1) Most people did not follow their advice – no matter how spectacular it was.
(2) They were not always as fully appreciated as they wanted to be.
(3) The same 'issues' always seemed to come back for people, over and over, without any discernible progress, clarity, commitment or resolution.
(4) They were never compensated for their brilliant advice.

The Steps in the Process

The primary aim is to help coaches shift from giving advice to focus on helping the client to know more fully and deeply his own Human Spirit.

In training new coaches, we have found the following two steps to be essential in helping them move into a more empowering partnership with clients who are ready, willing and able to take responsibility for their own lives and begin the courageous work to move towards living their dreams, visions and purpose.

Step 1: Facilitate Each Client to Get to Know his or her Unique Human Spirit

My greatest contribution to my coaching client is to facilitate her to get to know her unique Human Spirit.

We have a passion for supporting our new coaches to really know themselves and to train them in such a manner that they in turn can support their coaching clients to really know themselves. This work has to be the first step in establishing the coaching foundation. Without it, the client and coach are wandering in the wilderness and will have difficulty anchoring the client's goals and objectives to her Human Spirit. Instead, the client will remain caught in her conditioning that more money, the next promotion, or the approval of someone else will bring happiness or satisfaction – the payoff she is seeking. However, most of the time these payoffs are anchored to something that is outside of the client and, as a result, the payoffs lack sufficient meaning and personal significance for the client.

Based on our experience, we know that any achievement or payoff that is not directly linked to the person's Human Spirit is, by design, going to leave the person unfulfilled and frustrated in the end. We also know that the continual setting, and even achieving, of goals that are primarily externally driven lead to a loss of motivation and a growing sense of burnout. So if repetition of what the client has already been doing, even if it is with greater efficiency, is not the answer, what is? We have found that the answer is to help the client access (not assess) his or her Human Spirit. We have heard clients also call this soul, true self, core self, essential nature, or God self. We strongly encourage the coach to use and honour the language of the client during the coaching relationship; for the purpose of this chapter we will refer to it as the client's 'Human Spirit'.

How can I do it?

We have identified the following three stages that masterful coaches can use to support their clients to get to know and reconnect with their Human Spirit.

Stage 1

Facilitate the client in processes that will lead to a deeper awareness of herself. We use a model that incorporates four levels at which to work depending on the capability and readiness of the coach and the client.

- *Level 1*: Use assessment tools that employ classifications of preferences, e.g., relating, communicating, deciding. These can be helpful as a starting point with people who are new to this work – clients who are not ready to do the deeper work and/or coaches who are not trained in the use of techniques to access deeper levels.
- *Level 2*: Use list-making tools (e.g., values, purposes, talents) to surface how the client frames, interprets and responds to the world. Working at this level of access helps the client to make more refined distinctions, particularly between what she has adopted from her upbringing and environment and what she herself wants to bring forward in her life.
- *Level 3*: Ask the client to describe experiences, events and accomplishments that brought her joy. Working at this level helps the client access memories and emotions that provide glimpses into her Human Spirit and the values, purpose and talents that are present. It is important here to help the client separate behaviours or accomplishments that were rooted in pleasing others from those that came from being true to her own Human Spirit.
- *Level 4*: Invite the client to relax into a guided visualization where the client describes a place in the future or an ideal scene. While in this altered state of consciousness, ask her to describe what qualities, accomplishments, talents and passions are being visualized. This level bypasses the client's current ego, reality, limitations and past assumptions to get to what is innately important to and nourishes her Human Spirit.

Stage 2

Work with the client to articulate her core values, her life purpose, and her unique and natural talents from the deepest level she was able to access using the steps above. We have found the greatest success is in asking the client questions while in her altered state reached at level 4. At whatever level the client reaches, the coach writes down those words and phrases from the client that are filled with a passionate energy. We found in our work, that it is helpful to the process if the coach does not describe the process as a 'values clarification', 'life purpose' or 'talent identification' process because doing so often evokes a more linear, cerebral and predictable response from clients. Instead, masterful coaches position it as a 'discovery process' or 'foundational process' that is intended to assist the client during her coaching relationship. Using a more open term seems to enable greater access, based in the moment and not on pre-formed terms, to the client's Human Spirit.

In order to be effective, the masterful coach has become proficient at:

- Guiding the client to a level 4 depth of access (as described above).
- Distilling the client's words, phrases and energy into an accurate reflection of what the client has revealed (without consciously knowing it yet) as his or her:
  - Unique set of core values
  - Unique life purpose statement
  - Unique combination of natural strengths and talents

Stage 3

Invite the client to take the words and phrases written down by the coach and work with them and express them in a fashion that is personally meaningful and generative. Once the client feels complete with the process and her articulation of the results, the coach can then share with her the frame and terms for what she has developed – core values, life purpose and strengths/talents.

When these three stages of client discovery are done in the manner described here, the client is often moved to a humbled reverence of who she has always known herself to be, through being able to articulate it so succinctly, accurately and powerfully. As an example, a recent client wrote at the end of this discovery process:

My core values: Creative, connection, thriving, compassionate, of service.
My life purpose: I am the exquisite and playful orchestration of Spirit's oneness and Human's uniqueness that come together to create a bodacious flourishing of life.
My unique talents: Conceptual, easily articulate the complex, deep listener, patience, trust, visionary, designer, facilitator.

When a client is able to articulate key elements of her Human Spirit, the coach can listen for/on behalf of the client's best and brightest self. The coach can also use each of these three elements of her Human Spirit as the basis for asking powerful questions, creating plans, designing actions and making requests of the client for commitments to her own forward movement. As a result, the masterful coach no longer has to guess where to anchor the client's decisions and actions. The novice coach is now more able to make the transition from unconsciously giving advice and asking leading questions to consciously accessing the client's articulated Human Spirit for direction, clarity and decisions. For clients, there is quite often a sense of receiving, for the first time in their life, a clear and personal compass that is empowering and easy to apply in everyday situations and choices.

These three elements of the Human Spirit – values, purpose and talents – become the predominant focal point to which the masterful coach now listens for where the client is or is not aligned. The client is always revealing her underlying beliefs and aspirations, or some aspect of her decision-making, planning and goal-setting processes. The masterful coach can now listen through the client's own higher consciousness of herself.

Step 2: Facilitate the Client's Awareness to Choose (or not) Alignment with his/her Human Spirit

My second greatest contribution to my coaching client is to create awareness in her to choose if, when, where and how to live her life in alignment with her unique Human Spirit.

Once the client's Human Spirit is revealed and articulated, the second step is for the coach to support the client to be aware of:

(1) whether or how his goals, dreams, decisions, plans and action steps are aligned and anchored with his Human Spirit, and
(2) to make new choices accordingly.

When a coach is able to evoke the client's Human Spirit, the client has access to greater clarity of purpose and direction in every part of his life.

There are many paths

There are times when the client is aware that a planned action is not fully aligned with her own values, purpose or talents – for any number of reasons. In these cases the coach has done his job by bringing the client to this conscious awareness; it is the client's right and privilege 'to be or not to be' fully herself. In our experience, when a client has consciously chosen a path that was not fully congruent with what the individual knew and believed herself to be, this conscious choice of incongruence has always been the precursor to a significant and fulfilling turning point in the client's life.

When coaching from the perspective of the Human Spirit, a coach knows, without reservation, that even this seemingly incongruent (and yes, unanchored) path the client is choosing is the path that will best serve this client at this time. In part, this requires the coach to take a wider view on behalf of the client's path. Perhaps there is a lesson to be learned. Perhaps it is to understand the experiences of those people the client is being called to serve. Perhaps it is in the very experience of the struggle of trying to be someone they are not. Helping a client gain awareness of any incongruity or misalignment related to a particular course of action allows her to connect her incongruity with her results – including any undesirable fallout, e.g., internal feelings or external reactions. The client can choose to recalibrate her way of being and doing – or not. We believe it is the client's sole responsibility to make this choice whether to move into greater alignment with whom she now knows herself to be. *To be or not to be*... continues to be a powerful question the coach has a responsibility to ask and the client has the right to consciously choose.

Accessing the client's resourcefulness

The masterful coach facilitates the client to access aspects of herself that have lain in the shadows and remained mostly unexplored until now. Most clients do not know or believe what vast resourcefulness is available to them. There is so much more available to us than most people are able to see and know on their own, due to a lifetime of being told who they are and what they can and cannot do. The masterful coach is a professionally trained listener. However, questions remain, such as: What is the coach listening for? What is the coach missing as a result of their default listening modality? The type of listening used by the coach changes everything in the coaching relationship.

What is the coach listening for?

Most coaches, consciously or unconsciously, are primarily listening for one of the following:

(1)　What is *impeding* the client from reaching his or her goals and dreams? or
(2)　What is *inspiring* the client's actions, plans and decisions in support of reaching his or her goals and dreams?

The 'what-impedes-you?' approach

Based on most new coaches' past experience, training and compensation, they are delighted when a client has some fear, block or challenge into which they can dig. The new coach proceeds with a line of questions designed to eliminate or at least minimize these impediments to a client achieving her goals. However, when coaches listen for limiting beliefs, blocks, fears, tolerations, etc., that is what they will reflect back to their client. Our experience is that this approach to listening makes for arduous coaching for both the client and the coach. The client is led into the areas of low energy and low confidence and reconnected with an all-too-familiar state of struggle. When the coach then asks, 'So now what do you want to accomplish in this session?' or 'What's the next step for you to move towards your goal?' or 'How can you overcome this obstacle?', the client is in a diminished state of resourcefulness marked by her gremlins (protection from getting hurt), critical mind (limiting self-talk), and fears about moving forward. The client's mind is literally shut down to a wider range of possibilities.

Coaches we have observed who continue to utilize this approach are also more likely to interject their ideas, advice, strategies, resources, etc. to assist the client in moving forward. By doing so, the coach takes over the responsibility for finding the client's answers. The burden of having to move the client forward under this type of coaching process shifts from the client to the coach. As one would expect, this is fraught with all the down-sides of giving advice to friends. The client has not been empowered; she has again been told what to do. The client has little or no buy-in; the source of answers is still outside of her. The client has been once again robbed of the experience to learn more about herself and to know she is more resourceful than she has ever given herself credit for.

The 'what-inspires-you?' approach

When the coach listens for the client's natural strengths, passions, aspirations, core values and life purpose, these are what the coach has available to reflect back to the client, verify that is what the coach heard him say, and ask what he wishes to expand on. A client will still bring up his fears and blocks. The difference is that this approach to coaching moves him into his most resourceful space with an unlimited mind for solutions to appear.

The masterful coach can use this approach to engage the client in a vibrant celebration of his Human Spirit and in a co-creative process of new possibilities. Doing so can be exhilarating for both the coach and the client. The coach's role in this process is to know and hold the client's unique Human Spirit at all times and to start from this place in asking questions of, communicating with and acknowledging the client. When the coach comes from the client's self-articulated Human Spirit, the client cannot dissuade his coach that he is anything but innately magnificent, resourceful, purposeful and talented. At the same time, the coach accepts and allows the client to be stuck if the client is not prepared, for any reason, to move forward. This honours the client's path of learning and his humanness in that moment.

Table 10.1 depicts the two approaches to enquiry and listening – one that leads to openness and one that often leads to closure in clients. These two approaches are illustrated with common questions at each of the three different levels in terms of what the coach is listening for and seeking to access.

Table 10.1   Comparison of the two approaches.

	The 'what-impedes-you?' approach	The 'what-inspires-you?' approach
What mindset informs my questions?	Questions that often result in the client closing down.	Questions that often result in the client opening up.
What level of access informs my questions?	My-client-is-strictly-human approach: Questions that can restrict or limit the client.	My-client-is-a-Human-Spirit approach: Questions that can expand the client.
Accessing the client's internal world	• *What fears are holding you back? What are your internal obstacles?*	• *What part of this aligns with your core values, life purpose and natural talents?*
Accessing the client's external world	• *What blocks are in your way that you will need to overcome?*	• *What impact will your vision have in your world?*
Accessing the client's system or source of resourcefulness	• *What part of your past training or area of expertise can support your quest? What has made you successful in the past?*	• *What is that quiet connection to your Human Spirit saying to you now?* • *What is your inner guidance showing you?*

Establishing the client's Human Spirit

All coaches want the best for their client. However, we have found that in working with 'what-inspires-you', coaches are less likely to listen to clients through their own autobiographical filters of what may or may not be true for the client. By helping the client to articulate the client's own Human Spirit, coaches have a key to help their clients attain greater fulfilment, satisfaction, peace, love and an experience of heaven on earth. In the fourth and final section of this chapter we ponder the implications our work has had and will continue to have in coaches and on the coaching profession.

What Are the Implications of Coaching the Human Spirit?

Reconnect your Client with her Human Spirit and you Change the World

Each human being, regardless of nationality, profession, gender, age or religious belief has core desires and aspirations to live a fulfilling and purposeful life. Everyone wants to know they made a difference, their life was worthwhile and it stood for something or inspired someone. We have developed the Fulfillment Coaching Model utilizing the philosophy and principles of Coaching the Human Spirit so the coaches we train can empower their clients to reach this vision.

The future of coaching is linked to every individual we coach in the world. In the process, we have focused in particular on knowing a person's innate magnificence, or what we have referred to in this chapter as the client's Human Spirit. This is the basis for helping clients clarify, understand and reconnect to their core values, life purpose and unique combination of natural talents. We facilitate clients by shining a light of awareness on their patterns of response to the question of '*to be or not to be*' and whether or not they are living in alignment with who they know themselves to be.

The benefits of accessing the client's Human Spirit and being able to coach the depths of the client's Human Spirit are profound for the individual client, their family, work associates, community and, ultimately, the world. We have seen evidence of this in observing people heal decade-long torn relationships, redirect their lives towards life-affirming pursuits, stand up for those who have been disempowered, bring personal integrity to organizational governance, and fall back in love with themselves. We believe every act of inhumanity will cease when we are a planet of people who really know who we are, love who we are, and live in full alignment with who we are.

Conclusion: The Future of Coaching and Human Development are Connected

The profession of coaching has an unprecedented and historical opportunity to support healthy and responsible people to live more consciously and in alignment with their Human Spirit. We have the opportunity and privilege as coaches to foster fulfilment at the deepest and most meaningful levels of our clients. We need to continue to master the skills, knowledge and attitudes that evoke the very best of our clients' Human Spirit so it can be known, be expressed and be of service to their world in a manner that is 100% congruent with their Human Spirit.

In the most basic sense, coaching is about helping clients to move forward and achieve their desired goals. We have advocated here that, while this is effective in many circumstances, it may not produce a deep and meaningful sense of fulfilment for the client. However, by facilitating the client's articulation of her Human Spirit and using this new awareness to inform the coaching process, the masterful coach can anchor the client's goals, plans, decisions and actions in what will bring the highest personal and most meaningful fulfilment to the client. When our clients are guided by their Human Spirit they are better leaders who make better decisions; better parents who create better relationships; better teachers who provide better learning environments; and better human beings who grow more capacity for acceptance, have more passion for their world and compassion for their fellow humans.

We have developed our work to further these ends. Our philosophy and practices did not primarily come from the literature or research. Instead, out models and approaches, as addressed in this chapter, are based in an epistemology that is more phenomenological in nature. They emerged from our direct experience in applying commonly held beliefs and practices from numerous Spiritual Traditions. These beliefs, principles and philosophies include:

- There is a benevolent Spirit (God, Divine Presence, Higher Power, etc.).
- We are all connected, one, unified.
- We all have direct access to a benevolent Spirit.
- As humans, we embody some or all of Spirit's qualities.

- Spirit's guidance is always available.
- Our humanness causes us to forget our connection with Spirit.
- Our humanness requires daily practices to help our remembrance of our inalienable connection with Spirit.

Based on this commitment to the Human Spirit as the basis for meaningful and fulfilling goals in our clients' work and lives, we invite all current and future coaches to continue to develop their personal capacity to:

- Know their own Human Spirit.
- Develop a stronger relationship with their sense of Spirit.
- Open up to hear their calling of how and where they are to serve.
- Inspire their clients to go deeper.
- Expand their personal mastery every day.

We encourage all current and future coaches to support their clients to rediscover their innate magnificence and their unique Human Spirit. We encourage coaches to be fully prepared in every coaching interaction to remind their clients of who they really are, what they are here to do, and what natural talents they have to serve and inspire the world around them. You may be the only person in your clients' lives that is available and capable to do this with them.

11

Achieving Tangible Results: The Development of a Coaching Model

Sabine Dembkowski and Fiona Eldridge

Introduction

One of the things we notice when clients come to the first meeting is that the ones who have no experience with coaching will often ask, 'Well, what do you actually do?' 'How does it actually work? What exactly will happen if we start working together?' Without a clear and structured process these questions are almost impossible to answer and, as a consequence, it is hard to demonstrate to organizational buyers the value you will bring as an executive coach. In this chapter we will present a coaching model we have developed, reflections on that process, and insights we have gained in using it to produce tangible results through our coaching assignments.

After completing several training programmes and starting our journey, we noticed that there was an air of mystery around the whole coaching process. The answers to what was actually happening in a coaching programme or process appeared to be all too often in a 'black box'. We wondered which ideas, models and processes executive coaches actually used in their daily practices. Were there any 'trade secrets'? In order to better understand the coaching process, we reviewed the literature in coaching and related fields such as psychology and learning theory. To complement this review, we also worked with, observed, and interviewed executive coaches in the USA, England and Germany. Our guiding questions included:

The Philosophy and Practice of Coaching: Insights and Issues for a New Era.
Edited by David B. Drake, Diane Brennan and Kim Gørtz.
© 2008 John Wiley & Sons, Ltd.

- How does the executive coach achieve tangible results?
- What does the executive coach do to create a positive impact on a client's performance?
- What distinguishes an experienced coach from a novice coach?

We chose to adopt a qualitative approach for our research and model development as the coaching process is essentially concerned with working with aspects of human behaviour that do not readily lend themselves to quantification. In order to reflect actual best practice and provide a framework for future development we used an inductive process rooted in real world situations. In addition, we adopted a qualitative approach as the best way to examine what was happening within coaching assignments from the perspective of the coach and client.

We saw the benefits of a qualitative approach for our research as follows:

- Ability to progress understanding in a relatively new field of study
- Ability to address aspects of human behaviour which are not necessarily captured by quantitative approaches
- Ability to grasp a complex phenomenon
- Portrayal of the respondents' perspective
- Ability to uncover the less obvious
- Penetration of rationalized or superficial responses
- Greater richness and depth of information

In this chapter we will provide an overview of the Achieve Coaching Model®, how it evolved from our study and how it is applied in practice. The chapter is organized according to the stages of the model using the following headings:

- *General description.* Here we describe each stage of the model and how it evolved from our study.
- *Objectives.* Here we detail the specific objectives of the stage and the contribution to the overall outcome of the coaching programme.
- *Observations of the key effective behaviours of experienced coaches.* Here we describe the key behaviours of experienced coaches, shed further light into the 'black box' of coaching, and provide practical insights into what experienced coaches actually do in action.

The chapter concludes with a case study to provide an example of how the model is used in practice. This shows how a model developed in theory can be applied to a real coaching situation. As with any model you may choose to use, you will undoubtedly add other ideas drawing on your own experience and background to develop a model that suits your practice.

What Is The Achieve Coaching Model®?

Through our study we identified seven steps that were used, in one form or another, by many of the experienced coaches. The model was developed based on these steps and it was subsequently tested and refined through our coaching practice. In essence, we experimented with the steps we had identified and noted what worked. For example, in using the model we found that it is best used iteratively rather than merely pushing the client through one step after another.

The model provides a structure for coaching sessions without restricting the flexibility of individual coaches and can be used to create coaching relationships that are purposeful and have clearly defined outcomes. It also can be used to provide greater transparency about the process for clients and it has created credibility with a more analytically minded clientele. At each stage, a range of tools and techniques can be used according to the coach's own background and experience.

The seven stages that emerged and form the basis of the model are:

- **A**ssess the current situation
- **C**reative brainstorming of alternatives
- **H**one goals
- **I**nitiate option generation
- **E**valuate options
- **V**alid action programme design
- **E**ncourage momentum

As with any model, it simplifies the process but it still functions to explain the stages that a coach and client go through during a coaching assignment in order to achieve results. While it is presented here as a sequence, in real life it is much more of an iterative process in which each stage is often worked through more than once (Figure 11.1). What is important is that all the stages are covered. We have found, though, that if more time is devoted to the first three stages then the others flow more easily and relatively quickly.

Figure 11.1   The Achieve Coaching Model®.

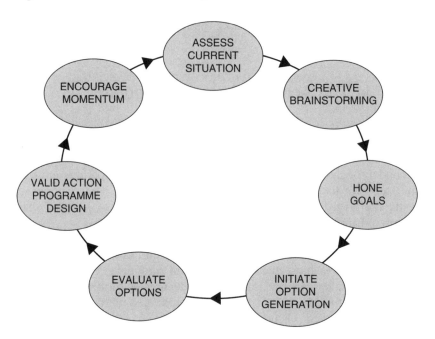

Developing the Model

Through our enquiry and interviews with experienced executive coaches
we identified that the GROW model was most often cited as the frame
for coaching assignments. The GROW model was developed by Graham
Alexander and Sir John Whitmore and is the best-known coaching model
in the UK. However, as we looked at what really happens in practice,
we recognized that experienced executive coaches were expanding their
repertoire beyond the GROW model in order to achieve tangible and
sustainable results with their clients. It was particularly evident that they
took time to really understand the situation from the client's perspective
before honing the client's goals and working on action plans for their
achievement. This differs from the GROW model which implies that the
client already knows the goal that he or she wishes to work upon.

In most cases clients have a good sense of the overall direction for
the coaching programme but no clarity about which specifics to focus
on. Generally most clients can describe what they do not want in great
detail, but are less articulate about what they actually do want. So, we
find that the specific goal is rarely clear at the beginning of a coaching

programme. Just asking the client, 'What is the goal for this coaching programme?', may result either in silence or seizing upon the first thing that comes to mind. This may not tackle the underlying issues or resolve the situation at all, resulting in a poor experience of coaching for client, coach and organization. This led us to the development of the first stage of the model.

Stage 1: Assess the Current Situation

This is the starting point for any coaching assignment. Typically it will be the main thrust of a first meeting and will probably extend to the second. We often found that experienced coaches revisit it throughout the coaching assignment as new challenges and issues arise for the client.

The first working coaching session is critical for developing a climate of trust, openness and honesty; these are essential for an effective coaching relationship. Without the appropriate climate and depth of rapport it is unlikely that the client will be able to achieve the deep reflection necessary for the success of this stage. Through carefully considering his current situation the client will increase his self-awareness and be more able to identify areas to work on with the executive coach.

Another advantage of reflecting on the current situation is that the coach gains an appreciation of the context for the sessions ahead. However, the most important benefit for the client is that she has time and space to consider all the factors that led to the current situation and how her behaviour has impacted on others. In fact, clients will often say, 'It's good to take time out; I don't often do that and just keep repeating the same things over and over again'.

The Johari Window model (Luft and Ingham, 1955) was developed by American psychologists Joseph Luft and Harry Ingham when they were researching group dynamics. The model helps to identify the areas a client needs to explore to enhance his self-awareness.

We identified that experienced coaches work with clients in the first session to guide them through the process of increasing self-awareness using a variety of techniques from a variety of perspectives, such as:

● the organization
● their superiors
● their peers
● their team
● the customers / clients

In addition, they may use additional information that is available such as appraisals, results of 360-degree surveys and psychometric tests. However, we noticed that experienced coaches never rely solely on these instruments but rather use them as part of a puzzle to complete the picture.

The objectives of this first stage are:

- Establishing the foundations of trust for an effective coaching relationship
- Understanding the issues, situation and context of the client
- Understanding and identifying the key development areas
- Identifying the most important development issues
- Understanding the world from the point of view of the client

Key behaviours of experienced coaches in assessing the current situation are as follows:

- Make informed use of assessment instruments but do not rely solely on them to gain an understanding of the client's situation
- Have a genuine interest and visible enthusiasm for the life stories of executives
- Take time to really understand the situation from the client's perspective
- Listen deeply so that the client is fully engaged and feels genuinely understood and valued
- Understand how to create a real sense of relatedness and comfort to foster a climate of openness and trust for the relationship
- Observe and take notice of all verbal and nonverbal communication.

Stage 2: Creative Brainstorming of Alternatives

Having established the current situation and begun to acquire a sense of what needs to change, this phase of the coaching assignment is all about the exploration of possibilities. It is about awakening the client's sense of excitement for exploration of these changes, be they behavioural, physical or a change of location. One of the objectives of coaching is to increase the options that a client has when approaching a challenge or specific situation.

All too often we see clients who are 'stuck' in a particular situation with no clear alternative course of action. In our study, clients often described feeling that they could not see a way out or were at the end of a dead-end street with nothing but a big wall in front of them. What this stage does is help the client discover a wider perspective and that there are ways out. Although this stage can be fun and enjoyable, as no judgements are made yet about the feasibility of alternatives, however wild, we noticed that experienced coaches often needed to be quite challenging to prevent the client from circling and clinging on to their old patterns of behaviour.

The objectives of this stage are:

- Assist the client to get out of the 'stuck state'
- Assist the client to get into a 'solution state'
- Assist the client to provide a platform to think about alternatives

Key behaviours of experienced coaches in creative brainstorming are as follows:

- Apply a variety of tools and techniques to take the client away from his habitual patterns *and* break his 'stuck state'
- Surprise the client with creative questions he does not expect at this stage
- Take time to brainstorm about real alternatives to the current situation
- Probe beyond the client's initial responses to uncover a broad spectrum of alternatives to the current situation

Stage 3: Hone Goals

In our own practice and in observing others, we learned that generating alternatives to the current situation helps the client begin to have a sense of what he wants to achieve. The next step is to refine these ideas into specific goals. It is the stage where the SMART model can be helpful in creating and/or refining the client's goals. The coach's role here is to help the client to specify exactly what he wants. In addition to setting SMART goals – a technique which most clients are familiar with in their work context – we have also found it useful to incorporate Sir John Whitmore's (2002) suggestion that goals also need to be PURE and CLEAR. These acronyms can be used by the coach to help the client clarify his goals so they are more likely to be achieved.

PURE means:
- **P**ositively stated
- **U**nderstood
- **R**elevant
- **E**thical

CLEAR means:
- **C**hallenging
- **L**egal
- **E**nvironmentally sound
- **A**ppropriate
- **R**ecorded

Once the client has set a goal, our experience and observation of other coaches suggests that the client should write down his goal so that there is a permanent record of it and to increase commitment. During our studies we observed many coaches omit this step, not wanting to set goals and/or record them. Today we see that more and more organizations have designed internal processes and even templates where the goals need to be clearly stated before a coaching assignment is approved. Having established and refined the goal it then serves as a focal point for future sessions. The coach's role is then to ensure that this goal is still important to the client as the programme progresses.

The objectives of this stage are:

- Assist the client to develop and/or hone her goal(s)
- Ensure that the chosen goal is of high personal relevance
- Help her to focus on the goal

Key behaviours of experienced coaches in the steps of honing goals are as follows:

- Encourage precise definition of goals in positive terms
- Take time to develop SMART goals
- Work with the client to develop goal(s) with high personal meaning and relevance
- Ensure goal is the client's
- Develop clear measures with client so that she has evidence of achievement of goal

Stage 4: Initiating Options

With a specific goal established and written down, the next stage is to work with the client to develop a wide range of ways of achieving the goal. It became apparent to us that this is important because if the client only has one course of action it is likely that any barrier will derail him and/or he may continue to waste energy thinking there may have been another, more suitable, option. This lack of focus on the action at hand increases the chances that the objective will not be reached.

By exploring a range of options the client is expanding his choices and breaking away from familiar patterns of behaviour. The coach needs to make sure that no option, however appealing and 'right', should form the sole focus of attention at this stage. The quantity, novelty and variety of the options are more important at this stage than the quality and feasibility. To help clients develop a spectrum of options we noticed that experienced coaches use creative process techniques. When we talked to them and observed them in action we noticed that they used a variety of approaches; Table 11.1 provides a number of examples.

We have incorporated some of these approaches in our work with clients and we have had good success in conducting this session away from the normal meeting place. Doing it this way aids the client to think 'outside of the box' as she has literally been taken away from the familiar context. In our study we found more examples on the left side of the creativity continuum (see Table 11.1) than on the right side. This may be the result of a number of causes, including the particular training and background of the executive coaches. The skilful use of paradigm stretching and paradigm breaking techniques will require in-depth training. In many executive coaching training programmes these techniques are either not covered at all or not covered in any depth to develop expertise in this area. It may also be that the whole reflective process of coaching, in combination with some creative techniques, may be sufficient to yield the desired results. However, it is a skill that we believe can be further exploited in executive coaching.

The client needs to take ownership of the options and generate as many as possible herself. However, sometimes we know of other clients who sought/are seeking similar goals or we have direct personal

Table 11.1   The creativity continuum (adapted from McFadzean, 2000).

	Paradigm reserving	Paradigm stretching	Paradigm breaking
Problem boundaries	Unchanged	Stretched	Broken
Creative stimulation	Low	Medium	High
Stimuli	Related	Unrelated	Unrelated
Association	Free	Forced	Forced
Expression	Verbal/written	Verbal/written	Unlimited
Examples of CPS	Brainstorming	Object stimulation	Wishful thinking
	Brain writing	Metaphors	Rich pictures
Techniques	Force field analysis	Assumption reversal	Picture stimulation
	World Diamond		Collage

experience in the area ourselves. Keeping in mind that client ownership is important, as we observed the other experienced coaches do, we make a clear offer of assistance. We might say, 'This is similar to an experience I had. Do you want to know what I did and how it worked?' In other words, we ask for permission before jumping in with suggestions.

The objectives of this stage are:

- Develop a wide range of (behavioural) options
- Encourage client to go off the 'beaten track', i.e., outside normal range of behaviours

Key behaviours of experienced coaches in initiating options are as follows:

- Exhibit confidence in the process and work with the client to develop alternative pathways to arriving at the desired goal
- Use a broad spectrum of questioning styles and other techniques to stimulate the client to generate options
- Provide space and time for the client to develop a range of options
- Ensure that the options are the client's and he has real ownership

Stage 5: Evaluating Options

Having generated a comprehensive list of options, the next stage is to evaluate the options systematically so that a comprehensive action plan can be developed. This is another important step in developing the client's focus and commitment to achieving his goal in the context of many other competing factors in his everyday life. This was a step that we drew from business planning processes in response to noticing that clients would otherwise become swamped often by a broad range of options. This feeling of being overwhelmed when presented with lots of options often led to clients failing to move forwards at all as they could not see a clear first step.

Strangely, we often find that clients who are skilled at evaluating options for business objectives often find it difficult to apply the same techniques to their personal development. As a result, we generally advocate the use of a simple evaluation matrix using criteria identified by the client (see Figure 11.2). The exact nature of the criteria will, of course, depend upon the situation and issue which is being addressed through coaching. The matrix will be defined by options as measured against these criteria. Once the matrix has been developed the client is

Figure 11.2 Simple evaluation matrix.

	Evaluation Criterion 1	Evaluation Criterion 2	Evaluation Criterion 3	Total
Option 1				
Option 2				
Option 3				

then asked to evaluate each option using a point system of 1–5 where 1 is low and 5 is high. Once all options have been assessed, the numbers are added up and a total is calculated for each option; the option with the highest number receives top priority. The coach's role in this situation is to remind the client of this skill and encourage him to apply it.

The objectives of this stage are:

● Identify a list of criteria against which the options can be evaluated
● Evaluate the options against the criteria
● Identify priorities

Key behaviours of experienced coaches in evaluating options are as follows:

● Encourage the client to develop his own criteria for the evaluation of options
● Ensure real ownership of the evaluation criteria as these form the basis on which options are chosen or rejected
● Take time to probe client to develop a full evaluation of each option
● Ensure that the key options and their evaluation are fixed in writing for future reference

Stage 6: Valid Action Programme Design

Once the client has a well-developed goal and a preferred set of options for achieving the goal, the next stage is to devise a concrete and practical plan. Our experience, and that of other coaches, is that many organizational sponsors and clients view the production of a written plan as tangible evidence that the coaching programme is achieving success. By breaking the actions necessary to achieve the goal into smaller steps the client can begin moving forwards without the sense of overwhelm which can be experienced if the goal is perceived as too large. In our study, the plans produced by clients ranged from simple action lists to comprehensive project plans using project management methodologies. However, it is not the format that is important – it has to be tailored to a client's individual preferences – it is the process of commitment to action which will lead the client forwards.

Action planning is not something that just happens towards the end of the coaching programme. We always ensure that each coaching session concludes with the client committing to specific actions. However, as the end of the programme approaches it is useful for the client to have a plan for the period after the coach has left. In this way, designing a plan can be seen as part of the preparation for closure, the ending of the coaching relationship. This is important as coaching is designed to be a short-term, focused process that should not create dependency in the client.

The objectives of this stage are:

- Gain commitment to action
- Identify concrete actions and/or exercises that help a client to progress towards his goal

Key behaviours of experienced coaches in valid action programme design are as follows:

- Create a detailed action plan with the client
- Gain commitment to the plan
- Probe client to develop a detailed action plan
- Work with the client to check the reality and achievability of the plan
- Put action plan in writing
- Ensure commitment to the action plan

Stage 7: Encourage Momentum

The final role for the coach is to assist the client to keep on track. This takes place in between each session as well as at the end of a programme. However obvious it may seem to encourage clients to move forward, we saw coaches in our study who do not take this step in a coaching relationship. Our finding is in line with a study by Lore International that found that nearly 40% of clients in their survey reported that the coach did not follow up after each coaching session to check that they were making the desired progress. It is important to reinforce even the smallest steps as this helps to build and maintain momentum and increase the client's level of confidence. Sustainable change is easier to achieve with continuous reinforcement and encouragement.

The objectives of this stage are:

- Assist the client to keep on track
- Ensure that the goals of the coaching programme are achieved
- Review progress

Key behaviours of experienced coaches in the step of ensuring momentum are as follows:

- Demonstrate continuing interest in the development of the client
- Organize regular sessions to check in, keep on track, and follow up
- Know when to end the relationship and take measures throughout the coaching programme to avoid dependency

Case Study

Over the last few years we have worked with many senior executives in large organizations and in the public sector. The example we have chosen to present here is from the public sector but it illustrates a common dilemma in any organization – how can a leader maximize his impact in the first 100 days of a new appointment? The difference in a public sector organization is in the degree of scrutiny from external stakeholders demanding value for money for the public purse.

Throughout the case study we have indicated where each stage of the model is being applied. As has already been stated, the coach moves between the stages of the model as appropriate to the situation; it is not a simple linear progression through the model but rather an iterative process, moving the client towards his goal over the course of his sessions. Let us begin by introducing Peter (name changed) and his coaching programme:

The Client

A Chief Executive of a public sector organization in his first year.
First experience heading up a national organization.
Late 40s, married with children.

The Context

As the leader and public face of the organization, he wanted to work on ensuring that both he and the organization engaged the support of internal and external stakeholders.

The Sessions

Session 1

We had a very wide-ranging discussion about Peter's current role, achievements, aspirations and concerns (*Step 1: Assess the current situation*). It was clear that he had a reasonably good understanding of his own strengths and areas for development and that he had devoted much time, energy and thought to establishing a good top team to support him and the organization in achieving its objectives. As we talked, Peter began to formulate some questions he thought were central for the success of the coaching programme. These were:

• How can I do my job better?
• What is it that I can do that would really make a difference?
• What is the role of the Chief Executive in the internal dynamics of the organization?
• How to strive for the balance between informal and casual?
• How to be more deliberate and make clear my vision so that others come with me?

As the organization was still in its infancy he had not received any formal appraisal and we decided that the next step would be to seek 360-degree feedback from both internal and external sources. This information would provide valuable input for the coaching sessions and add to his awareness of his own performance. We also looked at what success from the coaching sessions would look like for him. His overall outcome was to uncover valuable new ideas that would increase his performance as Chief Executive. He also said that he would find it helpful to learn more about what he did really well and what he currently did not do as well that would make a difference. Since we were not at the stage of formulating specific goals we noted his desired outcomes to use later to inform the goal-setting process.

It was a long session and the first time Peter had really spent time on thinking about himself. At this stage his days tended to be filled with worrying about contractors and builders who were building the physical structure of the organization. At the end of the session Peter committed to identifying and contacting the respondents for his 360-degree appraisal (*Step 7: Encourage momentum*).

Session 2

For our second session, Peter took the unusual step of inviting his executive team to our meeting to hear the results of the 360-degree feedback. He had seen a preliminary report and wanted to share the results with the team so that they could (a) see that their views had been taken on board and (b) engage them in activities which would take the organization forward and establish it as a key player in the sector.

I presented the results of the feedback and was able to elaborate on the written report. As a coach, this offered a fantastic opportunity to see the client in action in his everyday work context and added to my understanding of his current situation (*Step 1: Assess the current situation*). For Peter, there was an opportunity to try on the new behaviours and ideas he had proposed in our telephone session following the preliminary report (*Step 2: Creative brainstorming of alternatives*) in real time and receive feedback from me and from his team. After the group session Peter committed to identifying key actions (*Step 4: Initiate options*) on the basis of the appraisal and bring these to the next meeting.

Session 3

This was quite a challenging session as Peter viewed much of the feedback as organizational issues rather than personal. Without doubt his feedback respondents felt that in addition to the organization making its mark, Peter had to demonstrate his capabilities as well. Peter had begun work on an action plan but it was very focused on the organization. So I asked him to reflect further on the feedback as I wanted him to recognize the need for *him* to make changes. In summary, the key points from the feedback were as follows.

Strengths (keep doing and capitalize on)

- Personal commitment and energy for the aims of the organization
- Engaging stakeholders through meetings and public platform performance (but keep on message)

- Supporting staff
- Flexibility and ability to cope with change

Areas to work on

- Communication and engagement with top team
- Strategy development and implementation
- Written communication and 'paperwork'
- Getting 'big players' from external stakeholders on board
- Clear distinction about what the organization does – i.e., how does it differ from the other players?
- Demonstrating authoritative grasp of issues – illustrate with successful outcomes based on real case studies
- Focus on seeing things through – concrete delivery
- Communication and engagement with Central Government to demonstrate capability to deliver and enhance understanding of their demands

The central issues were becoming very clear to me, but I was unsure if Peter had grasped the situation. We went back through the feedback and Peter began to identify specific actions (*Step 4: Initiate and evaluate options*) for him rather than the organization. At the end of the session Peter tore up his draft action plan and committed to producing one with a more personal emphasis for the next session (*Step 6: Valid action plan* and *Step 7: Encourage momentum*).

Session 4

Just as I had thought that Peter had reverted to old ways and was circling he surprised me in the next session. Having reflected on the feedback he had finally identified where the root cause of the issue lay – his communication style. The way in which he spoke and presented was too general and made him appear woolly and ill-informed. He was seen as great at big picture vision but gave such little detail that people doubted his ability to deliver. It was now time to move on from this style.

We devoted much of the session to looking at ways he could do things differently (*Step 2: Creative brainstorming of alternatives*); in turn, this led to the formulation of specific goals (*Step 3: Hone goals*). Peter set himself goals relating to his communication with his Board and with specific external stakeholders, and he committed to revising his action plan to achieve these goals (*Step 6: Valid action plan* and *Step 7: Encourage momentum*).

Session 5

Peter had just come back from an away day with the Board. They had given him quite a tough time but he used the work we had been doing on his action plan to convince them that both he and the organization were on course. Nevertheless, there was still some scepticism from the Board about whether he had really changed or was just saying what they wanted to hear.

This prompted me to work with him to see things from their perspective. Putting himself in their shoes, what would it take to convince them? These exercises brought further insights and served to help Peter refine his strategy for achieving his goals (*Step 4: Initiate and evaluate options*). At the end of the session Peter decided to identify specific examples that provided concrete evidence of how he and the organization were achieving success.

Final Session

In our final session Peter was able to report that he had had a very good first year appraisal from his Chair. It had boosted his confidence and helped him to drive through some tough proposals that altered the internal structure of the organization to make it more responsive to its external stakeholders. These changes had been a by-product of our early 360-degree work that took into account the views of external stakeholders. Peter felt that he now had a good level of support from within the organization and its Board and that both the organization's and his personal influence was gradually becoming more highly regarded externally. To a large extent he had achieved his goals, although he was aware that it was an ongoing process to which he needed to continue to devote attention. We then took time to reflect back on the sessions and the progress that had been made (*Step 7: Encourage momentum*). Peter had valued our sessions, not only for the assistance in achieving his goals but also for the simple fact of having time to think things through with an independent sounding board.

We discussed his next steps and he decided to build in time for reflection and discussion by working with a colleague from his action learning set (from a top manager programme he had attended) to maintain a regular independent challenge session. Although we still exchange occasional emails (*Step 7: Encourage momentum*), my formal role was over and Peter now has sustainable strategies to take him forward into the next stage of his career.

Conclusion

In this chapter we described the development of the Achieve Coaching Model® and provided examples of how it is used in practice. In doing so, we aimed to contribute to the development of the discipline and practice of coaching in organizations by shedding light into our 'black box' and making the executive coaching process more transparent – for the benefit of coaches, coaching and clients.

We hope that the steps we have outlined provide openings for further research into the effectiveness of the coaching process and each stage in it, the impact it has on the client and her outcomes, and how we, as practitioners, can further improve our coaching practice. We welcome further conversation with scholars and practitioners about our model and its use as well as how to support ongoing development and advancement of the various models that inform and guide coaching practices across the globe.

References

Berg, I., and Miller, S. (1992). *Working with the problem drinker.* New York: Norton.

Luft, J., and Ingham, H. (1955). The Johari window, a graphic model of interpersonal awareness. *Proceedings of the Western Training Laboratory in group development.* Los Angeles: UCLA.

McFadzean, E. S. (2000). Techniques to enhance creative thinking. *Team Performance Management,* 6(3/4), 62–72.

Whitmore, J. (2002). *Coaching for performance: Growing people, performance and purpose* (3rd rev. edn.). London: Nicholas Brealey.

Reflections on Applications of Coaching

David B. Drake

This section provided a look at how coaching has been applied to address six important issues facing today's workplaces and communities. In addition to the authors' expertise, these chapters also provided a rare look at their lived experience in working with clients around their topic. Even if the applications are outside your usual practice domain, they still offer a lot of valuable insights about what it means to evolve as a mature professional. Accordingly, you are encouraged to track the process they are explicating as well as the great content. Whether you are new to coaching or consider yourself a seasoned professional, we invite you to reflect on the following questions as a catalyst for new ways of seeing yourself, your clients and your practice.

6. Sandy Gordon – An Appreciative Inquiry Coaching Approach to Developing Mental Toughness

(1) How would you describe and rate yourself in terms of your mental toughness? Based on the information in this chapter, where do you want to be more mentally tough in your life and how will you get there?

(2) How strengths-based and appreciative is your approach to coaching . . . really? Of the four Ds of the AI Cycle, which one comes easiest to you and which one is more of a stretch? How can you build out from what you do best?

(3) What is the key insight/inspiration you are taking from this chapter in terms of your resilience as a coach?

The Philosophy and Practice of Coaching: Insights and Issues for a New Era.
Edited by David B. Drake, Diane Brennan and Kim Gørtz.
© 2008 John Wiley & Sons, Ltd.

7. Charles Hamrick – Focus on Cultural Elements in Coaching: Experiences from China and Other Countries

(1) What are some of your earliest experiences that made you aware of 'culture' for yourself or in others? What are some of the stories you grew up with around these experiences and how has that shaped your approach to cultural dimensions in your coaching?

(2) How comfortable are you with silence . . . really . . . in your coaching conversations? How do/can you remain more conscious of culture, yourself and clients within these conversations?

(3) What is the key insight/inspiration you are taking from this chapter in terms of your epistemology as a coach?

8. Kristina Gyllensten – Coaching and Workplace Stress

(1) How do you manage stressors and stress in your own life and practice? What insights did you gain from this chapter about how to work more effectively with your stress and that of your clients?

(2) How do/can you study your own practice methods and outcomes as part of your continuous improvement and development? Do you have a place, such as in supervision, where you can talk through things in your practice that did not go well or as expected?

(3) What is the key insight/inspiration you are taking from this chapter in terms of your self-assessment as a coach?

9. Peter Webb – Coaching for Wisdom: Enabling Wise Decisions

(1) What do you see as the purpose for your coaching? What bodies of knowledge and experience inform that purpose, and how can you deepen your understanding of the development and nature of this aim?

(2) What stood out for you in terms of the various ways of looking at wisdom? In what ways do you see yourself as wise and how can you use this wisdom more fully in working with your clients?

(3) What is the key insight/inspiration you are taking from this chapter in terms of your epistemology wisdom as a coach?

10. Peter J. Reding and Marcia Collins – Coaching the Human Spirit

(1) What aspects of your life experience, your 'story', have impacted you in your development as a coach? How can you draw on this experience with vigour and rigour even as you focus on eliciting the client's 'own best answers'?

(2) How do you view the differences between the 'what-impedes-you?' and the 'what-inspires-you?' approaches? Which do you tend to use and how is that working for you?

(3) What is the key insight/inspiration you are taking from this chapter in terms of your advocacy for the human spirit as a coach?

11. Sabine Dembkowski and Fiona Eldridge – Achieving Tangible Results: The Development of a Coaching Model

(1) What models for coaching did you first use and how have you increased your repertoire since then? What would you recommend for next steps in building coaching models for a new era?

(2) What have you put in place to critically review and test the models upon which your coaching practice and behaviours are based – both on your own and from your peers?

(3) What is the key insight/inspiration you are taking from this chapter in terms of your diligence as a coach?

Part III

ORGANIZATIONS AND COACHING

12 Coaching the Team

David Clutterbuck

It is hard to envisage an organization without teams. Teams are the essential subcomponents that allow work to be divided, roles to be coordinated and chains of command to function. More academic study has been directed at teams than at almost any other aspect of organizational process, with the exception of leadership.

Coaching in the world of employment is a more recent topic for widespread study. There is very little empirical research to date and most of what exists tends to be qualitative, rather than quantitative, in nature – which suggests that we are still trying to define the process, rather than measure it. The small amount of qualitative work that exists focuses, by and large, on demonstrating the return on investment from executive coaching.

Research on coaching the workplace team, the combination of these two topics, is even sparser. In an extensive literature search, only one significant research-based article emerged. It builds on earlier research by the authors (Hackman and Wageman, 2005) on general team dynamics and by Gersick (1988), who established that project teams' approach to their task varies with the stage of their development and the stage of task completion. Extrapolating from this earlier work, Hackman and Wageman (2005) determined that team coaches need to adapt their approach to match a given team's stage of evolution and that the same principles can be adapted to other kinds of team than project teams. Their highly cogent extrapolation is, however, still theoretical – it has not to date been subjected to empirical testing with real teams.

The Philosophy and Practice of Coaching: Insights and Issues for a New Era.
Edited by David B. Drake, Diane Brennan and Kim Gørtz.
© 2008 John Wiley & Sons, Ltd.

It seems, therefore, that our knowledge base is sparse, to say the least. Yet, in searching the websites of 50 randomly selected coaching providers, I found that 29 claimed to be delivering team coaching in some form. A recent Google search produced 19 400 000 hits on 'team coaching'. The question arises: what knowledge base, if any, are providers of team coaching services building upon in offering such services? The extensive literature on team structure, typology, behaviours and effectiveness provides a valuable starting point for identifying the kind of coaching interventions, which may help teams develop greater insight into how they function and build the skills necessary to improve performance.

From my discussions with various coaching providers, it seems that there are two distinct categories. In one set, coaches simply transfer what they do in coaching individuals, add a dash of facilitation and/or team building, and wing it. In the other, coaches start from a deep understanding of the dynamics of teams, distinguish carefully between team coaching and team facilitation, and have a clear perception of the ethical and practical considerations involved in managing what can be a highly complex process. The latter was a much, much smaller group!

In this chapter, I begin by exploring some of the anthropological context behind our instincts to coach and to work in teams. I then review some of the key issues in team dynamics and present a typology of teams. I explore some of the differences between coaching individuals and coaching teams and between team coaching and team facilitation. Finally, I review some of the critical issues a team coach may need to help teams to manage and the nature of the relationship between an externally resourced team coach and the client organization.

An Anthropological Perspective

The emergence of our particular species of ape as the dominant animal on planet earth comes down to a series of accidents. Each accident gave us an ability and an instinct that worked together to increase our chances of survival and gain greater control of our environment. Which came first – the ability or the instinct – we can only guess, but the probability is that they developed in parallel, as a useful instinct became more manageable with the development of ways to control it. Three ability/instinct combinations, in particular, are relevant to this book:

- Intelligence and the instinct for curiosity and enquiry
- Speech and the instinct for passing on knowledge and skills
- Social skills and the instinct to collaborate to achieve collective goals

Human kind has all of these abilities and instincts to a greater degree than any other species, including our great ape cousins. The increasing pace of our societal and technological evolution is due to the combination and increasing competence of these ability/instinct pairings. It is probable that the pace of societal and technological evolution has already exceeded the capacity of our genetic evolution, hence the stresses and strains of everyday life in developed economies, and futurologists generally agree that the point where our own intelligence is insufficient to comprehend that of the thinking machines we create is only decades away (Kurzwell, 2005). For example, a 2001 study of over 400 commuters by scientists at the Centre for Psychotherapy Research in Stuttgart and the University Clinic in Ulm, Germany, found that commuters travelling more than 45 minutes each way had double the incidence and severity of pain, dizziness, exhaustion and severe sleep prevention compared to non-commuters.

The recent discovery of clues as to where the seat of intelligence may lie in the brain, in the lateral frontal cortex, is just part of a rapid expansion in our understanding of the nature and workings of various forms of intelligence. However, intelligence without curiosity is sterile. The combination led *Homo sapiens* to try to understand the world around him, to develop tools and strategies for achieving greater control, and to experiment and continuously improve the resulting technologies and skills.

Our ability to communicate, originally merely a means to coordinate activity within social groups for activities such as foraging and hunting, gave us the wherewithal to share knowledge and skills so we remained within the culture and advances in one place could rapidly be transferred to others. Without the instinct to share knowledge, however, that transfer would not have taken place, or at least would have been done so much more slowly. Sharing knowledge and ideas contributed incrementally to the increasing health, safety and viability of the social group. As our technologies become more and more effective – as well as faster and faster – at sharing, the elapsed time between major societal and technological changes becomes shorter and shorter. For our ancestors, a critical mediator in the communication speech/knowledge-sharing combination was the ability to represent abstract ideas through means such as numbers, drawings and metaphors. It is no coincidence that coaches in the modern world assist clients to quantify their commitment, their goals and their feelings; use conceptual models to draw out the relationship between complex factors in the client's situation; and make frequent use of metaphor and story to create comparisons and stimulate different perspectives.

The instinct to collaborate in social groups emerged in nature many times across many species. Survival of the individual is statistically more likely, if s/he protects and is protected by the group. Social groups develop rules about when and how to act for individual benefit and for the wider group benefit; they also establish rules for dealing with those who cheat. (Interestingly, humans have the most advanced skills of social cheating of all species. There seems to be an evolutionary race between our ability to cheat and other people's ability to recognize when we do so!) Numerous experiments investigating our sense of justice through game theory demonstrate that we have a built-in sense of fairness that leads us to punish those who cheat, even when we disadvantage ourselves by so doing. The social skills we develop have both genetic and environmentally learned components. Evolved for circumstances of small groups, with infrequent changes of membership, they do not always match the abilities increasingly required for operating in large groups, in small groups who change membership frequently, or in situations where individuals are members of multiple groups. Many of the problems we encounter relating to urban living and maintaining relationships with colleagues in remote teams are the result of a mismatch between our innate social skills and those demanded of us in a modern society.

Intriguingly, recent theories about the rise and decline of civilizations (Buchanan, 2005) suggest that groups who learn to cooperate better, develop the social cohesion that leads to the establishment of empires. Typically, they emerge in the relative chaos on the edge of existing empires. The collapse of empires, the same theory proposes, occurs when inequalities emerge between peoples within them. Eventually, the social competition between constituent groups within the empire overcomes the collaboration that brought them together. Similar experiences are often reported in strong work teams and companies, which emerge from the chaos within a large organization or in a disrupted marketplace; subsequently, the seeds of their undoing often emerge from internal conflict between groups.

These three combinations of ability and instinct – intelligence/curiosity; speech/sharing of knowledge and skills; social skills and instinct to collaborate – come to the fore in the work team. One would think these would be ideal situations to leverage our collaborative skills to drive the process of collective advancement most efficiently, most creatively and most enjoyably. Unfortunately, teams rarely operate at anything like optimum effectiveness. Like individuals, they are poor at recognizing their own strengths and weaknesses, and performance-sapping conflict is often sublimated for fear of undermining social cohesion. Yet social cohesion (getting on well together) does not necessarily translate into high levels of performance. Enter the team coach as a more or less objective observer who can help the team to:

- Recognize and understand its own dynamics and psychology.
- Surface and address issues, which hinder collective performance.
- Establish and pursue collective goals, not just in respect of the task, but also with regard to *how* the task is achieved (in particular how the team learns and how its members behave).
- Provide support and encouragement at critical points.

In terms of the three ability/instinct combinations, team coaches:

- Legitimize the process of enquiring about current practices and asking naive questions.
- Help the team develop the skills to communicate with each other and with external stakeholders.
- Help the team develop behavioural competencies that support collaboration.

In order to do this, team coaches need an extensive understanding of how teams function and how they react to both internal and external influences. They also need a repertoire of responses that balances the need to address immediate operational priorities against the need to develop processes and behaviours that support continuous learning both collectively and individually. The next section provides an overview of some of the critical areas of team functioning with which a team coach should be familiar.

Key Issues in Team Dynamics

The extensive research on teams throws up a number of key questions, some of which are more or less answered. These questions include:

- What *is* a team in the working environment?
- How does size affect its potential to achieve?
- What makes a work team effective?

What is a Team in the Working Environment?

It is clear that a random bunch of people, who come together, do not necessarily constitute a team. For that reason many of the groupings within organizations, particularly at senior levels, are clearly not teams, although they may often be referred to as such. There is something extra about the nature and quality of the interaction between members of a group that turns it into a team. John Katzenbach (Katzenbach and Smith, 1993), who has written widely on the common confusion between teams and groups, describes a team as: 'A small number of people with complementary skills, who are committed to a common purpose, performance goals and approach, for which they hold themselves mutually accountable'. Let us look at the words he uses.

Firstly, 'small'. There is a limit to the size of a team before it degenerates back into a group. Psychologists talk of 'social loafing' to describe the phenomenon, by which people are content to throttle back on their own effort and commitment as the team becomes larger. It seems that the average effort of an individual alone is more than twice that of the same person, when working with eight colleagues (Ringelmann, 1913). Various studies have tried to determine ideal team size, but it seems that this varies according to the nature of the team's task and, in particular, to the degree of interdependence of its members. The more integrated the team needs to be, the smaller the size, with highly integrated teams functioning best with five to eight members (Ratcliffe, Beckstead, and Hanke, 1999). Many teams in the workplace are either too small to generate diversity of perspective, or too large to function effectively. The latter often devolve into sub-teams, which may or may not cooperate with each other.

Secondly, 'complementary skills'. Groups do not necessarily capitalize upon the diversity of skills of their members, nor assign them roles accordingly. To become a team, members must actively collaborate and seek to manage a task or process together, rather than be managed by it.

Thirdly, 'common purpose or goals'. Where do the team's goals come from and are they collectively espoused? A team differs from a group in that the shared goal has similar meaning to all the members and that they have collectively agreed on how they intend to bring about the goals. Groups may have shared goals, at a very broad level, but lack cohesion about the method of achieving them and the roles each party plays in doing so. Teams also subordinate individual goals and priorities to those of the collective.

Fourthly, 'mutual accountability'. In a team, the success or failure of the task is shared by all of the members. Many sales teams, for example, undermine mutual accountability by overemphasizing individual bonuses at the expense of collective recognition and reward.

Other important factors in defining a work team include:

- A collective sense of membership, boundaries and what constitutes an insider versus an outsider. While groups may also adopt different language, assumptions and norms, teams perceive these as instrumental in achieving the task rather than as just a badge of social belonging.

- Teams use more structured and more varied forms of communication than groups. They invest more energy in maintaining the quality of communication and in networking both within the team and on behalf of the team externally.
- Team members give and expect more support from each other than group members. They recognize and respond to each other's needs for encouragement, practical help and guidance. They are prepared to put aside their own priorities and accept personal discomfort or disadvantage to provide this support when it is needed.
- Teams have a greater capacity to enable people to adapt what they do to meet the collective goals.

Therefore, a key initial task for a team coach is to establish whether the group he or she is working with is really a team. If it is a group instead, the coach needs to determine with the members and any other stakeholders:

- How important is it for this group to be a team? (What difference will it make? Could the same objectives be achieved from a lot of individuals working to a broadly shared agenda?)
- How prepared are they to invest in the learning and process management needed to become a team?
- How long realistically will it take?
- How well will the organizational environment, in which the group operates, support its efforts to become a team?
- What positive or negative experience of being in a team have the members had in the past? How does that influence their willingness to be a team now?

Understanding Team Dynamics

Assuming that there is a collective will to become a team, or that the group is already operating as a team, the coach needs to understand some of its basic dynamics. Some of the critical issues here are examined in the next few sections.

How Diverse is the Membership?

Diversity can be a strength or a weakness, depending on how it is managed. Recent research (Early and Masakowski, 2000; Fay, Borrill, Amir, Haward, and West, 2006), demonstrates that homogeneous teams (ones where members saw their colleagues as like themselves) tend to outperform heterogeneous teams (ones where people see colleagues as different from themselves) in the short term, especially in customer service. However, heterogeneous teams tended to be more creative and more able to initiate change from within. The least viable teams had a mixture of homogeneous and heterogeneous members – people tended to split into camps based on perceived affinities. Over time, however, some of these heterogeneous teams outperformed their homogeneous counterparts when they engaged in dialogues that allowed them to create their own unified culture and norms. The research does not tell us if coaching played a role in this transformation, but it would certainly appear that this is a fertile area to address through team coaching.

What Makes a Team Creative?

Research does not support the notion that giving teams greater autonomy makes them more creative. On the contrary, self-management can lead to even more restrictive and creativity-numbing rules and norms than existed before (Barker, 1993). The most common reason teams are less creative than they need to be is that people are too busy to step back and reflect. A key part of the team coach's role is to provide both the space and opportunity for reflective space and to equip the team with the skills to use it effectively. He or she can also encourage the team to become more open to ideas and naive questions. It is unfortunate that many teams and groups suffer from a tendency both to ignore the 'prophet in his own land' and to reject ideas from outside on the basis of 'not invented here'.

In one team I coached, I began to suspect that they had a very low opinion of their ability to be creative; this assessment was confirmed by their responses to my enquiries and led naturally to further questions:

- What value would being more creative bring to the team's ability to perform?
- Where does this self-limiting belief come from?
- When has the team been creative?
- What can you do to capture the quality of those creative moments more often?

In this instance, the team needed both to believe it *could* be creative and to *want* to be creative – in the face of a strong perception that creative people 'stuck out' and became targets within the organization as a whole. It was only when we had worked through those issues that it became appropriate to introduce them to a variety of practical creativity techniques.

How Effective is the Team's Communication both Internally and Externally?

Research by Ancona and his colleagues (Ancona, 1990; Ancona and Caldwell, 1988, 1992) indicates that teams need to be effective at communicating vertically upwards (*ambassadorial communication*) and horizontally (both internally and with other teams); they also need to be effective at scanning their environment, e.g., developing good communication networks that keep them informed of change in technology, markets and organizational politics. Accordingly, team coaches can explore critical issues such as how much time and energy the team spends on communication, how it manages its reputation (beginning with what reputation it already has among key stakeholders), how skilled the members are at communicating, and whether communication is an expected part of their role description. One team realized, for example, as a result of perceptive questions from the team coach, that the tickbox internal customer satisfaction forms it distributed every month were actually a barrier to communication. It opted instead to go talk to internal customers, a move that yielded immediate positive results in terms of team reputation and cooperation from other teams.

How does the Team Manage Conflict?

Conflict does not have to be destructive. *Relationship conflict* (based on antipathy towards others) is generally dysfunctional, but *task conflict* (how the task should be done) and *process conflict* (how duties and resources should be allocated), when well managed, can be a positive aid to team effectiveness (Jehn, 1995). These forms of conflict can help teams build greater understanding of complex issues, avoid groupthink and stimulate creativity. In general, the more complex the task, the more the potential for using conflict beneficially.

One useful approach we have developed in coaching encourages the team to examine incidents and sources of relationship, task and process conflict in the context of goals, motivations, values and methods. First, each individual within the team creates his or her own conflict matrix. Next, if there are subgroups within the team, they combine their thoughts into a more detailed matrix. Finally, the perceptions of the whole team are integrated into a composite matrix. Typical outcomes of this approach include a set of behavioural ground rules for recognizing and managing conflict and collective learning objectives for blame-free analysis of future conflict situations.

How does the Team Make Decisions?

It can be very revealing to ask a team how it makes decisions, not least because they have often not thought about it. For many teams, there is the perception that decisions just happen as a result of discussion, consensus just emerges, or the leader just determines what shall be done. In reality, effective decision-making involves a series of mental steps, including recognizing that there is a problem and trying to understand it, identifying and selecting from alternative solutions and following through with action that is well-planned and well-timed. Along the way there are numerous points where the process can go awry. As part of the initial assessment, a coach may wish to help the team determine the nature and quality of its current decision-making processes. Useful questions can include:

- How often do you have to make decisions in a rush?
- How often are decisions overturned once they are made?
- Do decisions usually lead to a collective commitment (not the same as a consensus!)?
- Is everyone clear why decisions are made?
- Is there agreement amongst the team about when decisions should be made on partial information and when full detail is required?
- Is it clear who should be involved in different types of decision and in what role?

What is the Team's Relationship with its Leader?

Leaders, both formal and informal, have a substantial impact on team performance. Over-management stunts initiative; the abdication of responsibility leads to intra-team conflict and confused objectives. In understanding how a specific team and its leader function, the coach needs to explore issues such as:

- How much respect is there between the team and its leader?
- Does the team have an atmosphere of psychological safety? (i.e., can people say what they think without fear?)
- How much time does the leader spend developing the talent in his or her team?

- How much belief do they express in what each member of their team can achieve? A lack of belief tends to become a self-fulfilling prophecy in terms of actual performance (Livingstone, 2003).

How Well does the Team Balance its Focus on Task, Behaviour and Learning?

Our studies of learning teams, reported below (Clutterbuck, 1999), aimed to build an understanding of how different types of team managed learning. One of the concepts to emerge from the interviews related to focus of team attention. The teams in our sample described their struggle to maintain a balance between attending to task, behaviour and learning. It appears (although it has not been tested in a rigorous study) that all three foci are essential. Failure to focus on the task tends to lead to a great deal of wasted effort; failure to attend to behaviour leads to negative conflict and hence detracts from performance; failure to learn makes the team's thinking and processes less and less relevant to the task. Some useful questions a coach can ask to assess the relative health and balance of each of the three foci include:

- Does everyone have the same understanding about the task priorities?
- What does this team avoid talking about?
- How do you know whether the pace of learning in your team is sufficient to keep pace with change in your environment?

It seems that effective team coaches need to add a number of skills to an existing portfolio of one-to-one coaching competences. In particular, they need:

- A deep understanding of team dynamics, based on both practical (hands-on) experience and a wide reading of research.
- A recognition of the different types of team in organizations and how differences in membership and task affect behaviour, task achievement and learning processes.
- A comprehensive awareness of the difference in relationship dynamics and interpersonal behaviours between coaching individuals and coaching groups (and between team coaching and team facilitation).
- An understanding of when it is the time and when it is not propitious to coach the team. For example, it appears from Gersick's (1988) research that project teams are much more open and responsive to coaching at some times than at others.

A Typology of Teams

A decade ago, I led a research team investigating the nature of learning within teams. Like with team coaching now, at that time there was very little empirical research on the phenomenon. Indeed, we carried out two literature searches through two different universities just to check that the volume of research was really as low as it appeared! One of the drivers for this research was a recognition that teams are not all the same. They differ considerably, for example, in the level of interdependability of their members. Some teams require very close, sequential collaboration between members; others require members to work on their own, but to coordinate regularly. Some teams do their tasks sequentially (e.g., an assembly line); others in parallel. Teams also differ in the level of stability of both task and membership.

This latter distinction provided the basis for a typology of teams; it has proven useful in focusing coaching interventions because each of the six team types identified from the research has its own pluses and minuses in terms of learning dynamics. The six types of team are shown in Figure 12.1. They are, in more detail:

- *Stable teams*, which perform the same task, or variations of it, over a long period, with relatively stable membership.
- *Project teams ('Hit teams')*, which are set up to deal with short-term, usually one-off tasks, with members typically drawn from several other teams.
- *Evolutionary teams*, which tackle longer-term developmental projects, such as the design and launch of a major new product or the

Figure 12.1   A typology of learning teams.

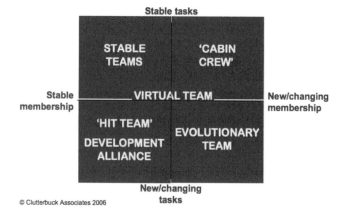

establishment of a greenfield factory site. Their membership is relatively fluid, with members entering and leaving according to the stage the project has reached.

- *Development alliances*, composed of two or more people not linked within a normal team, who agree to share learning – for example, off-line mentoring.
- *Virtual teams*, which typically have no formal recognition, but whose members work together for mutually understood goals, though often on an ad hoc basis. These are, in effect, a network with strong ties and influence and they often including people outside the organization such as suppliers or key customers.
- *Cabin crew teams* perform the same task, but with different members – sometimes with the membership changing every operation. Examples include film crew and repertory theatre.

Based on our research in UK-based workshops, each type of team has its own strengths and weaknesses from a learning perspective as follows:

- *Stable teams* easily fall into routines, where there is little stimulus to question how things are done. Only under crisis, normally externally generated, do they put great effort into learning, and sometimes not even then.
- *Cabin crew teams* meet infrequently, perhaps once only. Although the task remains the same, and must be performed consistently (as with the cabin crew on an airplane), the membership changes frequently.
- *Project teams* exist for such short periods that, by the time they have gone through the maturing stages of *forming, storming, norming* and *performing*, they are disbanded and the acquired learning is scattered. The need for speed in resolving problems or making things happen leaves little time for reflection and review of learning.
- *Evolutionary teams* suffer from the same learning difficulties as project teams, but usually have the breathing space to reach maturity. However, they encounter a second set of learning problems at that time in terms of how they deal with newcomers. The original members have coalesced into a functioning team and they have a strong, shared experience and understanding of the values, principles and reasoning behind the way the project is being run. Newcomers find it difficult to join the club. All too often, there are two teams – insiders and outsiders – because the newcomers cannot catch up with the learning the original members have undergone.
- *Virtual teams*, being mainly informal, rely on intuitive systems to ensure that learning takes place. Indeed, knowledge can be seen as

the currency of the virtual team, so people with low levels of influence and experience may not be invited to join. (This possibly explains why so few people at lower levels in organizations in our research had experience of working in virtual teams.)

* *Development alliances* have fewer inherent learning problems than other types of teams, in part because their focus is already on learning. The primary problems tend to revolve around *what* people learn in this mode. The attitudes, habits and behaviours of the more experienced partner will inevitably rub off, but it may be that not all of them are helpful. Another frequently reported problem is insufficient frequency of interaction necessary to make a significant difference.

Differences Between Coaching Individuals and Coaching Teams

Team coaching is frequently confused with individual coaching, team facilitation and team building. Coaching several individuals within a team, or all the team members individually, is not the same as coaching the team. Indeed, without the umbrella of collective coaching, based on team goals, behaviours and learning, coaching multiple individuals in the same team raises both practical and ethical issues. It is hard to be really open and honest about your views of team colleagues with someone, who will also be gathering information about how those colleagues feel about you. It also requires a high level of competence in systemic thinking for a coach to understand the complexity of the interpersonal dynamics and to avoid being influenced more by one set of individuals than another. As a result, the style and quality of supervision for coaches in these situations needs to be provided at a much higher level of awareness and sophistication.

Coaching the team differs from coaching individuals in several key ways. Firstly, there is a much lower level of confidentiality, so, it is a lot harder and more time-consuming to build a high level of openness and trusting dialogue than one-to-one. The thoughts and concerns an individual is willing to share on a one-to-one basis may be very different from those he or she is willing to share openly in front of working colleagues. Most of the team coaches we interviewed reported that they often had to supplement team coaching sessions with individual sessions. Some made a point of interviewing all team members in depth before team coaching sessions, to identify issues and perceptions, which they may be reluctant to articulate, but which the coach can introduce on their behalf.

Secondly, people think and learn at different speeds, so the coach is constantly balancing individual and collective learning, to ensure that no-one gets left behind – not least because this will have a significant impact on commitment to goals, plans and the coaching process itself. One technique we frequently use to assist this process in team meetings involves a period of reflection before any discussion of a topic is allowed. During these minutes of reflection, team members each record their response to three questions: 'What do I want to say, to hear and to achieve from this discussion?' Everyone then reads what he or she has written and the discussion begins. At key decision points, the coach (or team leader outside of team coaching sessions) can ask, 'Did you say what you wanted to say, hear what you wanted to hear, achieve what you wanted to achieve?' In this way, everyone is kept on board and dissension minimized.

The most effective team coaches (insofar as we were able to judge their effectiveness) all had a portfolio of approaches for managing individual variations in pace of thinking, learning and commitment. For example, one described how a team manager and one of his colleagues would race ahead in their thinking, produce a flurry of ideas and then become frustrated because colleagues took a long time to catch up. When this had happened a couple of times, she suggested that the two fast thinkers form a subgroup that pulled together all the potential counter-arguments to the new ideas. Not only did this take pressure off the rest of the team, so they could come to an understanding and view at their own pace, but it improved the overall quality of decision-making, because the two fast-thinkers identified issues they had not considered. The rest of the team also found that the counter-arguments helped them to structure and articulate some of the concerns they had.

A third major distinction between individual and team coaching relates to the scope of the issues discussed. By their nature, team coaching issues relate to the team as a whole, so individual concerns become relevant only insofar as they impact the team's overall performance and social cohesion. A challenge for the team coach is recognizing when an issue for an individual has the potential to affect team performance. One method I have used on occasion has been to encourage the team to coach each other in pairs, focusing on how the team environment is influencing each person's ability to perform and how, in turn, their ability to perform may affect that of the team as a whole.

Moreover, just as teams come in different shapes, sizes and purposes, so do team coaches. A useful analogy is the football stadium. One type of coaching role is that carried out by the captain of the team – the coach as supervisor. The captain guides and encourages colleagues, both individually and collectively, clarifying the performance required from them and helping them determine how they will deliver it. Engaged continuously in the play, the captain has principal responsibility for balancing task, behaviour and learning foci.

Out on the touchline (the edge of the playing field), the line-manager-as-coach can only watch the activity. He or she can reinforce the team's resources from time to time (for example, sending on a fresh player), but is limited in how far he or she can become involved in the play. An advantage of this position is that it gives a greater measure of objectivity, although the coach is still very much a stakeholder in the game.

Further away, in the boxes, sits another kind of coach, who can be compared to the internal professional coach now found in many large organizations. He or she is not engaged in the action at all, and can stand back and see the bigger, longer-term picture. Further away again, outside the stadium, the external coach does not observe the game at all. He or she is able to work with the team or with internal managers/coaches to help them make sense of their own experiences and use these to address performance issues.

These same perspectives can be applied to individual coaching as well. In both cases, the more distant the team coach's perspective, the wider the portfolio of coaching skills he or she is likely to require. The primary difference between individual and team coaching appears therefore to relate to the complexity of the team coaching role. Team coaches have a lot more to think about, both overall and simultaneously, and hence may need a higher level of skills. One of the necessary skill sets may be facilitation, but it is important to separate out the roles of facilitator and coach, even if they may sometimes overlap.

Differences Between Team Coaching and Team Facilitation

Team facilitation is also a different discipline, although a team coach may sometimes move into facilitation and vice versa. Both approaches are similar in that they work on the quality of the group's thinking and collective awareness. Among the many differences we identified in our research I will address two for our purposes here. (1) Team facilitation involves a 'directed' dialogue – the facilitator leads the team through a structure thinking process, which he or she believes will aid insight – while team coaching more typically involves an emergent dialogue – where the outcome and flow of the dialogue is far more open and the structure of the conversation comes from within the team. (In coaching jargon, it is client-led.) (2) Another difference relates to outcomes. For facilitation, the focus is normally on an agreement on team direction and method; for team coaching, the outcomes relate to team and individual achievement. The team coach is typically working more closely with the team, over a longer period and there is greater two-way learning (i.e., the coach learns with the team). This distinction can sometimes be compared to the difference between a reagent, which is changed by the experience, and a catalyst, which is not.

The ultimate aim of team coaching, as with individual coaching, is to develop the intrinsic skills and habits for self-coaching. At the end of the coaching intervention, the team should have the skills to identify and confront its own unresolved issues, to establish and pursue both collective and individual learning goals and enhance the quality of collective and individual thinking and decision-making. This is one more differentiating factor with facilitation, where there is not normally an expectation of long-term skills transfer.

Team building consultants sometimes describe what they do as coaching, but again, there are significant differences. Leaving aside very real doubts about how effective team building is beyond the very immediate short term, team building focuses more on 'how do we get on with each other?', while team coaching is more concerned with 'how do we learn together?' and 'how do we perform together?' Team building is usually a one-off event or a series of such events, often disassociated from the team task, whereas team coaching is more of a continuous process, intimately engaged with the team task.

Critical Issues a Team Coach May Face

The research that led to the book *Coaching the Team at Work* (Clutterbuck, 2007) identifies a range of issues that team coaches need to be aware of and, if those issues arise, to have appropriate (flexible, robust and insight-provoking) approaches to address. They tend to fall into three categories:

- *Managing interpersonal dynamics* is about helping the team develop the internal capability to surface and deal with conflict, to build the collective emotional intelligence and collective self-belief, and to manage stress and to establish and maintain a healthy coaching climate.
- *Temporal issues* relates to decisions about when and how the coach should intervene; to the nature of the team's temporal orientation (how it thinks about past, present and future and the appropriateness of this orientation to the team's task); and to time management. The only significant empirical study of team coaching (Hackman and

Wageman, 2005) deals specifically with timing the interventions. Investigating project teams only, it found that the coaching intervention was most effective when it was structured to address the issues most on the team's mind at each stage of its development. At the early stages, coaching needs to focus on clarifying the team task, gaining commitment to the shared goals, defining boundaries, roles and responsibilities and creating mutual motivation. Addressing strategic issues at this point does not appear to work. The collective will to address these emerges at about the midpoint of the project. Finally, towards the end of the project, the team is open to reflecting upon and codifying its learning. While there is no direct evidence to transpose these findings to other types of teams, the authors suggest that more permanent teams go through similar cycles of activity and, hence, readiness for coaching. So, at the beginning of any intervention, a team coach needs to assess what kind of need or issue the team is mentally prepared to address.

● *Managing key processes* relates to goal setting, understanding how the team functions and building its capacity in terms of creativity, systems thinking and communication. It also covers evaluating the impact of coaching. This category covers a wide range of issues, including, for example, how the team makes decisions. Processes may relate either to the team itself (what it does and how), or to the tools, techniques and approaches of team coaching.

Having a wide enough portfolio of approaches and frameworks to help the team tackle these often complex issues is a challenge for even the most experienced team coaches. Equally challenging is how they will ensure that the coaching process continues after the coach has backed off. The transition to self-coaching needs to be planned and agreed to well ahead with the team. Some of the practical steps, which can assist this transition, include:

● Helping the team determine its touchstone questions. These are questions against which it can benchmark decisions about priorities. For example: 'Will it make the customer come back?'
● Building the practice of networking and communicating with other teams and other resources to ensure the continued flow of ideas and information that will stimulate creativity and innovation.
● Creating regular forums for generating feedback for each other.
● Assigning team learning roles to each team member. Our studies identified eight such roles:
   – *Motivator* – providing vision and enthusiasm for learning.
   – *Skills coach* – transferring task knowledge and skills.

- *Reviewer* – championing and being a role model for creating and using reflective space.
- *Question-raiser* – raising issues the team needs to discuss, but may have been avoiding; sometimes taking a naive perspective to open up issues.
- *Gateway to permission and resources* – the ambassador role. (Although typically played by the leader, there are developmental and performance benefits in making this a role for several or all team members.)
- *Gateway to knowledge* – using informal networks to access expertise and information elsewhere.
- *Specialist* – a knowledge resource in a specific area useful but not central to the team's task.
- *Recorder* – capturing and recording learning, to prevent reinventing the wheel and help newcomers learn the ropes more quickly.
- Creating a team development plan, which contains the collective aspirations for task, behaviour and learning, and integrates these with both the business plan and the individual personal development plans.

The Unknowns of Team Coaching

Our knowledge of what makes an effective team coach is still relatively thin, but growing rapidly. There remain significant questions about the skills base required, particularly at the line-manager-as-coach level, and about the ethical parameters of team coaching. For example, is it appropriate to coach the team both collectively and individually? Will team members feel constrained in speaking openly to someone who also has intimate conversations with their boss?

Similarly, there is an emerging debate about whether team coaches should be expected to have a separate, additional qualification above that of executive coaches. How can a prospective client determine whether they have the appropriate knowledge and experience? In the next few years, we will see a lot more discussion about the role and scope of team coaching and, I hope, an expanding volume of empirical study that examines different situations, types and outcomes of team coaching.

References

Ancona, D. G. (1990). Outward Bound: Strategies for team survival in the organization. *Academy of Management Journal*, 33, 334–365.

Ancona, D. G., and Caldwell, D. E. (1988). Beyond task and maintenance: Defining external functions in groups. *Group and Organizational Studies*, 13, 468–494.

Ancona, D. G., and Caldwell, D. E. (1992). Bridging the boundary: External activity and performance in organizations. *Administrative Science Quarterly*, 37, 634–665.

Barker, J. (1993). Tightening the iron cage: Concertive control in self-managing teams. *Administrative Science Quarterly*, 38, 408–437.

Baron, R. A. (1991). Positive effects of conflict: A cognitive perspective. *Employer Responsibilities and Rights Journal*, 4, 25–36.

Buchanan, M. (2005). *Small world*. London: Weidenfeld & Nicholson.

Clutterbuck, D. (1999). *Learning teams*. Herts TEC: Exemplas.

Clutterbuck, D. (2007). *Coaching the team at work*. London: Nicholas Brealey.

Early, P. C., and Masakowski, E. (2000). Creating hybrid team cultures: An empirical test of transnational team functioning. *Academy of Management Journal*, 43(1), 26–49.

Fay, D., Borrill, C., Amir, Z., Haward, R., and West, M. A. (2006). Getting the most out of multidisciplinary teams: A multi-sample study of team innovation in health care. *Journal of Occupational and Organizational Psychology*, 79, 553–567.

Gerisck, C. J. G. (1988). Time and transition in work teams: Toward a new model of group development. *Academy of Management Journal*, 31, 9–41.

Hackman, J. R., and Wageman, R. (2005). A theory of team coaching. *Academy of Management Review*, 30(2), 269–287.

Jehn, K. A. (1995). A multimethod examination of the benefits and detriments of intergroup conflict. *Administrative Science Quarterly*, 40, 256–282.

Katzenbach, J. R., and Smith, D. K. (1993). *The wisdom of teams: Creating the high-performance organization*. Boston: Harvard Business School Press.

Kurzwell, R. (2005). Human life – The next generation. *New Scientist*, 24 Sept.

Livingstone, J. S. (2003). Pygmalion in management. *Harvard Business Review*, 81(1), 97–106.

Putnam, L. L. (1994). Proactive conflict: Negotiation as implicit consultation. *International Journal of Conflict Management*, 5, 285–299.

Ratcliffe, R., Beckstead, S. M., and Hanke, S. H. (1999). The use and management of teams: A how-to guide. *Quality Progress*, June.

Ringelmann, M. (1913). *Amenagement des fumiers et des purins*. Paris: Librairie Agricole de la Maison Rustique.

13 Leadership Coaching: The Impact on the Organization

Diane Brennan

Introduction

Leadership coaching is an increasingly prevalent focus in today's organization. The past ten or so years have produced numerous articles, journals, books and research documenting the practice and effectiveness of coaching. This chapter will explore the value of coaching for the leader and ultimately the organization. You will meet my client John (name changed) who is the chief executive officer (CEO) of a hospital organization in the United States. While the case example involves a healthcare executive based in the USA, the situation, concerns and process are applicable to just about any industry anywhere in the world. The chapter will examine coaching over a two-year period and connect the coach and client's work together in practice, process and results, to various theories and coaching competencies observed either during the coaching or in reflection afterward. Understanding one's own impact from the perspective of others may seem intuitive or even insignificant, yet it is the singular most important learning anyone in a leadership position can gain in a coaching relationship.

I say this reflecting on my learning as the coach and the client's feedback on his learning throughout our work together. Considering Robert Kegan's (1994) 'orders of consciousness', and how we construct meaning throughout our lives, coaching serves as a vehicle that allows for a shift in consciousness. The client presented in the third order of consciousness where he saw other perspectives and internalized these, yet he did

The Philosophy and Practice of Coaching: Insights and Issues for a New Era.
Edited by David B. Drake, Diane Brennan and Kim Gørtz.
© 2008 John Wiley & Sons, Ltd.

not resolve the conflict between his view and the view of others. Over time the client moved to Kegan's fourth order of consciousness where he not only saw other perspectives, he used these to strengthen his own, and he clearly recognized the impact of his learning which you will see influenced his ongoing work and behaviour.

Prior to beginning my journey as a coach, I spent over twenty years in healthcare in various clinical and leadership positions. I am one of those who learned management by doing and then later completed undergraduate and graduate degrees to match. Having had the practice, I appreciated learning the theory and using its power to grow in my career as a healthcare executive. I entered coaching in 2000 and enrolled in a coaching training programme which focused on skill building and practice. I recall noticing how valuable my management experience and learning were in my development, not to use as an adviser or consultant, but as context or background for understanding and informing my coaching. As a lifelong learner, I completed an Evidence Based Coaching Certificate (Fielding Graduate University, Santa Barbara, CA) in 2005 that provided me with a stronger connection between theory and practice in coaching. This coursework resulted in my ability to more consciously connect practice to theory, use theory to inform my coaching, and sometimes even 'educate' my clients.

For example, one day John came to our call full of energy and excitement about what was occurring for him and for the organization. Capitalizing on this energy I asked John what he noticed or observed about himself, how he felt, and what he noticed about others. John's description mirrored what Mihaly Csikszentmihalyi (1990) describes as flow, where you are so caught up in an activity that time becomes irrelevant; there is a sense of continual energy and satisfaction. Being engaged in a flow activity pushes us to higher levels of performance. I referenced Csikszentmihalyi and we talked about the concept of flow: how to recognize, recreate and strengthen his 'flow' experience for further personal growth. Had I not engaged in the EBC work as part of my own professional development, I would have missed this opportunity for connection to theory and the opportunity for deeper discussion and learning for the client and for the coach.

Case Description

John, an experienced executive in his mid-fifties, came to coaching at the recommendation of a team of consultants working with his organization. The hospital had received a poor rating on an employee satisfaction survey, and while senior leadership 'fixed' many issues identified by the employees, the survey results continued to worsen over a two-year period. It was difficult for John and the leadership team to understand what happened to cause this continuing decline in satisfaction. There was a palpable sense of scepticism among John and the senior team around the engagement of yet another consultant and process. What would be different this time?

Initial Findings

In my initial interviews with John and the senior team I heard frustration and fear around whether change was even possible. I also heard an element of blame in conversations with consultants and senior staff directed toward John. John voiced his responsibility as the one ultimately in charge. He was not new to his role as CEO. The organization was in financial difficulty when John arrived nearly ten years prior and he successfully turned the situation around to create a financially thriving resource for the community. The senior leadership team also included long-term employees, a few even longer-term than John, and in contrast to what was present in the surveys, employees voiced a strong sense of commitment to the organization which to them represented a family with a culture of caring for generations.

Under John's leadership, the hospital had years of increasing growth in facilities and services, a positive reputation in the community, a tradition of long-term employees from within their town and surrounding areas, and a genuine feeling of family and community. This was a growing organization in an evolving complex industry with challenges and obstacles that were difficult for the senior leadership team to navigate and difficult, if not impossible, for the regular worker to even consider. Declining reimbursement and increasing operating costs had a negative impact on employee benefits over the years. In addition, the increasing age and acuity of the patient population along with a shortage of nursing and skilled clinical professionals resulted in staffing challenges.

Current Reality

In *The Fifth Discipline*, Peter Senge (1990) talks about the learning organization, 'an organization that is continually expanding its capacity to create its future. John's organization was expanding and growing, though more in what Senge calls 'survival or adaptive learning', learning what is important or necessary to survive. The organization engaged consultants and identified problems and the leadership team tackled many of the concerns. There was a feeling of value and accomplishment only to learn their work was not enough as evidenced in the employee satisfaction survey results.

The hospital had conducted an annual employee satisfaction survey for over ten years. They used the same survey company for multiple years and had confidence in the survey tool, method and company. They were surprised when suddenly two years ago, the survey reported a decrease in employee satisfaction. Was it a one-time occurrence or did this represent a concern that needed further attention?

Senior leadership decided to gather follow-up information and to resurvey soon thereafter to more clearly assess the situation. Consultants were hired to assist leadership with objectively analysing the results, interviewing employees and providing recommendations for correcting concerns. All levels of leadership worked hard to eliminate concerns only to have the next survey demonstrate a continued decline in employee satisfaction with both management staff and the senior leadership team. The consultants recommended the organization consider management training and leadership development. Senior leadership was not sure if this was really what was needed. The solutions seemed to touch the surface concerns and the senior leadership team wondered if there was something deeper to explore. The senior leadership team along with human resources contacted several consulting firms requesting proposals to provide services to conduct face-to-face interviews with employee groups, assess the environment and make recommendations. I was contacted by one of the consulting groups submitting a proposal in the process. The consultants had personal experience with a coach and wanted to include coaching for the CEO as part of their proposal.

Why a Coach?

This was 2004 and coaching was gaining currency as a successful management tool. Consultants were already engaged with the organization. Articles were increasingly found in publications such as *Harvard Business Review*, the *Wall Street Journal* and *Fast Company* among others. The traditional problem-solution approach was not working and John and the senior leadership team were ready to try something different. They said they were ready for a change.

Metrics indicating a need for change were as follows:

- declining employee satisfaction scores
- increasing employee turnover
- higher employee turnover created gaps in staffing and limited ability to cover the staffing needs
- growing concern about the ability to continue to deliver the quality and service the community had grown to expect
- feedback from managers of an overwhelming sense of concern, uncertainty and apathy about the ability to correct the downward trend
- stories within staff ranks of negativity and uncertainty about the future

The Coaching Assignment

While the consulting team conducted focus group interviews with various staff (employees and managers) throughout the organization, my initial assignment was to interview the CEO and senior leadership team. I heard a lot of judgement in the organization that started with John, was echoed by the senior leadership team and evident in the employee and manager interviews I observed. Expectations were cloudy and there was uncertainty around accountability. Fear and blame seemed to permeate many of the conversations. As the consultants and I spoke with John and the senior leadership team in a debriefing session about the employee interviews, the terminology that surfaced was around corporate culture: the attitudes, assumptions, beliefs, values and experience of being part of this organization (Schein, 1985). Our work became known as the 'culture project'.

The First Steps

I vividly recall my first meeting John. He was not sure what coaching was all about or whether it was really what was needed though he stated that he was willing to engage. This was good – yet I had a sinking feeling in my stomach that perhaps he was not entirely ready to engage. As I consider Prochaska's Six Stages of Change (Velicer, Prochaska, Fava, Norman, and Redding, 1998), in retrospect I would say John was probably in the contemplation stage: he was considering making a change, but had not yet done so. There seemed to be something more underneath his feelings around coaching but I was not exactly sure what that was. My sinking feeling was the result of my own experience within a culture of fear and blame. What was the underlying cause? Was John part of the problem? Was coaching the right fit for this individual and organization? Was I the right coach?

I knew I could not stay with the sinking feeling as it was distracting me from being present with John (Rogers, J., 2004). I took a deep breath and asked John what he understood about coaching. He had read a few articles and knew a little about coaching. He had not considered a coach until this project. We discussed coaching, what it is and what it is not. John wanted to understand what coaching would mean for him personally. What was involved, how much time, how could he take the time in an already full schedule? As we talked, I asked if we might begin coaching now explaining that it is easier to understand coaching when you experience the process. John was willing so we agreed to engage in the process.

I explained some basic tenets of coaching:

- the confidential nature of the relationship
- an equal partnership
- the expectation for openness and honesty flowing in both ways
- a trusting and safe environment
- the importance of direct communication and feedback
- choice and responsibility

The Nature of the Coaching Relationship

I appreciate the special nature of the coach–client relationship. We have the opportunity to witness the power of the human spirit and the amazing work that can and does occur. My approach to beginning a coaching relationship has foundations in Humanistic Psychology and holding the client in unconditional positive regard (Rogers, C., 1980), believing in clients and their worth and capability even when they do not see this in themselves. This means creating a safe environment that encourages trust, accepting the client for who he is and being without judgement no matter what.

I remember in my coach training hearing, 'You can say anything as long as you say it from a caring place'. This is *unconditional positive regard* in action. Holding the client in unconditional positive regard creates trust, openness, honesty and it allows for deep dialogue. If done well, this is demonstrated in the coaching relationship as we build trust, and allow and encourage full self-expression and disclosure without judgement (Rogers, J., 2004). Unconditional positive regard is a key element in establishing the agreement and foundation of trust with the client.

John and I first met face-to-face in his office one morning for about two hours. We began the relationship with a tentative nature in our dialogue. This introductory conversation was more of a mutual interview, a gathering of information for both of us. For John it was to determine whether, in fact, he wanted to engage in work with a coach and, specifically, with me; and for me it was to listen to, and begin to learn about, who this individual was as a leader and a human being.

John and I established a foundation of trust that allowed for open and honest communication. I listened intently to what John said without assumption, judgement or agenda. Being in person allowed me to also observe his body language and expression and notice his tone of voice. If I had been working with John as an individual executive coaching client, we might have done all of our work together over the telephone. It is amazing what you hear when you are truly listening. With organizational clients, I have found it is important to have an opportunity to be face-to-face, at least for an initial meeting, to have an opportunity to observe the client within his environment.

An Opportunity to Listen and Learn

Listening was my primary coaching tool – listening at a deeper level beyond the client's story (Rogers, J., 2004). Early on, John related an incident involving a revolving door at the hospital entrance that had occurred a few days before our meeting. An elderly man was entering the hospital through the revolving door. The door stopped because of the man's slow motion and he panicked and fell. An emergency crew was called and after a few minutes, the man was free. John was away from the hospital at the time but he returned immediately when he was notified of the incident. The man was taken to the emergency room where he was examined and later released in good condition. John spoke with the man and his family in the emergency room and the incident ended; there was no further concern from the man or his family.

However, John's concern continued; he saw this incident as reflective of the lack of attention to detail among his senior team. As I listened, I noticed the incident was one among a long list of incidents John saw as similar in nature evidencing for him a lack of performance and commitment by many on the team reinforcing John's need to intervene. The revolving door was immediately shut down, labelled out of order and taped shut, which is how it was marked when I arrived at the hospital. John said he wanted the staff to really investigate the matter in order to understand what occurred and how to prevent such problems in the future. He felt that what he got back from the staff were excuses and a sense they missed his point of the importance of a full investigation. To John this meant there was a risk of recurrence.

I heard of the incident the day before in several focus groups with staff. In each of the groups, staff spoke of how they admired John and his genuine caring, concern and calm approach with the man and his family. The staff was respectful and complimentary of John's ability as CEO. At the same time they expressed frustration and a wish that John would find the same calmness and care in follow-up with staff. This message repeated in a variety of stories throughout the day and some staff even described John as a micromanager.

The following is an excerpt from our first conversation:

Coach: What did you say to the staff after the incident?
John: I told them to do everything possible to prevent an incident like this in the future.
Coach: What I heard is that you asked for a 100% guarantee that it would never happen again.
John: I probably did mean I wanted them to guarantee it would not happen again.

John said he felt like he had to set this tone or the staff would not do their jobs to the best of their ability. As CEO, he saw himself as ultimately responsible for everything. I could hear John's commitment to quality and to delivering the best possible results.

John related additional incidents reflecting similar concerns. He said he did not want to micromanage but this was unfortunately what was really necessary. He was not confident that others shared his commitment given his experience with concerns such as the revolving door. He saw his staff as unaware or maybe even unwilling to obtain complete information and understand the full implications of their work. He felt this resulted in the need for his intense oversight, contributed to a feeling of heavy responsibility, and called into question his confidence in what he could expect from others.

John's assessment of whether staff shared his commitment to quality was built on repeated disappointment with performance that did not measure up with his (John's) expectations. We spent time talking about expectations and how these were communicated. John's assumption was that the staff should know the importance of their work and they should ask if they were not clear on expectations.

I asked John how he knew that the staff were clear on what he expected. John said he explained what was needed. When they did not deliver, he sent them back to rework and showed them what was missing. This type of interaction resulted in disappointment, decreased confidence and eroding trust for all involved. The predominant culture had become one of fear and blame (Heifetz and Linsky, 2002).

The revolving door served as an apt metaphor throughout our initial work together. John and his team seemed to be stuck inside the door going round and round, seeing the same things over and over, resulting in more rules and causing a sense of feeling trapped with no way to move forward. John and the team were stuck in a pattern of behaviour that kept repeating itself. John's reaction was to become more intense and do exactly what the team feared – micromanage.

Metaphor as a Tool for Learning

Metaphor is a powerful tool (Heifetz and Linsky, 2002), when it has meaning for the client. The revolving door metaphor appeared from the story John shared in our conversation. I could have easily gone past it or overanalysed the meaning. I simply made the connection and observation, and this resonated with John and in later discussions with the team. It was their language and their situation, and it described what they were feeling inside. The story of the revolving door created an opportunity for learning both individually and collectively.

Our first step was to raise John's awareness around judgement, expectations and the opportunity for increasing clarity. We spoke of reflective practice and developing a practice of looking for the learning (Schön, 1987). This was a shift in thinking as John was used to looking for the cause.

It would have been easy to assume that indeed John was a micromanager as described by several staff early on. However, it would be a mistake to make such an assumption; even if it had an element of truth. My responsibility as a coach is to hold the client in unconditional positive regard, to accept him as he is and without judgement, to not make assumptions. Had I taken on the assumption that John was a micromanager, it would have negatively influenced our relationship. I was not hired as a consultant to solve the problem. I was hired as the coach to work with John, a very different task. As John's coach my role was to stay objective, ask questions, challenge what I heard, notice connections or themes and provide honest and direct feedback. Having spent many years in various roles in hospitals and as a consultant, I could have easily led John to a solution. I had the experience and I might have provided the answers. That might solve the immediate concern and John would likely learn some skills in the process, but it would not allow John to develop what he needed for growth and long-term success.

When John asked for my opinion I asked him for clarification on what he really wanted with his question. What I learned he wanted were questions and observations more than specific answers. John said the most valuable part of our work together was the safe place to explore, voice concerns and engage in sparring. John used the term sparring, connecting to the sport of Tae Kwon Do – a Korean form of martial arts I have practised with my family for several years. During my work with John, I earned my black belt in Tae Kwon Do. Part of my testing for the black belt involved sparring, actual fighting with an opponent. I am all of five feet tall and was never very athletic as a child so this was a major accomplishment. John enjoyed the idea of sparring and defined it as an invigorating event.

Coaching: An Adventure

John and I had the initial in-person meeting and then began work by telephone for about one hour every other week. He described our initial work together and the engagement in the culture project using the metaphor of a roller coaster: willingly getting on the ride, knowing you will face unexpected twists and turns. There may be a sense of, 'Oh, my gosh, why did I do this', but you know you will enjoy the ride. John said he appreciated the adventure of a roller coaster. He saw this engagement as a similar adventure. The experience might at times feel out of control and uncomfortable. There is uncertainty and a loss of control though it is safe and it is a ride he chose to get on, and in the end he will have enjoyed the experience.

John's metaphor captured the idea, reflected commitment and a spirit of adventure as we began this process (Heifetz and Linsky, 2002). His vivid description allowed me to hear creativity and excitement that was not apparent early on.

Communicating Commitment

John chose to communicate his commitment to engage in coaching to the senior team at the very beginning. They knew this was a possibility as coaching was part of the engagement proposal. John asked the team for assistance to help raise his awareness around his impact on their work. John said he valued their work and did not want to create concern. He wanted the team to be clear on expectations and accountable for their area's results. John told the team that he would be available for guidance and advice as they requested, but that he did not want to interfere. This was a courageous move for John. As a leader, particularly as the CEO, it is opening yourself up to vulnerability and humility – not something traditionally characteristic at the top of an organization.

A few senior team members questioned whether John was serious or if he understood what he was asking. The team looked to John for the answers which he always provided. Now John was looking to the team for feedback to better understand and support learning, growth and performance within the organization. He purposefully stepped back from the intense oversight on projects. This was an important learning for John and for the team. John felt he delegated authority in the past but could not always trust the work would be done to his satisfaction. John's openness with the team allowed him to begin to discuss authority and accountability and clarify expectations up front. This change in approach elicited positive and negative responses from the team.

There was a sense of understanding and freedom that started to emerge for some as opposed to confusion and stress for others. Peter Senge (1990) talks about creative tension, the gap between vision and current reality. While there was a desire for change or a new vision of this working relationship, the current reality did not match the experience creating tension and anxiety and resulting in uncharacteristic behaviour among some of the team members at times. I asked John to raise his awareness through observing his interactions with others, noticing their reaction, listening for cues to assess where they were intellectually and emotionally and being conscious of safety within the conversation to encourage the openness, honesty and learning.

Learning as a Leader

In one of our calls, John shared what he described as an interesting conversation with Josie, one of the senior team. John was increasingly aware of his desire to influence decisions and understanding this allowed him to intentionally stop himself from interfering. When he met with Josie, she clearly asked for his input. She wanted his assistance and directly asked him not to hold back. Josie's clear request allowed for an open dialogue that furthered John's awareness around the importance of clear direct communication and provided the opportunity for both of them to clarify expectations and to expand perspective.

John spoke of his reflections after this encounter, specifically around giving input versus giving direction. He saw the need for occasional input and an opportunity for good dialogue with his team. What he noticed was a tendency to give direction with the underlying assumption this was needed in order for the project to achieve the desired outcome.

As Goleman (2000) observed in his work on emotional intelligence in leaders, John's actions created uncertainty and frustration leading to decreased accountability and commitment – the exact opposite of what he wanted to achieve.

Another skill John took responsibility to practise was listening. He was becoming increasingly aware of his impact and influence on others. He expanded his request for feedback to key board members and to leadership a level below the senior team. John's openness and willingness to accept feedback encouraged more and more sharing. At times he heard more than perhaps he wanted. At the end of one of our calls, John observed that much of the time it was not so much about the content of the conversation, but rather the context of what he learned in the unspoken message he received. He said, 'What I am learning they hear from me is "you screwed up"'. He was not sure if this was real or simply 'dancing around problems'. John was concerned with this negative perception and wanted to know where it was coming from; he wanted to find the source so he could correct the perception.

The reality is John could not correct the problem by finding the source as there was likely no one source to find. In *Leadership on the Line*, Heifetz and Linsky (2002), talk about 'accepting responsibility for your piece of the mess'. As the leader, John is part of the problem. To search for the source of the negative perception sets him up for continuing the culture of fear and blame. Even if his intent is good, his desire to track down the negative perception feeds into the story surrounding him.

The revolving door incident helped us understand the strength of the hospital's 'grapevine' where stories, mostly negative, travelled rapidly throughout the organization. What John or the team said to clarify or correct the story, even if they were right, did not really matter. The employees perceived the situation differently from leadership's intent and perception is reality. Here is an excerpt of a conversation we had around finding the source:

John: I would like to find out how these negative comments get started. Who spends their time making up these stories?

Coach: I hear your desire to find the source so that you can change the message. Though I have a sense there is not one individual or even one group responsible for the stories.

John: I would probably agree.

Coach: John, you already acknowledged your role in contributing to the negative messages with interactions you have had with the team. Your action now is to be the leader. What will allow you to let go of the need to find someone responsible – to blame?

John: This is something I need to consider further. This feels like touchy-feely stuff and I don't like touchy-feely.

Coach: Tell me more about what you mean by touchy-feely.

John: It feels like I cannot address a concern directly, that I have to be careful or I will be accused of micromanaging. My hands are tied.

Coach: John, I am not asking you to avoid addressing the concern. You are right that it is best to address problems directly and as we talked before timely. This is good management practice. What I am asking you to do here is to stay away from blame.

John and I spoke for a while about blame and fear and how his wanting to find the source would hurt rather than help him in getting to what he really desired which was to create a culture of trust and accountability. We talked about gaining understanding or learning rather than finding the blame. I referred to Jim Collins' work in *Good to Great* (2001) where he writes about conducting autopsies without blame as a way to examine and learn from situations that do not turn out as intended or expected.

In a follow-up conversation, John spoke about his concern that the leadership was not delivering results he expected. Here is how it went:

Coach: How do you see the team around you?

John: Competence is high though there is significant resistance to change.

Coach: What's your role?

John: To provide the leadership. To bring clarity, focus and consistency to the team.

Coach: Anything else you need to say to the team?

John: I need to tell them when I see progress. I told Josie I was pleased with something earlier today and I could see it was very well received. I need to clearly communicate the expectation of results with the latitude of how to get there.

Coach: I want to acknowledge you for your awareness of the power of your words in conversations with your team over the past several weeks. Also, for your acknowledgement of Josie. Acknowledgement is a powerful tool (Rogers, J., 2004). As you said in looking at your conversation with Josie, it is important you share your insight and expectations clearly. You do not want to withhold information that can trip them up or set them up to fail. Your objective is to support them to succeed for the organization and as an individual.

Jim Collins' (2001) quote, 'Under the right conditions, the problems of commitment, alignment, motivation and change largely melt away', occurred to me as I listened. I shared the quote as another piece of information for reflection or not, it was John's choice. John was familiar with the book though had not yet read it. A while later, John came across the monograph written by Collins (2005), *Good to Great and the Social Sectors*. He embraced this book eventually using it as vehicle for establishing common context and expanding discussion and thinking with the leadership team.

The Importance of Observation

During an early on-site session, I attended a meeting with John and his leadership team that included an expanded management team. The consultants I worked with were presenting the results from the focus groups. I was there as part of the consulting team though my role was as an observer to notice connections, themes or actions by John or the team in their work together. John was standing near his seat at the board table and spoke about his vision for the organization, work that was occurring, and generally encouraged the team. John finished speaking, took his seat and proceeded to write something on his tablet. Within seconds I noticed almost everyone else in the room was writing. It seemed odd to me that they would each have something to write in that moment. It occurred to me that perhaps they thought John said something they needed to note. Now, John's message was good but it was not anything that seemed to require additional writing – no new information or message that I could hear. We took a break shortly after this experience and I asked John what he wrote when he sat down. He asked why. I shared my observations that the team began writing immediately after he sat down and wrote on his tablet. He had not noticed this occurring. John was reluctant to tell me what he wrote. I pushed harder as I had a sense we had a potential learning opportunity at hand. John sheepishly said, 'I wrote a reminder to myself to pick up bread and milk on the way home'.

My response was to exclaim, 'How wonderful! What a perfect opportunity to check in with the team'. I could tell by his expression that John was not so sure it was wonderful, though he trusted my instinct to raise the observation with the team.

John and I spoke to the team about my observation around their writing. He told them what he wrote. There was an audible gasp followed by laughter. There was a powerful learning around this observation and conversation that followed. John learned how the team grew to depend on his words interpreting cues for how to process – sometimes they were accurate and other times they were far off the mark resulting in frustration for everyone. This discovery was a breakthrough for John as well as for the team. John and the team shared a common understanding about how they related to each other up to this point (Patterson *et al.*, 2002). The unspoken belief among the team was, 'It's all about John', meaning all about 'what John wants'. The perspective shifted when everyone realized that perhaps it was not really all about John but rather it was all about what they *thought* John wanted.

Learning occurred for the individuals as well as for the organization (Argyris, 1990) where John and his team were able to discuss something that was previously unknown or under the surface. Recognizing the assumption and the resulting actions allowed for reflection and the opening for learning – to reinforce the importance of clarifying expectations, questions, assignments, and doing this without fear or concern. All clearly understood they could no longer allow themselves to manage to what they thought John wanted. This was unfair to John and created unnecessary work and worry, and, not uncommonly, resulted in misunderstanding and dissatisfaction. This experience, along with John's willingness to be open and honest with the team, resulted in a pivotal moment creating awareness for John and for all present (Peltier, 2001).

We acknowledged significant learning in the moment creating an open and safe space for dialogue with John and the team. Looking back I believe this situation was foundational in creating a common understanding, safety and new awareness for John around the magnitude of his impact on the organization.

Follow-up Action

The client's commitment to action is a key part of a successful coaching relationship. The process of action supports practical application as an important ingredient for adult learning (Cox, 2006). Actions do not need to be physical to produce value. John's action was commitment to raising his awareness in conversations with the team: noticing their response, being aware of his own reaction, clarifying expectations and working through differences with the individuals. His action was to notice his personal reaction and involvement in conversations or projects. He became an observer rather than a judge, noticing, reflecting (Schön, 1987) and responding rather than reacting around preconceived ideas or judgement about specific outcomes or people. We talked about differences in communication and conversational style (Tannen, 1994), language, and creating meaning and action (Pearce, 2004). We used the questions noted in *Crucial Conversations* around learning to look at the situation objectively (Patterson *et al.*, 2002) as a guide for examining the situation. Together we:

- Explored his reactions, emotions, attachments, triggers, etc.
- Sought to identify his real concerns.
- Asked what he really wanted in this situation.
- Considered how he might go about this from a different perspective.
- Looked at what he could learn from others.
- Discussed his role and the work he wanted to do.

Coaching the Team

John and I worked together in a one-on-one coaching relationship for an initial three months as part of the overall culture project. After our on-site meeting, we met by phone twice per month for one-hour sessions. During this initial period, John requested expanding the coaching to include meetings with the senior team, both individually and as a group. The overall coaching objective we established was: Coaching to evolve corporate culture and leadership style from a 'command and control' to one of 'commitment and learning' for inspired leadership.

While I appreciate the value of carefully chosen and validated assessments, there is a very real concern about the over-use or sole reliance on such tools. My experience and preference is to engage fully in and appreciate the power of the coaching conversation.

As we began the group work, we did decide to use a behavioural and communication styles assessment. The assessment provided a simple way to succinctly gather information about the group that gave a common context and voice to their experience (Rogers, J., 2004). It was a tool that allowed for a more in-depth discussion and examination of how the group related with each other and the larger team.

Reviewing the group's profile, John's style was strongly dominant while the four senior team members were more of a consistent steady style. John liked quick decisions while the others liked to discuss and deliberate. The potential for misunderstanding and conflict, particularly under stress, was immediately apparent.

A Team Retreat

I facilitated a day-long retreat with John and the senior team. The recurring theme throughout the day was on trust or the lack thereof among the team and how this flowed through the organization.

The focus was around communication within the senior team. The group created the following acronym (that unintentionally spelled TRUST) and definitions as a guide for how they wanted to relate with each other:

- *Trust* – Build trust among the senior team and extend to the larger team. Communicate with each other when concerns occur.
- *Respect* – Respect, honour and integrity (consistent with the organization's values). Speak with and encourage the truth.
- *Understanding* – Listen to and understand each other. The diversity and value of a broader perspective. Be aware of and let go of attachment and judgement.
- *Support* – Use meetings effectively. Incorporate 'round table discussion' time into the weekly meeting to keep each other informed. Implement critical incident debrief (from Collins' autopsies without blame) as a tool for learning. Request support when needed and give support when requested or if you observe delays or struggle.
- *Team* – Build upon and maximize the strengths of the team.

Action items committed to by John and the senior team:

(1) Have a conversation before opinion or critical judgement.
(2) Talk with people and not about them.
(3) Incorporate time for debriefing as a routine to build learning, ownership, acceptance of responsibility and action.
(4) Raise awareness of responsibilities and priorities as a team.
(5) Keep each other in the loop.
(6) If you are not in on a project and are concerned, do not make assumptions. Ask yourself, 'Do I need to be involved or do I want to be involved?'

Ongoing Work

Team meetings with the coach continued for six months. During this period John and his team established a safe environment for regular and clear communication with each other. John and I continued our individual work together moving to about every three weeks. I attended two follow-up retreats with the group and had the good fortune to witness their progress and evolution as team over a two-year period. The group focus shifted from what was wrong to acknowledging and celebrating what was right (Seligman, 2002). They addressed concerns and conflict more easily and incorporated the debrief process into their routine. Most notable was that the word 'trust' never again entered into the conversation. It was evident John and the team were modelling trust rather than talking about trust.

While John and I worked together in the coaching relationship, the consultants continued work with the organization to support process improvement in key areas identified as concerns through focus groups and employee surveys. In addition, John requested the senior team begin plans for manager and supervisory skill training to provide a strong management foundation that defines the scope of their responsibilities and provides guidelines/processes to manage within and support to turn to for new or unusual situations. John and the team acknowledged the importance of providing clear definition, expectations and channels of support to the management team (Collins, 2001).

Measures of Success

The impetus for hiring me as coach for this assignment was the steadily decreasing employee satisfaction results. The survey completed one year after beginning the culture project showed an increase in employee satisfaction with summary comments from the survey company stating, 'The hospital culture is improving in many areas of employee satisfaction thus strengthening the commitment of employees and managers'. According to the survey company, there was a statistically significant increase in the employee satisfaction scores compared with the surveys from each of the two prior years. All of the satisfaction measures demonstrated improvement. Those related to the coaching assignment that had a statistically significant change included:

- attention to employee needs
- communications
- employee involvement
- leadership – organizational
- leadership – departmental
- fairness

A resurvey was done the following year as the organization moved to a more specific instrument with enhanced reporting capability to include comparative data for organizations within their region and size range. John and the team were very proud to report scores that ranked above the comparative data in each area. The survey company asked what the organization had done to achieve such an increase in satisfaction. While the organization engaged in work other than coaching to improve their employee satisfaction, I would posit that the work which was most significant was related to coaching and John's commitment to the process, the learning and the change. John's willingness to engage, listen, reflect, explore, experiment and to trust me and the process of coaching made the difference in the results John and the organization achieved.

I had the opportunity to speak with the senior leaders as part of two feedback evaluations John requested during this process. There was noticeable change from one year to the next. One indicator of this change was that people reported that John seemed more aware of his behaviour and there has been a shift from:

- telling to listening
- blame, judgement and defensiveness, to awareness, flexibility and a willingness to explore and engage in a conversation
- controlling to acknowledging
- fear and blame to trust

I met one of the managers at a meeting one day while on-site toward the end of my work with John. She knew me as part of the 'culture project'. She was unaware of my role as the coach. She commented how amazed she was at the progress that was made in such a short time. She continued, unsolicited, to state that of all who contributed to the dramatic change in culture, she saw John as the leader and the one who did the most significant work. I never mentioned I was John's coach as that would be violating my confidence with John. I simply encouraged her to share this observation with him to acknowledge his contribution and impact on the organization.

John's metaphor of a roller coaster aptly described this adventure. Along the way and in our final evaluation, John mentioned that although there were times he dreaded coming to our calls he always walked away feeling glad to have engaged in them. He especially liked the challenging, spirited dialogue.

The Coach's Development

This assignment provided significant learning for me as a coaching professional and as a lifelong student of human and organizational behaviour and development. I began the assignment ready to work with John. This was modified when John requested I also work with the team. In addition to talking this through with John and the team to ensure all were in agreement, I sought out the wise counsel of coaches more experienced in organizational and team coaching work. I had my own coach who served as a mentor/supervisor allowing me the safe space to reflect and learn from successes, mistakes and reactions to recognize my own learning (Cox, 2006). I strongly recommend engaging in reflective practice and having the support of a mentor/supervisor for your own professional and personal development.

Final Thoughts

I am thankful to John for allowing me to partner with him in this adventure and for granting permission for me to document our work together for this case. I encourage those of you who are coaches to begin to document your work with clients and to reflect on the theories that influence our practice. Strengthening the connection between theory and practice enhances our knowledge and skill as a coaching professional, supports our personal development and growth and ultimately increases the value we bring to our clients. Coaching is a continuous opportunity for learning – for both our clients and ourselves as coaches.

References

Argyris, C. (1990). *On organizational learning*. Malden, MA: Blackwell.
Collins, J. (2001). *Good to great*. New York: HarperCollins.
Collins, J. (2005). *Good to great and the social sectors*. Boulder, CO: Jim Collins.
Cox, E. (2006). An adult learning approach to coaching. In D. Stober and A. Grant (Eds.), *Evidence based coaching handbook: Putting best practices to work for your clients*. Hoboken, NJ: John Wiley & Sons, Inc.
Csikszentmihalyi, M. (1990). *Flow: The psychology of optimal experience*. New York: Harper & Row.
Goleman, D. (2000). *Leadership that gets results*. Boston: Harvard Business Review.
Heifetz, R., and Linsky, M. (2002). *Leadership on the line: Staying alive through the dangers of leading*. Boston: Harvard Business School Publishing.
Kegan, R. (1994). *In over our heads: The mental demands of modern life*. Cambridge, MA: Harvard University Press.
Patterson, K., Grenny, J., McMillan, R., and Switzler, A. (2002). *Crucial conversations: Tools for talking when stakes are high*. Hightstown, NJ: McGraw-Hill.
Pearce, W. B. (2004). The coordinated management of meaning (CMM). In W. Gudykunst (Ed.), *Theorizing about intercultural communication*. Thousand Oaks, CA: Sage.
Peltier, B. (2001). *The psychology of executive coaching*. New York: Brunner-Routledge.
Rogers, C. R. (1980). *A way of being*. Boston, MA: Houghton-Mifflin.
Rogers, J. (2004). *Coaching skills: A handbook*. Milton Keynes, UK: Open University Press.

Schein, E. (1985). *Organizational culture and leadership: A dynamic view.* San Francisco: Jossey-Bass.

Schön, D. (1987). *Educating the reflective practitioner.* San Francisco, CA: Jossey-Bass.

Seligman, M. (2002). *Authentic happiness.* New York: Free Press.

Senge, P. (1990). *The fifth discipline: The art and practice of the learning organization.* New York: Doubleday Currency.

Tannen, D. (1995). *The power of talk: Who gets heard and why.* Boston: Harvard Business Review.

Velicer, W. F., Prochaska, J. O., Fava, J. L., Norman, G. J., and Redding, C. A. (1998). Smoking cessation and stress management: Applications of the Transtheoretical Model of behavior change. *Homeostasis, 38,* 216–233.

Creating Corporate Coaching Cultures for Resiliency and Performance

14

Vicki Escudé

Imagine being poised comfortably, able to shift directions with grace and facility, like a tennis pro going for an overhead smash to score the winning point. As in tennis, success of the corporation today is not only about gaining and applying technical knowledge; success is also about resiliency, changing gears and learning new things easily and rapidly. It is about embracing and adapting quickly to change.

Corporations, however, cannot make this significant shift toward valuing resiliency and change without the support of its base of knowledge and power – the employees. Historically, employees have been trained by corporate leadership to follow directions and perform within structured guidelines. A hierarchical, authoritarian relationship with employees in which 'telling, training, teaching and directing' are the primary modes of communication may be detrimental to the organization which wants to develop into a successful, creative and flexible entity.

According to several corporate thought leaders of today, shifting to a corporate culture that honours independent thought, creativity and opportunities to learn and grow is the path of survival for organizations. A 'coaching culture' in organizations is one that would support this creative and rich, productive environment through use of coaching leadership styles and coaching relationships.

What are 'coaching' and 'coaching relationships'? According to the International Coach Federation, 'Coaching is partnering with clients in a

The Philosophy and Practice of Coaching: Insights and Issues for a New Era.
Edited by David B. Drake, Diane Brennan and Kim Gørtz.
© 2008 John Wiley & Sons, Ltd.

thought-provoking and creative process that inspires them to maximize their personal and professional potential. . . . Coaches help people improve their performances and enhance the quality of their lives. . . . They seek to elicit solutions and strategies from the client; they believe the client is naturally creative and resourceful. The coach's job is to provide support to enhance the skills, resources, and creativity that the client already has' (accessed October 25, 2007: www.coachfederation.org).

In a coaching culture, leaders foster greater productivity by nurturing among employees a willingness to grow and learn through rapport and trust building. Leaders do not solve all the problems. They are neither the heroes nor do they wield heavy-handed authority. They skilfully provide problem-solving models for employees that empower them to explore their own solutions and develop their own means of motivation. Employees are more likely to have ownership of and responsibility for positive corporate results.

This chapter presents four key questions for corporations interested in moving to an environment that can be described as a coaching culture where learning and creativity are valued and encouraged:

(1) How can a corporation integrate coaching principles into practice at work?
(2) What are the benefits of establishing a coaching culture?
(3) What is required to make the transition to a corporate culture?
(4) What do you need to create a strong foundation for doing so?

Integrating Coaching Principles within the Corporate Environment

Recognizing that strategically designed change is essential for corporate survival, organizations traditionally provide employees with training workshops and retreats, teaching the cutting-edge information designed to keep abreast of rapidly shifting trends. However, employers and employees are afraid of lost productivity, an overload of more information, and an encroachment into their personal time. They ask themselves, 'How can we integrate this new information into our already over-taxed system?'

Playing the Game

According to Timothy Gallwey, author of *The Inner Game of Work* (2000), teaching often has an adverse effect on learning. In traditional approaches to teaching, people try to follow someone else's directions while ignoring their own inner experience and wisdom. From teaching tennis, he noticed that when people were supported and encouraged to observe their own behaviours, they quickly developed and refined their skills without teaching and telling. Naming this learning style the 'inner game', Gallwey successfully applied his learning principles not only to tennis, but also to golf, skiing and music, and ultimately, to the corporate environment.

In the 1970s, Gallwey dramatically demonstrated to American television audiences his 'inner game' approach to teaching tennis, which also illustrated his philosophy of teaching, in general. Harry Reasoner, who hosted a current events television show, challenged Gallwey to teach tennis to a woman named Molly, who had never played the game. The tennis lesson was to be videotaped, and later shown on national television. Gallwey accepted the challenge, and began by having Molly choose how to hold the tennis racquet as well as how to move on the court. Amazingly, she began to return volleys. Within minutes, her skill level was that of someone who had worked for several months with a professional instructor using traditional teaching methods. Molly's success was based on intuitively choosing and refining racquet swings and steps as *she* solved the problem of returning the tennis ball back over the net.

Corporate leaders began asking Gallwey to apply these same 'inner game' principles to the corporate arena. AT&T, Coca-Cola, Apple, IBM and many other companies hired Gallwey as consultant-coach to bring these principles into their workplace in support of better learning cultures. A key use of these principles, to increase learning and performing, was to help organizations redefine work.

Gallwey's principles support a new way for employees to relate to work, as well as a new way for corporate management to relate to employees. It is about making the work environment more satisfying and productive. When an employee is free from strict dictates and is able to approach his tasks with curiosity and a sense of purpose, he engages his creativity, which, according to Gallwey, leads to higher job satisfaction, greater productivity and enhanced bottom-line results.

Another 'inner game' proponent and thought leader, John Whitmore, connects empowerment and coaching in the corporate environment. He relates motivation at work to Maslow's hierarchy of needs in *Coaching for Performance* (Whitmore, 1998). Once a worker's basic need of pay, housing and community are fulfiled, employees then look for the higher-level fulfilment of greater self-esteem and self-actualization. They become increasingly motivated at this point by values and meaning in work and life. Whitmore states in his book, 'Self-esteem is not met by prestige and privilege, which are more symbolic than substantial. It is built when someone is seen to be worthy of making choices, in other words, by genuine empowerment and by having the opportunity to express potential. This is the very stuff of coaching. Telling, on the other hand, negates choice, disempowers, limits potential and demotivates' (Whitmore, 1998, p. 105).

Gallwey notes that the primary purpose of work for the top of the organization is to produce bottom-line results. It is about greater profits, better service and economic viability. This stance, according to Gallwey, is called the '*outer game*', and is, of course, essential for corporate survival. For employees, however, work takes on a broader meaning. Yes, there is a need to make money, however, more and more people are also concerned with their relationships at work and how they can contribute their skills in fulfiling ways. The inner fulfilment speaks to the '*inner game*'.

Rather than relying only on information from workshops and training, he suggests that becoming adaptable to change, and learning how to change, gives 'performance' a new meaning. Gallwey discovered that people who are high performers are those who tend to learn faster. They learn faster when they are encouraged to be aware of their surroundings and not to be stuck in old habits, patterns and beliefs. Through his approach to sports training, Gallwey demonstrated the learning principle that individuals who are supported to trust their inner resources are able to learn quickly and perform effectively. Applying this knowledge to the corporate environment today, we see workers who are contending with rapid change and need more of an atmosphere of encouragement in support of their success. The only way an individual can adapt and change readily is to learn how to learn.

The workplace can support and encourage inner learning and personal development, just as Gallwey did on the tennis court. Gallwey contends that both the 'inner game' and the 'outer game' can be realized, but only when corporations begin to embrace the idea that a worker who is learning and growing is also one who is more productive and a better contributor to the 'bottom-line'. For many organizations this is a shift in focus.

The Importance of Learning

The case that learning and performing are interwoven has also been made through extensive corporate survey and research by the Gallup Organization (2001) which resulted in an assessment tool named 'The 12 Elements of Great Managing'. Gallup set out to identify elements of employee engagement, a term that speaks to employee satisfaction and productivity, and impacts employee loyalty and retention. The twelve statements that resulted from their research, known as the Q12, are measures of a corporate culture and the degree to which employees experience it as caring, supportive, and affording opportunities for learning and self-development. In *Feedback for Real*, Gallup researcher John Thackray (2001, p. 2) explains how the tool was developed, and how it has subsequently been used:

> [T]his tool has been used by more than 87,000 divisions or work units within corporations, and approximately 1.5 million employees have participated. For companies that were able to provide data across units, comparisons of engagement scores reveal that those with high Q^{12} scores have also experienced lower turnover, higher sales growth, better productivity, better customer loyalty, or other manifestations of superior performance.

To make the shift to a more engaging and learning-based culture, organizations are being asked to let go of some of their control and to encourage their employees to become more aware – of themselves and what is happening around them.

In writing on emotional intelligence, Daniel Goleman (1997) speaks to the importance of a positive corporate management environment in relationship to learning and decision-making. 'When emotionally upset, people cannot remember, attend, learn or make decisions clearly. As one management consultant put it, "stress makes people stupid"' (p. 149). As an executive coach, I have worked with CEOs who put undue pressure on employees because they believed that others in the corporation were not as committed, could not see the bigger picture, and were not as capable as they were. Their micromanagement not only demotivated the employees, but also created time-management problems and stress for the CEOs. The ensuing environment was not optimal for high performance.

The fact that stress from heavy-handed coercion affects performance is noted in an article by Goleman (2000), 'It's easy to understand why of all the leadership styles, the coercive one is the least effective in most situations. Consider what the style does to an organization's climate. Flexibility is the hardest hit. The leader's extreme top-down decision making kills new ideas on the vine. People feel so disrespected that they think, "I won't even bring my ideas up – they'll only be shot down"' (p. 82). Goleman also makes the point that employees in this atmosphere become resentful, and no longer feel responsible for their performance.

Some of my CEO clients chose to make the transition to coaching leadership which is a necessary step toward developing a coaching culture. Once their limiting patterns and beliefs about leadership were explored, they were introduced to a coaching style of leadership which helps employees explore options for action and encourages them to choose the options that might give them the greatest traction toward goals. By keeping the 'ball in the employee's court', the employee gains the satisfaction of solving the problem. This coaching approach gives ownership of goals back to the employees while freeing the CEOs and executives to oversee and provide accountability.

Enjoying the Benefits of a Corporate Coaching Culture

Professional coaching purports that individuals have their own answers and the ability to find their own answers, similar to Gallwey's (2000) learning principle of relying on greater awareness and inner resources. When a corporation embraces this philosophy and provides coaches and coaching leaders to partner with employees, the resulting culture helps those within the organization keep focused on desired outcomes while achieving results in a way that engenders satisfaction.

In organizations where there is a serious commitment to creating a coaching culture and a learning environment is established, everyone has an opportunity to become coach-like by supporting each other to problem-solve and by trusting each person to find his or her own path to the bigger goals. Learning and growing can become so compelling that the individual is motivated to succeed while encouraging others to do the same. Undue competition, which creates anxiety, is seen as a deterrent to learning. Coaching partnerships between employee and boss, or employee and peers encourage collaboration, high performance and success. According to John Whitmore (1998), 'Coaching brings out the best in individuals and in teams, something that instructing does not even aspire to do . . .' (p. 137). This foundational principle of coaching supports creativity and learning in the workplace. Whitmore (1998) goes on to cite the benefits of coaching in organizations, 'Improved performance and productivity, staff development, improved learning, improved relationships, improved quality of life for individuals, more time for the manager, more creative ideas, better use of people, skills and resources, faster and more effective emergency response and greater flexibility and adaptability to change' (pp. 137–138).

CEOs who adopt a coaching approach to leadership from being coached by my organization have reported many benefits. These leaders were bolstered by greater support from employees, experienced more effective time management, and reversed their slide toward burnout. Their shift to a more positive experience is echoed by research from Boyatzis, Smith, and Blaize of Case Western Reserve University in the article 'Developing sustainable leaders through coaching and compassion'. They state:

By integrating recent findings in affective neuroscience and biology with well documented research on leadership and stress, we offer a more holistic approach to leadership development. We argue here that leader sustainability is adversely affected by the psychological and physiological effects of chronic power stress associated with the performance of the leadership role. We further contend, however, that when leaders experience compassion through coaching the development of others, they experience psychophysiological effects that restore the body's natural healing and growth processes, thus enhancing their sustainability. We thus suggest that to sustain their effectiveness, leaders should emphasize coaching as a key part of their role and behavioral habits. (Boyatzis, Smith, and Blaize, 2006, p. 8)

Corporations are already seeing the benefits of hiring coaches to strengthen the effectiveness of their leaders, as indicated by recent surveys. Writing in *Fast Company*, Jim Bolt (2006) cites a study on executive coaching ('High-Impact Executive Coaching') which surveyed 48 organizations and 86 leaders who were coached. It found that

the vast majority of our respondents indicated 'leader development' to be the primary reason coaches were engaged. The biggest change is from coaching being used as a 'fix it tool' for leaders with problems, to helping successful leaders get even better. In many firms, having a coach is seen as a badge of honor. And we found that coaching now reaches into the highest levels: 43% of CEOs and 71% of the senior executive team had worked with a coach. And here's the bottom-line: 63% of organizations say they plan to increase their use of coaching over the next five years. Most telling, 92% of leaders being coached say they plan to use a coach again.

If this survey is an indication, coaching seems to be not only more widely used, but is growing in its acceptance by senior management.

Transitioning to a New Coaching Culture

There are several ways a corporation can evolve into a coaching culture. Developing leaders is essential for survival in the corporate arena, and, according to Terry Bacon (2003) in a white paper series for the Lore International Institute, executive leadership can be enhanced through coaching. '[C]oaching is regarded as one of the most effective means of executive development because it provides focused, one-on-one attention in areas the executive most needs to develop and offers help and guidance from someone who should be expert at diagnosing developmental needs and helping executives resolve problems and develop their skills' (Bacon, 2003, p. 1). Often, an employee in the corporation who has had a positive personal experience with a professional coach becomes a champion for the coaching philosophy. This employee, whether of the senior leadership team, or a high-level manager, encourages colleagues to get coaching for themselves and others. Building on the positive coaching experiences of executives, a steady, organic path toward a coaching culture may peak early without sufficient infrastructure or support, or it may continue until it reaches a tipping point, and coaching becomes more widely accepted.

Another path can be seen when senior management decides, based on an assessment of the current organizational climate and/or position in the marketplace, they need to embrace the coaching philosophy as the driver for a strategic change. To support a wholesale culture change, a three-step process can be implemented leading to create a learning/coaching environment.

(1) Create agreement within the organization about the need and the vision for the establishment of an environment that promotes learning and coaching as well as accountability, performance and results. This step may include orientation workshops for all executives and managers to promote a common understanding and an appreciation of coaching as a leadership and communication approach and set of skills. In addition, it is imperative that coaching be defined within the organization as a desirable vehicle for self-discovery and a stepping-stone for success.

(2) Key managers and executives are coached by professional coaches in order to experience the value of coaching, address their goals, and develop their own coaching skills. Coaches would work with individuals to enhance leadership competencies and work–life balance, often using formal and informal assessments. As noted earlier in the Bolt study, there are some indications that coaching is already making headway in organizations.

(3) Individuals are chosen to become internal coaches within the organization in order to provide coaching as needed and to support the ongoing evolution of a learning and coaching-based culture. These coaches often receive professional coach training to equip them to handle the demands of coaching in their own organization. From my experiences with internal coach training, effective internal coaches are mindful to support the initiatives of the organization, to model the coaching approach in meetings, and to encourage an acceptance of coaching as a path toward personal and professional growth rather than remediation.

To keep abreast of the high rate of change in today's marketplace, the creation of better coaching culture and learning environments is essential for organizations to survive and flourish. A key part of these strategies is the development of leaders, managers and employees who have learned to value change, self-direction and self-motivation. Corporations that attract and nurture these individuals increase their chances for long-term success.

Coaching Competency-Based Guidelines as the Foundation for a Coaching Culture

Just as guidelines for individual coaches are useful in setting the stage for coaching engagements, corporations and organizations would benefit from guidelines to help define and create a corporate coaching culture. The International Coach Federation (ICF) has established coaching competencies that are the foundation for one-on-one coaching relationships. For the purposes of this chapter, I will apply these competencies as guidelines and subjective indicators of the readiness of a corporation to support a coaching culture and as a basis for guidelines on how to do so. The eleven coaching competencies are discussed as they relate to corporate values, actions and the design for corporate coaching initiatives.

The Competency of Ethics: An ethical corporate culture is one in which people, integrity and safety are valued, and these values are visible and demonstrated daily in the activities of the organization. The importance of corporate ethics has been highlighted in the past few years with the example of corporate giant Enron and the lack of ethics concerning accounting and the misuse of employee funds. Unethical practices leading to negative consequences for employees were a wake-up call for corporate ethics. On the other hand, some corporations have clear ethical standards which contribute to employee trust, loyalty and ultimately performance. According to James C. Collins and Jerry I. Porras (1996), 'Companies that enjoy enduring success have core values and a core purpose that remain fixed while their business strategies and practices endlessly adapt to a changing world. The dynamic of preserving the core while stimulating progress is the reason that companies such as Hewlett-Packard, 3M, Johnson & Johnson, Procter & Gamble, Merck, Sony, Motorola and Nordstrom became elite institutions able to renew themselves and achieve superior long-term performance' (p. 65).

The Competency of Establishing Agreement: A coaching culture is based on the establishment of clear agreements with employees. Employees know what is expected of them and are clear about their roles and responsibilities in the corporation. Personal accountability is the norm and people are able to make clear requests and commitments. Everyone is knowledgeable about coaching relationships, coaching conversations and the conditions and expectations for their place in the organization and its daily life. When the coaching philosophy is embraced, coaches and coachees form partnerships of mutual exploration. Coachees are supported to retain ownership of their development and performance.

The Competency of Trust and Intimacy: Trust is engendered when the corporation and employees have shared values and ethics, and when there is positive regard for each other. Employees are encouraged to be open to coaching as a resource for their own development, balance and performance. Employees understand that coaching is a means for self-discovery, and feel free to choose coaching to grow personally and professionally. Leaders view coaching as a positive step for employees who wish to advance in the organization.

The Competency of Coaching Presence: For an effective coaching culture, executives and managers are well trained in the use of coaching skills and coaching leadership, demonstrate confidence in their skills, and are seen by others as good coaches for both their style and their results. Education about coaching is imperative among senior leadership, managers and direct reports via presentations, workshops and/or direct experience of one-on-one coaching.

The Competency of Active Listening: The corporation must create vehicles within the organizational structure to actively listen to employees and support and encourage open lines of communication. Regularly taking the pulse of the climate, letting employees know they are heard and visible helps to create a coaching environment. Listening in an open and receptive manner engenders trust and helps to establish a strong rapport, loyalty and employee engagement. The senior management must embrace the value of listening, and be well-trained in communication skills.

The Competency of Powerful Questioning: Powerful questioning in a coaching engagement implies that the manager or coach is open to exploring options and ideas with direct reports and peers. A corporate environment supportive of learning and coaching promotes this non-judgemental approach with employees, which enables them to maintain focus on the corporate goals while empowering them to creatively problem-solve, clarify issues and find solutions.

The Competency of Direct Communication: When the foundations of communication are laid through active listening and powerful questioning, employees can trust that feedback in the form of direct communication will be respectful and relevant. Corporations may have their own systems to assess performance which can be shared with employees in a direct yet coach-like way by focusing on strengths and inviting self-observation. Formal and informal assessments with timely feedback sessions also support a coaching and learning culture. Use of 360-degree feedback assessments and personality assessments help employees learn, grow and self-correct behaviours, as well as provide a foundation for effective, reality-based development plans.

The Competency of Creating Awareness: When the corporate leadership establishes regular feedback mechanisms with assessments and development plan reviews, the employee can trust that the organization supports his or her personal and professional growth. The organization that provides coaching, coaching leadership and other growth opportunities is setting the stage for greater employee engagement.

The Competency of Designing Actions: Corporations need to have a clear sense of their vision, mission, values and goals in order for employees to be able to effectively align their actions with the needs of the organization. Managers and coaches need to have a firm grasp on these organizational signposts as the bases for assisting those they coach in designing meaningful and productive action steps. Facilitating actions through a coaching approach keeps ownership of the actions in the employee's hands.

The Competency of Goal Setting: Agreed-upon, value-based strategic goals set the stage for coaching cultures. With them, employees can be clear how they can best fit in and contribute to the attainment of those goals. As a result, they often develop a greater sense of intrinsic motivation and esteem. In a more advanced coaching culture, the employees have a greater voice in setting these corporate goals, and their individual goals as part of the larger picture.

The Competency of Managing Progress and Accountability: As a foundation for a coaching and learning culture, the corporation continually reviews the goals, objectives and strategic plan as they relate to coaching, and the progress is communicated to everyone in the organization. Individuals also have frequently scheduled coaching conversations about progress on their own personal development plan. Taken together, these measures keep both the corporation and employee focused on the important tasks at hand, both for handling the present and preparing for the future, and send the message that everyone in the organization is visible and valuable.

Reference Guide to Coaching Competencies for Organizations

Table 14.1 provides a summary of the individual coaching competencies as they can be used to assess the level of readiness and progress within an organization in terms of creating a coaching culture. The table is based on the ICF Individual Coaching Competencies (2007), with permission from the International Coach Federation.

Table 14.1 Indicators for an organization's readiness to support a coaching and learning culture.

Competency	Indicators
1. *Ethics*	• The corporate values are well-known • The corporate values are demonstrated daily with integrity • Confidential coaching conversations and relationships are respected
2. *Establishing Agreement*	• The corporation provides a clear organizational structure • Job descriptions are clear and agreed-upon • Agreements are valued and maintained with employees, management and external relationships • Customer service is valued and demonstrated • Employees and management accept the coaching philosophy of partnership, exploration and problem-solving
3. *Trust and Intimacy*	• The corporation and employees share similar values • There is a high level of trust between management and direct reports • Trusting relationships are evident in the support of new ideas, exploration and creativity
4. *Coaching Presence*	• The leadership and management understand and embrace the coaching philosophy • Management is trained in, confident about and uses coaching skills as a leadership style • Management encourages individual coaching as a positive support for employee development

Table 14.1 *Continued*

Competency	Indicators
5. *Active Listening*	• Various vehicles exist for listening to employees • Open lines of communication exist between management and employees • The corporation values employee feedback
6. *Powerful Questioning*	• Management is skilled in non-judgemental questioning as a means of mutual exploration with employees • Managers as coaches use powerful questioning to support employees to find their own solutions
7. *Direct Communication*	• Employee feedback mechanisms exist with 360-degree assessments, personality assessments and employee reviews
8. *Creating Awareness*	• Employee feedback systems are used to support employee awareness and personal/professional growth • Management demonstrates skill in communication and leadership by employing active listening, powerful questioning and direct communication for the purpose of enhancing individual awareness and professional growth
9. *Designing Actions*	• Management coaches employees to design meaningful actions based on clear performance goals and assessments • The corporation has clear objectives and action steps based on strategic goals • Employee action steps support corporate goals
10. *Goal Setting*	• Corporate goals are clear, actionable and with timelines • Employees have a voice in creating corporate goals • Employees' goals support their ability to further the corporate goals • Employees' goals are clear, actionable and with timelines
11. *Managing Progress and Accountability*	• Management schedules periodic coaching conversations with individuals to evaluate development plans and progress • Management schedules coaching conversations to discuss corporate strategic plans • The corporation provides employees with an ongoing progress report and status of corporate goals

Conclusion

In conclusion, many present-day thought leaders in the fields of corporate behaviour and productivity have applied the 'inner game' framework and strategies to enhance coaching and learning in the corporate setting. In doing so, they have laid the groundwork for building environments that support a high-level of corporate productivity while fulfilling the employee's need to learn, grow, create and succeed. Personal fulfilment and the corporate bottom-line are not mutually exclusive. In fact, they are deeply intertwined and mutually supportive goals.

A coaching culture is one that supports learning. In addition to releasing their need for authoritarian control and stress-driven performance, corporations are encouraged to create a new relationship with employees, one that supports 'learning' rather than fostering competition, invites creativity rather than following rules, and offers opportunities to grow and develop, rather than adhering to predetermined paths and patterns. By encouraging everyone in the corporation to learn to think for themselves, employees can develop a sense of ownership.

Corporations can now benefit from the strong foundation developed by leaders, coaches and organizations that have been down this path towards a coaching culture, and from the ongoing research related to productivity and employee engagement. The more an organization is able to integrate the competencies and elements of a coaching culture as has been identified in this chapter, the greater the potential for both improving the bottom-line and enhancing the corporate work environment. Using the guidelines above to assess their readiness and plan for development, organizations can begin taking specific action steps on the journey toward corporate change and positive growth.

References

Bacon, T. R. (2003). Measuring the effectiveness of executive coaching. White Paper, Lore International Institute.

Bolt, J. (2006). Coaching: The fad that won't go away. *Fast Company*, retrieved from http://www.fastcompany.com/resources/learning/bolt/041006.html on September 13, 2007.

Boyatzis, R. E., Smith, M. L., and Blaize, N. (2006). Developing sustainable leaders through coaching and compassion. *Academy of Management Learning and Education*, (5)1, 8–24.

Collins, J. C., and Porras, J. I. (1996). Building your company's vision. *Harvard Business Review*, September–October, 65–77.

Gallwey, T. (2000). *The inner game of work*. New York: Random House.

Goleman, D. (1997). *Emotional intelligence*. New York: Bantam Books.

Goleman, D. (2000). Leadership that gets results. *Harvard Business Review*, March–April, 78–90.

International Coach Federation. *Coaching competencies: What is coaching?* retrieved from www.internationalcoachfederation.com on October 25, 2007.

Thackray, J. (2001). Feedback for Real. *Gallup Management Journal*, retrieved from http://gmj.gallup.com/content/811/Feedback-Real.aspx on October 12, 2007.

Whitmore, J. (1998). *Coaching for performance*. London: Nicholas Brealey.

Coaching and Leadership in the Six Cultures of Contemporary Organizations

15

William Bergquist and Vikki G. Brock

Introduction

Susan Stracker (name changed) is an executive coach. She is deeply involved with three clients right now who absolutely drive her crazy. They have made her professional life difficult not because they are problematic; rather, it is because they are each quite different in their approaches to leadership and in what they want and expect from their coach. Susan feels like a chameleon who must constantly change its colour (coaching style) depending on the divergent needs of her clients. How can Susan expect to offer a coherent and consistent message regarding her coaching if she must constantly change her approach and style to meet the diverse needs of her clients? We would suggest that Susan Stracker is not alone in this state of confusion and inconsistency. Many coaches, including the authors, have faced a similar dilemma. So we would propose to Susan that the dynamics of her diverse coaching strategies are, in part, a result of the differing organizational cultures in which her clients work and in which they come to 'know' the reality of their organizations. Furthermore, we would propose that her frustration is a product of her own coaching culture – her assumptions, values and aspirations as an organizational coach.

In this chapter we will identify and discuss six different organizational cultures that we believe strongly influence the ways in which

The Philosophy and Practice of Coaching: Insights and Issues for a New Era.
Edited by David B. Drake, Diane Brennan and Kim Gørtz.
© 2008 John Wiley & Sons, Ltd.

contemporary organizational leaders and organizational coaches frame their work and their expectations regarding the assistance that a coach might provide. We then turn to the intercultural dynamics created by the interplay among these six cultures and focus, in particular, on two aspects: the ways in which culture and coaching help to create meaning among coaching clients and the ways in which culture and leadership help contain the anxiety that inevitably exists in contemporary organizations. We conclude by examining the specific ways in which each of the differing cultures of coaching help the client (and the coach) create meaning and reduce anxiety associated with their daily work.

Six Organizational Cultures

Over the past twenty years, one of us [W.B.] has recognized the need for cultural analyses of organizations from the perspective of those who lead and work in these organizations (Bergquist, 1993; Bergquist, Guest, and Rooney, 2003; Bergquist and Pawlak, 2007). He assumed that those inside the organizations might welcome an understanding of organizational culture because many organizations seem to be particularly resistant to influence and change. The dynamics of contemporary organizations are often difficult to understand. Any framework that can help bring order to the complexity of these organizations will be greatly appreciated. One of us [V.G.B.] has recently conducted a series of interviews with leading practitioners in the field of coaching. She has discovered widely divergent perspectives on the field and believes (with W.B.) that these differing perspectives relate to differing organizational cultures and, in turn, to differing notions about effective leadership and coaching in each of these cultures. This chapter represents a blending of the conceptual work and research done by both authors.

It has become increasingly fashionable to describe organizations as cultures. Anthropologists, management consultants, organizational psychologists, and other social scientists have become enamoured of this concept and have helped to popularize the notion that cultural analyses yield important insights about the life and dynamics of an organization. The definitions of organizational culture and the methods used to study organizational cultures are as diverse as the disciplines involved (for example, Pettigrew, 1979; Peters and Waterman, 1982; Schein, 1985, 1992, 1999; Kotter and Heskett, 1992; Deal and Kennedy, 2000; Alveson, 2002; Martin, 2002; Cameron and Quinn, 2006). Here we will use Philippe Rosinski's (2003) view that 'a group's culture is the set of unique characteristics that distinguishes its members from another group'

(p. 20). Rosinski's definition encompasses visible and invisible manifestations and sees culture as a group phenomenon as opposed to an individual reality. While Rosinski is primarily focusing on the 'big C' (cultural differences across national and ethnic boundaries), his analysis – as Rosinski himself suggests – also applies to the 'small c' (cultural differences within organizations and other social groups). Rosinski (2003) states that 'once differences can be seen as cultural, there is the possibility of understanding and developing skills to manage, or better yet leverage, those differences' (p. 17). The purpose of this chapter is to provide an analysis of culture with regard to organizational coaching as one of the most important of these skill sets.

Four different, yet interrelated, cultures of leadership and coaching are often found in contemporary organizations. These cultures have a profound impact on the ways in which leaders and coaches view their current work and the ways in which they perceive the potential for personal benefit and organizational improvement. These four cultures also influence how those outside the organization perceive the purposes and appropriate operations of organizations, and how they believe they themselves should interact with these organizations. Two of the four leadership and coaching cultures can be traced back several centuries. They are the *professional culture* and the *managerial culture*. The other two have emerged more recently, partially in response to the seeming failure of the two original cultures to adapt effectively to changes in contemporary organizations. The first of these more contemporary cultures is referred to as the *alternative culture* and the second is referred to as the *advocacy culture*. The four cultures are briefly described in Figure 15.1. While these four models are aligned in some ways with the work of Bolman and Deal (1991), and Morgan (2006), we are attempting in this chapter to move beyond cultural analysis into the implications of these differing cultural properties for the field of professional coaching.

There are additional external influences in our global culture that are pressing upon the contemporary organization, forcing it in some ways to alter the way it goes about its business. Two new leadership and coaching cultures are emerging in organizations as a result of these external, global forces, and they interact with the previous four, creating additional dynamics. The first one, the *virtual culture*, was prompted by the technological and social forces that have emerged over the past 20 years. The second new one, the *tangible culture*, has existed in various forms for quite some time, yet has only recently been evident as a separate culture partly in response to emergence of the virtual culture and the concern about the loss of continuity and stability in contemporary culture. We propose that these six distinct cultures (each with its own history and values) yield a specific perspective with regard

Figure 15.1 Six Cultures of Contemporary Organizations.

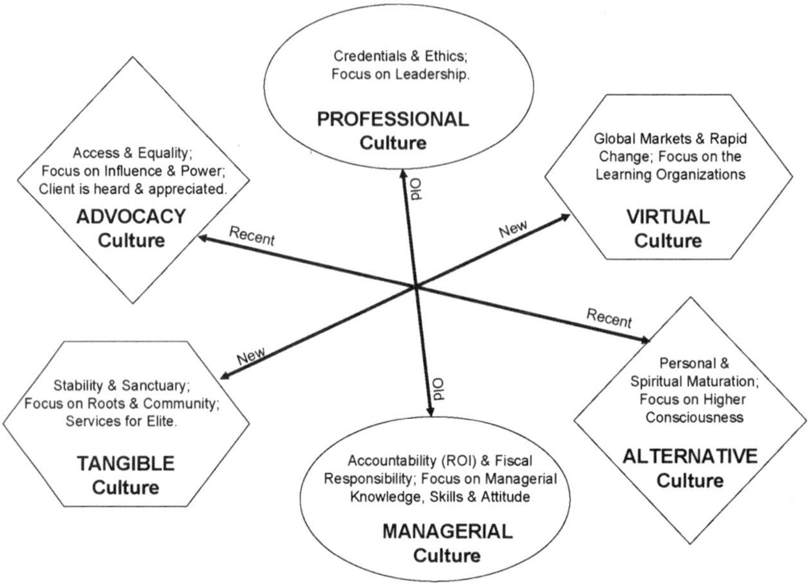

Credentials & Ethics;
Focus on Leadership.

PROFESSIONAL
Culture

Access & Equality;
Focus on Influence & Power;
Client is heard & appreciated.

ADVOCACY
Culture

Global Markets & Rapid
Change; Focus on the
Learning Organizations

VIRTUAL
Culture

Recent   New

Old

New   Recent

Stability & Sanctuary;
Focus on Roots & Community;
Services for Elite.

TANGIBLE
Culture

Old

Personal &
Spiritual Maturation;
Focus on Higher
Consciousness

ALTERNATIVE
Culture

Accountability (ROI) & Fiscal
Responsibility; Focus on Managerial
Knowledge, Skills & Attitude

MANAGERIAL
Culture

to organizational coaching and, in turn, generate assumptions about ways in which to work most effectively with organizational leaders (see Figure 15.1). Coaches such as Susan bring their own cultural preference to their work and are often called to adopt other approaches and styles in order to synchronize with the organizational culture of the client, at least temporarily. The question here is how far do coaches stretch, and for how long, such that they do not lose their authenticity.

The Professional Culture

Coaches and the users of coaching services who are aligned with the professional culture conceive of coaching as a 'profession' and seek to build its credibility through establishing a code of ethics, professional organizations (such as International Coach Federation (ICF), Professional Coach and Mentor Association (PCMA), European Mentoring and Coaching Council (EMCC) and International Consortium for Coaching in Organizations (ICCO)) and publications (such as the *International Journal of Coaching in Organizations* (IJCO) and *International Journal of Evidence Based Coaching and Mentoring* (IJEBC&M)), and research and scholarship regarding coaching. In many cases, the established professions (for example, psychology and business consulting) have claimed that they alone can certify coaches or, at the very least, that the field of coaching should be closely monitored and controlled. The motives behind this professional concern are laudable: concern for quality of service and for an adequate foundation of theory-based and evidential research to support coaching practices. However, underlying these legitimate motives is often an unacknowledged thirst for control of the field (with its potentially rich source of money and capacity to influence personal and organizational lives).

Professional associations often play a central role in promoting this culture. These organizations address 'a need for status, a sense of commitment or calling, a desire to share in policy formation and implementation . . . a feeling of duty, a wish for fellowship and community' (Houle, 1980, p. 171). They create excitement and energy – a 'zest' for promotion of a specific profession – in this case, coaching (Merriam and Brockett, 1997). While those aligned with the professional culture support research on coaching, they are inclined to identify coaching as an 'art' rather than a 'science', and cringe at any efforts to quantify (and therefore constrain or trivialize) the specific outcomes of coaching. In his book *Coaching to the Human Soul*, Sieler (2003) supports both practice and theory when he references an ancient Chinese proverb: 'theory without practice is foolish; practice without theory is dangerous' (p. xi). In this sense, coaching is an art in its full integration of theory and practice.

Let us assume for a moment that our bewildered coach, Susan Stracker, is strongly associated with the professional culture. She and other coaches who associate with this culture are likely to embrace many untested assumptions about the dominance of rationality in organizations. Susan is likely to find it hard to work with an 'irrational' client – someone who seems to dwell only in the heart rather than in the head. Susan is likely to read quite a bit (hoping to keep up in her 'field') and expects her clients also to be knowledgeable. Susan will embrace a perspective on coaching that is systemic in nature – she believes that a 'knowledgeable' leader must always look at the 'big picture' and she assists her clients in seeing and carefully analysing this big, systemic picture. At a fundamental level, Susan and her colleagues in the professional culture conceive of the coaching enterprise as the generation, interpretation, and dissemination of knowledge and the development of specific values and qualities of character among leaders in the organization – and they tend to differentiate between managers and leaders.

As 'professional' coaches, Susan and her colleagues are inclined to associate their work with leadership, rather than the more 'mundane' (in their view) operations of managers in the organization. Managers may need coaching, but the 'real' value of coaching concerns engagements with men and women who operate in a leadership position. Viewing management from a professional culture orientation, Warren Bennis (2003), suggests that managers administer, ask how and when, focus on systems, do things right, maintain, rely on control, and have a short-term perspective. Bennis also suggests that managers tend to accept the status quo, have an eye on the bottom line, and imitate. They are the classic good soldier and are copies of the stereotypical manager of the 60s and 70s. Given Bennis's limiting perspective on management, the role to be played by coaches with a professional culture orientation is quite clear. They are not to assist managers in performing specific organizational functions; rather, they are to assist leaders who decide what these managerial functions should be.

The Managerial Culture

Coaches and the users of coaching services who are aligned with the managerial culture conceive of coaching as a vehicle for improvement of performance in Bennis's managerial areas. Coaches and clients with a managerial orientation are much less enamoured, compared to those oriented to the professional culture, of 'big pictures' and the focus on leadership. Management is where the action is – not so-called 'leadership'. Management and managerial coaching are often identified with a specific set of organizational functions and responsibilities. For example, Fournies (1978) proposed many years ago that 'the coaching process is a technique that helps managers more successfully bring about performance achievements in business that relate directly to the survival of that business' (p. vii). Megginson and Boydell (1979) similarly indicate that 'coaching is a process in which a manager, through direct discussion and guided activity, helps a colleague to learn to solve a problem, or to do a task, better than would otherwise have been the case' (p. 5). Some authors even go so far as to identify coaching as a specific managerial skill. For instance, Peltier (2001) identifies coaching as a 'set of day-to-day skills exercised by managers at all levels of the organization' (p. xv). Many other definitions of coaching from the late 1970s to the 2000s are similarly oriented towards the management culture.

What if we turn Susan Stracker into a coach who is oriented towards the managerial culture? For Susan and her colleagues in this culture, coaching is seen as a vehicle for improved managerial performance. Coaches aligned with this culture are often engaged in the planning, implementation and evaluation of a manager's work – this work being directed toward specified goals and purposes. Susan would love working with a client who has a specific request to make regarding the way Susan can be of assistance: 'Help me prepare for this meeting' or 'I'm having a particularly difficult time working with my male subordinates. Can you help me?' As a coach oriented toward the managerial culture, Susan is not likely to perceive any important differences between management and leadership. Managers *are* leaders, as far as Susan and her managerially-oriented colleagues are concerned. In fact, managers are the employees who really make an organization work.

Those who are aligned with this culture – both clients and coaches – tend to value fiscal responsibility and the quantifiable measurement of coaching outcomes (for example, return-on-investment (ROI)). They tend to believe that management (and therefore leadership) skills can be specified and developed through a blend of training and coaching. Coaches who associate with this culture often embrace many untested assumptions about the capacity of an organization's managers (leaders) to clearly define and measure its goals and objectives. They conceive of the coaching enterprise as the inculcation or reinforcement of specific knowledge, skills and attitudes in the men and women they are coaching, so that they might become successful and responsible managers (leaders). Clients with a managerial orientation want Susan, as their coach, to be able to assist them in a very tangible manner to become more skilful and therefore successful and 'promotable' in the organization. One of Susan's clients actually fits this mould. He wants her to help him find the 'keys to success' in his organization. To the extent that Susan is oriented toward the managerial culture, she is likely to feel comfortable with this client's expectations; to the extent that Susan is oriented toward the professional culture, she is likely to feel constrained by these expectations – that's why she would like to work as a professionally-oriented coach with leaders who are interested in the big picture rather than the 'trivia' of specific performance skills or job promotions.

The Alternative Culture

Coaches and the users of coaching services who are aligned with the alternative culture conceive of coaching as a vehicle for the creation of programmes and activities that further the personal (and often the spiritual) growth of all members of the organization (or even more broadly the entire community). Flaherty (2005) says 'coaching is a way of working with people that leaves them more competent and more fulfilled so that they are more able to contribute to their organizations and find meaning in what they are doing' (p. 3). Sieler (2003) supports this assertion, 'The human soul is the hidden side of business. Coaching to the human soul is about supporting people to be at their best in living, learning and working. Coaching to the human soul makes good business sense, for when people are at their best, organizations benefit from their enhanced performance, productivity and creativity' (p. xiii). Those leaders who are aligned with this culture turn to coaches who value personal openness and service to others, as well as the integration of mind, body and spirit (see Stoneham, Weger, and Rocco, 2006). Neither group accepts what they see as an artificial distinction between personal and organizational coaching.

If Susan Stracker were aligned with the alternative culture, she would feel most comfortable working with clients who want to share freely their feelings and their life issues inside and outside the workplace. Susan and her fellow coaches who associate with this culture often embrace many untested assumptions about the inherent desire of all men and women to attain their own personal maturation. Susan does not just want her client to think systemically; she also wants her client to reflect on his own aspirations for the organization – his own vision, his own future in the organization, the alignment between his own values and those of the organization. Both coaches and leaders who embrace this alternative culture wish to assist in the development of others in the organization (or even the broader community). They conceive of the coaching enterprise as the encouragement of potential for cognitive, affective, physical and spiritual development among all members of the organization – not just the formal leaders. They do not want to just assist a client become more skilful in working with subordinates or in successfully completing a specific task – as would a coach oriented toward the managerial culture. They want their client to ask fundamental questions and find answers to these deeper questions: Why work with subordinates in a specific manner? Why successfully complete this task? Of what ultimate importance is the work I do and what do I sacrifice in my life to complete this work in a successful manner?

The Advocacy Culture

Coaches and the users of coaching services who are aligned with the advocacy culture conceive of coaching as a vehicle for the establishment of equitable and egalitarian policies and procedures regarding the distribution of resources and benefits in the organization. Rosinski (2003) views this as the equality end of the 'hierarchy/equality' continuum and at the universalist end of the 'universalist/participant' continuum. Rosinski (2003) defines equality as an organizational arrangement in which 'people are equals who often happen to play different roles'. The universalist framework is one in which 'all cases should be treated in the same universal manner, adopting common processes for consistency and economies of scale' (p. 54). Those who embrace this culture often have been associated in their past life with the formulation and/or enforcement of HR (human resources) policies and procedures (serving as 'policy police' in a large corporation or government agency).

Leaders who are aligned with this culture turn to coaches who value confrontation and equitable, enabling and empowering strategies that bring all stakeholders 'to the table'. Susan Stracker has one client who is strongly oriented toward this culture. This client wants to know that Susan's own value system is aligned with his commitment to broad-based participation in the decision-making processes of his organization. Leaders with an advocacy orientation turn to coaches who recognize the inevitable presence of (and need for) multiple constituencies with vested interests that are inherently in opposition. These leaders and coaches aligned with this culture believe that coaching is essential to this broad-based engagement. Both leader and coach worry about ways in which organizational coaching might be inequitably provided in an organization – producing even greater division between the 'haves' and the 'have nots'.

For a moment, let us assume that Susan Stacker is oriented toward this culture. Susan and other coaches and leaders associated with this culture are likely to embrace many untested assumptions about the ultimate role of power in the organization. Susan would frequently identify the need for outside mediation to deal with these power-based issues. She is likely to conceive of the coaching enterprise as the surfacing of existing (and often repressive) social attitudes and structures. As an advocate for social justice, Susan is likely to recommend, whenever possible and appropriate, the establishment of new and more liberating attitudes and structures in the organizations with which she coaches. As an advocate, Susan is clearly not 'neutral' about her work or the men and women she coaches. She would not hide her own beliefs and is likely to be quite selective regarding the organizations and specific clients with whom she contracts.

The Virtual Culture

Coaches and the users of coaching services who are aligned with the virtual culture conceive of coaching as a vehicle for the engagement and use of knowledge and expertise that is being produced and modified at an exponential rate in our postmodern world. This organizational arrangement, labelled 'change' by Rosinski (2003), 'values a dynamic and flexible environment, promotes effectiveness through adaptability and innovations, and avoids routine which is perceived as boring' (p. 54). Those aligned with this culture tend to value a global perspective and make extensive use of open, shared and responsive learning systems. They are participants in what Thomas Friedman (2006) describes as a 'flat world' which has abandoned organizational and national boundaries.

Leaders who are aligned with this culture turn to coaches who speak about learning organizations. As Peter Senge (1990, p. 4), one of the early proponents of the learning organization, has noted: 'The organizations that will truly excel in the future will be the organizations that discover how to tap people's commitment and capacity to learn at *all* levels in an organization. Learning organizations are possible because, deep down, we are all learners.' Furthermore, as learners, we should not avoid taking risks and making mistakes, yet we should avoid repeating the same mistakes and taking the same unsuccessful risks. We learn from our mistakes (as well as our successes).

If Susan Stracker were aligned with the virtual culture, she and her fellow coaches and leaders associated with this culture would embrace many untested assumptions about their ability to make sense of the fragmentation and ambiguity that exists in the postmodern world (Bergquist, 1993; Bergquist and Mura, 2005). Susan would undoubtedly be quite wise and skilful in making use of digital technologies. She might even do some of her coaching via the Internet and is likely to work with clients who are also technologically savvy. Susan would be frustrated in working with clients who are not readily accessible via some portable digital device, and would be inclined to work quickly and decisively with clients via many different media. Coaches and leaders who are oriented toward the virtual culture are likely to conceive of the coaching enterprise as linking the leader's learning needs to technological resources that enable the leader to access a global market and learning network. As a virtually oriented coach, Susan would be actively engaged in setting up her own network of coaches and in accessing coaching resources from throughout the world.

The Tangible Culture

Coaches and the users of coaching services who are aligned with the tangible culture conceive of coaching as a vehicle for the identification and appreciation of an organization's roots, community and symbolic grounding. This organizational arrangement is at the opposite end of the continuum from the virtual culture. Labelled 'stability' by Rosinski

(2003), it 'values a static and orderly environment, encourages efficiency through systematic and disciplined work, and minimizes change and ambiguity which is perceived as disruptive' (p. 54). Those aligned with this culture tend to value the predictability of a value-based, face-to-face coaching process. They like to work with people they can see and 'touch' (tangible) and work in relationships that are long-term and grounded in reality (tangible). Leaders who are aligned with this culture turn to coaches who focus on deeply embedded patterns (traditions) in the organization. Cultural change is either considered impossible or unwise. A strong emphasis is placed on the full appreciation of the existing and often long-standing dynamics of the organization – this emphasis being most fully articulated by those embracing an 'appreciative approach' to leadership (Srivastva, Cooperrider, and Associates, 1990) and coaching (Bergquist, Merritt, and Phillips, 2004).

Susan is in fact oriented towards the tangible culture (as well as the professional culture). One of her points of frustration concerns the desire of one client to always meet by phone. He has 'no time' for in-person meetings. Susan does not feel like she really 'knows' this client and would much prefer, at least on occasion, to meet in person for at least an hour. Much more could be accomplished and she would be much more comfortable in picking up his subtle phone-cues if she at least had an opportunity to work with him in person once in a while. As a coach oriented toward the tangible culture, Susan Stracker would like to see all of her clients face-to-face, but must agree to some phone coaching, given the location and busy schedule of her coaching clients.

Coaches and leaders associated with this culture embrace many untested assumptions, not only about the value of personal relationships, but also about the ability of organizations and their leaders to 'weather the storm' and to move beyond the seduction of faddish change. They conceive of the coaching enterprise as the honouring and reintegration of learning from the existing sources of distinctive wisdom located in their specific organization. These coaches and leaders tend to be appreciative, loyal – and sometimes a bit narrow-minded and resistant to new ideas.

Culture and Coaching: The Creation of Meaning

Although most organizational coaches and leaders tend to embrace or exemplify one of these six cultures, the other five cultures are always present and interact with the dominant culture in an actual coaching session. The dynamic interaction among these six cultures is critical. We would suggest that each culture has an 'opposite' on which it depends and with which it shares many features and assumptions. Thus, the alternative culture, which has evolved primarily in response to faults associated with the professional culture, is nevertheless dependent on it and shares many values and perspectives with this culture. Similarly, the advocacy culture grew out of opposition to the managerial culture, yet looks to it for identity and purpose – and shares values and perspectives with it. We similarly suggest that the tangible culture has reared its head in opposition to the virtual culture's lack of acknowledgement of the value of face-to-face contact or historical context; tangibility and virtuality need one another. It is often in the interaction among cultures that organizations create shared meaning – usually in an attempt to bridge the gap and reconcile the perspectives offered by these cultures. In addition, it is often in the coach's sensitive probing of her client's culture-based assumptions that the coach and client gain greater clarity regarding the client's current meaning and even create new personal meaning for the client. We will focus briefly in this section of the chapter on this dynamic process of creating meaning through culture.

A culture provides a framework and guidelines that help to define the nature of reality for those people who are part of that culture. People belong to multiple groups and cultures, each of which provides the lens through which its members interpret and assign value to the various events and products of this world. Culture is composed of *artefacts and products* (visible and conscious manifestations), *norms and values* (groups' collective answers to universal challenges) and *basic assumptions* (invisible and unconscious beliefs about universal challenges) (Rosinski, 2003,) If we are to understand and influence men and women in their daily work inside contemporary organizations, then we must come to understand and fully appreciate their implicitly held models of reality. Schein agrees with this view: 'The bottom line for leaders is that if they do not become conscious of the cultures in which they are embedded, those cultures will manage them. Cultural understanding is desirable for all of us, but it is essential to leaders if they are to lead' (Schein, 1992, p. 15). Equally critical is for coach practitioners to understand the particular norms, values and basic assumptions that shape their perspectives (and their clients').

Ultimately, culture provides 'guidelines for problem-solving, decision making, influencing, establishing mindsets and directing behaviors' (Rosinski 2003, p. 42). More generally, culture (both big C and small c) serves some overarching purpose – a dimension that was often ignored in cultural analyses and traditional coaching prior to the publication of *Coaching across Cultures* by Rosinski in 2003. A culture is established around the production of something valued by its members. A culture does not exist for itself; rather, as Lessem (1990) notes, it exists to provide a context for successful achievement and interpretation of fundamental organizational intentions – it creates meaning.

At an even deeper level, culture is the collective programming of the mind that distinguishes members of one group or category of people from another and distinguishes between different ways in which members of organizations find meaning and purpose in their work. Therefore, the cultures of organizations must be understood within the context of each organization's multiple purposes. The ceremonies, symbols, assumptions and modes of leadership in an organization are usually directed toward the organization's purposes and derive from its cultural base. Precisely because of its subordinate (though critical) role, culture is a phenomenon so elusive that, unless it is explicitly targeted, it can often be seen only when an organization is struggling with a particularly complicated or intractable problem – as often is the case with contemporary organizations. It is in those situations where coaching can be of great value. A coach rather than a crisis can bring culture (and the untested assumptions, values and beliefs associated with culture) to the foreground – and provide support and resources to address the situation. This coaching process can also be of great value in helping members of organizations not only cease waiting for a crisis to create insight, but also more effectively contain the anxiety that is inevitably associated with the crises that do occur. We turn now to this matter of anxiety and the role played by culture and leadership in the interpretation and containment of organizational anxiety.

Culture and Leadership: The Containment of Anxiety

Beyond the understanding of the cultures themselves and how they are formulated, it is important for organizational coaches to recognize that organizational cultures serve the purpose of containing the anxiety and fear that is faced by organizational leaders. We have identified three ways in which anxiety is created in organizations relative to culture. One, anxiety is generally created in the midst of organizational crises. Two, it is present in relation to the work of the leader and the formal and informal processes of evaluation and monitoring that are associated with this work. Three, anxiety is often stirred when the assumptions of one culture collide with those of other cultures in the organization. In a reciprocal manner, a group forms assumptions and develops a culture in order to adapt to external circumstances and establish internal integration. The group feels better (at first) because the culture provides a solution – a way of perceiving, thinking and feeling about the challenges it faces.

For a variety of reasons, organizational cultures do not change easily (as those aligned with the tangible culture tend to emphasize). Not the least of these reasons is the ability of culture to assuage the anxieties and fears that inherently develop through the course of organizational life and leadership work. If the assumptions and beliefs upon which a culture is based are challenged through external or internal situations, or through an organizational change process, people will tend to resist the challenges. People tend to avoid the fear and anxiety associated with instability because they want to avoid the pain that is provoked. So they avoid change. Schein (1992) specifically suggests that anxiety is released when basic assumptions are unstable. The human mind needs cognitive stability. Therefore, any challenge to or questioning of a basic assumption will release anxiety and defensiveness. In this sense, the shared basic assumptions and beliefs that make up the culture of a group can be thought of as psychological defence mechanisms that permit the group to continue to remain viable and manage its anxiety.

Anxiety and Culture

We long for an existence that is comfortable, even joyful, and certainly free from anguish or surprise. Instead, we find ourselves living in a world that is filled with the demands for change and the accompanying demands for learning. To the extent that the hazards of learning are unknown and unpredictable, specific fears translate into a diffuse anxiety about that which cannot be clearly defined. Culture provides a container. It establishes roles, rules, attitudes, behaviours and practices. It prescribes ways for people to feel safe. Culture provides predictability and ascribes importance to one's actions and one's presence in the world. It says that when you participate in this culture you are not alone. There are specific roles and responsibilities.

Psychologists tell us that when we become anxious, we tend to regress to a more primitive state of mind and feelings. We become more like we were as children. In particular, we are likely to become dependent, and look forward to being taken care of by a person who in certain respects is superior. This anxiety and resulting dependency often serves us well. Anxiety, however, is a source of major problems with regard to learning. Anxiety not only keeps people from embracing major new learning in their lives, it contributes to the inability or unwillingness of leaders to learn about their own organization and to learn about ways they must confront the emerging challenges of our postmodern era (Bergquist and Mura, 2005). We propose that anxiety blocks the personal and organizational learning required in our contemporary systems. When we as coaches and leaders come to understand the nature and effect of this anxiety and its interplay with organizational culture, we will begin to unravel many of the Gordian knots associated with resistance to learning and change.

Organizational Culture as a Container of Anxiety

The fundamental interplay between the containment of anxiety and the formation of organizational cultures was carefully and persuasively documented by Isabel Menzies Lyth (1988). She describes ways in which nurses in an English hospital cope with the anxiety that is inevitably associated with issues of health, life and death. Menzies Lyth notes how the hospital in which nurses work helps to ameliorate or at least protect the nurses from anxiety. She suggests that a healthcare organization is primarily in the business of reducing this anxiety and that on a daily basis all other functions of the organization are secondary to this anxiety-reduction function.

It is specifically the culture of the organization that serves as the primary vehicle for addressing anxiety and stress. The culture of an organization is highly resistant to change precisely because change directly threatens the informal system that has been established in the organization to help those working in it to confront and make sense of the anxiety inherent in the operations of the organization. Menzies Lyth's observations have been reaffirmed in many other organizational settings. Anxiety is to be found in most contemporary organizations and efforts to reduce this anxiety are of prominent importance. Somehow an organization that is inclined to evoke anxiety among its employees must discover or construct a buffer that both isolates (contains) the anxiety and addresses the realistic, daily needs of its employees.

How exactly does anxiety get addressed in organizations? Menzies Lyth (1988) suggested that it gets addressed through the 'social defense system' – that is, the patterns of interpersonal and group relationships that exist in the organization. Other organizational theorists and researchers, for example Deal and Kennedy (2000) and Schein (1992), similarly suggest that the rituals, routines, stories and norms (implicit values) of the organization help members of the organization manage anxiety inside the organization. Yet, these rituals, routines, stories and norms are not a random assortment of activities. Rather, they cluster together and form a single, coherent dimension of the organization – they create meaning as well as contain anxiety. This single, coherent dimension is known as the 'culture' of the organization. As Edgar Schein (1999) has noted, the culture of an organization is the residue of the organization's success in confronting varying conditions in the world. To the extent that an organization is adaptive in responding to and reducing pervasive anxiety associated with the processes of organizational learning and related functions of the enterprise, the existing cultures of this organization will be reinforced, will deepen and will become increasingly resistant to challenge or change.

The Culture of Coaching: Creating the Meaning and Reducing the Anxiety

How might Susan Stracker best operate as a coach? How can she embrace the multiple perspectives of her clients and appreciate the strengths to be found in all six coaching cultures? How can she best help her clients create meaning and reduce anxiety in their work? Perhaps Susan and other organizational coaches can best help clients do so through their work by bringing forward the diverse perspectives that the six cultures offer to their clients. Taken in isolation, each of the six cultures provides a vehicle that is only partially successful in providing meaning and reducing the anxieties of people about their own learning. Furthermore, even when successful, each culture produces only part of the cluster of values and meaning associated with a specific organization and alleviates only the symptoms of the anxiety not its ultimate source. Meaning and anxiety will only be fully addressed when people feel they are being valued by their organization. They will feel valued when their own concerns are effectively addressed by other members of the organization, regardless of culture.

We propose that it is crucial for organizational coaches like Susan Stracker to appreciate each of the cultures so that they can help their clients to operate effectively within and among them. With this knowledge, Susan's clients can more effectively influence and improve the quality and efficacy of change that is required in their twenty-first-century organizations. With this sense of appreciation, coaching clients can ensure that each culture becomes a force for improvement rather than destruction in their organization. Each culture can contribute to the ability of coaching clients to learn rather than reinforcing limiting and inflexible assumptions about the nature and direction of the enterprise in which these leaders are engaged. Building on our proposition that all six cultures should be appreciated by the coach and client, we will consider the specific contributions to be made by each culture.

Professional Culture

The primary vehicles for the creation of meaning and the containment of anxiety in the professional culture are the demonstration of wisdom and credibility on the part of the coach. If she can exhibit extensive knowledge of the particular business in which her client is working or if she can exhibit a broad-based knowledge of how organizations work and how leaders lead, then her client is likely to feel more at ease, clearer about the purpose of his work, and less vulnerable to the leadership challenges that he faces. If a coach can show that she is credentialled (such as having an ICF certification), or if she can relate her client's leadership issues to a specific theory (e.g., a model of leadership) or specific research findings (e.g., leadership competencies that have been studied), then she gains credibility with her client and is likely to be influential in her coaching interactions with him.

Managerial Culture

When a leader and coach interact under the auspices of this culture, meaning is likely to be created and anxiety is likely to be contained if the coach can provide services that yield measurable results – the leader improves her performance in a specific way (such as being able to increase revenues in her department by 30%). The coach is likely to be particularly effective in creating meaning and reducing his client's anxiety if the performance improvement is linked to specific rewards. Thus, it is not only important that revenues increased by 30%, it is also important that this leader receive a substantial bonus, salary increase, increased responsibility, or promotion in recognition of her improved performance. The coach who is aligned with the managerial culture holds an advantage over coaches aligned with the other five cultures in this regard because he can commit to specific goals (and this commitment itself creates meaning and reduces anxiety). On the other hand, with explicit coaching goals, there is always the danger that if these goals are not met, the anxiety of both leader and coach will be increased, not diminished, and the fundamental assumptions about work-related meaning will be challenged.

Alternative Culture

The leader and coach who are aligned with this culture tend to equate meaning with personal satisfaction and ongoing learning and maturation.

The client and coach are likely to feel less anxious when the client 'feels better', feels more aligned with some greater purpose or higher level of consciousness, or feels that he has access to some higher (spiritual) source of energy or inspiration. In many ways, this culture offers the most accessible and intimate vehicles for the production of meaning and reduction of anxiety. The client senses that he is physically 'more alive', he is experiencing 'less stress', or he is 'energized' by some external power or presence. There are no standardized criteria for determining the success of coaching in this culture. Success in each case is defined by the client or by the particular community of belief and values through which this specific coaching process is engaged.

Advocacy Culture

This specific culture is often filled with anxiety, given that it inevitably involves some confrontation and some tension between the 'haves' and 'have nots'. The client that is receiving the coaching is likely to feel less anxious when he feels 'heard' and 'appreciated'. He will assume that his work is meaningful if he believes he has been influential in the area(s) of greatest concern to him. As in the case of the managerial culture, meaning is likely to be clarified or created and anxiety is often reduced in the advocacy culture if the coach and client can be explicit about their coaching goals. An advocacy-oriented coach is likely to help her client identify specific ways in which (and times and places when) he can be more influential. If 'influential' can be stated in measurable terms, then the advocacy leader and coach can celebrate victory (yet also risk the increased anxiety and collapse of meaning that comes with defeat).

Virtual Culture

The leader and coach who operate out of this particular frame of reference are involved in a balancing act with regard to the creation of meaning and the reduction or elimination of organizational anxiety. On the one hand, the coach is often in the business of challenging his client with new information regarding her postmodern world or with new points of access into a dynamic network of relationships, even though these challenging queries can shake up existing patterns of meaning and can certainly increase anxiety. On the other hand, the virtual coach is trying to be supportive of his client, providing her with some sense of coherence in a world that is filled with complexity, unpredictability and turbulence (Bergquist and Mura, 2005). The virtual coach faces a difficult task in helping his client make sense of her world. It is not only a matter of digesting a large amount of information; it is also a matter of thinking and acting at a very high level. Kegan (1994) suggests that we, of the postmodern era, are 'in over our heads' (certainly a challenge to existing patterns of meaning and a source of profound anxiety). It would seem that coaches to these virtual, postmodern leaders are particularly needed to help their clients address these major twenty-first-century challenges.

Tangible Culture

Given the challenges facing contemporary leaders, it is obvious that the tangible coach is potentially of great value – for leaders long for coaching strategies that are directly aligned with the tangible culture. They want to be able to meet with their coach face-to-face; they seek out a time and space that is safe. When effective, the coach who is aligned with the tangible culture will help create a 'sanctuary' in which her client can talk about anything and feel deeply. This coaching client may have no specific agenda, nor does he necessarily want to improve his performance, find a higher level of consciousness, or become more influential. He mostly wants to find a safe place where he can 'be himself', 'talk to someone who holds no agenda other than being there for him', or 'simply be listened to by someone who cares about his personal welfare'. These tangible needs are not easily articulated in a formal coaching contract. However, as in the case of the alternative culture, the coaching strategies associated with the tangible culture may be immediately effective in helping to create (or sustain existing) patterns of meaning and to reduce postmodern anxiety. Unfortunately, this type of coaching is often reserved only for those with sufficient power, wealth or opportunity to meet in person with a coach (often in some retreat site). Thus, the tangible culture – more than any of the other five cultures – is often associated with coaching services that are reserved for the elite.

Beyond and Beneath the Organizational Meaning and Anxiety

Our analysis would suggest that there are not only many sources of meaning and of anxiety associated with leadership in a twenty-first-century organization, there are also many different ways in which coaches can help to create or clarify meaning and contain the anxiety.

Many psychological theorists suggest that human service providers should not be in the business of clarifying or creating meaning – this is the job of a spiritual director or religious counsellor. We disagree with these assessments and believe that Susan Stracker will be able to do her best work by directly addressing both the challenge of meaning and the challenge of anxiety. The meaning we are talking about here is not reserved for the domain of spirituality; work and organizational life are often just as important sources of meaning as are religious institutions and spiritual communities. Furthermore, just as pain is an important source of information for the healthcare provider regarding the nature of an injury or illness, so anxiety might be a source of information about the 'malady' facing an organizational leader regarding his own behaviour or some broader systemic problem.

An organizational coach such as Susan Stracker might wish to examine the ways in which her coaching strategies and perspectives not only help to create meaning and alleviate anxiety, but also reveal the underlying problem(s) that have led to a sense of alienation from the work or helped to generate the anxiety associated with this work. In this chapter we have identified several of the strengths associated with each culture and the coaching strategies aligned with each culture. We have also identified some of the potential blind spots. We encourage Susan Stracker and other organizational coaches to explore assumptions arising from their cultural perspective. We further encourage organizational coaches and their clients to explore what lies beyond and beneath the meaning and anxiety associated with their work and their organization. The bottom-line is that none of these six cultures will be going away in the near future. Furthermore, all six play a critical role in the vitality of virtually every twenty-first-century organization. Therefore, it is crucial for organizational coaches and their clients to appreciate all six cultures in order for the clients to be effective leaders within and among the cultures of the organization.

References

Alveson, M. (2002). *Understanding organizational culture.* Newbury Park, CA: Sage.

Bennis, W. (2003). *On becoming a leader.* Cambridge, MA: Perseus Publishing.

Bergquist, W. (1993). *The four cultures of the academy.* San Francisco: Jossey-Bass.

Bergquist, W. (1993). *The postmodern organization.* San Francisco: Jossey-Bass.

Bergquist, W., and Mura, A. (2005). *Ten themes and variations for postmodern leaders and their coaches.* Sacramento, CA: Pacific Soundings Press.

Bergquist, W., and Pawlak, K. (2007). *Engaging the six cultures of the academy.* San Francisco: Jossey-Bass.

Bergquist, W., Guest, S., and Rooney, T. (2003). *Who is wounding the healers?* Sacramento, CA: Pacific Soundings Press.

Bergquist, W., Merritt, K., and Phillips, S. (2004). *Executive coaching: An appreciative approach* (rev. edn) Sacramento, CA: Pacific Soundings Press.

Bolman, L. G., and Deal, T. E. (1991). *Reframing organizations: Artistry, choice, and leadership.* San Francisco: Jossey-Bass.

Cameron, K. S., and Quinn, R. E. (2006). *Diagnosing and changing organizational culture.* (rev. edn) San Francisco: Jossey-Bass.

Cervero, R. M. (1992). Adult education should strive for professionalization. In M. W. Galbraith and B. Sisco (eds.), *Confronting controversies in challenging times: A call for action. New Directions for Adult and Continuing Education, No. 54.* San Francisco: Jossey-Bass.

Deal, T. E., and Kennedy, A. A. (2000). *Corporate cultures: The rites and rituals of corporate life.* Perseus Publishing.

Flaherty, J. (2005). *Coaching: Evoking excellence in others.* Amsterdam: Elsevier Butterworth-Heinemann.

Fournies, F. F. (1978). *Coaching for improved work performance.* New York: Van Nostrand Reinhold.

Freidman, T. (2006). *The world is flat.* New York: Farrar, Straus & Giroux.

Houle, C. O. (1980). *Continuing learning in the profession.* San Francisco: Jossey-Bass.

Kegan, R. (1994). *In over our heads: The mental demands of modern life.* Cambridge, MA: Harvard University Press.

Kotter, J. P., and Heskett, J. L. (1992). *Corporate culture and performance.* New York: Free Press.

Lessem, R. (1990). *Managing corporate culture.* Aldershot, UK: Gower.

Lyth, I. M. (1988). The functioning of social systems as a defense against anxiety. In *Containing anxiety in institutions* (pp. 43–85). London: Free Association Books.

Martin, J. (2002). *Organizational culture: Mapping the terrain.* Newbury Park, CA: Sage.

Megginson, D. and Boydell, T. (1979). *A manager's guide to coaching.* London: Broadwater Press.

Merriam, S. B., and Brockett, R. G. (1997). *The profession and practice of adult education.* San Francisco: Jossey-Bass.

Morgan, G. (2006). *Images of organization.* Thousand Oaks, CA: Sage.

National Institute of Mental Health, retrieved July 20, 2006 from http://www.nimh.nih.gov/HealthInformation/anxietymenu.cfm.

Peltier, B. (2001). *The psychology of executive coaching: Theory and application.* New York: Brunner-Routledge.

Peters, T. J., and Waterman, R. H. (1982). *In search of excellence: Lessons from America's best-run companies.* New York: HarperCollins.

Pettigrew, A. M. (1979). On studying organizational cultures. *Administrative Science Quarterly,* 24, 570–581.

Rosinski, P. (2003). *Coaching across cultures: New tools for leveraging national, corporate, and professional differences.* London: Nicholas Brealey.

Schein, E. (1985). *Organizational culture and leadership: A dynamic view.* San Francisco: Jossey-Bass.

Schein, E. H. (1992). *Organizational culture and leadership* (2nd edn). San Francisco: Jossey-Bass.

Schein, E. H. (1999). *The corporate culture survival guide.* San Francisco: Jossey-Bass.

Sieler, A. (2003). *Coaching to the human soul: Ontological coaching and deep change.* Blackburn, Victoria, Australia: Newfield Australia.

Senge, P. (1990). *The fifth discipline.* New York: Doubleday.

Srivastva, S., Cooperrider, D., and Associates. (1990). *Appreciative management and leadership: The power of positive thought and action in organizations.* San Francisco: Jossey-Bass.

Stoneham, D., Weger, P., and Rocco, D. (2006). Integral intelligence™: Unleashing potential in leaders and organizations. *International Journal of Coaching in Organizations,* 4(3), 40–51.

Coaching, Lean Processes, and the Concept of Flow

16

Kim Gørtz

Flow makes us feel better in the moment, enabling us to experience the remarkable potential of the body and mind fully functioning in harmony.

Mihaly Csikszentmihalyi

Introduction

The first half of this chapter explores two meanings of the word 'flow', one from Csikszentmihalyi's (1990, 2003) work in psychology and the other from a key element in Lean processes. In the first case, 'flow' signifies a state in which an individual or a group is fully immersed in an activity that has an appropriate level of challenge, heightened awareness and satisfaction. In a Lean context, 'flow' refers to a holistic route by which a product is developed in tandem with what creates value for the customer and serves his or her needs. This route partners the organization with the customer and demands a high degree of engagement from the employees, where focus, awareness and the ability to really listen to the needs of the customer are essential. The hypothesis here is that coaching can be used to foster this psychological state and, in so doing, become a tool for successful Lean implementation. The aim of this chapter is to use the conceptual framework of flow in an integrated manner, where organizational implementation of Lean processes and coaching can be understood and further developed.

The Philosophy and Practice of Coaching: Insights and Issues for a New Era.
Edited by David B. Drake, Diane Brennan and Kim Gørtz.
© 2008 John Wiley & Sons, Ltd.

The second half of the chapter offers a case study based on my research at Nordea Bank, which outlines how coaching can be used to support organizational change and the implementation of Lean processes. I will argue that this is of great importance for business-oriented coaches as Lean processes are exerting immense influence on every level of modern business life. The chapter concludes that, in order to be successful in implementing Lean processes, companies need to develop a 'responsible self-leadership culture' as a foundation and invest in coaching as a key component in this process. As a result, I advocate the view of coaching as an integrated skill in leadership practice and demonstrate how it can be used in organizational change, and Lean processes in particular.

The Concept of Flow in Psychology

There has been no study to date on the links between psychological flow theories, flow within Lean processes and coaching. In order to make the case for my hypothesis, I begin here with a look at flow within positive psychology. Flow, as developed and used by Mihaly Csikszentmihalyi (1990, 2003), is achieved when a challenge or task requires everything we've got, while simultaneously offering continuous and immediate feedback on how well we are succeeding. Flow occurs solely when focus on clear goals matches the willingness and capabilities of the person involved in accomplishing them. In Csikszentmihalyi's view, flow combines initiative and mental absorption and often leads to a greater sense of self and of making a difference in the world.

A major part of Csikszentmihalyi's work stresses that our performance reaches its zenith when we are operating at our limit in a generative manner. To reach this place requires definite goals, clear rules and immediate feedback (i.e., a context that focuses and maintains attention while at the same time making near-capacity demands on our capabilities). It is a question, then, of working at an optimal level of performance. Furthermore, when people pay close attention to each other while working together and invest mental energy in common goals, the chance of achieving a shared sense of flow is quite considerable and the power of cohesion increases. However, two conditions must be met in order to create such a level of consciousness: (1) a reasonable agreement between personal goals and the goals of others; and (2) a willingness to invest attention – i.e., empathy – in another person and his or her goals.

For a manager to create flow, he or she must consider the entire team and have the grace and skill to attend to others within the organization to further their goals and ambitions. Highly developed communication skills are essential to creating an atmosphere where flow can flourish. This, however, presupposes that both management and employees engage fully in the dialogue. Therefore, the state of psychological flow in the workplace demands continuous structured reflection, systematic evaluation, performance measurement and self-conscious control. Once developed, a sense of flow among employees can be converted into a usable strategy at every organizational level in ways that are beneficial in Lean processes. It will become apparent through the organizational case later in this chapter that leadership embedded in a coaching culture increases the ability for employees to focus, maintain and fully engage their awareness. In other words, leaders promote a culture of challenge, relevant feedback and clear goals to guide the organization towards optimal learning and high performance in a state of psychological flow.

Kaufmann (2006) outlined seven ways in which the theory of flow was applicable in coaching. Two of them seem particularly important in thinking about coaching within a Lean context: (1) increase the capacity to self-reflect and incorporate performance feedback; and (2) become aware of, and flexibly respond to, new information coming in the periphery (p. 229). They are relevant here because they highlight how coaching can be used to help employees meet their basic needs so they can perform more effectively and hone their abilities to increase customer value as well as help leaders gauge the impact of Lean processes in everyday work. As such, the next section looks at the organizational side of our integrated framework of flow in order to clarify: (1) the notion of flow within Lean processes; and (2) how coaching can be a great tool for successful Lean implementation by increasing the capacity to self-reflect, incorporate performance feedback and develop awareness and flexibility in responding to new information and organizational changes.

The Concept of Flow in Lean Processes

Lean production is built around the concept of continuous flow processing.

Cynthia Swank (2003)

The research suggests that a holistic approach to the implementation of Lean processes is required in order to achieve optimum change and improvement. At the same time, it is also important that managers and employees are fully engaged in, and take ownership of, the organizational process of change (Banner and Gagne, 1995; Morgan, 1993). Garrahan and Stewart (1992), among others, point out that this holistic approach and need for total engagement is often overlooked by those who approach Lean processes from a Tayloristic perspective. The establishment of self-learning teams and an overall learning culture are two of the key elements for success (Brochner, 1995; Koskela, 1992).

These are essential because Lean processes are, above all, about the primacy of value as it relates to the customers and their ever-evolving needs. As Swank (2003) put it: 'Always measure performance and productivity from the customer's perspective' (p. 4). From a strategic perspective, Womack and Jones (2005) stress that it is a question of defining value, defining a process that provides the desired value, and then creating an organization able to carry out the process. This focus on customer needs and requirements requires a continuous value-based dialogue with the customer about how, from their point of view, the product or service offers its value in the best possible way (Atkin and Pothecary, 1994; Bennett, Pothecary, and Robinson, 1996; Gray, 1996).

Broadly speaking, the vision of the Lean philosophy is to stay oriented to the customer's needs and value orientation. The goal is to reduce actions irrelevant to the value chain while at the same time focusing on where there is room for improvement. The process of optimization is infinite and requires the constant assessment of the production chain – what is being done, how it is being done, by whom and how well. It is necessary to engender a constant process of change to progress towards the optimal situation (Garnett, Jones, and Murray, 1998). For it to become embedded in the organization, it is necessary to establish a learning culture with improvement at its core. Furthermore, it is vital that everyone takes responsibility for the entire process and that a culture is developed clearly defining the concept of customer value.

Parallel with the elimination of what is irrelevant or an impediment to generating customer value is the creation of a state of flow and sense of motion within the organization. This 'good path' is based in, and created by, the state of flow (Bennett and Jayes, 1998). In contrast to the psychological conceptualization of flow, the good path takes place outside the individual. It is the flow of the product or service (e.g., in the Toyota production model, where the cars move through an assembly line and the workers engage in it to optimize quality and reduce time – and cost). In this conception of flow, we witness an outward continuous activity where employees know when and how to support the product on its way to the customer.

Hence, within a Lean context, flow is about making processes run smoothly and, thereby, allowing activities to move forward as efficiently and effectively as possible without undue delay. Flow is about creating a balanced working rhythm that optimally matches performance requirements and customer demands, facilitates the process flow accordingly, and systematically identifies hold-ups and lack of flow in the process (Eriksen, Fischer, and Mønsted, 2005). Achieving flow, therefore, requires the active elimination of any obstacles. Processes that achieve high levels of flow in this sense: (1) create value; (2) are flawless; (3) are accessible and reliable; (4) have sufficient capacity and match the activity; and (5) are flexible enough to allow a switch between variations in the process and tasks (Christensen, Ahrengot, and Leck, 2006; Womack and Jones, 2005).

The goal is the uninterrupted, direct and swift movement of the product towards the customer. However, this process is not just about the manufacturing or operational elements; it also requires the flow of information, documentation, learning and employee engagement. The latter requires people to have the ability to combine initiative and mental absorption in order to know where to be and when in the process line and value chain. It is here we see that the function of the manager is crucial and rather delicate. Since the manager isn't always along the process line, he or she needs to cultivate a harmonious environment among the people in order to get the workers on the line to buy into a sense of a common goal.

Bhasin and Burcher (2006) emphasize three common problems in connection with the unsuccessful implementation of Lean processes: lack of direction, lack of planning, and undue subdivision of projects. They observed that only 10% or less of companies succeed in implementing Lean manufacturing practices. Writing along similar lines, Sohal and Eggleston (1994) found that only 10% of organizations properly instituted the requisite philosophy. They concluded that the lack of knowledge of tools and techniques is rarely the problem. Instead, they stress that a combination of the following elements is an excellent guide to the successful implementation of Lean processes: (1) implement simultaneously five or more Lean techniques; (2) consider Lean processes as a mindset and a prolonged journey; (3) define and articulate the constant improvement perspective; and (4) introduce cultural change by including empowerment and supporting the Lean philosophy throughout the value chain.

It is not so much a question of bringing about change, but about how behaviour and communication stimulate and support the successful implementation of organizational change. Allen (2000) supports the significance of communication and recommends a change of focus, which I will rephrase as a mental and emotional shift from controlling to helping; from evaluating to empowering; from planning to listening; from directing to coaching. This notion of a Lean learning enterprise is supported by Philips (2002), who writes that human skills such as communication, problem solving, teamwork and leadership dialogues are vital for the success of Lean processes. As we shall see, coaching is a critical component in efforts to increase the capacity of employees to self-reflect, give performance feedback, and develop greater awareness and flexibility in responding to new information and organizational changes.

The Role of Coaching in Achieving Flow in Lean Processes

By engaging in coaching dialogues with employees, the manager helps articulate goals that are tailor-made to the capabilities and skill level of the person carrying them out. By investing empathetic attention and giving feedback to the entire team, the manager can help them further their goals and ambitions. As a result, coaching contributes to greater learning, growth and a sense of making a meaningful difference. The capacity to work close to the maximum individual and team performance levels, and attention to the psychological dimensions of flow, are critical in successful Lean process implementations.

However, as the organizational case will show, a broader perspective, planned strategy and systemic framework are also needed for a fuller understanding of the role of coaching in these initiatives. While there has not been much study in this area, Brown *et al.* (2003) provide some important insights on the importance of a planned strategy for the use of coaching in supporting a Lean implementation in large organizations. The essential lessons to be gleaned from their study can be seen in the six questions below as they are applied in the formulation of a Lean coaching strategy:

1. What is the scope of responsibilities for the coaching staff to support Lean processes?
2. What are the credentials needed to select coaches to support Lean processes?
3. What is the mix of external and internal coaches needed to support Lean processes?
4. What tools do coaches need to have knowledge and experience of to support Lean processes?
5. What performance measures are needed to manage coaches to support Lean processes?
6. What are the incentives coaches need to support Lean processes? (p. 120)

A key component of their approach is the recommendation that different coaching strategies be used for each of the three phases of the

Lean process: (1) the introduction phase; (2) the growth phase; and (3) the sustainability phase. In the *introduction* phase, the function of coaching should be to clarify new guidelines and standard operational procedures and ensure that the qualifications, systems and processes required to create the intended change are in place. On this level, coaching provides a canalization function in terms of the reorganization of a specific department and group of employees. In the *growth* phase, the function of coaching should be to create a more trusting environment between managers and employees and between employees, as the basis for a sense of solidarity and teamwork in connection with the change.

In the *sustainability* phase, the function of coaching should be to support employees in finding deeper meaning and perception of purpose in the process of change. Brown *et al.* (2003) remind us that the key words at this level are communication and dialogue. In their view, these three levels are essential for a successful Lean coaching strategy and incorporate nine critical components, including: (1) establishing several levels of coaches with different degrees of responsibilities; (2) selecting and clarifying internal coaches to an organizational standard; and (3) selecting a standard set of primary tools for coaches to use (p. 131).

As we have seen, attempts to run Lean processes often fail due to lack of coaching strategies, communication and dialogue – in a word, a failure to see 'the human side' of the equation in managing organizational culture change and its impact on people's mental and emotional state of mind. Therefore, it is the human side of things I'd like to address now, based on my investigations, observations and experience from the last two years at Nordea Bank, the biggest bank in Scandinavia and the site for my doctoral research.

Coaching, Lean and Flow – An Organizational Case

An ideal organization is one in which each worker's potentialities find room for expression. A healthy organization is marked by communication based on trust.

Mihaly Csikszentmihalyi

Introduction

Nordea Bank is located in the four Scandinavian countries and has business interests all around the world. It is one of the top 25 largest banks in the world, with around 30,000 employees. This case study shows how coaching has been embraced as a serious tool and method within a large organization, but has relevance for other applications as well. The case draws on my observations and findings from work within Nordea Life & Pension, their subsidiary insurance company with 460 employees, as well as across the large banking organization. It illustrates the integrated conceptual framework of flow and highlights some of its important features and practical applications.

Lean Processes in Nordea Bank

On 19 January 2006, Jarle Haug, then Head of Lean Banking – a department in the bank that was created to run the implementation of the Lean processes – announced that Lean processes were to be applied throughout Nordea. He stated, 'It is a provable fact that Lean processes will increase our productivity. This way of working has become popular because it increases staff engagement, enhances teamwork and offers numerous enhancement measures' (Nordea Bank's intranet, 19/1-06). The Lean Banking pilot projects in Retail Banking, Group Processing and Technology had proven successful, and a new goal was set to create a new bank based entirely on Lean processes, enhanced customer focus, increased productivity and the constant pursuit of improvement.

By enhancing in-house efficiency, Hang believed that Nordea would be able to attend to customers much faster while at the same time handling an increasing number of customer contacts. Lean Banking was therefore based on a platform for constant improvement and it used three Lean principles in particular: (1) *waste* – i.e., eliminating anything which does not add direct value to the product and the customer; (2) *minimizing variation* – i.e., attaining a high degree of standardization and the subsequent reduction in the number of errors; (3) *flexibility* – i. e., removing restrictions which prevent the immediate and efficient response to changes in customer demands.

Only four days after the announcement, I joined a kick-off event at Brøndby Stadium where the management team of Nordea Life & Pension announced the plan to implement Lean processes in the course of the coming year. The main ideas behind the management's initiative were that employees must be happy for the customers to be happy; work must be easy and comfortable; and everybody must be engaged in the success of the process. The idea behind the Lean process was clear: enhancing customer satisfaction, employee and management satisfaction and, last but not least, ensuring that the right Lean competencies were available at the managerial level. The management team stated that all processes had to become increasingly simple and, therefore, production, workflows and case handling had to be thoroughly reviewed to eliminate what were termed 'bottleneck problems'.

Senior management supported the necessary initiatives, changes and enhancements, even as they recognized that ambition would exceed performance for a while given that it would take time to change the mindsets as a prerequisite for changing the system. It was evident that the mindset and focus must shift vis-à-vis the customers through new ways of communicating with customers, increased engagement of the employees, and greater competency in both Lean skills and coaching among the managers. There were expectations of increased production, reduced procedure time and enhanced quality that were simultaneously supported by the development of the managers' ability to coach and perform Lean behaviour in the daily practices. A general feeling of optimism arose and everybody felt confident that change and growth would occur.

Nordea Life & Pension decided to do a step-by-step implementation of Lean processes and hired a trained coach to head the implementation process at the department level, in cooperation with a number of Lean experts. A steering group, a project management group and a project group were established to support the delivery on the plan. The coach's primary function was to support the Lean process through developing the space and time for coaching dialogues in which challenges to the reorganization could be termed, reflected and acted upon by the three groups. In meetings, workshops and seminars the coach played an essential role, at times challenging the participants to reflect more deeply and ask the harder questions and at other times encouraging a greater sense of team spirit among the participants.

As Lean processes require managers to think and act in new ways in production terms, Nordea Life & Pension developed workshops specifically for managers to define their roles and new core competencies. At the same time, specific resources within the project group were dedicated to providing coaching and feedback on managers. The goal was to both increase the managers' skills and their engagement through designing the workshops to match their practical experience, operational requirements and real-time challenges of managing within a new Lean context. A vital element in gaining their buy-in was to demonstrate how the performance management support generated value at an individual level and supported the success of each employee on a day-to-day basis. One particular question was repeatedly raised in this process: 'What is the specific role and purpose of leadership in a Lean context?'

Leadership Requirements for Coaching within Lean Processes

The Leadership Development (LD) Department within the Nordea organization had been the driver of a large-scale coaching programme that had been running for more than four years. The programme had evolved to include several levels of courses on individual and team coaching, examinations and degrees of certification. As a result of a plan for subsequent coaching development, it was decided at the highest executive level of the bank in autumn 2007 that all managers had to go through at least the coaching basics course (coaching level 1) offered internally. It was now expected that all managers in the bank should learn and use coaching as a part of their daily leadership practice. The question then became: 'How can these coaching competencies – which more than 1500 managers had already learned to varying degrees through the internal coaching skills courses – be supportive of the overall implementation of the Lean processes?' In addition, it was asked how the overall leadership-based coaching function could be used to ensure success in implementing Lean processes throughout the bank.

At a higher organizational level, the LD Department, as part of the overall Human Resources Department, discussed what would emerge from viewing the development of managers in the context of the overall Lean process. It should be noted that Lean Banking approached the implementation process with a very sure touch and, therefore, the LD Department had to address these issues as soon as – and for as long as – Lean processes impacted various managerial levels of the organization. The LD Department saw it as an opportunity to integrate the managerial skills required to handle Lean processes, the identified coaching abilities and overall leadership competencies in one overall developmental plan. One of the primary and central questions was whether the LD Department could manage the relationship between coaching and the Lean processes as well as integrate the Lean philosophy and strategies with the coaching philosophy and purpose to shift the overall leadership practices and organizational culture?

The goal now was to bring these coaching resources and competencies to bear on the upcoming Lean initiatives involving all managers and employees in the bank. The complexities in integrating Lean processes and coaching were frequently discussed. In other words, as coaching was further embedded in the Nordea leadership style, a process was simultaneously launched in which coaching would serve as a key element in implementing Lean processes. To support this effort, the LD Department created a Lean Academy, a Lean-specific leadership programme, which included master Lean principles, team leadership and coaching in an integrated Lean/coach training process to support the Lean implementation process within Nordea.

Whereas Lean leadership was aimed particularly at performance management, the coaching component was aimed to support improvements in communication skills in service to a successful implementation. The GROW coaching model (Whitmore, 2002) was used in designing and teaching different phases of the process as a tool for implementing the Lean strategies. All efforts were made to make the new coaching initiatives consistent with the existing terminology and use of coaching within Nordea Life & Pension (i.e., a tool whereby a manager engaged in a dialogue with an employee to determine how the employee could put his or her skills to the best possible use when solving a particular task within the Lean processes). As an outcome of reflections and discussion in the LD Department on what kind of leadership competencies and styles should be promoted in Nordea in service to the overall initiative, three types were identified. The LD Department developed and delivered internal courses to train managers on how to apply them in a Lean context.

1. The first type of leadership and coaching offers simple guidelines and makes sure that the qualifications, systems and processes required to create the intended change are in place. At this level, coaching and leadership serves a canalization function in order to handle the reorganization of a specific department and group of employees. The manager must be able to address the state of confusion, helplessness and distrust which may be the result of an employee's lack of comprehension of what he or she is capable of, and expected to do, in the context of the Lean implementation process.

2. The second type of leadership and coaching builds a trusting environment between managers and employees and between employees, fostering solidarity and teamwork in connection with the change. On this level, leadership and coaching provide a uniting function at the team level designed to create focus on, and appreciation of, internal departmental and team goals. It is the responsibility of the manager to address wasted resources, resolve political issues and conflicts, and reassure and encourage those employees who feel that they are not making a valuable contribution because of stultifying routines or personal conflicts.

3. The third type of leadership and coaching allows employees the space to find the deeper meaning and purpose in the process of change. On this level, leadership and coaching requires close attention to the individual employee to bolster his or her sense of purpose

in the Lean process. The manager must be able to address concerns about the risk of loss, bureaucratic procedures and repeated routines as well as the lack of actual innovation. In brief, managers need to be able to harness and steer the intrinsic energy and creativity that employees bring to the workplace.

Following the suggestions from Brown *et al.* (2003), the primary functions of coaching within a Lean process and executed through developed leadership skills are: (1) directing through reorganization the new professional challenges the employees face; (2) unifying the team, focusing its goals and increasing its social orientation; and (3) articulating meaning and purpose in the employees' everyday work lives. In the first phase, a manager can use coaching to address any confusion, helplessness and distrust in people in order to enable the processes to run smoothly. In this sense, coaching can serve as a way to create a balanced workflow rhythm that matches the performance requirements and the customer demands/needs. Furthermore, this leadership approach, through its emphasis on individual coaching, helps to mitigate frustration through the active elimination of inner and outer obstacles and anxiety through active support for the development of employees' capabilities to succeed in a Lean environment.

In the next phase, the manager can invite the employee into a dialogue – or the employee can ask for it her/himself – to address wasted resources, political issues and conflicts within the team in order to gain maximum customer value. In the process, the manager can help the employee develop a greater ability to enter a psychological flow state through regaining a balance between her/his perceived capacity and the perceived demands at a higher level. In this sense, coaching enhances people's internal and external flexibility so they can accommodate variations in the process and related tasks. Furthermore, this leadership approach incorporates team coaching to decrease the victimization mentality among employees who feel that they are not making a valuable contribution because of internal routines and conflicts.

In the third and final phase of sustainability, the manager can invite the employee into a dialogue – or the employee can ask for it her/himself – to address concerns about the risk of loss, bureaucratic procedures and persistent routines that inhibit innovation in order to keep a clear focus on the direct and swift movement of the product towards the customer. In this sense, coaching serves to harness the energy and creativity that employees bring to the workplace. Furthermore, this leadership approach, through its attention to organizational coaching, supports the emergence of a shared meaning and purpose for the everyday organizational practices.

These functions of coaching within the three phases of Lean processes, if embedded in a leadership practice and culture, illustrate the connection between the personal psychological state of flow and the organizational process sense of flow within change initiatives. An integrated approach to Lean implementation provides the opportunity for the inner and external states of flow to meet in developing managers, the processes and the culture. Both dimensions of flow are critical for success and, given their interdependence, coaching can be used as a key resource for development at both levels. Based on my observations, questionnaires and interviews, there is evidence of the need for a greater capacity to self-reflect, incorporate performance feedback, and become more aware and flexible in responding to new information in the periphery (Kaufmann, 2006). Thinking about coaching at individual, team and organizational levels and across the three phases seems to be an important step in this direction.

Observations from the Study

Getting employees to give their best does not mean exploiting their talent as a means of generating higher profits. It is first and foremost a way to make it possible for them to grow as individuals.

Mihaly Csikszentmihalyi

The function of coaching in a Lean context may be broken down into several parts, each of which I observed in their effects on Nordea leadership at various levels. In terms of employees, the basic idea of coaching was to unleash otherwise hidden talents, support them in identifying new potential, and help them become better team players and increasingly more open. The assumption was that the atmosphere within a department would improve if the manager was a good coach and understood how to make his or her employees thrive. It was further assumed that, done well, coaching would result in increased productivity, job satisfaction and customer satisfaction. These were also the stated goals of the Lean initiative. The question then became, 'Was it coaching and/or the Lean process improvements which enabled the first part of the Lean implementation process in Nordea Life & Pension to be a success?'

According to my research among managers and employees in Nordea Life & Pension, coaching was perceived as being highly effective in the Lean processes whether practised in an informal, spontaneous manner or in a formal, scheduled manner. The benefits of spontaneity in coaching were particularly significant with regard to 'canalizing coaching', and showed an effect through increased ability to take responsibility among employees during the first phase of the Lean processes. The benefits of more formal approaches, particularly through team coaching – what I have termed 'uniting coaching' – were significant and included such gains as a more open culture of communication among employees. Other benefits of formal coaching emerged from what I termed 'extending coaching', including increased enthusiasm and a deeper understanding on both the personal and overall organizational objectives. According to an internal survey of 60 employees throughout the bank, I found that coaching – according to those surveyed – was seen to contribute to positive personal and social emotions, and expansion of cognitive abilities to be both 'sharp and decisive' *and* 'mentally flexible'. Furthermore, coaching raised employees' energy levels and their degree of engagement 67% on average. Certainly, the bank's five years' involvement in coaching has contributed to a culture conducive to these approaches.

From my own observations, interviews, questionnaires, etc., coaching added value to the Lean implementation process in several ways. First and foremost, coaching made employees focus on what is possible. Further, a culture of enquiry changes thinking in the workplace and streamlines production. In that sense, those surveyed in my investigation viewed coaching as a prerequisite for Lean – that is, supporting both a change of mindset and a change of culture. Moreover, coaching seems to encourage people to find better and more innovative ways of working. Coaching is seen as inspiring people to develop other kinds of problem solving, such that employees do the right things in the right way. In addition to this, a lot of employees and managers viewed coaching as a key factor in increasing their efficiency and use of time. On a team level, plenty of the respondents experienced coaching as a brilliant tool to promote suggestions, give compliments, propose improvements and foster courage to approach new situations. In an organizational context and as part of leadership practice, coaching can function within Lean implementation across a wide spectrum – from performance improvement to the emergence of meaning.

Conclusion

The main conclusion from this chapter, as supported by my findings and observations, is that coaching increases business results, leadership engagement and team interaction. This is, according to my point of view, precisely what is needed in order to implement Lean processes properly. When Lean processes and coaching activities are integrated, managers can function at higher levels – from promoting greater personal responsibility, fostering more open communication and dialogue, to enhancing the flow of processes at the organizational level. Coaching brings together both internal and external flow to promote feedback, trust, meaning, learning and performance. In doing so, it contributes to an environment characterized by increased confidence, an openness to social thinking and an enriched capacity to learn and respond flexibly. As a result, coaching promotes higher quality and productivity at the individual, team and organizational levels. Therefore, my advice to coaches working within a strategic, organizational context is: 'When the objectives are clear, the foundation is settled and there is an appropriate pacing in the coaching process, managers become more effective in managing their people, collaborating with peers and accomplishing their business objectives.'

A key use of coaching in supporting Lean processes is asking provocative questions to inspire and increase employee involvement in the customer value process. A second use of coaching is in introducing an appreciative approach to create greater energy and a more pleasant atmosphere in the workplace. Thus, coaching may be said to make an active contribution at all levels in an extensive organizational process of change. This can be seen in the case study outlined here, where the LD Department helped managers – and thereby employees – to redefine themselves as a consequence of new work routines, methods and relations. To support these efforts, internal coaches from the LD Department were engaged to support coaching at the inter-managerial level and at the team level.

Overall, coaching can inspire the desired Lean behaviour and mindset in an organizational initiative. Through internal workshops and seminars, coaching can lead to an increased focus on what generates customer value and what does not, and what is considered waste and must therefore be eliminated. Coaching can therefore be seen as a method to support managers and staff, at both the internal and external levels, to handle complexity and support the desired workflow. Coaching also inspires staff members to improve their work procedures. As an implementation tool, coaching enables managers to encourage and empower their staff on the journey through constant change.

Coaching enhances the desired degree of staff flexibility, allows for a better flow through the entire value chain to the customer, and creates a greater sense of meaning and engagement in employees by helping them appreciate how they contribute to the overall goals of the business. Finally, the appreciative and attentive quality of coaching may inspire the recognition that errors and problems are opportunities for improvement. In such a culture, managers and employees can work together to address conditions and problems that inhibit flow – both individually and procedurally – by engaging in an open and trusting dialogue using their coaching skills. As a coaching culture and a Lean culture are created in tandem, the overall outcome can be seen as a 'responsible self-leadership culture'. This seems like both an essential and a noble pursuit for all organizations as they seek to integrate coaching and Lean methods in order to mature and thrive in the twenty-first century.

References and Bibliography

Alarcon, L. F. (1997). *Lean construction*. Rotterdam: A. A. Balkema.

Allen, J. H. (2000). Making Lean manufacturing work for you. *Journal of Manufacturing Engineering*, June, 1–6.

Andersen, F. Ø. (2006). *Flow og fordybelse*. Copenhagen: Hans Reitzels Forlag.

Atkin, B., and Pothecary, E. (1994). *Building futures*. Reading: University of Reading.

Banner, D. K., and Gagne, T. T. (1995). *Designing effective organizations: Traditional and transformational views*. London: Sage Publications.

Bennett, J., Pothecary, E., and Robinson, G. (1996). *Designing and building a world class industry*. Center for Strategic Studies in Construction. Reading: University of Reading.

Bennett, J., and Jayes, S. (1998). *The seven pillars of partnering*. Reading: University of Reading.

Bhasin, S., and Burcher, P. (2006). Lean viewed as a philosophy. *Journal of Manufacturing Technology Management*, 17(1), 56–72.

Brochner, J. (1995). *Pattern transfer; Process influences on Swedish construction of the automobile industry*. Proceedings of the 3rd Workshop on Lean Construction, Albuquerque, NM.

Brown, S., Miller, S., and Schvaneveldt, K. (2003). Recommendations on coaching strategies for implementing Lean. *Journal of Defense Acquisition Review*, August–November 2004, 117–133.

Christensen, T. B., Ahrengot, N., and Leck, M. (2006). *Lean. Implementering i danske virksomheder*. Copenhagen: Børsens Forlag.

Clutterbuck, D., and Megginson, D. (2005). *Making coaching work. Creating a coaching culture*. London: CIPD.

Csikszentmihalyi, M. (1990). *Flow: The psychology of optimal experience*. New York: Harper & Row.

Csikszentmihalyi, M. (2003). *Good business: Leadership, flow and the making of meaning*. New York: Penguin Group.

Eriksen, M., Fischer, T., and Mønsted, L. (2005). *God Lean ledelse. I administration og service*. Copenhagen: Børsens Forlag.

Flaherty, J. (2005). *Coaching. Evoking excellence in others* (2nd edn). Oxford: Elsevier.

Garnett, N., Jones, D. T., and Murray, S. (1998). *Strategic application of Lean thinking*. Homepage (accessed on 18 October 2007), http://www.ce.berkeley.edu/~tommelein/IGLC-6/GarnettEtAl.pdf.

Garrahan, P., and Stewart, P. (1992). *The Nissan enigma, flexibility at work in a local economy*. London: Mansell.

Gray, C. (1996). *Value for money; Helping the UK afford the buildings it likes.* Reading Construction Forum. Reading: University of Reading.

Kaufmann, C. (2006). Positive psychology: The science at the heart of coaching. In D. R. Stober and A. M. Grant (Eds.), *Evidence based coaching.* New Jersey: John Wiley & Sons.

Koskela, L. (1992). *Application of new production theory in construction.* Technical Report No. 72. CIFE, Stanford University.

Lyhne, J. (2004). Kollektivt flow – et interview med musikeren Peter Bastian. In *Kognition & pædagogik. Tidsskrift om tænkning og læring*, No. 52. Copenhagen: Psykologisk Forlag A/S.

Morgan, G. (1993). *Imaginization: The art of creative management.* California: Sage Publications.

Philips, E. (2002). Pros and cons of Lean manufacturing. *Forming and Fabricating*, October, 1–5.

Sohal, A., and Eggleston, A. (1994). Lean production: Experience amongst Australian organizations. *International Journal of Operations & Production Management*, 14, 1–17.

Spear, S. J. (2004). Learning to lead at Toyota. *Harvard Business Review*, May, 78–86.

Swank, C. S. (2003). The Lean service machine. *Harvard Business Review*, October, 1–8.

Whitmore, J. (2002). *Coaching for performance* (3rd edn). London: Nicholas Brealey Publishing.

Womack, J. P., Jones, D. T., and Roos, D. T. (1991). *The machine that changed the world.* New York: Harper Perennial.

Womack, J. P., and Jones, D. T. (1996). *Lean thinking: Banish waste and create wealth in your corporation.* London: Touchstone Books.

Womack, J. P., and Jones, D. T. (2005). *Lean solutions: Companies and customers can create value and wealth together.* New York: Free Press.

Taking Coaching to the Next Level: Critical Insights from ROI Evaluations

17

Merrill C. Anderson

Overview

Over the past five years our firm has conducted several evaluations of leadership coaching and development initiatives. The first ROI (return on investment) study we conducted in 2001 with Nortel Networks demonstrated an ROI over 500% (Anderson, Dauss, and Mitch, 2002). Most recently, our firm and Linkage, Inc. conducted the second annual Coaching in Organizations Benchmark Study (Anderson, Lynch, and Brill, 2007), which revealed how coaching delivers a broad range of both tangible and intangible benefits. These evaluations have shed light on what leaders have learned during the coaching process, how they have applied what they learned, and the impact these actions have had on the business. In the process, monetary benefits were also documented, with returns on investment ranging from 50% to 500%.

As impressive as these business results have been, even more impressive is how these evaluations have made visible the underlying dynamics by which leadership coaching delivers this level of value. Leadership coaching is defined here as a process that translates insights into meaningful actions to realize potential. ROI studies reveal ways in which coaching initiatives can best be leveraged for creating strategic value. This chapter begins with a representative case study showing how ROI

The Philosophy and Practice of Coaching: Insights and Issues for a New Era.
Edited by David B. Drake, Diane Brennan and Kim Gørtz.
© 2008 John Wiley & Sons, Ltd.

is determined for a coaching initiative. Then, I will share insights and explore the implications of this study, along with similar studies that we have completed, in order to identify ways to take coaching to the next level with even greater strategic impact.

Case Study: A Manufacturing Company Pilots Coaching

A coaching programme, designed and delivered by Coaching–Partnership, Ltd (see references), was intended to be a comprehensive effort to accelerate the development of leaders at a manufacturing facility. Specifically, the facility leaders expected the coaching programme to increase the site's competitiveness, e.g., doing more with less in a highly competitive market and enabling the leaders to deal more effectively with change and promote culture change across the organization.

The coaching programme was tailored and targeted to meet these expectations and a pilot was conducted. The leaders who participated in the programme were drawn from the leadership team and other up-and-coming leaders. The comprehensive programme included self-assessments and feedback, emotional intelligence assessments, individual coaching sessions, a coaching skills workshop, and coaching skills mentoring. Because the intention of this programme was not just for leaders to be coached, but for leaders to be coaches, additional support was provided to the participants: a coaching 'buddy trio' system was made available to participants, as was a resource library, and ongoing communications with Coaching–Partnership through telephone and email.

The purpose of the programme evaluation, commissioned by Coaching–Partnership, was to better understand what participants learned during the programme, how they applied what they learned in the work environment, and the impact that these actions had on the organization. The results from this evaluation were intended to support the development of a site coaching strategy and the design and delivery of the next wave of the coaching programme for the organization. Each of the 17 participants in the programme was contacted to participate in a 40-minute conversation. Twelve were available to participate in the evaluation (71% response rate).

The impact of the programme was viewed as both intangible (e.g., improved team work) and tangible (e.g., increased productivity). Whenever appropriate, the tangible impact was converted to monetary value following a proven and conservative process described in Anderson (2003) and Anderson and Anderson (2005). The effects of coaching were isolated from other potential influencing factors. The total cost of the whole programme and the follow-on coaching phase was determined as part of the overall value determination; this included opportunity costs (for all 17 participants). In the end, the return on investment was calculated (based on data from the 12 in the study) and recommendations were sought from the participants on how to enhance the impact and value of the coaching programme in light of considerations to expand the programme within the organization.

Key Lessons Learned from the Coaching Programme

Participants reported some profound shifts in how they think about situations with others and how they can use coaching approaches to increase their effectiveness. Many reported moving from controlling or directing to being more empowering; from giving answers to asking questions. Participants gained new appreciation for taking time for reflection and engaging in open dialogue. They learned how to recognize coaching opportunities, and when these opportunities arise, how to open up new possibilities with their direct reports and other colleagues.

For example, one participant noted, 'I deal with many teams and products; work with cross-functional teams and help them with action plans. I learned how to use coaching approaches and give structure to conversations with team members. Before I just gave advice and now I explore options; I help others see implications and see both sides of the situation.' Other participants noted that being coached themselves helped them to better understand the coaching approaches and how to be more effective in coaching others. One participant observed, 'I learned how powerful coaching could be not just for me but for my direct reports; how coaching opens up possibilities and creates more of an empowering culture'.

Many participants noted how the programme complemented what they learned from their leadership development initiative. All participants viewed the programme as a positive experience, which enabled them to increase self-knowledge, improve relationships with others and, in some cases, influence career direction.

How Participants Applied What They Learned

Most participants reported using coaching approaches on a day-to-day basis, a fact that was viewed as an important ingredient in creating an empowerment culture. Those who had direct reports noted that coaching helped clarify what had to be done as a team and to focus on the high priorities for the team and for the customers. Teams became more engaged and brought more enthusiasm to their roles.

Participants reported how coaching was increasing the performance of their individual team members. One noted, 'I use coaching with each of my direct reports, treating each one differently based on their needs. I gave feedback to each direct report regarding his or her strengths and improvement opportunities. I then had coaching conversations with each person, gaining increased commitment and engagement.' The direct reports of the participants noted changes in their boss's leadership styles. One participant reported preparing the direct reports in advance for changes in leadership style, noting there might be some rough patches. This preparation seemed to smooth the transition to a coaching style for both the participant and the direct reports.

Participants are seeing changes in their direct reports as well. They are better prepared, identifying and thinking through the options before coming to see their manager and, when they get there, the direct reports are not just coming to them to give the answer. Rather, this approach is building the decision-making capability of the direct reports and preparing them for increased responsibility. One participant noted that the coaching approach is especially well suited to managing the younger generation, who often have higher needs for autonomy and engagement. A main reason that younger workers leave is not connecting with their immediate manager. Using coaching approaches may prove to be a critical retention tool for those younger workers, increasingly important in a tight job market.

Those participants who do not have direct reports indicated other ways in which coaching had been applied very successfully. Those who work with peers or managers reported an increased ability to influence and solve problems and an increased focus on priorities and getting to root causes. For example, one participant noted that coaching approaches were used to enable a manager to more quickly understand the deeper problem regarding a product recall in a situation with a very tight timeframe. Some participants also noted how coaching has improved work–life balance. Participants are making better life choices, improving family relationships, and approaching their day in a more structured way.

Intangible Impact

I have organized the impact of the coaching programme in creating intangible value into two broad categories: intangibles related to personal abilities; and those related to communication, collaboration and teamwork.

Intangible Value: Personal Abilities

Figure 17.1 presents the percentage of respondents who said coaching had a significant impact or some impact on each area of personal ability. Respondents in the conversation were presented with each potential impact area and asked if coaching had a 'significant impact, some impact, no impact, or if the area was not relevant'.

About 60% or more of the respondents indicated that the programme had a significant impact or some impact on each of the six areas in Figure 17.1. Every respondent said that the programme improved their ability to coach and develop others, building upon their earlier

Figure 17.1   Percentage of respondents who said coaching had a significant impact or some impact on each area of personal ability.

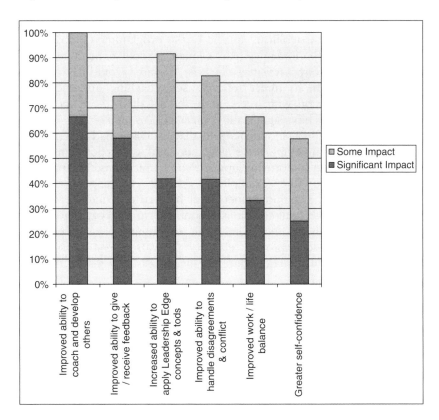

comments about what they learned and how they applied what they learned. For example, one respondent said that, as a result of the programme, 'the light bulb went off. I gained insights into what I enjoy doing and what's important to me. I changed my role to one that's a better fit for me. I now have more enthusiasm. People see this and are more engaged.'

Between 40% and 60% of the respondents noted that the programme had significantly increased their abilities to give and receive feedback, apply leadership development concepts and handle disagreements and conflicts. About 35% reported a significant improvement in work–life balance, while about 25% reported a significant increase in self-confidence. Many respondents noted, however, that their self-confidence was already very high with little room for the programme to increase it.

Intangible Value: Collaboration, Communication and Team Work

Turning our attention to Figure 17.2 we will address the impact on the areas of collaboration, communication and team work. Respondents noted that the most significant impact of the programme (almost 60%) was on improving performance management. Of course, many respondents did not have direct reports; otherwise this area would have scored higher. Those without direct reports used coaching approaches to improve collaboration with peers, with about half of the respondents indicating that coaching significantly impacted this area.

About 40% of the respondents said that coaching had a significant impact on increasing employee engagement and satisfaction, improving decision-making and improving upward communications. The previous section highlighted other examples, e.g., how coaching approaches have increased team empowerment and helped team members make their own decisions about situations. About 25% to 30% of the respondents reported significant improvements in communications with employees, team work and improved relationships with others. Almost 20% saw significant gains in delegation or accomplishing results through others.

Tangible Impact

The tangible value produced by the coaching programme was explored in terms of four areas: personal productivity of the respondents, productivity of their immediate team, the quality of their work and the cost of their work.

Figure 17.2 Percentage of respondents who said coaching had a significant impact or some impact on each intangible area of collaboration, communication and team work.

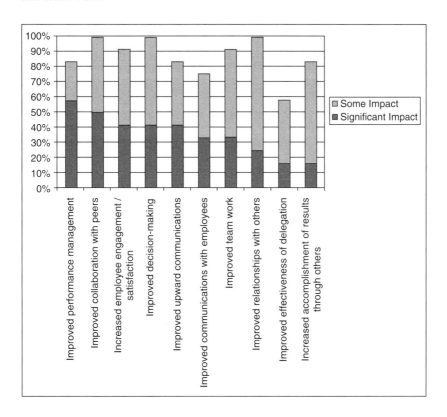

As can be seen from Figure 17.3, the greatest impact of the programme reported by the respondents was in the area of increased productivity, with over 90% of the respondents indicating some or significant improvement. Two-thirds of the respondents noted the quality of their work increased, often due to improved decision-making, while about 25% noted cost reductions.

Monetary Impact and Return on Investment

Those respondents who noted that the actions they took as a result of their participation in the coaching development programme had significant impact on a tangible benefit area were asked additional questions in order to convert the value to monetary benefits (see Anderson and

Figure 17.3 Percentage of respondents who said coaching had a significant impact or some impact on each tangible benefit area.

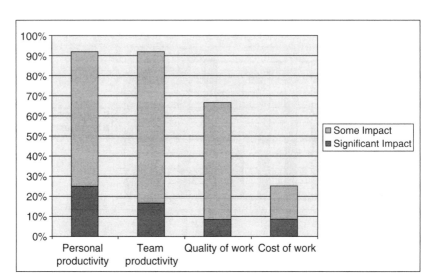

Anderson, 2005). A process described by Anderson (2003) was used to make this conversion in a way that isolates the effects of the coaching to produce the benefits from other potential influencing factors. Isolating the effects of coaching was accomplished by asking the respondent to:

(1)   Estimate the contribution of coaching, on a percentage basis, to produce the benefits.
(2)   Estimate their degree of confidence, also on a percentage basis.

Then, the monetary benefits were multiplied by these two percentages to produce the final monetary benefits that were gained solely from this programme.

Examples of Converting Value to Monetary Benefits

Personal Productivity

A respondent reported a significant impact in personal productivity due to getting more focused and setting priorities. She was further asked to quantify this increase in terms of hours gained per week (or as a percentage productivity increase). She noted a gain of at least half a day (4 hours) per week.

The person was also asked how much of this productivity gain, on a percentage basis, was directly due to participation in the coaching programme and the person replied that 75% was due to coaching. The person was then asked how confident she was, again on a percentage basis, in this estimate, and she replied 90% confident. The confidence factor gives us the error of the estimate and is used to discount the benefits in order to give a conservative and credible figure.

In order to convert these responses to monetary benefits, the value of 4 hours per week was annualized by multiplying it by 48 weeks (rather than by 52 weeks, to account for time away from work). Then this value was multiplied by the average compensation and benefits for the group of respondents, which was determined by the Human Resources function. For illustration purposes, we will say the average compensation and benefits value was £40.

Annualizing the benefit:

- *4 hours × 48 weeks × £40 average remuneration = £7680 annualized benefit*
- *Isolating the impact from other potential influencing factors:*
- *£7680 Annualized benefit × 75% attribution × 90% confidence = £5184 isolated benefits*

Team Productivity

Another respondent noted that, as a result of the coaching programme, he was able to effectively use questioning techniques with his team members. Before his approach was to just state what was needed and hope people got on board. He now is able to build more rapport, look at what others are looking for, and increase their commitment. He said that his direct reports gained, on average six hours of time per week; 50% of this gain was directly due to coaching and he was 50% confident in the estimate. For purposes of illustration we will use £40 for the average compensation and benefits value and an average of 10 direct reports.

Annualizing the benefit:

- *6 hours × 48 weeks × £40 average remuneration × 10 number of direct reports = £115 200 annualized benefit*
- *Isolating the impact from other potential influencing factors:*
- *£115 200 Annualized benefit × 50% attribution × 50% confidence = £28 800 isolated benefits*

Tally of All Monetary Benefits

The monetary benefits described in this case study derived from increases in personal and team productivity. These benefits, while real in terms of creating greater capacity in the organization, do not necessarily show up on the financial statement and therefore cannot be considered 'bottom-line' benefits. However, by creating greater capacity, these benefits become an enabler to take other actions and realize other benefits.

The total productivity benefits were over £190 000, comprising personal productivity (£25 000) and team productivity (£165 000). (Note: the exact values of the monetary benefits and the programme cost have been altered to respect the private financial aspects of the coaching engagement.)

Return on Investment

Determining the Fully Loaded Cost of the Initiative

The fully loaded cost of the initiative was about £75 000. This cost includes programme design and delivery, administration and expenses, facilities, materials, opportunity costs (the time people spent by all participants in programme activities times their average remuneration and benefits) and other costs.

It should be noted that the cost was based on all 17 programme participants, while the benefits were drawn only from the 12 study respondents. Although it seems likely that those not included in the study would have created value, an assumption was made, again to be very conservative, that those five who were not included in the study created no monetary value as a result of the programme. In addition, one respondent noted a cost reduction benefit of over £40 000. This benefit was eliminated from consideration to be included in the benefits pool as an extreme (high) value. This, again, is an extra conservative measure that lowers the tally of monetary benefits when calculating the return on investment.

Calculating the Return on Investment

The return on investment and benefits/cost ratio are useful tools to better understand how the value delivered by the programme compares to the investment required to deliver the value. These monetary benefits are based on increased productivity and are not to be considered as 'bottom-line' benefits.

The return on this investment was calculated as follows: *ROI = (£190000 − £75000) / £75000 × 100 = 153%.*

The benefits/cost ratio was calculated as follows: *BCR = £190000 / £75000 = 2.5:1.*

It should be noted that this ROI calculation is based on the benefits from one year only. The productivity benefits are sustainable and will likely be realized in years to come, while almost all of the investment in the programme was made in year one. ROI projections beyond year one would likely show a substantially higher ROI. However the ROI is calculated, it is clear that the coaching development programme more than paid for itself through the productivity benefits identified by the respondents.

Wrap-Up of the Case Study

The coaching programme, designed and delivered by Coaching–Partnership, had a positive and significant impact on both the participants and on the organization in which they worked. Participants have incorporated coaching into their leadership and communication styles. The use of coaching approaches on a day-to-day basis is an important ingredient in creating an empowerment culture. Those who have direct reports noted that coaching has helped clarify what has to be done as a team and to focus on the high priorities for the team and for the customers. As a result, teams are more engaged and bring more enthusiasm to their roles.

Those participants who did not have direct reports indicated other ways in which coaching had been applied very successfully. Those who work with peers or managers reported an increased ability to influence and solve problems. There is an increased focus on priorities and getting to root causes. Some participants also noted how coaching has improved work–life balance. Participants are making better life choices, improving family relationships, and are approaching the day in a more structured way.

The impact of applying coaching approaches has been felt across a broad spectrum of communication, collaboration and team activities. Performance management has been improved; collaboration and engagement have increased; and decision-making and team work have been improved. These actions created sustainable tangible value for the organization and produced a return on investment of over 150%.

This case study example shows how a meticulous and conservative evaluation methodology can be used to describe the full picture of value creation for a coaching programme. The weaving together of the stories told by the coaching programme participants shaped this picture of value creation. Impressive intangible benefits were produced that will help enable the organization to achieve its strategic goals. The analysis of tangible benefits, some of which were converted to monetary benefits, revealed that the coaching programme more than paid for itself in terms of increased productivity.

Key Lessons Learned

What makes a coaching programme, like the one depicted in the case study, so valuable to the programme participants as well as to the organization? This case study reveals three key success factors enabling coaching programmes to create strategic value:

- Coaching must be integrated with other developmental activities.
- Coaching programmes must support leaders being coaches, not just being coached.
- The strategic context for coaching must be established.

Integrating Coaching with Other Developmental Activities

As effective as coaching has proven to be, it is not an end unto itself. The purpose of coaching is, in part, to develop leaders to be more effective. It is up to each organization to define 'effectiveness'. One way of defining effectiveness is through the development and application of a competency model. Leadership competencies – in areas such as cross-organization collaboration, business acumen and performance management – can serve as a lynchpin for all developmental activities. In the case study example, developmental activities, such as mentoring, assessments and workshops, were utilized in addition to coaching. All of these activities were dedicated to increasing the effectiveness of the leaders against prescribed outcomes. Coaching was therefore well integrated into a broader developmental process.

The development and utilization of an educational curriculum represents another area of integration with coaching. The curriculum presents a longer-term developmental path for leaders to take. The curriculum includes specific topic areas that typically relate to the expected leadership competencies, as well as a wide variety of potential developmental activities that may be utilized to build the competencies. Examples include: action learning, job rotations, day-in-the-life visits or job shadowing, leaders serving as teachers, mentoring, and other activities. As the developmental paths are defined for leaders, coaching gains a stronger developmental focus and foundation. Coaching is viewed as a key enabler for leaders to successfully travel down their developmental paths.

Leaders as Coaches

In the case study example, the leaders who participated in the programme received coaching; however, these leaders were also mentored in how to be effective coaches with their team members and others. Workshop experiences supplemented their learning in how to be coaches. This programme is illustrative of a broader trend for leaders to incorporate coaching approaches into their leadership styles. Increasingly, the 'leader as coach' style is replacing the more traditional 'command and control' style. Moreover, as the number of leaders who embrace coaching approaches increase, these leaders contribute to creating a coaching culture (Anderson and Anderson, 2006). These cultures emphasize development and epitomize empowerment.

Evaluations of coaching and of leadership development initiatives have shown that integrating coaching approaches into leadership styles has many benefits. People who work for leaders who use coaching approaches begin to find their own answers to questions. They feel more empowered to explore solutions without a need to gain permission from their leader. As a result, these people become more resourceful. They are more open to new possibilities with each problem they solve or each new skill set they adopt. The learning that coaching facilitates becomes self-reinforcing and people incorporate coaching approaches in their interactions with others. Indeed, coaching can have a 'cascading effect' throughout the organization as people's experience and success with coaching grows. In the case study, the leaders talked about how they instilled coaching capabilities with their team members. The leaders became role models for coaching so that even those direct reports who did not receive formal training in coaching began coaching others.

Not all benefits are intangible in nature. Drawing from the case study, we saw how the programme increased both the productivity of the leaders and the productivity of their work teams. For example, as leaders coached their team members, these team members became more independent and resourceful, which required less time of the leader to provide day-to-day direction for the team members. Consequently, leaders were able to free up additional time. This enabled the leaders to devote more time to the strategic aspects of their job. Leaders were also more effective in dealing with their peers. Meetings were more focused and more was accomplished in less time.

We also saw in the case study how the leader's team members became more productive as a result of the coaching programme. Their increased sense of empowerment and increased resourcefulness enabled them to reduce the time it took to accomplish their tasks. They too were able to accomplish more in less time. As these team members began to use coaching approaches in their work with others, a broader, more informal support network for coaching was established. This support network supplemented the more formal 'buddy system' that was used in the coaching programme, served to 'legitimize' coaching and reinforced its broader application in the organization. This reinforcement served to increase the sustainability of coaching as well as the productivity gains that were produced as a result. As this trend continues, coaching is no longer an 'event', but rather a continuous process of learning.

The Strategic Context for Coaching

Evaluations of coaching and leadership development programmes have revealed that coaching programmes risk going adrift in the organization when these programmes are not aligned to the business strategy. Coaching programmes must be placed in the appropriate strategic context. The outcomes of the programme must be articulated and be perceived as having strategic value for the organization. Organizations that have corporate universities or strong, centralized training and development functions, have additional resources and capabilities to drive the strategic context (Anderson, 2007). In the case study example, the facility leaders expected the coaching programme to advance strategic and cultural change. The business rationale and strategic context for the coaching programme was well understood and accepted throughout the leadership ranks.

Strategic coaching programmes require strong sponsorship. Sponsors not only provide the funding for the programme, they provide vision, advocacy and guidance for the programme. The more strategic the programme, the longer the time horizon is likely to be for this programme to bear fruit. For example, incorporating coaching approaches throughout multiple levels in the organization takes years. Building the bench strength of leadership in the organization, as was the objective in the case study example, also takes years to accomplish and so the sponsors must have a long-range view of the programme and its impact. Sponsors develop a story about the programme and its impact that reflects their long-term vision and becomes the centrepiece for their advocacy of the programme.

Addressing these three success factors – integration, leaders as coaches and strategic context – is essential for coaching programmes to be successful. The case study illustrated these three factors in the context of a formal evaluation process. This evaluation process was especially important, given that the coaching programme was a pilot and under consideration for broader deployment in the organization. Evaluations that assess the application of coaching to the workplace and the impact that these actions have in the organization are a source rich in insights about how to maximize the value of coaching. While much has been made in recent years about the ROI and the monetary value of coaching, the greatest value of coaching is more likely intangible in nature. In the case study example, increased productivity was certainly important – and the source of the ROI. However, increasing the bench strength of leadership, while intangible, was critical for long-term business success. It seems safe to say that the coaching programme at least paid for itself and along the way created strategic value for the organization.

Conclusion

The coaching profession is evolving and insights from ROI studies are opening possibilities for taking coaching to the next level and creating even greater strategic value. Coaching initiatives are moving beyond simply being a series of one-on-one coaching relationships to becoming initiatives that impact leadership styles and company cultures. Leaders are not just being coached; they are becoming coaches. As more and more leaders embrace coaching approaches in their leadership styles, subtle and yet important shifts in the company culture can emerge. There is a greater emphasis on leaders developing people throughout the workday. Leaders become teachers, asking questions and not just giving answers. Employees take on more responsibility for problem solving and feel greater empowerment for the solutions.

ROI studies reveal critical success factors for realizing these possibilities of evolving leadership styles and company cultures. Coaching initiatives must be integrated with other development activities, enable leaders to be coaches and establish a strategic context. For those who manage coaching initiatives, either as an internal manager or external coach, it is important to keep an eye on the 'big picture', asking questions such as: 'How will this coaching initiative . . .

- contribute to achieving business goals?'
- enable leaders to become coaches?'
- leverage other developmental activities?'
- contribute to evolving the culture?'

By addressing these questions, initiative managers and coaches will increase the strategic value of coaching for the organization. As the present ROI case study shows, this value is tangible, as well as intangible, and can be expressed in monetary terms. Demonstrating ROI underscores that the coaching initiative is also a business initiative. This is a key message for business leaders and sponsors of coaching: an investment in coaching is also an investment in the business. Coaching has proven to deliver important intangible benefits while more than paying for itself in terms of productivity benefits.

References

Anderson, M. C. (2003). *Bottom-line organization development*. Boston: Butterworth-Heinemann.

Anderson, M. C. (2007). The strategic contributions of corporate universities to leadership coaching. In M. Allen (Ed.), *Corporate universities* (2nd edn). San Francisco: Berrett-Koehler Publishers.

Anderson, M. C., and Anderson, D. L. (2005). *Coaching that counts*. Boston: Butterworth-Heinemann.

Anderson, M. C., and Anderson, D. L. (2006). Leaders who coach create coaching cultures. In D. Kirkpatrick (Ed.), *Improving employee performance through appraisal and coaching* (2nd edn). New York: AMACOM.

Anderson, M. C., Dauss, C., and Mitsch, B. (2002). The return on investment in executive coaching at Nortel Networks. In D. J. Mitsch (Ed.), *In action: Executive coaching*. Alexandria, VA: American Society for Training and Development.

Anderson, M. C., Lynch, J., and Brill, P. (2007). The business impact of leadership coaching: results from the second annual bench mark survey of leadership coaching. *International Journal of Coaching in Organizations*, September.

Coaching–Partnership, Ltd, www.coachinginpartnership.com.

Reflections on Organizations and Coaching

David B. Drake

This section provided a look inside the uses, expectations, impact and value of coaching in organizations. Whereas the first section focused largely on psychology and philosophy as the bases for coaching, this section drew on coaching's roots in organizational and leadership development. Accordingly, these authors addressed some of the issues facing organizations that are seeking to create better and more sustainable results from coaching. Whether you are new to coaching or consider yourself a seasoned professional, inside an organization or outside, we invite you to reflect on the following questions as a catalyst for new ways of seeing yourself, your clients and your practice.

12. David Clutterbuck – Coaching the Team

(1)   What have you done to prepare yourself to work with teams, if you do, or with your client types, if you do not? How deep is your theoretical and practical understanding of their nature and needs? Where are your developmental edges here?

(2)   How do you address the realities that individual clients face when they are working at making shifts within a variety of systems at home and/or work? What insights did you gain from this chapter to help you in becoming more effective with clients in these relational/systemic domains?

(3)   What is the key insight/inspiration you are taking from this chapter in terms of your expertise as a coach?

The Philosophy and Practice of Coaching: Insights and Issues for a New Era.
Edited by David B. Drake, Diane Brennan and Kim Gørtz.
© 2008 John Wiley & Sons, Ltd.

13. Diane Brennan – Leadership Coaching: The Impact on the Organization

(1)   What did you learn in following the play-by-play narrative of this coaching intervention as a way of informing your work with leaders? What questions did it raise for you in terms of our need for a greater understanding of how people and organizations change?

(2)   Do you have opportunities to openly and honestly share your cases with peers for review and development? If so, how can you deepen your self-reflection and these conversations? If not, where can you begin to create what you need in this regard?

(3)   What is the key insight/inspiration you are taking from this chapter in terms of your openness as a coach?

14. Vicki Escudé – Creating Corporate Coaching Cultures for Resiliency and Performance

(1)   How would you define and characterize a coaching culture? How does this chapter inform that view and your efforts in working with systems, e.g., organizations, communities, families, that are seeking such a culture?

(2)   What do you think of the application of individual coaching competencies to gauge readiness for change in organizations and to identify and deliver appropriate coaching interventions? How would you describe your strengths and challenges with these competencies?

(3)   What is the key insight/inspiration you are taking from this chapter in terms of your competency as a coach?

15. William Bergquist and Vikki G. Brock – Coaching and Leadership in the Six Cultures of Contemporary Organizations

(1)   What culture type is most prominent in the organization(s) with which you work? Which of them are the best fit for your coaching style? Based on your self-assessment, what advice would you give the coach in this chapter and why?

(2)   How do you tend to relate and respond to anxiety – in yourself and in others? How do your preferences show up in your coaching practice? What connections do you see between anxiety and meaning?

(3)   What is the key insight/inspiration you are taking from this chapter in terms of your preferences as a coach?

16. Kim Gørtz – Coaching, Lean Processes, and the Concept of Flow

(1)   At what level and scope do you prefer to engage clients around coaching? Where do you most often experience *flow* in your work? What would it take to expand your capabilities and/or scope if that is what you want?
(2)   What are the links between the emotional, cognitive and behavioural benefits from coaching and the development and success of a system, e.g., organization, community, family?
(3)   What is the key insight/inspiration you are taking from this chapter in terms of your epistemology role as a coach?

17. Merrill C. Anderson – Taking Coaching to the Next Level: Critical Insights from ROI Evaluations

(1)   What experience do you have with ROI or other evaluative processes related to coaching? How has reading this case added to/ shifted your thinking – particularly around measuring the tangible versus the intangible benefits of coaching?
(2)   What questions – and their answers – matter most to you and your clients (and sponsors) in terms of the process and outcomes of coaching and coaching initiatives? Are these the right questions? If not, what else would you like to ask?
(3)   What is the key insight/inspiration you are taking from this chapter in terms of your efficacy as a coach?

Conclusion

David B. Drake

Like many others with an eye to the larger forces at play in the world, we see the emergence of a new era faced with unprecedented challenges and opportunities. It is time for coaching to step more fully onto this global stage. To do so will require a deeper understanding of our roots, our research, our relationships and our results. This book was designed to support coaches and coaching to rise to this challenge through more candid self-reflection and more courageous collective expression.

In drawing this book to a close, I would like to focus on the key implications from each chapter for the development of coaches and the future of coaching. As reflected in the title of the book, our aim has been to address both the philosophy and the practice of coaching through sharing insights on important issues we face in coaching. We have taken a scholar-practitioner approach to doing so in order to be both grounded and applicable. We hope we have been successful in fulfilling our aim on behalf of our readers and coaches everywhere. I leave you with 17 wishes, one from each author, on behalf of the future of coaching and those we serve.

We need a better understanding of:

The foundations of coaching

1. The taxonomy of coaching's foundations so coaches can develop a coherent plan for their ongoing development and performance.

2. The nature of coaching relationships and their link to outcomes along with a greater commitment by coaches to increase their capabilities to manage themselves in those relationships.
3. The dynamics of the 'field' that is created within coaching conversations and the powerful opportunities for coaches in working with clients and their emergent narrative material.
4. The best ways to move beyond a culture of pragmatism within coaching and distinguish among the types and uses of evidence.
5. The mechanisms to more fully connect the dots between theory, research and practice so that more coaches take a scholar-practitioner approach to their practice.

The applications of coaching

6. The best ways to support people to become more resilient and mentally tough so they can tackle the complex issues and decisions in productive and healthy ways.
7. The components necessary for a truly global framework for coaching that incorporates non-Western and non-dominant epistemologies, values and practices.
8. The ways in which coaching can be used effectively to address specific problems and attain specific outcomes.
9. The place of advocacy in coaching as a way to enrol clients on a path to greater wisdom and engagement in the critical issues of the day.
10. The role of spirituality in human and social development and how best to engage these issues with clients.
11. The best methods – and the necessary will – to study the various models of coaching so as to develop common points of reference and more sophisticated distinctions.

Organizations and coaching

12. The basis for a relational view of coaching and the means by which to align expertise, experience and evidence in support of effective coaching with teams.
13. The different roles and modalities through which coaching occurs, e.g., formal sessions, consultation, facilitation and what it takes when the same professional (internal or external) has multiple roles.
14. The definition and essential elements of a coaching culture, the competencies necessary to nurture one, and finer distinctions among types of coaching within such cultures.

15. The resources needed to support coaches to be successful in contemporary organizational cultures and to address the issues inherent in a time marked by increased anxiety and a greater need for meaning.
16. The means for creating flow experiences within complex systems and to sustain rich, relationship-based coaching conversations within Lean environments.
17. The measures of coaching that will ultimately prove useful in enriching the process and the profession of coaching – particularly around the intangibles in our work.

Which item(s) calls to you in thinking about the future of your work and the evolution of coaching? Stop by our website at www. PracticeOfCoaching.com to tell us your story and join in conversations with your peers.

David B. Drake
Sebastopol, CA, USA
April 2008

Index